NO PEACE, NO HONOR

Nixon, Kissinger, and Betrayal in Vietnam

LARRY BERMAN

The Free Press   *New York London Toronto Sydney Singapore*

THE FREE PRESS
A Division of Simon & Schuster, Inc.
1230 Avenue of the Americas
New York, NY 10020

For information regarding special discounts for bulk purchases,
please contact Simon & Schuster Special Sales at 1-800-456-6798
or business@simonandschuster.com

Designed by Jeanette Olender
Manufactured in the United States of America

10 9 8 7 6 5 4 3 2 1

Library of Congress Cataloging-in-Publication Data

Berman, Larry.
    No peace, no honor : Nixon, Kissinger, and Betrayal in Vietnam / Larry Berman.
        p. cm.
    Includes bibliographical references and index.
    1. Vietnamese Conflict, 1961–1975—United States. 2. United States—Politics and
government—1969–1974. 3. Nixon, Richard M. (Richard Milhous), 1913– 4. Kissinger,
Henry, 1923– I. Title.

DS558.B467 2001
959.704′3373—dc21
                                                                    2001023904

ISBN 0-684-84968-2

In memory of two mothers,

Selma Berman and Bertha Costantini

The only guide to a man is his conscience; the only shield to his memory is the rectitude and sincerity of his actions. It is very imprudent to walk through life without this shield, because we are so often mocked by the failure of our hopes and the upsetting of our calculations; but with this shield, however the fates may play, we march always in the ranks of honor.

Winston Churchill, November 1940

CONTENTS

CAST OF CHARACTERS

ABRAMS, CREIGHTON

General, U.S. Army; Commander, U.S. Military Assistance Command, Vietnam (COMUSMACV), July 3, 1968–June 29, 1972; Chief of Staff, U.S. Army, October 12, 1972–September 1974

BINH, MME. NGUYEN THI

Vietcong leader, Provisional Revolutionary Government representative to the Paris Peace Talks

BO, MAI VAN

Chief of Democratic Republic of Vietnam's commercial delegation in Paris and secret peace contact

BREZHNEV, LEONID

Secretary General of the Central Committee and President of Presidium, Communist Party of the Soviet Union

BRUCE, DAVID

U.S. representative to the Paris Peace Talks, August 1970–July 1971

BUNKER, ELLSWORTH

U.S. ambassador to South Vietnam, April 1967–May 1973

COLBY, WILLIAM

Deputy COMUSMACV for Civil Operations and Rural Development Support, November 1968–June 1971

DIEM, BUI

South Vietnamese ambassador to the United States and adviser to President Thieu

DIEM, NGO DINH

Former president of South Vietnam, 1955–1963; toppled in a coup and assassinated by Big Minh

DON, TRAN VAN

South Vietnamese lieutenant general, previous chairman of Senate and House Defense Committees, and temporary minister of defense, April 1975

DONG, PHAM VAN

Premier of Democratic Republic of Vietnam, 1955–1987; member of the Political Bureau, 1951–1986

DUAN, LE

Secretary general of Lao Dong (Vietnam's Communist party), 1960–1986

DUC, NGUYEN PHU

South Vietnamese special assistant for foreign affairs, career diplomat, ambassador to Belgium, 1974

DUNG, VAN TIEN

North Vietnamese general, member of the Politburo, and commander of North Vietnam's final offensive

ENLAI, CHOU

Premier of People's Republic of China

GIAP, VO NGUYEN

North Vietnamese general, member of the Politburo, and minister of defense, 1941–1981

GROMYKO, ANDREI

Foreign minister of the Soviet Union

HAIG, ALEXANDER, JR.

General, U.S. Army; Kissinger's military assistant at the National Security Council, 1971; army vice chief of staff, 1973; White House chief of staff, 1973

W. HARRIMAN, AVERELL

U.S. undersecretary of state for political affairs, 1963–1965; ambassador at large ("peace ambassador")

HO CHI MINH

President and founder of Vietnam's Communist party, 1929–1969

HOA, LE QUANG

North Vietnamese major general, North Vietnamese chief of delegation to the Four-Party Joint Military Commission

HOFFA, JAMES

Former Teamster boss

HUONG, TRAN VAN

Vice president and brief successor to President Thieu in April 1975

KHIEM, TRAN THIEN

South Vietnamese general, former prime minister, and briefly president of South Vietnam in 1964

KIEM, TRAN BUU

National Liberation Front diplomat; Provisional Revolutionary Government representative to Paris Peace Talks

KISSINGER, DR. HENRY

Assistant to the president for national security affairs, January 1969–September 1973; secretary of state, September 1973–January 1977; U.S. secret negotiator with Xuan Thuy and Le Duc Tho of North Vietnam

KY, NGUYEN CAO

Air vice marshal, former commander of the air force, premier, and vice president, 1967–1971; without official command in 1975

LAIRD, MELVIN

Secretary of defense, January 1969–January 1973

LAM, PHAM DANG

South Vietnamese representative to the Paris Peace Talks, 1969–1973

LAM, TRAN VAN

South Vietnamese foreign minister, 1969–1973; signatory to the Paris Peace Agreement, 1973; president of the South Vietnamese Senate, 1973–1975

LAU, HA VAN

Deputy chief of North Vietnam's negotiating team in Paris, 1969–1973

LE, NGUYEN THANH

North Vietnam's official press spokesperson in Paris during peace negotiations, 1968–1972

LODGE, HENRY CABOT

U.S. ambassador to Republic of Vietnam, 1963–1964, 1965–1967

LOI, LUU VAN

North Vietnamese colonel, senior North Vietnamese diplomat, 1954–1974; member of the Four-Party Joint Military Commission, 1973; party to secret negotiations with Kissinger and Le Duc Tho, 1969–1973

MARTIN, GRAHAM

Member of American peace negotiating team in Paris; last U.S. ambassador to South Vietnam, 1969–1974; career diplomat

MCGOVERN, GEORGE

South Dakota senator, 1963–1981; author of McGovern-Hatfield amendment, 1970; 1972 Democratic party presidential nominee

MILES, PAUL

Major, U.S. Army. Planning Staff for U.S. Delegation, Four-Party Joint Military Commission

MINH, DUONG VAN

> General; president of South Vietnam, during surrender to the North in April 1975

MOORER, THOMAS

> Admiral, U.S. Navy; chairman, Joint Chiefs of Staff, July 3, 1970–July 1, 1974

NEGROPONTE, JOHN

> Aide to Henry Kissinger, 1969–1973; specialist on Asia

NHA, HOANG DUC

> Previous minister of information, cousin, special assistant, and adviser to President Thieu, 1967–1974

NIXON, RICHARD

> President of the United States, January 20, 1969–August 9, 1974

NOL, LON

> Premier of Cambodia, 1970–1971; president of Cambodia, 1972–1975

PHUOMA, SOUVANNA

> Premier of Laos; neutralist leader

PHUONG, TRAN KIM

> South Vietnamese ambassador to the United States

PORTER, WILLIAM

> U.S. representative to the Paris Peace Talks, September 1971–January 1973

ROGERS, WILLIAM

> Secretary of state, January 1969–September 1973

SAINTENY, JEAN

> French businessman; facilitator of secret talks between Kissinger and Le Duc Tho

SULLIVAN, WILLIAM

> Deputy assistant secretary of state, East Asian and Pacific affairs, April 1969–July 1973

THIEU, NGUYEN VAN

> President of South Vietnam, October 31, 1967–April 21, 1975

THO, LE DUC

> North Vietnamese Politburo member and peace negotiator; secret negotiator with Henry Kissinger; member of the Lao Dong Political Bureau, 1951–1986

THUY, XUAN

> North Vietnamese minister for foreign affairs, 1963–1965; North Vietnamese representative to the Paris Peace Talks, 1969–1973; secret negotiator with Le Duc Tho and Kissinger, 1969–1973

TIN, BUI

One of Hanoi's most prominent journalists; in 1973 official spokesman for North Vietnamese delegation in Saigon; on April 30, 1975 he witnessed South Vietnamese surrender at Independence Palace. Defected in 1990.

TRA, TRAN VAN

North Vietnamese general, B-2 theater; head of the Vietcong delegation in the Four-Party Joint Military Commission in Saigon

TRINH, NGUYEN DUY

North Vietnamese foreign minister, 1965–1975; member of Political Bureau, 1975–1981

VIEN, CAO VAN

South Vietnamese general, chairman of the Joint General Staff

WESTMORELAND, WILLIAM

General, U.S. Army; Commander, U.S. Military Assistance Command, Vietnam, 1964–1968; chief of staff, U.S. Army, July 3, 1968–June 30, 1972

WEYAND, FRED

General, U.S. Army; U.S. Military Assistance Command, Vietnam (COMUSMACV), September 1970–June 29, 1972; COMUSMACV June 29, 1972–March 29, 1973

WHITEHOUSE, CHARLES

Deputy ambassador to South Vietnam under Ambassador Bunker, 1967–1974

WICKHAM, JOHN

Brigadier general, U.S. Army; deputy chief, U.S. delegation to Four-Party Joint Military Commission, 1973

WOODWARD, GILBERT HUME

Major general, U.S. Army; chief of staff, Military Assistance Command Vietnam, May 1972–March 1973; chief, U.S. delegation to Four-Party Joint Military Commission in Vietnam, January–March 1973

YI, CHEN

Foreign minister of the People's Republic of China

ZUMWALT, ELMO

Admiral, U.S. Navy; chief of naval operations, July 1, 1970–July 1, 1974

GLOSSARY

ARVN	Army of the Republic of Vietnam
CJCS	Chairman, Joint Chiefs of Staff (U.S.)
CMJC	Central Military Joint Commission
CNR	Committee of National Reconciliation
CINCPAC	Commander in Chief, Pacific (U.S.)
COMUSMACV	Commander, U.S. Military Assistance Command, Vietnam
DMZ	Demilitarized Zone
DRVN	Democratic Republic of Vietnam (North Vietnam)
FPJMC	Four-Party Joint Military Commission
FPJMT	Four-Party Joint Military Team
GVN	Government of Vietnam
ICCS	International Commission of Control and Supervision
Khmer Rouge	Cambodian Communists
JCS	Joint Chiefs of Staff
JGS	Joint General Staff of South Vietnam
JMC	Joint Military Commission
MACV	Military Assistance Command Vietnam
NCRC	National Council of National Reconciliation and Concord
NLF	National Liberation Front
NSC	National Security Council
NVA	North Vietnamese Army
Pathet Lao	Laotian Communists
PLAF	People's Liberation Armed Forces (Vietcong)
PRG	Provisional Revolutionary Government
RVN	Republic of Vietnam (GVN)
RVNAF	Republic of Vietnam Armed Forces
TPJMC	Two-Party Joint Military Commission
VC	Vietcong
VNLAF	Vietnamese Liberation Armed Forces

Prologue

The great enemy of clear language is insincerity.

George Orwell

President Richard Nixon spent New Year's Eve 1972 watching his beloved Washington Redskins defeat the Dallas Cowboys 26–3. Afterward, Nixon wrote in his diary, "As the year 1972 ends I have much to be thankful for—China, Russia, May 8, the election victory, and, of course, while the end of the year was somewhat marred by the need to bomb Hanoi-Haiphong, that decision, I think, can make the next four years much more successful than they otherwise might have been. 1973 will be a better year."

It was a fair assessment of 1972. It was, of course, wildly wrong about the years to come, thanks to Watergate, but on that New Year's Eve, Nixon had reason to be optimistic. His biggest foreign policy problem, inherited from LBJ, had been the ongoing Vietnam War. Heading into 1973, it seemed likely that a peace treaty was just around the corner. Indeed, as he wrote, peace negotiations were getting restarted. The *New York Times* reported that Hanoi's negotiator, Le Duc Tho, was en route to Paris for a new round of meetings with Henry Kissinger. As we now know, Tho was first making a secret stop in Beijing in order to consult with Chou Enlai. The Chinese premier summarized the state of affairs nicely. He began by noting that Nixon's effort "to exert pressure through bombing has failed." Observing that Nixon faced numerous international and domestic problems, Chou advised Tho to "adhere to principles but show the necessary flexibility" that would produce a settlement. "Let the Americans leave as quickly as possible. In half a year or one year the situation will change," Chou Enlai advised Le Duc Tho. As he knew full well, 150,000 North Vietnamese troops were still in the South. The North was positioned for eventual victory; America was fed up with the war to the point of exhaustion. The ally that America had long supported, and continued to guarantee the safety of, was facing almost certain doom.

While Le Duc Tho was in China, Strom Thurmond, South Carolina's senior Republican senator and one of Nixon's strongest supporters, penned a personal message to the president. Nixon had always valued Thurmond's advice and support. In 1968, Thurmond had delivered the crucial Republican southern delegates to Nixon's nomination for president. A certified hawk on the war and a strong supporter of the Christmas bombing of North Vietnam, Thurmond wrote to the president on January 2 that any final settlement negotiated in Paris between Henry Kissinger and Le Duc Tho that allowed North Vietnam's troops to remain in the South would be viewed as a betrayal of those who had fought and died in the war. "I am pleased that the bombing of North Vietnam has brought the communists to the negotiating table. This proves once again that the firmness of your policies brings results. It is my hope that the forthcoming negotiations will produce a revised draft agreement, which will explicitly provide that all non-south Vietnamese troops will be required to evacuate South Vietnamese territory. I am deeply concerned that past draft agreements indicate that North Vietnamese troops would be allowed to remain in South Vietnam. This could be the foundation for North Vietnam to take over South Vietnam after our final withdrawal in the future. In such an outcome, history will judge that the sacrifice of American lives was in vain."

Three weeks later, on Tuesday, January 23, 1973, at the International Conference Center in Paris, the test of his assumption was launched. Le Duc Tho and Henry Kissinger, about to conclude their Nobel Prize–winning negotiations on the Agreement on Ending the War and Restoring Peace in Vietnam, were joking together. Kissinger said, "I changed a few pages in your Vietnamese text last night, Mr. Special Advisor, but it only concerned North Vietnamese troops. You won't notice it until you get back home." They shared a good laugh.

* * *

Two years later there would be no laughter.

By 1975, Watergate had unraveled the presidency of Richard Nixon.

Throughout the negotiation and signing of the agreement, Kissinger and Nixon had privately promised to South Vietnam's president, Nguyen Van Thieu, that America would intervene if any hostilities broke out between North and South, but Thieu knew that these promises were fragile. In a final plea for assistance, President Thieu penned a personal letter to a man he had never met, President Gerald Ford: "Hanoi's intention to use the Paris agreement for a military take over of South Vietnam was well-known to us at the very time of negotiating the Paris Agreement. . . . Firm pledges were then given to us that the United States will retaliate swiftly and vigorously to any violation of the agreement. . . . We consider those pledges the most important guarantees of the Paris Agreement; those pledges have now become the most crucial ones to our survival."

But President Ford had already accepted the political reality that Congress would not fund another supplemental budget request and that America's involvement in Vietnam would soon be over. Reviewing the first draft of his address to a joint session of Congress, the president read his speechwriter's proposed words: "And after years of effort, we negotiated a settlement which made it possible for us to remove our forces *with honor* and bring home our prisoners." Ford crossed out the words *with honor.*

Henry Kissinger also knew that American honor was in danger. In the cabinet room on April 16, the secretary read aloud a letter from Sirik Matak, one of the Cambodian leaders who had refused the American ambassador's invitation to evacuate Phnom Penh. The letter was written just hours before Mitak's execution: "Dear Excellency and Friend, I thank you very sincerely for your letter and your offer to transport me towards freedom. I cannot, alas, leave in such a cowardly fashion. As for you, and in particular for your great country, I never believed for a moment that you would have this sentiment of abandoning a people, which has chosen liberty. You have refused us your protection, and we can do nothing about it. You leave, and my wish is that you and your country will find happiness under this sky. But, mark it well, that if I shall die here on the spot and in my country that I love, it is too bad, because we are all born and must die one day. I have committed this mistake of believing in you, the Americans."

In Saigon, the fate of thousands of Vietnamese was on the line. The American ambassador, Graham Martin, cabled Kissinger that "the one thing that would set off violence would be a sudden order for American evacuation. It will be universally interpreted as a most callous betrayal, leaving the Vietnamese to their fate while we send in the marines to make sure that we get all ours out." Martin pleaded with Kissinger to delay the evacuation for as long as possible because any signs of the Americans' taking leave could set off panic and "would be one last act of betrayal that would strip us of the last vestige of honor."

Nonetheless, evacuation plans proceeded. By April 29, the situation at the American embassy was in chaos as Ambassador Martin flagrantly disregarded the president's evacuation order. By April 30, the top-secret transmissions came in quick bursts from the CH-46 Sea Night helicopters and the larger CH-53 Sea Stallions, which were ferrying evacuees from the American embassy rooftop to the U.S. fleet offshore. All communications between the pilots and their Airborne Battlefield Command and Control Center were simultaneously transmitted to U.S. command-and-control authorities in Hawaii and Washington. The final transmissions confirmed the bitter end of the evacuation.

"All of the remaining American personnel are on the roof at this time and Vietnamese are in the building," reported the pilot of a CH-53. "The South Vietnamese have broken into the Embassy; they are rummaging around . . . no hostile acts noticed," reported another transmission. From the embassy rooftop, Marine Major James Kean described the chaos below as similar to a scene from the movie *On the Beach*.

Finally, at 7:51 A.M. Saigon time, the embassy's Marine ground security force spotted the CH-46 and its call sign, "Swift 22." It was the last flight from Saigon that would take the Marines home.

The final transmission from the CH-46 arrived with just seven words: "All the Americans are out, Repeat Out."

But not everyone was out. A breakdown in communication had occurred between those running the evacuation from the ground and those offshore, with the fleet controlling the helicopters and those making the decisions in Hawaii and Washington. "It was the Vietnam war all over again," observed Colonel Harry G. Summers, Jr. "It was not a proud day to be an American." There, on the embassy rooftop, over 420 Vietnamese stared into the empty skies looking for signs of returning American helicopters. Just hours earlier, they had been assured by well-intentioned Marines, "Khong ai se bi bo lai" ("No one will be left behind").

The helicopters did not return.

From the White House, President Gerald Ford issued an official statement: "The Government of the Republic of Vietnam has surrendered. Prior to its surrender, we have withdrawn our Mission from Vietnam. Vietnam has been a wrenching experience for this nation. . . . History must be the final judge of that which we have done or left undone, in Vietnam and elsewhere. Let us calmly await its verdict."

* * *

It has been over thirty years since the United States and Vietnam began talks intended to end the Vietnam War. The Paris Peace Talks began on May 13, 1968, under the crystal chandeliers in the ballroom of the old Majestic Hotel on Avenue Kleber and did not end until January 27, 1973, with the signing of the Agreement on Ending the War and Restoring Peace in Vietnam at the International Conference Center in Paris. Despite the agreement, not a moment of peace ever came to Vietnam. This book uses a cache of recently declassified documents to offer a new perspective on why the country known as South Vietnam ceased to exist after April 1975.

Since the very first days of his presidency in January 1969, Richard Nixon had sought an "honorable peace" in Vietnam. In January 1973 he characterized the Paris agreement as having achieved those lofty goals: "Now that we have achieved an honorable agreement, let us be proud that America did not settle for a peace that would have betrayed our allies, that would have abandoned our prisoners of war, or that would have ended the war for us, but would have continued the war for the 50 million people of Indochina."

A speakers' kit assembled within the White House on the evening of the president's announcement of the cease-fire described the final document as "a vindication of the wisdom of the President's policy in holding out for an honorable peace—and his refusal to accept a disguised and dishonorable defeat. Had it not been for the President's courage—during four years of unprecedented vilification and attack—the United States would not today be honorably ending her involvement in the war, but would be suffering the consequences of dishonor and defeat. . . . The difference between what the President has achieved and what his opponents wanted, is the difference between peace with honor, and the false peace of an American surrender."

A White Paper drafted for distribution to members of Congress offered more barbed attacks on his critics.

For four agonizing years, Richard Nixon has stood virtually alone in the nation's capital while little, petty men flayed him over American involvement in Indochina. For four years, he has been the victim of the most vicious personal attacks. Day and night, America's predominantly liberal national media hammered at Mr. Nixon, slicing from all sides, attacking, hitting, and cutting. The intellectual establishment—those whose writings entered America into the Vietnam war—pompously postured from their ivy hideaways, using their inordinate power to influence public opinion. . . . No President has been under more constant and unremitting harassment by men who should drop to their knees each night to thank the Almighty that they do not have to make the same decisions that Richard Nixon did. Standing with the President in all those years were a handful of reporters and number of newspapers—nearly all outside of Washington. There were also the courageous men of Congress who would stand firm beside the President. But most importantly there were the millions upon millions of quite ordinary Americans—-the great *Silent Majority* of citizens—who saw our country through a period where the shock troops of leftist public opinion daily propagandized against the President of the United States. *They were people of character and steel.*

Meanwhile, the North Vietnam heralded the Paris agreement as a great victory. Radio Hanoi, in domestic and foreign broadcasts, confined itself for several days to reading and rereading the Paris text and protocols. From the premier's office in Hanoi came the declaration that the national flag of the Democratic Republic of Vietnam (DRV) should be flown throughout the country for eight days, from the moment the cease-fire went into effect on January 28 through February 4. For three days and nights, Hanoi's streets were filled with crowds of people celebrating the fact that in 60 days there would be no foreign troops in Vietnam.

The *Nhan Dan* editorial of January 28, titled "The Great Historic Victory of Our Vietnamese People," observed, "Today, 28 January, the war has ended completely in both zones of our country. The United States and other countries have pledged to respect our country's independence, sovereignty, reunification, and territorial integrity. The United States will withdraw all U.S. troops and the troops of other foreign countries and their advisors and military personnel, dismantle U.S. military bases in the southern part of our country and respect our southern people's right to self-determination and other democratic freedoms."

Premier Pham Van Dong was more forthcoming to American broadcaster Walter Cronkite that "the Paris Agreement marked an important victory of our people in their resistance against U.S. aggression, for national salvation. For us, its terms were satisfactory. . . . The Paris agreement paved the way for our great victory in the Spring of 1975 which put an end to more than a century of colonial and neo-colonial domination over our country and re-stored the independence, freedom and unity of our homeland."

Perhaps the most honest response came from a young North Vietnamese cadre by the name of Man Duc Xuyen, living in Ha Bac province in North Vietnam. In a postcard, he extended Tet New Year wishes to his family. "Dear father, mother and family," the letter began. "When we have liberated South Viet-Nam and have unified the country, I will return."

Only in South Vietnam was there no joy or celebration over the signing of the Paris agreement. By the terms of the deal, over 150,000 North Vietnamese troops remained in the South, whereas the United States, over the course of Nixon's presidency, had unilaterally withdrawn over 500,000 of its own troops. President Nguyen Van Thieu and his fellow countrymen understood that the diplomatic battle had been won by Le Duc Tho. President Thieu was agreeing to nothing more than a protocol for American disengagement. True, President Nixon had guaranteed brutal retaliation if the North resumed any aggression. But could these guarantees be trusted? The fate of his country depended on them. Twenty-eight months later, South Vietnam would disappear.

* * *

To date, there have been two quite different explanations for the failure of the Paris Accords and the subsequent end of the country known as South Vietnam.

Richard Nixon and Henry Kissinger have always maintained that they won the war and that Congress lost the peace. The treaty itself, they said, although not perfect, was sound enough to have allowed for a political solution if North Vietnam had not so blatantly violated it. North and South Vietnam could have remained separate countries. When the North did violate the agreement, Watergate prevented the president from backing up his secret guarantees to President Thieu. Kissinger goes even further, insisting there was nothing secret about the promises Nixon made to Thieu. In any case, by mid-1973 Nixon was waging a constitutional battle with Congress over executive privilege and abuse of powers; he could hardly start a new battle over war powers to defend South Vietnam. "By 1973, we had achieved our political objective: South Vietnam's independence had been secured," Nixon later told Monica Crowley, former foreign policy assistant and confidante, "But by 1975, the Congress destroyed our ability to enforce the Paris agreement and left our allies vulnerable to Hanoi's invading forces. If I sound like I'm blaming Congress, I am."

Kissinger has put it this way: "Our tragedy was our domestic situation . . .

In April [1973], Watergate blew up, and we were castrated. . . . The second tragedy was that we were not permitted to enforce the agreement. . . . I think it's reasonable to assume he [Nixon] would have bombed the hell out of them during April."

The other explanation for the failure of the Paris Accords is known as the "decent interval." This explanation is far less charitable to Nixon or Kissinger because it is premised on the assumption that by January 1973, U.S. leaders cared only about securing the release of American POWs and getting some type of accounting on MIAs, especially in Laos. The political future of South Vietnam would be left for the Vietnamese to decide; we just did not want the communists to triumph too quickly. Kissinger knew that Hanoi would eventually win. By signing the peace agreement, Hanoi was not abandoning its long-term objective, merely giving the U.S. a fig leaf with which to exit. In his book *Decent Interval,* Frank Snepp wrote: "The Paris Agreement was thus a cop-out of sorts, an American one. The only thing it definitely guaranteed was an American withdrawal from Vietnam, for that depended on American action alone. The rest of the issues that had sparked the war and kept it alive were left essentially unresolved—and irresolvable."

Kissinger was asked by the assistant to the president, John Ehrlichman, "How long do you figure the South Vietnamese can survive under this agreement?" Ehrlichman reported that Kissinger answered, "I think that if they're lucky they can hold out for a year and a half." When Kissinger's assistant John Negroponte opined that the agreement was not in the best interests of South Vietnam, Kissinger asked him, "Do you want us to stay there forever?"

Nixon yearned to be remembered by history as a great foreign policy president; he needed a noncommunist South Vietnam on that ledger in order to sustain a legacy that already included détente with the Soviets and an opening with China. If South Vietnam was going down the tubes, it could not be on Nixon's watch. "What really matters now is how it all comes out," Nixon wrote in his diary in April 1972. "Both Haldeman and Henry seem to have an idea—which I think is mistaken—that even if we fail in Vietnam we can survive politically. I have no illusions whatsoever on that score, however. The US will not have a credible policy if we fail, and I will have to assume responsibility for that development."

* * *

No Peace, No Honor draws on recently declassified records to show that the true picture is worse than either of these perspectives suggests. The reality was the opposite of the decent interval hypothesis and far beyond Nixon's and Kissinger's claims. The record shows that the United States *expected* that the signed treaty would be immediately violated and that this would trigger a brutal military response. Permanent war (air war, not ground operations) at acceptable cost was what Nixon and Kissinger anticipated from the so-called peace agreement. They believed that the only way the American public would accept it was if there was a signed agreement. Nixon recognized that winning the peace, like the war, would be impossible to achieve, but he planned for indefinite stalemate by using the B-52s to prop up the government of South Vietnam until the end of his presidency. Just as the Tonkin Gulf Resolution provided a pretext for an American engagement in South Vietnam, the Paris Accords were intended to fulfill a similar role for remaining permanently engaged in Vietnam. Watergate derailed the plan.

The declassified record shows that the South Vietnamese, North Vietnamese, and the United States disregarded key elements of the treaty because all perceived it was in their interest to do so. No one took the agreement seriously because each party viewed it as a means for securing something unstated. For the United States, as part of the Nixon Doctrine, it was a means of remaining permanently involved in Southeast Asia; for the North Vietnamese, it was the means for eventual conquest and unification of Vietnam; for the South Vietnamese, it was a means for securing continued support from the United States.

The truth has remained buried for so long because Richard Nixon and Henry Kissinger did everything possible to deny any independent access to the historical record. As witnesses to history, they used many classified top-secret documents in writing their respective memoirs but later made sure that everyone else would have great difficulty accessing the same records. They have limited access to personal papers, telephone records, and other primary source materials that would allow for any independent assessments of the record pertaining to the evolution of negotiating strategies and compromises that were raised at different stages of the protracted process. The late Admiral Elmo "Bud" Zumwalt, Jr., former chief of naval operations, said that "Kissinger's method of writing history is similar to that of communist historians who took justifications from the present moment and projected backwards, fact by fact, in accounting for their country's past. Under this method, nothing really was as it happened." This is how the administration's history of "peace with honor" was written.

The personal papers of Henry Kissinger are deposited in the Library of

Congress with a deed of gift restricting access until five years after his death. For years we have been denied access to the full transcripts of Kissinger's negotiations. Verbatim hand-written transcripts of the secret meetings in Paris were kept by Kissinger's assistants, Tony Lake, Winston Lord, and John Negroponte. Negroponte gave a complete set of these meeting notes to Kissinger for writing his memoirs, but they were never returned. In his deposition to the Kerry Committee investigation, which examined virtually all aspects of the MIA issue and gave special attention to the Paris negotiations, Winston Lord stated that there were "verbatim transcripts of every meeting with the Vietnamese. I'm talking now about the secret meetings, because I took, particularly toward the beginning, and we got some help at the end, the notes as did Negroponte or Smyser or Rodman and so on." Only now have notes of these secret back-channel meetings become available. Furthermore, the North Vietnamese have published their own narrative translation of the Kissinger-Tho negotiations.

This is the story of a peace negotiation that began with Lyndon Johnson in 1968 and ended with the fall of South Vietnam in 1975. Many secret meetings were involved. The principal sources include transcript-like narratives of documents from Hanoi archives that have been translated by Luu Van Loi and Nguyen Anh Vu and published as *Le Duc Tho–Kissinger Negotiations in Paris;* declassified meeting transcripts from a congressional investigation of MIAs in Southeast Asia; declassified meeting notes from the papers of Tony Lake and memoranda of conversations from recently declassified materials in the National Archives or presidential libraries. These three have been triangulated to connect minutes as well as linkages between events. In many cases, I have been able to fill in classified sections through materials in back-channel cables from Kissinger to Ambassador Ellsworth Bunker or President Nixon.

Here, then, is the emerging story of what Nixon called "peace with honor" but was, in fact, neither. This story of diplomatic deception and public betrayal has come to the light only because of the release of documents and tapes that Richard Nixon and Henry Kissinger sought to bury for as long as possible. Prior to these declassifications, we knew only what Nixon or Kissinger wanted us to know about the making of war and shaping of the so-called honorable peace in Vietnam.

CHAPTER ONE

"Search for Peace"

> [Ambassador Averell] Harriman told me at least
> twelve times that if I called a halt, the North
> Vietnamese and Vietcong would stop shelling
> South Vietnamese cities. But nothing happened.
> Every one of the bombing halts was a mistake.
>
> Lyndon Baines Johnson to Richard Nixon
> during 1968 presidential transition

By 1968 Lyndon Johnson had become a war president. Hoping to be remembered as the president who used his office and powers to build a truly Great Society of equal opportunity and justice for all Americans, Johnson now feared a legacy shaped by the chants, "Hey, hey, LBJ, how many kids did you kill today?" and "One, two, three, four. We don't want your fucking war!"

The optimistic rhetoric of kill ratios, body counts, attrition, weapons loss, order of battle, and population control no longer held credibility with the American public. By 1968 a dwindling number of Americans doubted that they would ever see the long-promised "light at the end of the tunnel."

Despite 525,000 troops committed to the war, thousands upon thousands dead, wounded, and missing, billions of dollars and resources allocated, extensive bombings of South and North Vietnam, and the defoliation of forests with deadly toxins that destroyed jungles and poisoned civilians and soldiers alike, the pace of the war and the capacity to sustain it were controlled not by America but by the enemy.

During the early morning hours of January 31, the Vietnamese New Year known as Tet, a combined force of approximately 80,000 North Vietnamese regulars and Vietcong guerrillas attacked over 100 cities in South Vietnam. The military goal was to achieve a popular uprising and, as captured documents revealed, "move forward to achieve final victory."

This final victory was not achieved, but there were psychological and political gains in the offing. The front page of the February 1 *New York Times* showed the picture of the U.S. embassy in Saigon under assault. Guerrillas had blasted their way into the embassy and held part of the ground for nearly six hours. All 19 guerrillas were killed, as were four MPs, a Marine guard, and a South Vietnamese embassy employee.

The story of Tet has been told elsewhere and will not be repeated here. The enemy sustained major losses from which it would take years to recover. As Don Oberdorfer explained, "The Viet Cong lost the best of a generation of resistance fighters, and after Tet increasing numbers of North Vietnamese had to be sent South to fill the ranks. The war became increasingly a conventional battle and less an insurgency." But Tet also demonstrated the enemy's great skill in planning, coordination, and courage. North Vietnam regular and Vietcong forces had successfully infiltrated previously secure population centers and exploited Saigon's claims of security from attack.

Johnson's field commander, General William C. Westmoreland, now requested additional troops to regain the strategic initiative. Westmoreland believed that the enemy was throwing in all his military chips to go for broke. In late February 1968 the chairman of the Joint Chiefs of Staff, General Earle G. Wheeler, went to Vietnam for three days of consultations with Westmoreland and the senior American commander in each of the corps areas. Secretary of Defense Clark Clifford described President Johnson during this period "as worried as I have ever seen him."

On February 27 Johnson received Wheeler's report with recommendations on military requirements in South Vietnam, which amounted to a request for 206,000 additional troops. To many, this was proof of the bankruptcy of the Army's strategy in Vietnam. Despite the large enemy losses during Tet, the United States was no closer to achieving its goal in Vietnam than it was in 1965. There appeared to be no breaking point in the enemy's will to continue the struggle indefinitely. The new reinforcements would bring the total American military commitment to three-quarters of a million troops. It seemed increasingly evident that no amount of military power would bring North Vietnam to the conference table for negotiations without stopping the bombing.

That very evening of February 27, CBS television anchorman Walter Cronkite told the nation that the war was destined to end in stalemate: "We have been too often disappointed by the optimism of the American leaders, both in Vietnam and Washington, to have faith any longer in the silver linings they find in the darkest clouds. . . . For it seems now more certain than ever that the bloody experience of Vietnam is to end in a stalemate. To say that we are mired in stalemate seems the only realistic, yet unsatisfactory, conclusion."

The president appointed a task force under the direction of Secretary of Defense Clifford to evaluate the Wheeler-Westmoreland troop request. The president's final instructions to Clifford were, "Give me the lesser of evils." Clifford took the lead among a small group of LBJ advisers who believed that the war had become a sinkhole and that no matter how many forces the U.S. put in, the enemy would match it. "I see more fighting with more and more casualties on the U.S. side with no end in sight to the action," Clifford would tell the president. For weeks, Johnson wavered between a bombing halt and upping the ante by another 206,000 troops. For weeks, an anguished president awakened in the middle of the night and walked the halls of the White House or called downstairs to the situation room for an update on American casualties. Meanwhile, Clifford led a cabal trying to convince their president that he ought to stop the bombing and thereby start the negotiations that might end the war. "Is he with us?" a phrase used from the French Revolution, became the code for the group.

Johnson was torn between instincts that told him the North Vietnamese could not be trusted and fears that a bombing halt would be exploited by domestic political opponents. At the National Farmers Union convention in late March 1968, Johnson spoke of his desire to "achieve an honorable peace and a just peace at the negotiating table. But wanting peace, praying for peace, and desiring peace, as Chamberlain found out, doesn't always give you peace." Johnson also believed that there was political capital in a bombing halt. If things did not work out, he had gone the extra mile, only to be rebuked, and therefore the bombing could be renewed. Johnson had grave doubts about the sincerity of the men in Hanoi's Politburo but he felt he had no choice except to move ahead. "It's easier to satisfy Ho Chi Minh than Bill Fulbright," Johnson told Clifford. (From 1959 to 1974 J. William Fulbright served as chairman of the Senate Foreign Relations Committee. His was a powerful voice of dissent during the Vietnam War, leading Johnson to refer demeaningly to the senator as "half-bright.")

Johnson would be wrong in his judgment of Ho. But at this crucial juncture in the history of the war, LBJ was rolling the dice, believing that his decisions might result in negotiations but most certainly would allow him to renew the bombing if Hanoi did not cease its military activities. He would not stop all of the bombing until Hanoi agreed to cease attacking the cities. Addressing the nation on March 31, 1968, the president spoke of his willingness "to move immediately toward peace through negotiations." Johnson announced, "There is no need to delay talks that could bring an end to this long and this bloody war." He was "taking the first step to de-escalate the level of hostilities" by unilaterally reducing attacks on North Vietnam, except in the area north of the demilitarized zone, known as the DMZ. "The area in which we are stopping our attacks includes almost 90% of North Vietnam's population and most of its territory," said Johnson. "Even this very limited bombing of the North could come to an early end if our restraint is matched by restraint in Hanoi."

Johnson called on North Vietnam's leader, Ho Chi Minh, to respond favorably and positively to these overtures and not to take advantage of this restraint. "We are prepared to move immediately toward peace through negotiations." The United States was "ready to send its representatives to any forum, at any time, to discuss the means of bringing this ugly war to an end." To prove his sincerity, Johnson named the distinguished American ambassador W. Averell Harriman as his "personal representative for such talks," assigning Harriman the task to *search for peace.*"

Then, in a dramatic gesture toward national unity, the president renounced his chance at reelection. "With America's sons in the fields far away, with America's future under challenge right here at home, with our hopes and the world's hopes for peace in the balance every day, I do not believe that I should devote an hour or a day of my time to any personal partisan causes or to any duties other than the awesome duties of this office—the presidency of your country. Accordingly, I shall not seek and I will not accept the nomination of my party for another term as your President."

Three days later, Radio Hanoi broadcast the news that North Vietnam had accepted Johnson's offer and would agree to establish contact between the representatives of the United States and North Vietnam. This was the first time that Hanoi had said publicly it was willing to talk. It nevertheless was careful to stipulate that these initial contacts would focus first on bringing about the unconditional end to American bombing and other acts of aggression against Vietnam.

Johnson's announcement that he would not seek reelection stunned the country. To many, the hawk was dead. To others, the war had claimed as victim a man of immense talent and heart. Tragedy then further unraveled the fabric of the Great Society on April 4 when the Rev. Martin Luther King was assassinated in Memphis, igniting riots in America's cities. The Great Society was dead.

Recently declassified documents from communist archives disclose that Hanoi's positive response to initiate contacts with the U.S. engendered a serious rebuke from China, whose leaders believed that there was no reason to begin negotiations until the North Vietnamese post-Tet military position had improved. Two weeks after the March 31 announcement, North Vietnam's prime minister, Pham Van Dong, was told by Chou Enlai, "In the eyes of the world's people, you have compromised twice." Chou asked how it was possible for Hanoi to have contacts while the United States still bombed north of the DMZ. "We entirely believe in your fighting experience. But we are somewhat more experienced than you as far as conducting talks with the United States is concerned," observed Chou. The Chinese believed that Hanoi was helping to transform Johnson from a man of war to a man of peace, and there was no need to have done so before improving their military situation.

A few days later, Chou Enlai told Pham Van Dong that the North Vietnamese needed to be prepared to fight for at least two to three more years, through at least 1970. "Comrade Mao said that the question is not that of success or failure, nor of big or small success, but of how you gain the great victory. It is high time you gain a complete victory. That task gives rise to the need for large-scale battles." Chou described LBJ's March 31 speech as "a wicked and deceitful scheme."

It would soon become apparent to the Chinese as well as the Soviets that North Vietnam was determined to be master of its own fate in these negotiations. Le Duc Tho and other members of the Hanoi Politburo possessed lingering memories of betrayal in 1954 at Geneva, when the Vietminh were pressured into compromise by their allies, the Chinese and Soviets. When Japan had finally admitted defeat in World War II, the Vietnamese had hoped for freedom. Ho Chi Minh, who four years earlier had founded the League for Revolution and Independence—the Vietminh—had been preparing his entire lifetime for the August 1945 revolution. Here was the opportunity to rid Vietnam not only of the Japanese but the Vichy French colonial regime as well. Military Order No. 1, issued by Vo Nguyen Giap on August 12, called for a general insurrection throughout Vietnam. Within weeks the Vietminh had taken control of major cities throughout the country.

Following Emperor Bao Dai's abdication on August 24, Ho Chi Minh quickly moved to proclaim a new independent Democratic Republic of Vietnam (DRV). The People's Republic of China (PRC) was the first country to recognize the new DRV. It was an exciting time. Eighteen-year-old Bui Tin had come to the ornate French-style Opera House in Hanoi that August to witness the end of French colonialism. "I too was fired with enthusiasm. Like the rest of my generation and indeed most Vietnamese people, we were bursting with optimism and excitement," he recalled.

Throughout Vietnam, banners proclaimed "Vietnam for the Vietnamese." Saigon was seething. Truong Nhu Tang described the moment: "Caught in a tide of emotional patriotism and excited by danger and the idea of independence, all of Saigon's young people seemed to be joining." On August 21 Tang was in the crowd marching from one end of Saigon to the other chanting, "Da Dao de quoc, Da Dao thuc dan dhap" ("Down with the Imperialists, Down with the French colonialists").

Two weeks later, on September 2, 1945, Bui Tin was in the crowd in Hanoi's Ba Dinh Square to witness Ho Chi Minh's historic proclamation of independence in which he borrowed words from the American Declaration of Independence: "We hold the truth that all men are created equal, that they are endowed by their Creator certain inalienable rights, among them life, liberty and the pursuit of happiness. . . . Do you hear me distinctly my fellow countrymen?"

Born Nguyen Sinh Cuong in 1890, Ho left Vietnam in 1911 for a variety of jobs in Western Europe; he traveled to the United States, where he lived briefly in Brooklyn and Boston, and by 1917 had returned to France. He became one of the founders of the French Communist party and agitated for Vietnamese rights. He was later sent to South China, where he organized and recruited Vietnamese students and dissidents. He became known for his writings as a pamphleteer, editor, and organizer. His writings attracted the attention of young Vietnamese like Vo Nguyen Giap and Pham Van Dong, who would remain forever loyal to their leader and themselves played important roles in Vietnam's diplomatic and military history.

In September 1945 the DRV controlled the region of Hanoi and the northern part of the country, but the French, determined to stop their declining world reputation, focused on reasserting control over Indochina. Following the shelling of Haiphong by French cruisers in November 1946, full-scale war broke out between the French and Vietminh. As the cold war developed, Washington became more sensitive to the colonial interests of its allies than to the decolonization of Indochina. Ho was a Leninist and pro-Moscow. Not surprisingly, the U.S. indirectly supported the French military action in Indochina against the Vietminh. After the communist victory in China in 1949 and the outbreak of the Korean War in 1950, its contribution became direct. A month after the outbreak of hostilities in Korea, Secretary of State Dean Acheson announced the first increment of American aid to the French for the Indochina war.

In 1954 the French were defeated in battle at Dien Bien Phu. The Vietminh controlled most of Vietnam and sought a political settlement at Geneva that would lead to the withdrawal of French forces and the establishment of an independent government led by Ho Chi Minh. But four of the men sitting around the large horseshoe shaped table at the old League of Nations building with a map of Southeast Asia on it put their own interests ahead of the fifth person at the table, Pham Van Dong. The four—Foreign Secretary Anthony Eden of the United Kingdom, Premier Pierre Mendes-France of France, Foreign Minister Vyacheslav Molotov of the Soviet Union, and Foreign Minister Chou Enlai of China—pressured the DRV to accept much less than it had won in battle. The Vietnamese would never forget this "negotiation."

The Pentagon Papers make clear that the United States intended to disassociate itself from the results at Geneva, fearing a "sellout" of U.S. interests. A May 4, 1954, meeting of the National Security Council established U.S. policy: "The United States will not associate itself with any proposal from any source directed toward a cease-fire. . . . In the meantime, as a means of strengthening the hands of the French and the Associated States during the course of such negotiations, the United States will continue its program of aid and its efforts to organize and promptly activate a Southeast Asian regional grouping for the purpose of preventing further expansion of communist power in Southeast Asia."

The Chinese and Soviets, fearing American intervention under Secretary of State John Foster Dulles, forced Ho to accept two major concessions: a demarcation line drawn at the 17th parallel and free nationwide elections supervised by an international commission scheduled for 1956. The elections would settle the question of political control over Vietnam. Vietnam was to be neutralized, meaning that no military alliances were to be made by either side.

The Geneva settlement partitioned Vietnam at a nominally temporary "line of demarcation" between North and South at the 17th parallel, with the Vietminh taking control of the Northern zone and France and an opposing Vietnamese government, ultimately led by Ngo Dinh Diem, controlling the South. The Vietminh surrendered two strongholds in Quang Nam and Quang Ngai. They had wanted the elections to be held in six months, not two years. All in all they gave up quite a bit.

Nguyen Khac Huyen later explained that at the time of Geneva, the Vietminh did not yet have any experience with diplomacy or multilateral discussions. They had just fought a ten-year war in the jungles; there were few diplomats among them. "Literally, we were stepping out of the jungle and going to Geneva, at the invitation of our friends; our allies, the Chinese and Soviets."

Robert McNamara later observed, "At Geneva, they compromised in order to secure a promise, which was broken. In the future, their willingness to compromise would seem virtually nonexistent to Washington. At Geneva, they tried to play the game of diplomacy with the big powers and lost. In the future, 'diplomacy' with the United States would be conducted only between Washington and Hanoi—or not at all. And, most importantly, one suspects, at Geneva they felt they had, in effect, betrayed their counterparts south of the 17th parallel, who had already suffered most in the war with the French."

"All in all, the 1954 Geneva Agreement was a disaster for us," said Luu Doan Huynh, "because the big powers were the architects and the Vietnamese the victims." Why did Ho Chi Minh accept these compromises? As Ziang Zhai's recent scholarship shows, "Ho Chi Minh must have realized that without Chinese and Soviet assistance, he could not have defeated the French and achieved the position he now had. He could not afford to resist the pressure of his two communist allies." He must also have believed that in two years, "all Vietnam would be his."

Instead, Vietnam would remain divided for over two decades. Indeed,

Geneva would prove an important prelude to the Paris Peace Talks in more than one way. Richard Nixon was vice president at the time of Geneva, and Pham Van Dong headed the DRV delegation. By 1970 both men would be the leaders of the United States and the DRV, respectively. Both drew lessons from the Geneva experience that would influence how each approached the negotiations in Paris. Dong believed that the Vietminh were betrayed by their friends. For example, two weeks after Nixon's election in 1968, Dong would visit Mao in Beijing. "Twenty three years have passed since the Japanese surrender in 1945 but your country is still existing," said Mao. "You have fought the Japanese, the French, and now you are fighting the Americans. But Vietnam still exists. . . . It was difficult for Ho to give up the South, and now, when I think twice, I see that he was right. The mood of the people in the South at that time was rising high. . . . I see that it would be better if the conference could have been delayed for one year, so the troops from the North could come down [to the South] and defeat [the enemy.]"

Pham Van Dong responded, "Ultimately, it is we who make the decisions based on the actual situation in Vietnam and how we understand the rules of the war. . . . We are determined to fight until the final and total victory is gained."

North Vietnam negotiator Le Duc Tho would hold a similar view. On September 7, 1971, Tho would meet Ieng Sary, Pol Pot's closest collaborator in the Cambodian Communist party Politburo, who was then living in Beijing. "We will always remember the experience in 1954. Comrade Chou Enlai admitted mistakes in the Geneva Conference of 1954. Two or three years ago, comrade Mao also did so. In 1954, because both the Soviet Union and China exerted pressure, the outcome became what it became. We have proposed that the Chinese comrades admit their mistakes and now I am telling you, the Cambodian comrades, about this problem of history."

In short, North Vietnam had learned the hard way that it should trust no one and give up nothing in negotiation. Richard Nixon had learned from Geneva to use Hanoi's friends, the Soviets and Chinese, to force concessions that would lead to a political settlement whose terms could be ignored.

* * *

Northern memories of past betrayals colored the peace process from the start. In 1968, after Johnson's overture met its tentative response from Hanoi, he wanted to situate them in Geneva again. After all, Switzerland was a neutral country, and the city could accommodate the large number of diplomats and members of the world press who were expected to attend the plenary sessions. But the memories of the Vietminh were too long to allow them to consider it. The comically long list of cities that was bandied about should have been taken as a bad omen.

Hanoi wanted the meetings to be held in Phnom Penh, Cambodia, but that was out of the question to the Americans. The president offered four Asian sites—Vientiane, Rangoon, Djakarta, or New Delhi. All were unacceptable to the North Vietnamese, who countered with Warsaw and the date of April 18 for the first session. Warsaw was unacceptable to President Johnson because Poland had given so much assistance to the North Vietnamese, and in no sense could Warsaw be considered a neutral site. "I don't want any part of Warsaw, Czechoslovakia, or any other Eastern European country," Johnson told Harriman.

The Joint Chiefs of Staff's *Command History of the Vietnam War* concluded that Hanoi rejected all subsequent future suggestions made by the U.S. out of deference to China. The United States then proposed another six sites in Asia and four in Europe: Colombo, Tokyo, Kabul, Katmandu, Rawalpindi, Kuala Lumpar, Rome, Brussels, Helsinki, and Vienna. The North Vietnamese rejected all on grounds that they were either not neutral or were in countries that did not have diplomatic relations with North Vietnam.

On May 2, Hanoi rejected the U.S. proposal for a secret meeting in the Gulf of Tonkin on an Indonesian ship, but just a few hours later finally agreed to meet in Paris. United States officials, including President Johnson, were concerned that President Charles de Gaulle, a critic of American involvement in Vietnam, might now be credited for his country's role in brokering the peace, yet Paris seemed the only possible site. On May 3, 1968, President Johnson announced that both sides had agreed to Paris. He quietly added, "This is only the first step. There are many, many hazards and difficulties ahead."

The talks were scheduled to begin on May 9. But who, exactly, would take part?

President Johnson knew that the Government of South Vietnam, headed by President Nguyen Van Thieu, opposed any bilateral discussions with the North Vietnamese on issues that would affect the South. Thieu believed that North Vietnam would use these initial contacts to demand direct negotiations between the Government of Vietnam (GVN) and the National Liberation Front (NLF) in the hope of creating the conditions for a coalition government. He was correct, and the issue of who sat at the table became a major sticking point.

The NLF had been created in 1960 as part of the North Vietnamese Communist party's strategy of combining political with military tactics to destroy the Saigon regime. The period 1954–1960 had proven to the party leaders that political struggle alone would be insufficient for uniting the country. The NLF was active in the South and had many followers, but no real hope of winning an election. The revolutionary goals now aimed for socialism in the North and liberation in the South. After eight years of armed conflict, the liberation of the South seemed entirely possible.

The party's Political Bureau formulated a strategy for dividing their enemy for any negotiations with the United States. As historian Robert Brigham explains, "Party leaders correctly predicted that they could use the NLF's participation in the upcoming negotiations to alienate the United States from Saigon. In a secret meeting in Hanoi in early April [1968], the Political Bureau instructed the southern diplomats to promote the NLF as a political entity with a significant role in the settlement. . . . The communists therefore linked the negotiations to the Front's right to participate, a position the Saigon government had opposed from the beginning." For the North, getting the NLF recognized as a player would be a victory.

Tran Van Do, South Vietnam's foreign minister, told the *Gazette de Lausanne* on April 16, "We do not deny the existence of the National Liberation Front as a powerful organization, but we do deny its existence as a government. It is logical. It is a principle. For us, the negotiations have to be conducted between Saigon and Hanoi who have a common basis for discussions: the Geneva Accords accepted by the two Vietnams. Once that is settled, we are ready to talk to the National Liberation Front as Diem did after 1954, such as with the armies and the dissident parties." In other words, the NLF had to be treated as a minority party within an autonomous South, not as a principal actor in international affairs.

Meanwhile, the South prepared its own strategy. A secret special committee under the leadership of Tran Van Do prepared position papers on such topics as coalition government, neutralization, and the 1954 Geneva Accords. Do had been chief of South Vietnam's delegation at Geneva in 1954, but some, like Vice President Ky, did not believe he was tough enough to head South Vietnam's delegation in Paris. Nguyen Cao Ky told Thieu that Do "might break down and cry again," as Do, who was from the North, had done in 1954 when he was presented with the final design. Ky offered to head the delegation himself, but that job fell to Pham Dang Lam, South Vietnam's ambassador to France. Bui Diem went to Paris as an observer.

The group included the most respected South Vietnamese: Vuong Van Bac, a Saigon lawyer; Senator Tran Chanh Thanh, chairman of the Senate Foreign Affairs Committee; Pham Dang Lam; Senator Dang Van Sung; Tran Thanh Hiep, a lawyer; and Dr. Pham Huu Chuong, former civilian member of the Directorate.

By May, with the parties, location, and strategy in place, the North Vietnamese and the United States were set to begin talks. But how serious were they? On the ground, in 1968, the North and Vietcong had accomplished little; in fact, they had suffered serious setbacks on the military front. Nevertheless, they believed that time was on their side. Although Hanoi had spurned Chou Enlai's suggestion of putting off the talks until there was a discernable improvement in the military situation, the North agreed to attend the meetings in Paris in order to discern Johnson's motives and garner public support for the cause. There were several layers to Hanoi's strategy, but until the balance of power shifted dramatically in their favor, the Politburo had no intention of negotiating, seeking only to frustrate Lyndon Johnson as peacemaker.

* * *

On May 8, a day before departing for Paris, LBJ summoned Ambassador Harriman to the White House so that the two men could review the ambassador's final instructions for the negotiations. President Johnson was under great domestic pressure from hawks as well as his Joint Chiefs not to stop all the bombing as a precondition for beginning talks, and Johnson was inclined to agree. Just a few weeks earlier, General Westmoreland had told him that "in the negotiations, Governor Harriman will have a hand with four aces, and the enemy will have two deuces. I do not see any acceptable ceasefire. We would just like the North Vietnamese to go home and turn in their weapons." But that was not going to happen, and Johnson now provided Harriman with four U.S. objectives in Paris:

1. Prompt and serious substantive talks looking toward peace in Vietnam, in the course of which an understanding could be reached on a cessation of bombing in the North under circumstances that would not be militarily disadvantageous
2. Creation of some control mechanism to oversee any peace or cease-fire
3. Reestablishment of the DMZ as a genuine border

4. The full involvement of the government of the Republic of Vietnam in any talks on the future of South Vietnam

The American and Vietnamese delegations reached Paris on May 9. The talks at the International Conference Center in the old Majestic Hotel began on May 13.

The NLF was not officially present, but its propaganda campaign for parity with Thieu's government was growing each day. Hanoi's delegation was headed by Nguyen Xuan Thuy, the former foreign minister who had faced Harriman at the negotiating sessions at the 1962 Geneva Conference on Laos. His deputy was Ambassador Ha Van Lau, who aside from extensive General Staff experience had been a member of the DRVN delegation to the 1954 Geneva Conference on Indochina as well as the 1961–1962 Geneva Conference on Laos.

Xuan Thuy, like so many others of his generation, had joined the nationalist movement in Vietnam's fight against the French in his early teens. In 1926 he joined Ho Chi Minh's Communist Revolutionary Youth League, was arrested twice during the 1920s, and later was imprisoned and tortured by the French for six years at Son La. While in prison, he edited a communist newspaper that was secretly circulated among his fellow prisoners. After his release from prison, he became chief editor and director of *Cuu Quoc,* the official newspaper of the Vietminh League.

Thuy's diplomatic career began in 1953 when he was named secretary general of North Vietnam's Peace Committee and representative on the Communist World Peace Council. He was known for his close affinity to the Chinese. Kissinger later described him as "tiny, with a Buddha face and a sharp mind, perpetually smiling even when saying the most outrageous things . . . His job was psychological warfare."

Unbeknown to the American negotiators, just two days prior to the opening session in Paris, Xuan Thuy was in Beijing, meeting with Chou Enlai at the Great Hall of the People in a strategy meeting that paralleled LBJ's with Harriman. "The fundamental question is that what you cannot get on the battlefield, no matter how you try, you will not get at the negotiation table. Dien Bien Phu set up the 17th parallel, therefore the Geneva Conference could reach an agreement," said Chou. The Chinese still believed the North Vietnamese had agreed to negotiate too quickly, "which might have left the Americans with the impression that you are eager to negotiate." Xuan Thuy was reminded that the Americans and their allies still had a military force of over 1 million, and "before their backbone has been broken, or before five or six of their fingers have been broken, they will not accept the defeat, and they will not leave." The Chinese position was clear: stall. War was the only way to further the cause. Xuan Thuy did not necessarily follow orders from Beijing, but he did eventually take Chou's advice.

Arriving in Paris from Beijing, Xuan Thuy also carried explicit instructions from Hanoi's Politburo. He was not in Paris to reach a settlement. The public talks would serve only as a vehicle to gain worldwide public support for their people's war of resistance, gain a complete halt to the bombing, and figure out the United States's diplomatic strategy. To date, all available archival materials from Hanoi, China, and the former Soviet Union show that Johnson's bombing restriction south of the 20th parallel had caught Hanoi by surprise. Communist leaders needed time to calculate a diplomatic and fighting strategy that would be effective against the American's new diplomatic overture.

For the next five months, very little progress would be made. Both sides had preconditions prior to negotiations. For Hanoi, it was the demand for a total bombing halt, as well as the NLF's full participation in the talks. For the United States, it was that Hanoi desist from infiltrating the DMZ, stop attacks on South Vietnam's cities, and welcome the Republic of Vietnam into the negotiations.

Xuan Thuy used the opening session to assail the United States for "monstrous crimes" and its puppet regime in Saigon. He repeated what at the time constituted Hanoi's four points: withdrawal of all U.S. forces, temporary restoration of the North and South zones as delineated under the 1954 Geneva Accords, self-determination for South Vietnam, and peaceful reunification of North and South. "The opening statement by the chief North Vietnamese delegate could have been an editorial in Hanoi's Communist party newspaper," said President Johnson. "Their solution was for us to stop the bombing and pull all our forces out."

Averell Harriman, who was joined by Cyrus Vance, former Deputy Secretary of Defense, who now held the rank of Ambassador; Lieutenant General Andrew Goodpaster, then Commandant of the National War College, serving as military advisor; Phillip Habib of the State Department; and William Jorden of the NSC, used the first plenary session to restate that the United States's sole objective was for South Vietnam "to determine their own future without outside interference or coercion." Harriman had been instructed to tell the North Vietnamese that the bombing would stop only if Hanoi promised not to take advantage of the halt and if they showed they were ready to begin serious negotiations. Hanoi rejected all of these "ifs" on grounds that "if" constituted reciprocity and a bombing halt needed to be unconditional.

The talks proceeded at such an unproductive pace that Johnson sought the advice of his Joint Chiefs for military recommendations in the likely event that the talks fell apart. On May 8, May 15, and May 21, Secretary of State Dean Rusk and JCS chairman Earle Wheeler pressed Johnson to renew the bombings in areas between the 19th and 20th parallels. Rusk kept warning Johnson that the communists were engaging in a propaganda offensive. By May 29, the Joint Chiefs produced a plan calling for a greatly expanded air campaign over North Vietnam, except areas close to the Chinese border. The Joint Chiefs' *Command History* shows that the JCS emphatically rejected any mere extension of bombing from the 19th to the 20th parallel and even rejected a one-time big strike. Indeed, their recommendation was that if the talks broke down, it would be time for such aggressive actions as mining the harbors and bombing the North almost without constraint.

The declassified record shows that any serious debate about the Joint Chiefs' proposal subsided when a new figure arrived in Paris: Le Duc Tho, a ranking member of Hanoi's Politburo, special adviser to Minister Thuy at the talks. The Joint Chiefs' *History* notes that "no one knew what instructions he might bring with him, but Ambassador Harriman considered that his arrival might at least signal a degree of flexibility in the enemy's position." Harriman recommended that any consideration of bombing be deferred.

Le Duc Tho was unknown to the general public when he arrived in Paris, but French and American intelligence services had long dossiers on him. Born in October 1911 in Nam Ha Province in Tonkin, North Vietnam, the young Phan Dinh Khai, as he was known before taking his nom de guerre, was an early member of Ho Chi Minh's circle and in 1930 was one of the founders of the Indochina Communist party. During the mid-1960s he supervised military and political activities in the South; during the French Indochina war, he was chief commissioner for southern Vietnam. He would spend over ten years in French jails, including forced labor at Poulo Condore, later called Con Son, a prison island known for its brutal and harsh conditions. During World War II, he was imprisoned in the Nam Dinh jail, from which he wrote the poem "Cell of Hatred," with the words, "Rage grips me against those barbaric imperialists, so many years their heels have crushed our country . . . a thousand, thousand oppressions."

When seen in public, the gray-haired Le Duc Tho, five feet eight inches tall, was invariably dressed in a plain, well-tailored black Mao suit. Beneath the smiling exterior was a hardened revolutionary. "Mr. Six Hammer" was the name his cadres gave to him.

Harriman hoped Le Duc Tho's arrival was a signal that the other side was prepared for private meetings between the heads of the two diplomatic delegations. He was right. Just two weeks earlier, Harriman had confided to Soviet ambassador Valerian Zorin that the lack of progress in Paris was creating pressure on Johnson to renew the bombing. Soviet premier Aleksei Kosygin now sent LBJ a private message that "my colleagues and I believe, and we have grounds for this, that a full cessation by the United States of bombardments and other acts of war against the DRV could promote a breakthrough in the situation that would open perspectives for peaceful settlement" without "adverse consequences whatever for the United States." Kosygin recommended that there be "unofficial contacts" between the delegations. Johnson had serious doubts about Soviet motives and North Vietnam's flexibility, but at tea break during the June 12 session, Harriman and Vance suggested to Le Duc Tho that private talks be held parallel to the public discussions. Tho agreed.

The first of these meetings took place on the evening of June 26 at the home of the North Vietnamese delegation in Vitry-sur-Seine and lasted over two hours, ending past midnight. These initial private meetings produced no progress because both sides still held firm positions. Le Duc Tho insisted that the negotiations could not begin until the United States completely stopped the bombing; Harriman insisted that Le Duc Tho negotiate with the South Vietnamese delegates. At one of the private meetings, Xuan Thuy told Harriman, "I should frankly tell you that the Saigon administration is not the representative of the Vietnamese people. We do not recognize the Thieu-Ky clique, don't you know that?"

Harriman responded, "You are distorting things. This is not a condition. If you want war, bombs will fall on your heads."

Xuan Thuy then said, "Do you threaten with the resumption of bombing in North Vietnam? We are prepared to cope with it. Our people have been opposing aggressors; we have been fighting against you for decades. You cannot threaten us with war."

For the next three years, U.S. negotiators would often resort to this same type of threat, and Xuan Thuy's or Le Duc Tho's response would always be the same.

The unyielding stance of the North Vietnamese negotiators was viewed by the Joint Chiefs' historian as the result of "their belief that the United States had entered the talks merely to find a face-saving formula for a surrender. This conviction was reflected in their arrogant self-assurance. Little progress could be expected so long as they remained under this impression."

The Politburo knew that LBJ would never agree to Hanoi's conditions and devised a strategy of *dividing* the United States from Saigon. The communists, as President Thieu had anticipated, insisted on the right of the NLF to participate in the talks, which they knew Saigon would oppose from the very beginning. Slowly but steadily, the U.S. was tempted to cave in.

Johnson's patience was wearing thin. He did not want to stop all the bombing of North Vietnam when the communists had not ceased infiltration and were poised for another offensive. On July 26, 1968, he invited Republican candidate Richard Nixon to the White House in order to hear the probable Republican nominee's views on Vietnam. Rusk and Rostow were the only others present. Nixon made it very clear that he did not favor a bombing pause because bombing was "one piece of leverage you have left." As Nixon was leaving the White House, he told LBJ, "I do not intend to advocate a bombing pause." LBJ was certainly leaning the same way. On August 22 he told the cabinet that "we want peace now worse than anything in the world—but with honor, without retreat." He added that "61% of the people don't want to halt the bombing."

LBJ tried to break the impasse in Paris with a stern warning, but already he had set a pattern of weakness that undercut attempts at resolve. On September 15, he sent a message to the Soviet leaders. "Setting all political arguments aside, the simple fact is that the President could not maintain a cessation of the bombing of North Vietnam unless it were very promptly evident to him, to the American people, and to our allies, that such an action was, indeed, a step toward peace. Cessation of bombing which would be followed by abuses of the DMZ, Viet Cong and North Vietnamese attacks on cities or such populated areas as provincial capitals, or a refusal of the authorities in Hanoi to enter promptly into serious political discussions which included the elected government of the Republic of Vietnam, could simply not be sustained."

On October 12, the Soviets passed a message to the U.S. delegation that North Vietnam would agree to the participation of the Saigon government, but only if the bombing stopped totally. Valentin Oberenko, the Soviet deputy chief of mission, told Cyrus Vance that "if the U.S. stops unconditionally and completely the bombardments and other acts of war against the DRV, the delegation of North Viet Nam will agree to the participation of the representatives of the Saigon government in the talks on the problem of political settlement in Viet Nam. Thus, these talks would be held by the representatives of the DRV, of the United States of America, of the NLF, and the Saigon government."

Oberenko added that the time had arrived to "move the talks off dead center and that this view was shared by the North Vietnamese yesterday afternoon after our meeting with them." He emphasized that "the situation is most favorable right now and this opportunity should not be lost."

The U.S. soon learned that this message was not only a transmission from the DRV but an instruction from the Soviet government. What Harriman had long predicted had been finally borne out. Moscow wanted to deny Richard Nixon, a certified cold warrior, victory in November. They would rather deal with Hubert Humphrey, as would the North Vietnamese. Moscow's ambassador, Anatoly Dobrynin, later wrote that he was instructed to help Humphrey win the 1968 election: "Moscow believed that as far as its relations with Washington were concerned, Humphrey would make the best president at that time."

After the August 1968 Democratic convention, however, the Soviets had begun to worry that Nixon might win the election. "As a result the top Soviet leaders took an extraordinary step, unprecedented in the history of Soviet-American relations, by secretly offering Humphrey any conceivable help in his election campaign—even financial aid." Dobrynin claims that he communicated this information to Humphrey, but that the candidate declined any assistance from the Soviet Union. It was the start of a complicated dance of domestic interference by Hanoi that would stutter forward again in 1972.

At this point, Le Duc Tho tried to launch the talks by posing two questions to Harriman: Would the United States stop the bombing after Hanoi answered the U.S. condition on GVN participation? And, after the answer was given, would the U.S. consider it a "condition" or "reciprocity" for stopping the bombing? The North Vietnamese were prepared to allow Saigon into the talks in exchange for a total U.S. bombing halt, but on October 13 Le Duc Tho received new instructions from Hanoi: the United States would not only have to stop the bombing and other acts of aggression, but if Hanoi was going to talk with the GVN, then the U.S. would have to talk with the NLF. With all these conditions, the chances for a deal before the election were dim. Yet with so many variables—North, South, NLF, Johnson, Humphrey, and Nixon—the temptation to play the election card only grew.

On the same day Le Duc Tho told Harriman that Hanoi would talk with the South Vietnamese, "unbeknownst to anyone in the Johnson administration, Henry Kissinger secretly informed Nixon's campaign manager, John Mitchell, that there was a strong probability that the Johnson administration would stop the bombing before the election." Kissinger had obtained this information earlier from Harriman and Vance, who were still negotiating in Paris.

Could LBJ achieve a deal in time to help Humphrey? Not if China could help it. Stopping in China on his way to Hanoi on October 17, Le Duc Tho was severely chastised by the Chinese foreign minister, Chen Yi, for having already lost the diplomatic initiative by agreeing to talk with the Americans while the U.S. had only partially stopped the bombing. The North Vietnamese had accepted quadripartite negotiations with the South Vietnamese, albeit only as an observer. Chen Yi stated that the United States had gained legitimacy for its "puppet government," and the "NLF's status as the unique representative of the people had lost its prestige. This makes us wonder whether you have strengthened the enemy's position while weakening ours. You are acting in contradiction to the teaching of President Ho, the great leader of the Vietnamese people, thus destroying President Ho's prestige among the Vietnamese people. . . . You do not liberate the people of the South, but cause them more losses." Chen Yi closed by accusing North Vietnam of falling into a trap set by the "compromising and surrendering proposals put forward by the Soviet revisionists."

By now Le Duc Tho could take no more: "We have gained experience over the past 15 years. Let reality justify." Tho harkened back to Geneva when the Vietnamese had listened to China and made a mistake. "But this time, you will make another if you do not take our words into account," warned Chen Yi.

Two weeks of difficult negotiations ensued in Paris, but finally a breakthrough occurred on October 27, when all sides agreed that President Johnson would announce a complete bombing halt on October 31 and that the talks would start on November 2. Presidential candidate Richard Nixon and South Vietnam's Thieu had other ideas. A declassified CIA cable reported that President Thieu believed LBJ's motivation for seeking a bombing halt was "to carve his niche in history at the expense of the GVN." Thieu also sensed that Johnson was "trying to pull off a near miracle which. . . . will be needed to stave off defeat for Mr. Humphrey and the Democrats in November." Vice President Ky "wonders whether this is not a bad time to tie oneself too closely to the present Washington leadership."

Johnson decided he would stop the bombing but first called a meeting requesting that "the man who bore the heaviest burden for the safety of the men under fire," General Creighton Abrams, be present so that he could look him in the eyes and ask about the implications of a complete bombing halt.

Abrams boarded a C-141 in Saigon and flew all night, arriving at Andrews Air Force Base about 1:00 A.M. where he was met by Colonel Robert Ginsburgh and was taken directly to the White House. They went directly to the cabinet room, where the president and his team were waiting. It was 2:30 in the morning of October 29, and Dean Rusk, Clark Clifford, General Earle Wheeler, Maxwell Taylor, Richard Helms, and Walt Rostow were in the room.

LBJ reviewed the course of negotiations to that point, beginning with Kosygin's June 5 note, saying that North Vietnam's agreement to GVN participation was a major concession—"potentially setting the stage for an honorable settlement of the war."

Turning to General Abrams, the president asked whether, in the light of what he knew, he had any reluctance or hesitance to stop the bombing.

"No, sir," was the reply.

LBJ then asked, "If you were President, would you do it?"

General Abrams replied that he had "no reservations," although he understood that it would be "stepping into a cesspool of comment." He continued, "I do not think it is the right thing to do; it is the proper thing to do."

The president told Abrams, "I am going to put more weight on your judgment than that of anyone else." He followed with another specific question: "General, do you think they will violate the DMZ and the cities?"

Looking the president directly in the eyes, Abrams said, "I think they will abide by it on the DMZ, Mr. President. On the cities, I am not so sure. I am concerned about Saigon."

It was 5:00 A.M. when the president finished his questions of Abrams. In fourteen hours, the bombing halt would be initiated.

Lewis Sorley, in his biography of Abrams, describes a scene where, following this meeting, the president privately awarded Abrams his fourth Distinguished Service Medal in an upstairs bedroom of the White House. As Abrams was leaving the White House, LBJ gave him a handwritten letter that reflected just how little faith Johnson had in the bombing halt: "Dear Abe, you and I know that the really crucial stage of both diplomatic and military operations is now upon us. If we are to win the kind of peace in Paris we want, you must keep the enemy on the run—in South Vietnam and in Laos. . . . Your President and your country are counting on you to follow the enemy in relentless pursuit. Don't give them a moment's rest. Keep pouring it on. Let the enemy feel the weight of everything you've got."

All that was left was to get President Thieu's okay to the negotiations. Yet, as would be the pattern for the next four years, President Thieu was not ready. Thieu insisted that the NLF should attend only as part of the North Vietnamese delegation, not as a separate entity, which would appear to give recognition to Hanoi's puppet and set the stage for a coalition government in the South. Thieu said that the South Vietnamese could not attend the Paris forum on November 2 and asked for a delay in the first meeting. "There is no honor in talking to thieves, let alone the servants of thieves," said Thieu of talking with the NLF. "In whose Army do the Generals of the other side hold rank?" he asked. Thieu saw the generals of what he always referred to as the "so-called" NLF as being little more than lackeys of the North.

President Thieu by now recognized that the United States was entering talks with the North Vietnamse without having obtained any agreement with their ally on the most fundamental questions: What are we going to talk about? What is the process to conduct the talks? What will be the format? "The South Vietnamese wanted these questions to be at least agreed upon between allies and put forward to the communists as the allied unified position. As the record shows, the U.S. did not listen as they had already made the decision and they moved quickly to pin the blame on the South Vietnam President," recalled Thieu's press secretary, Hoang Duc Nha.

But with the NLF delegation on its way to Paris, it would embarrass the U.S. if the South Vietnamese boycotted the talks. By now, Clark Clifford had had enough of Thieu's machinations, telling the president that he should "force them to attend." General Earle Wheeler instructed Abrams to use his personal influence on Thieu, saying, "I wish you to know that I consider the position taken by President Thieu to be intolerable." Clifford described Thieu's motivations as "horseshit." What he meant by this was that Thieu appeared to be trying to influence the American election.

* * *

The 1968 presidential campaign between Vice President Hubert Humphrey, Governor of Alabama George Wallace, and Richard Nixon did nothing to soothe the nation's turmoil. Nixon, who had defeated Nelson Rockefeller and Ronald Reagan in the Republican primaries, ran on a platform of law and order, reductions in welfare expenditures, and an honorable end to the Vietnam War.

Humphrey, the once-happy warrior, found himself in a no-win situation. He led a bitterly divided party, having lost much of his liberal backing at the Democratic convention in Chicago. The conservative South was in the hands of candidate George Wallace and his running mate, General Curtis LeMay, both hawks and known as "the bombsy twins." Humphrey found it difficult to escape being linked to LBJ's Vietnam policy since he could not repudiate an administration in which he was still vice president. Instead, Humphrey tried to distance himself slowly from Johnson. But not until September 30 in Salt Lake City did Humphrey finally say, "As President, I would stop the bombing of North Vietnam as an acceptable risk for peace." The Salt Lake speech had a significant effect in Saigon, where President Thieu now believed that a Humphrey victory would bring a coalition government and a United States withdrawal. Thieu had good reason and hope for a Nixon victory.

"A Humphrey victory would mean a coalition government in six months. With Nixon at least there was a chance," recalled Thieu. This view was shared by Vice President Ky, who remembered that "we had little desire to sit down with the communists at all, and no intention of sitting down with, and thereby recognizing, the National Liberation Front." Thieu thus decided he would not go to Paris even if there were a bombing halt. A declassified CIA cable quoted Thieu as describing LBJ's actions as a "betrayal comparable to the U.S. abandonment of Chiang Kai-Shek as a result of Yalta, Teheran and Casablanca conferences."

President Thieu had two contacts in Washington: Anna Chennault, the widow of Flying Tigers hero General Claire Chennault, and Bui Diem, the respected South Vietnam ambassador. Chennault was a key figure in the China lobby, a fierce anticommunist, and chair of Republican Women for Nixon. During the campaign, Nixon asked her to be "the sole representa-

tive between the Vietnamese government and the Nixon campaign headquarters." Known in the White House as "Little Flower," Chennault, with
Nixon's encouragement, encouraged Thieu to defy Johnson. Johnson knew
all about it, but his information had been obtained from illegal wiretaps and
surveillance so he could not do much with it.

Chennault passed information through Bui Diem to President Thieu.
John Mitchell, Nixon's campaign manager, called Chennault every day during the last week of the campaign in an effort to keep Thieu from going to
Paris. Bui Diem sent at least two cables to Thieu, the first on October 23
stating, "Many Republican friends have contacted me and encouraged us to
stand firm. They are alarmed by press reports to the effect that you had already softened your position." Then, on October 27, "The longer the present situation, the more we are favored. I am regularly in touch with the
Nixon entourage."

Chennault later recalled that Mitchell told her, "Anna, I am speaking on
behalf of Mr. Nixon. It is very important that our Vietnamese friends understand our Republican position and I hope you have made that clear to
them."

Vice President Ky later wrote, "I had reservations about the support we
might get from Humphrey if he became President. . . . Then, out of the blue,
Nixon's supporters stepped into the picture. Approaches were made to Bui
Diem, the Vietnamese Ambassador in Washington, to the effect, 'Hold on!
Don't accept the invitation to go to Paris. If Mr. Nixon is elected President
he promises he will increase support for the Vietnam War.'"

By this time, Johnson's wiretaps and surveillance were paying dividends,
and the evidence was political dynamite. On October 29, 1968, Walt Rostow cabled Johnson about "the explosive possibilities of the information
that we now have on how certain Republicans may have inflamed the South
Vietnamese to behave as they have been behaving. . . . The materials are so
explosive that they could gravely damage the country whether Mr. Nixon is
elected or not. If they get out in their present form, they could be the subject
of one of the most acrimonious debates we have ever witnessed."

On October 31, the day that LBJ announced the bombing halt and that
negotiations would begin, Rostow wrote to him that if Thieu still refused to
go along, then Nixon should be brought into the White House for a private
meeting. "Give him the evidence . . . that the South Vietnamese are thinking
that they can turn down this deal and get a better deal after the election."
Rostow recommended that LBJ tell Nixon that the president was confident

that the candidate has nothing to do with this, but "it is your considered judgment that if it becomes known that Thieu is holding up a deal which would lower U.S. casualties and bring peace near, the basis in the United States for support of the enterprise would dissipate. . . . We simply cannot let these inexperienced men snatch defeat from the jaws of victory."

Ambassador Ellsworth Bunker was instructed to see President Thieu first thing on October 31 and deliver the message that the president would announce a bombing halt the next day at 8 P.M. Washington time, that the North Vietnamese would be told that evening, and that the next meeting would not be before November 6, after the U.S. presidential election. President Johnson hoped that President Thieu would join in this announcement.

Instead, President Thieu defied LBJ publicly. He went before South Vietnam's National Assembly, giving perhaps the greatest speech of his political career, interrupted by applause no fewer than fifteen times. Ambassador Bunker described the speech as "electrifying." Afterward, Thieu's supporters streamed into the streets for a parade to the U.S. embassy and a demonstration against the Paris talks.

LBJ bitterly commented, "It would rock the world if it were known that Thieu was conniving with the Republicans. Can you imagine what people would say if it were to be known that Hanoi has met all these conditions and then Nixon's conniving with them kept us from getting it."

FBI reports declassified in December 2000 and made available to researchers in January 2001 reveal the extent of Chennault's contacts with both the South Vietnamese government and the Nixon camp. On November 2, 1968, Chennault contacted Vietnamese Ambassador Bui Diem and advised him that she had received a message "from her boss, which her boss wanted her to give personally to the Ambassador." The message was "to hold on, we are gonna win." Chennault's "boss" wanted Ambassador Diem to tell "his boss" (President Thieu) to "hold on," the clear implication being that Thieu should not send a delegation to Paris. Chennault then made a fateful disclosure—"her boss had just called from New Mexico." Vice Presidential candidate Spiro Agnew was in New Mexico, and Agnew, of course, had to be representing candidate Nixon.

Election night 1968 brought much uncertainty. Wallace, with 45 Electoral College votes, came very close to denying either Nixon or Humphrey the necessary 270 votes in the Electoral College. For a time, it appeared that Humphrey would win the popular vote but not the electoral vote. But when all the votes were counted, Nixon had won a 0.7 percent margin in the popular vote and a majority in the Electoral College. The Democrats retained control of both houses of Congress.

Nixon had asked for a "mandate to govern" and failed to receive one. Rather, he had the inauspicious distinction of being the first president not to carry at least one house of Congress since Zachary Taylor in 1848. The new Republican president, the first since Eisenhower, faced a Senate composed of 57 Democrats and 43 Republicans and a House composed of 243 Democrats and 192 Republicans.

A December 2000 declassified FBI report from the FBI director to the White House Situation Room on November 7 revealed Chennault had "requested that Ambassador Diem be advised that she, Mrs. Chennault, had been talking to 'Florida'. . . ." President-elect Nixon was in Key Biscayne, Florida, on that day, and this FBI report reached President Johnson because Chennault's activities involved maintaining contacts between President-elect Nixon and President Thieu.

At the request of LBJ, Walt Rostow compiled the complete Chennault file and instructed Rostow to seal all of the contents and hold it personally because of its sensitive nature. In the case of LBJ's death, the materials were to be turned over to the LBJ Library under whatever conditions Rostow deemed appropriate. "At the time President Johnson decided to handle the matter strictly as a question of national security; and, in retrospect, he felt that decision was correct," Rostow later wrote. Much of the Chennault files remain sealed. Following Johnson's death, Rostow transmitted the sealed files to Harry Middleton, director of the LBJ Library, with "my recommendation to you that this file should remain sealed for fifty years from the date of this memorandum, June 26, 1973."

The Watergate tapes later revealed that in January 1973, when the Congress was investigating the Watergate break-in, Nixon came up with the wild idea of pressuring LBJ to call his Democrat friends in Congress and request that they stop the investigation. Nixon threatened LBJ with public disclosure that Johnson had bugged the Nixon and Agnew planes and campaign offices during the 1968 campaign, thus embarrassing Johnson and also proving that Nixon was not the first to wiretap illegally those suspected of leaking information. On a January 9, 1973, tape, Nixon says, "LBJ could turn off the whole Congressional investigation." But LBJ trumped Nixon by threatening to release the complete National Security

Agency (NSA) Chennault files showing that the Nixon campaign had "illegally interfered with the Paris Peace talks by convincing Saigon to stay away until after Nixon came to office."

Vice President Ky wrote, "By holding out we deprived the Democrats of their election victory, and Nixon became president instead." The question is whether Richard Nixon believed he owed Thieu something in return.

At his November 9 morning staff meeting, Secretary of Defense Clark Clifford told his staff that "LBJ now thinks Thieu is a liar and a double-crosser. The 'Little Flower' contact is still going on—Nixon seems unwilling/unable to help. His people are still playing their Black Games." Clifford told his staff that LBJ was receiving calls from "Senators who say tell Thieu 'Kiss your behind,' 'tell Thieu to go to Hell.'"

Years later, in a memorandum for the record in the LBJ Library dated May 14, 1973, Walt Rostow offered the following reflection, which in retrospect is one of the most perceptive observations of his career: "First, the election of 1968 proved to be close and there was some reason for those involved on the Republican side to believe their enterprise with the South Vietnamese and Thieu's recalcitrance may have sufficiently blunted the impact on U.S. politics of the total bombing halt and agreements to negotiate to constitute the margin of victory. Second, they got away with it. Despite considerable press commentary after the election, the matter was never investigated fully. Thus, as the same men faced the elections of 1972, there was nothing in their previous experience with an operation of doubtful propriety (or, even, legality) to warn them off; and there were memories of how close an election could get and the possible utility of pressing to the limit— or beyond."

CHAPTER TWO

Nixon Takes Control

Arriving at Dulles International Airport at 5:45 P.M. on July 14, 1969, on Air France Flight 039, Jean Sainteny was taken immediately to the Hays-Adams Hotel, where a room had been reserved by the White House in the name of Mrs. Edward McCarthy, American Optical Co. The former French delegate general in Hanoi and leader in the French Underground, Sainteny was an ideal intermediary for contacts between President Nixon and Ho Chi Minh. He was personally known by Ho as well as Pham Van Dong. In 1946 Sainteny, on behalf of France, had negotiated directly with Ho. He was also a personal friend of Henry Kissinger. Sainteny's wife, Claude, had been one of Kissinger's summer students at Harvard. Kissinger credited Sainteny with providing him with "my first insights into the Vietnamese mentality." Whenever he was in Paris, Kissinger would try to visit his friends in their luxurious downtown apartment on Rue de Rivoli.

This was not the first time Sainteny had been brought to Washington. Nixon had previously asked him to travel secretly to Hanoi so that he might try to deliver a letter to Ho Chi Minh. Sainteny was able to speak with Hanoi's representatives in Paris, but nothing came of this initial effort at jump-starting the secret negotiations because Hanoi did not know if Sainteny really represented the president. Sainteny had also served as an intermediary with the North Vietnamese during the 1968–1969 presidential transition. Kissinger and Nixon had now decided to bring Sainteny back to Washington for an assessment of the situation in Vietnam and, as Kissinger put it, to "suggest that he help arrange a meeting between me and Le Duc Tho." Kissinger's advice to Nixon was straight to the point: "I now think I should deliver the letter to Ho Chi Minh via Le Duc Tho. . . . You should inform Sainteny you are determined to achieve an honorable settlement, [and that you will] not be pushed beyond a certain point (just in case Sainteny leaks your conversation to the other side)," advised Kissinger.

Secrecy was paramount. No one could know why Sainteny was in Washington. The next day, he was scheduled to accompany Vice President Spiro Agnew to the moon launch at Cape Kennedy. How could Kissinger explain Sainteny's presence? Kissinger wrote to Agnew that "for the purpose of his visit here, I am portraying him strictly in the context of a personal friend, although he is actually providing us with some important information with respect to the Vietnam conflict. It is important, however, that he not be linked with any official role with the U.S. Government. Nor should his past duties in Hanoi become known in informal conversations with your guests. Mr. Sainteny is very much aware of this problem and can be expected to remain discrete and play the role as a personal friend of mine whom you have graciously included in your official party." Nixon's official presidential negotiations with both Hanoi and Saigon thus began where his candidacy had left off: with secrecy and layers.

In preparation for the president's July 15 meeting with Sainteny, Kissinger recommended that Nixon make clear he would not compromise on the objective of free choice for the South Vietnamese people, but that he would be "most flexible on the means to attain this objective." The U.S. had no intention of unilaterally disengaging, but if Hanoi was ready for serious negotiations, the U.S. was prepared to talk. "We would hope to employ Sainteny as an informal spokesman to reiterate directly to Hanoi our concern that nothing can be gained by further delay in substantive negotiations. The president is offering them reasonable terms, which have stretched our flexibility to the limit. If it is not now possible to reach a satisfactory settlement quickly, important decisions will have to be made. We are convinced that all parties are at a crossroads and that extraordinary measures are called for to reverse the tide of war. For this reason, the President is requesting that Mr. Sainteny carry his personal communication to Ho Chi Minh which would directly and personally reiterate his conviction that a just peace is achievable and which would underline the importance of both sides to arrive at a settlement promptly."

At their private meeting in which Kissinger served as translator, Sainteny told Nixon, "I will try to meet with Mai Van Bo in the presence of Xuan Thuy and will give him the letter destined for Ho, calling to his attention that *this time* I have the latitude to let him know that President Nixon has authorized me to give it to him. I will ask him to have this letter sent to Hanoi as rapidly and safely as possible. I will inform him of Mr. Kissinger's [forthcoming] trip to Paris on August 4 [to meet Xuan Thuy] and his desire to learn of Hanoi's reaction to the message of the President."

Sainteny was instructed to tell Xuan Thuy and Mai Van Bo that President Nixon sincerely wanted to end the war and was prepared to initiate high-level secret negotiations in order to accomplish that end, "but he will not allow himself to be snared by the tactic of drawing out the negotiations in the hope that American public opinion, having become weary, would finish by accepting unconditional withdrawal—a trap into which he will not fall under any circumstances. He has decided to hope for a positive outcome from the conversations at Paris by *November 1* . . . but if, however, by this date—the anniversary of the bombing halt—no valid solution has been reached, he will regretfully find himself obliged to have recourse to measures of great consequence and force. . . . If this diplomatic approach fails, he will resort to any means necessary." Here was the first of many ultimatums.

Sainteny left the White House carrying two letters. The first conveyed his letter of credential: "The bearer of this letter, M. Jean Sainteny, has my full confidence. I have asked him to act as my personal messenger from me to top senior officials of the Government of the Democratic Republic of Vietnam, including the President of the Republic, Ho Chi Minh. Any written communication, or oral comment thereon, has been reviewed by me personally. M. Sainteny is thoroughly cognizant of my views on the subjects he will discuss, and will, I know, present them accurately."

The second was Nixon's private letter to Ho Chi Minh described by Kissinger and Nixon in their respective memoirs as conciliatory, containing such language as, "The time has come to move forward at the conference table toward an early resolution of this tragic war. You will find us forthcoming and open-minded in a common effort to bring the blessings of peace to the brave people of Vietnam. Let history record that at this critical juncture, both sides turned their face toward peace rather than toward conflict and war." The letter also carried the specific warning that unless there was a diplomatic breakthrough by November 1, Nixon would be forced to turn "to measures of great consequence and force."

The penultimate draft of Nixon's letter to Ho reveals that Nixon was just as torn by the war as LBJ had been. It possessed all the conciliatory language described by Nixon and Kissinger—but without the threat:

Dear Mr. President:

I realize that it is difficult to communicate meaningfully across the gulf of four years of war. But precisely because of this gulf—and because the question of our sincerity has been raised by your side in Paris—I wanted to take this opportunity to reaffirm in all solemnity my desire to work for a just peace. I deeply believe that the war in Vietnam has gone on too long and delay in bringing it to an end can benefit no one—least of all the people of Vietnam. My speech of May 14 laid out a proposal which I believe is fair to all parties. It takes into account the reasonable conditions of all sides, but we stand ready to discuss other programs as well. We have one fundamental purpose: to assure the right of the South Vietnamese people to determine their own fate free of outside coercion. As I indicated on May 14, this includes the right to reunify Vietnam "if that turns out to be what the people of South Vietnam and the people of North Vietnam want." Your side seems to agree on this point, though we differ on means to achieve this end. Important decisions face us all. The time has come to move forward at the conference table toward an early resolution of this tragic war. You will find us forthcoming and open-minded in a common effort to bring the blessings of peace to the people of Vietnam.

But these "blessings of peace" would be appended to an explicit threat from Nixon. Ho's response, when it was finally received, made clear that no threat would be a precondition for seeking a negotiated settlement.

After meeting with Mai Van Bo and Xuan Thuy in Paris, Sainteny immediately reported to Kissinger via Alexander Haig. The content of Sainteny's letter was considered so secret that Haig would not risk normal delivery channels; instead, he personally gave it to John Ehrlichman, who hand-delivered it to Kissinger. "The message has been delivered to Xavier in the presence of Maurice," wrote Sainteny in code. Yes, Xuan Thuy and Mai Van Bo desired to meet with Kissinger, but "my interlocutors repeatedly stated that they had some doubts about my belief when I told them of your desire to put an end to this war and of bringing an acceptable solution for the two parties. . . . It is always the lack of confidence in your good faith which is opposed. They seem to be convinced that the U.S. never will withdraw their troops entirely from the territory of Vietnam and that they have installed some bases there, which they will maintain, in any case. Finally, they reproach you for maintaining in power a government which hasn't the confidence of the people and which is incapable of uniting them."

The first meeting between Kissinger and Xuan Thuy (with Mai Van Bo) was held on August 4, 1969, in Sainteny's Paris apartment. Kissinger was accompanied by his assistant Tony Lake and attaché General Vernon Walters, who recalled that they arrived before the Vietnamese and Sainteny offered them a drink while they waited. "As I waited, I wondered how one talked with the enemy. Did one shake hands with them? How did one behave? I had no idea."

The Vietnamese delegation soon arrived, headed by Xuan Thuy, who was accompanied by Mai Van Bo and interpreter Nguyen Dinh Phuong. After introductions, Sainteny brought the group into his living room, arranged for beverages, and left the diplomats alone. The meeting would last over three hours because it required double translation: Kissinger spoke in English, which Walters translated into French, which Xuan Thuy's interpreter rendered into Vietnamese. Almost immediately, Kissinger asked whether there had been a reply to Nixon's July 15 letter to Ho. "We have received from Mr. Sainteny the undated letter addressed by President Nixon to President Ho Chi Minh. The letter had been forwarded to Hanoi," said Xuan Thuy.

Kissinger then explained that the United States had taken several significant steps toward peace since Nixon took office, including the withdrawal of 25,000 combat forces. Kissinger, referring to notes that he told Xuan Thuy had personally been approved by the president, said that the United States hoped to have a settlement by November 1, 1970. In order to do so, the United States was willing to withdraw all of its troops without exception from Vietnam and was willing to accept the outcome of a free political process. As part of that process, the United States realized that neither side could be expected to give up at the conference table what had not been conceded on the battlefield; that a fair political process must register the existing relationship of political forces; that the United States would differ from the North Vietnamese on how to achieve this "but that neither side should be asked to accept the proposition that it can be defeated without noticing it."

The president wanted the North Vietnamese to know that he was prepared to appoint Kissinger as his personal representative to begin high-level negotiations designed to bring the war to a conclusion. If no progress was made by November 1 (the anniversary of the bombing halt), however,

Kissinger warned Xuan Thuy that the United States would take "measures of the gravest consequences." Kissinger also added that it was a mistake for the North Vietnamese to keep calling this "Mr. Nixon's War," because if this was so, Mr. Nixon could not afford not to win it.

Xuan Thuy responded as Hanoi's negotiators would repeatedly do for the next four years. He gave a very long exposition of the history of foreign aggression in Vietnam. As Kissinger later described it, "They would give us lectures about the heroic history of Vietnam and the certainty of our defeat, which would go for hours. The second lecture we received was the impossibility of separating military from political objectives and, they consistently rejected the proposition with which we started—that we settle the military issues first by way of cease-fire, POWs and so forth, and leave the political evolution to Vietnam, to the evolution of Vietnam, as long as it was done by reasonably democratic processes."

Xuan Thuy's exposition fit Kissinger's characterization perfectly. The Vietnamese wanted their independence, sovereignty, unity, and territorial integrity. They wanted the North to be independent, free, and socialist; they wanted the South to be free of foreign troops, neutral, no military bases, no alliances, no military block. Reunification could then occur in a step-by-step process, by peaceful means, by agreement between the two zones. "We wonder why the United States could bring in its troops rapidly and it could not pull them out rapidly. Why don't you propose 5 or 6 months for the complete withdrawal of troops from South Vietnam? . . . The withdrawal of 20,000–25,000 troops out of 540,000 troops is insignificant. If the United States withdraws some more troops, say, a larger number than 25,000, it is still meaningless. Your policy is to withdraw troops by droplets and to prolong your military occupation in South Vietnam. We doubt your goodwill." He insisted on a "Ten Point Overall Solution," introduced by the NLF on May 8, that called for a complete U.S. withdrawal, the release of all prisoners of war, and the creation of a coalition government.

Xuan Thuy disagreed with Nixon's claim that the government in Saigon was legal and constitutional: "Should the United States maintain this administration, the problem cannot be solved, it is necessary to change the men and the policy of that administration. We admit the existence of the Saigon administration as a reality, but there should be a three-component [the GVN, the NLF and PRG] coalition government to organize the election. This is logical and reasonable."

Kissinger reiterated that the Nixon administration would not dump President Thieu and that a settlement must reflect the existing balance of power. "We have too much respect for Xuan Thuy to believe that we could trick him into a solution which does not respect their dignity. But they cannot impose a dishonorable solution on us," Kissinger said. For the next three years, Xuan Thuy and Le Duc Tho would insist that peace could be achieved only if the United States withdrew all troops (which it was doing) and force President Thieu to step aside. For three years, the United States would gradually remove all of its troops but refuse to oust Thieu. Was it that Nixon owed Thieu for his 1968 victory? Or was Thieu merely code for the continued American bombing of Hanoi after the troops left? That is, did Nixon and Kissinger believe that another leader of South Vietnam might not accept what the Americans would offer because they might be more inclined toward a neutralist position and coalition government? Tens of thousands of lives were lost while the negotiations dragged on.

Kissinger concluded by saying that when he was a professor, he had started out with problems of philosophy and art. "He recognized that the most difficult problems are not where good people meet evil people, but are where two strong people with strong convictions confront each other." Kissinger restated that the United States would prefer to have the Vietnamese as friends rather than enemies and he hoped that by the end of the year, November 1, the two would not test each others' resolution and that a diplomatic rather than military solution could be found. Xuan Thuy needed to understand the president's sincerity but also his determination. "He would also like to tell him personally of his respect for him and his people. This will continue whether they found a way to be friends or whether fate forces us into an expanded confrontation."

Although little was accomplished, this first meeting opened the door for the secret parallel negotiating meetings that would soon begin between Kissinger and Le Duc Tho. The story of Paris would henceforth be a dual tale of the official talks (the plenary sessions), with South Vietnam present, and the real talks (private meetings) between the United States and the North Vietnamese. Nixon and Kissinger's obsession with secrecy would have disastrous consequences. Aside from a handful of NSC aides, Kissinger, the president, and Ambassador Ellsworth Bunker would be the only ones aware of the parallel diplomatic track. Until January 25, 1972, the State Department, the Joint Chiefs of Staff, the CIA, and the Defense

Department were kept out of this loop. Even worse, although President Thieu had been assured by Kissinger and Nixon that he would be consulted and kept abreast of any private discussions, especially on issues that pertained to the internal political processes of South Vietnam, he was "informed" but never "consulted." Nixon had set up a process by which he could cut a deal directly with the enemy and keep much of his own government and even his ally in the dark about it. In the end, he would tell a different story to each side—to Thieu, to his advisers, and to the public.

Certainly Nixon's strategy with the North seemed to make more sense than LBJ's, insofar as he made clear threats and intended to use more force to back them up. Yet the use of threats would have no effect. In fact, the greater the threat, the more rigid Le Duc Tho would become. Nixon and Kissinger firmly believed that when the threat became an act, as it did in the punishing B-52 bombings of May and December 1972, it would bring the communists into compliance. But by then the balance of forces had changed in Hanoi's favor and after several crucial U.S. concessions. To be sure, the bombings hurt the North, but the bombing could not break the North's resolve to unify Vietnam. In fact, Nixon's belief in the efficacy of B-52s took on a life of its own, leading to retrospective arguments that *had* the U.S. taken such aggressive action in November 1969, the war *would* have ended then. Nixon's faith was misplaced. The Linebacker bombing brought the North back to the table, but in fact Hanoi never took the resumption of the negotiation process seriously. All along, their plan was a long stall that aimed at dividing the U.S. from Saigon and world opinion against the U.S. It succeeded brilliantly.

Heyward Isham, the deputy director of the Vietnam Working Group who later functioned as a principal staff person during the Paris peace meetings, made the interesting observation that "the very fact that we had to resort to B-52 bombings was to an Asian an admission of ultimate weakness, because it was saying we cannot do this on the ground, we or our allies together cannot prevail on the ground; therefore, we will resort to this super-weapon, for them. And although they had to yield to it to some degree and certainly were terribly punished by it, their reading was that this reflected a fundamental vulnerability . . . and I think a lot of our people did not understand that. This is a psychological thing. This is a little bit like jujitsu, where you use the superior power of the enemy to force him to tumble over himself. You let him make a lunge at you then you just trip him. You let him use all that force. You don't block that force directly. You just use it so he himself is his own worst enemy."

* * *

During the presidential campaign in Hampton, New Hampshire, on May 5, 1968, Nixon had replaced the term "victorious peace" with winning an "honorable peace" in Vietnam. Crucial to his plan was the concept of linkage—using the Soviet Union to get the North Vietnamese to negotiate seriously.

By the time Nixon reached the Republican party convention, he was telling delegates that "critical to the settlement of Vietnam is relations with the Soviet Union. That is why I said over and over again it is going to be necessary for the next president to sit down with the Soviet leadership quite directly, not only about Vietnam, you have got to broaden the canvass—because in Vietnam they have no reason to end the war; it's hurting us more than it's hurting them."

In what Nixon believed was an off-the-record discussion with southern delegates at the 1968 Republican convention, the nominee described another way for ending the war in Vietnam: "How do you bring a war to a conclusion? I'll tell you how Korea was ended. We got in there and had this messy war on our hands. Eisenhower let the word get out—let the word go out diplomatically to the Chinese and the North Koreans that we would not tolerate this continued round of attrition. And within a matter of months, they negotiated."

In October 1968 Nixon met with Harrison Salisbury, assistant managing editor of the *New York Times*, to discuss his foreign policy views. The candidate was adamant that "we can't have a foreign policy with Vietnam hanging around our necks. I will deal with it within six months." Just months earlier, in March 1968, he had announced that "if in November this war is not over, I say that the American people will be justified in electing new leadership and I pledge to you that the new leadership will end the war and win the peace in the Pacific." He hinted that he had such a plan, but it would remain secret until after the election.

When Nixon took office in January 1969, the United States had been involved in combat operations in Vietnam for nearly four years. U.S. military forces exceeded 540,000, the bulk of them ground combat troops. Over 30,000 Americans had lost their lives and the war had cost $30 billion in fiscal year 1969. Over 14,500 U.S troops had been killed in 1968 alone. "The fighting seemed to be stalemated," wrote Kissinger. In other words, the war was impossible to win militarily, but not impossible to stalemate endlessly. In 1969 this stalemate played to Hanoi's long-term strategy; in 1973 it would be to the U.S. advantage.

Nixon was determined that Vietnam would not ruin his presidency. He slept only four hours during his first night in the White House, awaking at 6:45 A.M. Before beginning his first day on the job, the new president recalled the hidden safe that LBJ had shown him during their transition meeting. Going directly to the safe, inside he found a single folder—the Vietnam Situation Report for the previous day, LBJ's last in office. After reading the casualty reports, Nixon closed the folder and put it back in the safe, where he left it "until the war was over, a constant reminder of its tragic cost."

He would, of course, fail to end the war in six months. The war became a focus of Nixon's entire presidency and, as many have observed, there very likely would have been no Watergate if not for Vietnam since the secret Plumbers group was established to find and stop the source of leaks on Vietnam. It was Nixon who would set the terms in Paris; he who would force Thieu to accept the agreement that finally emerged; he who would tell the public that we were finished with Vietnam while telling the South Vietnamese that we would be back if need be. The man who would work most closely with him for the entire period was Henry Kissinger. Much has been written about Henry Alfred Kissinger, the German-born Harvard professor of political science who rose from White House consultant to LBJ and adviser to Nelson Rockefeller to the architect of foreign policy in the Nixon years. A man of great charm, wit, and intellect, Kissinger has elicited controversial assessments about his core truthfulness. Helmut Sonnefelt, who worked for Kissinger, once explained, "Kissinger doesn't lie because it's in his interest. He lies because it's in his nature." After working with Kissinger, former presidential press secretary Ron Nessen concluded that "the Kissinger character trait that troubled me most was his lack of commitment to the truth as a matter of morality. Kissinger bent the truth to serve what he believed were worthwhile foreign policy maneuvers."

One of the very first things Admiral Elmo Zumwalt came to understand about dealing with Kissinger was that what he said meant very little: "I found that I could not believe what Henry told me, that his assent to a recommendation or proposal I made to him—and he assented more often than he dissented—did not at all mean that he agreed or intended to follow my suggestion, but could very well be a mere ploy to defuse or dismiss me. To put it another way, I seldom could learn what Henry thought about a given situation, much less what he was going to do about it, from what Henry told me."

Kissinger and Nixon made a formidable team—but in the years to come, it would not always be clear where the truth lay.

From the beginning, during the presidential transition, President-elect Nixon met with his foreign policy team and directed them, under Kissinger's coordination, to develop a set of realistic options by Inauguration Day, so that he might develop a "coherent strategy" for Vietnam. During the transition, Kissinger began a review of all possible policies toward Vietnam, distilling them into specific options that ran the gamut from massive military escalation to immediate unilateral withdrawal. "A strong case could be made for each option," Nixon wrote in his memoirs.

The original twenty-seven-page options paper draft developed by Daniel Ellsberg (then of the Rand Corporation) and given to Kissinger on December 27 contained a withdrawal option on which General Goodpaster declined to comment. That option was deleted by the time it was presented to the principals at the very first NSC meeting after the inauguration, but the option of a de facto partition of Vietnam was added to the list.

Morton Halperin, who had worked with Kissinger at Harvard, was part of the original team that developed option papers on Vietnam. "When I arrived there may have been a plan in the President's head. There was nothing written down," he recalled. Throughout most of December and January, Kissinger's team, meeting frequently at the Pierre Hotel, developed a series of questions on Vietnam that eventually evolved into a series of options. "The only thing that was excluded was the option of a simple, unilateral American withdrawal," recalled Halperin. As for escalation, Halperin recalled that Kissinger was critical of the lack of a win option. "His response was that one ought to take that much more seriously as an option, and my response to that was to be quite nervous about it, because I thought it was a mistake, a fundamental mistake, and that it would recreate the illusion that we could somehow win this war."

In his memoirs, Nixon writes of receiving a call from "a friend [anonymous] in Congress" who advised the new president to pull out of Vietnam. Kennedy and Johnson had started it, and no one would blame Nixon "even if you end up with a bad peace." In fact, Nixon would be a hero for bringing the troops home and ending the terrible war. Nixon concluded the story by writing, "We simply could not sacrifice an American ally in such a way"— especially an ally who had just delivered the presidential election.

As Nixon prepared to take office, Hanoi made clear just how far apart the two sides were. Mai Van Bo commented to Sainteny in late December, "At the beginning, I believe that the question is to know if the U.S. wants peace, if it really wishes to withdraw its troops from South Vietnam, or if it only talks of this to make it possible to do nothing. For the rest, evidence indicates that the Saigon Administration does not want peace. Instead it wishes that the U.S. remain in Vietnam so that it can continue to make a living from the war." As long as the Thieu government remained in power, it was going to be difficult to settle any of these problems—so claimed Mai Van Bo.

Kissinger's memoir account of this response was that it was concerned with neither "honor [nor] self respect. It stated brutally two fundamental demands: the total withdrawal of all American forces and the replacement of what Hanoi called the 'Thieu-Ky-Huong' clique,' its pet phrase for the leadership in Saigon with which Hanoi was supposed to be negotiating. . . . Thus was the Nixon administration first exposed to the maddening diplomatic style of the North Vietnamese."

In a memorandum stamped "SECRET" to the president-elect dated January 2, 1969, Kissinger provided a more nuanced assessment of Hanoi's December 31 message: "The tone of the Hanoi message is more conciliatory by far than is customary; there is the usual effort to drive a wedge between Saigon and Washington; Hanoi, which always drafts very carefully, emphasizes that its point of primary concern is U.S. willingness to withdraw troops (no reference to ceasefire, de-escalation, etc.)."

On January 2 the president-elect wrote again to the North Vietnamese, and on January 13 he again received an uncompromising set of demands: "If the U.S. really desires to settle the Vietnamese problem it must end the war of aggression in Vietnam, withdraw in the shortest possible period all American and satellite troops from South Vietnam and leave the South Vietnamese population to settle itself its own affairs without foreign interference. The U.S. must as soon as possible start without delay the Conference of Four to discuss these profound questions."

A few days following the inaugural, Kissinger received a letter from Sainteny that painted gloomy prospects for peace. Kissinger immediately forwarded the letter to Nixon, first explaining the code names ("Maurice" is Mai Van Bo, "Louis" is Le Duc Tho, and "Paul" is Pham Van Dong) and then concluding from the letter that "in view of Hanoi's present state of mind, new overtures will probably not make much difference. However, I believe we should make another overture both for the record and because of the lack of real movement in the Paris negotiations. I therefore think we should bring Sainteny over here. This represents some hope of unfreezing the situation, and the record would then show that at least we tried."

One of the most revealing recent declassifications is Kissinger's "Talking Points on Vietnam," prepared for his first meeting with Soviet ambassador Dobrynin on February 21, 1969. Nixon instructed Kissinger to tell Dobrynin that "he will not be the first American President to lose a war, and he is not prepared to give in to public pressures which would have that practical consequence. The President is convinced that a North Vietnamese victory would pose an intolerable threat to future peace and stability in the Far East by feeding Mainland China's aggressive drive. The President has therefore decided that he will make one more effort to achieve a reasonable settlement. If it fails, other measures will be invoked. These measures could not help but involve wider risks." Kissinger was to link progress explicitly on the limitation of strategic armaments with progress toward an acceptable settlement to the Vietnamese conflict. Nixon was prepared to send a "high-level representative" to meet the North Vietnamese negotiator at any location, including Moscow, in order to negotiate a military and political settlement. "The President visualizes that this negotiation would be conducted distinct from the existing Paris framework in order to circumvent the sluggish and heretofore cumbersome mechanisms that have evolved in Paris. The President will give this peace effort just six weeks to succeed."

* * *

By March 1969 Nixon had a plan of action. He dispatched Secretary of Defense Melvin Laird to Vietnam, accompanied by General Wheeler, with a clear message: "The American people expected the new administration to bring the war to a satisfactory conclusion . . . and a satisfactory conclusion to most Americans meant eventual disengagement of United States troops from combat." Laird told the American commanders that their task was to find the means to shift the combat burden 'promptly' and 'methodically' to the South Vietnamese."

Upon his return, Laird met with Nixon, discussing Termination Day (T-Day) planning, a detailed program for withdrawal of U.S. troops and the transfer of equipment to the South. The United States would start winding down its role, seeking terms for a negotiated settlement premised on the idea of mutual withdrawal of North Vietnamese troops in South Vietnam. When peace came, both the United States and North Vietnam would have withdrawn their troops from the South.

The Nixon plan to "de-Americanize" the war became known as "Vietnamization," which involved building up the South Vietnamese armed forces so that they could assume greater combat responsibility while simultaneously withdrawing U.S. combat troops. The U.S. military role would shift from fighting to advising the South Vietnamese, buttressed with a massive influx of military equipment and weaponry. Perhaps most important, Nixon changed the political objective for U.S. intervention from guaranteeing a free and independent South Vietnam to creating the opportunity for South Vietnam to determine its own political future. Vietnamization *and* negotiation were Nixon's twin pillars for achieving an honorable peace.

During the first weeks of his presidency, Nixon also began to consider options for dealing with Cambodia, including the feasibility and utility of a quarantine to prevent equipment and supplies from coming into South Vietnam. Under code name MENU, B-52 strikes began on March 18, 1969, against enemy sanctuaries in that country. They were kept secret from the American public, in part because Cambodia was a neutral country, but even more important because Nixon had not been elected to expand the war after just three months in office.

According to the JCS *History,* "Knowledge of the operation was limited to individuals essential to its successful execution, and a procedure was carefully devised to conceal the bombing." This procedure was called double billing: General Creighton Abrams, commander of the U.S. Military Assistance Command, Vietnam, would request strikes through CINCPAC to the Joint Chiefs, who then obtained the approval of the secretary of defense. Simultaneously, in order to account for the resources, COMUS-MACV presented a routine request for a B-52 strike in a South Vietnam target. "Both strikes were approved, but normally only the MENU one was carried out."

Secrecy was so tight that even flight crews were not told that they would be dropping bombs in Cambodia, but they certainly knew that they were over Cambodia. Still, prior to their mission, the B-52 crews were briefed on targets in South Vietnam and told to fly over South Vietnam and avoid Cambodia. The flights were at night and therefore under guidance from ground control, so the pilots and navigators were told to react to all changes in directions for bomb release from ground control tones. Upon return, false reports were submitted through routine channels that showed the strike being carried out on Vietnamese targets. The real reports were submitted through a separate MENU channel. The JCS *History* notes, "The precaution to prevent disclosure of MENU proved quite successful. In fact, while the MENU attacks were taking place, only a few United States officials were aware of the B-52 operations in Cambodia, and the U.S. public had no knowledge of the attacks at all." The MENU operations included B-52 strikes against enemy base areas along the Cambodia–South Vietnam border, code-named BREAKFAST, DINNER, SNACK, SUPPER, LUNCH. They lasted fourteen months, through May 26, 1970. A total of 3,875 sorties were flown, expending 180,823 tons of munitions. In the summer of 1973, a congressional investigation provided official verification on the existence and extent of MENU operations, and the bombings became the subject of public controversy (although reports of the bombing appeared as early as May 1969 in many newspapers).

With MENU operations ongoing, President Nixon held a nationally televised address on May 14, 1969, unveiling a major eight-point peace initiative for ending the war in Vietnam. The May 14 proposals were a response to the ten-point proposal put forth by the NLF on May 8. The cornerstones of Nixon's new proposals were simultaneous or mutual withdrawal of both U.S. and North Vietnamese troops from South Vietnam and the maintaining of the current government in South Vietnam. The speech also contained important language for the North Vietnamese: "A great nation cannot renege on its pledges. A great nation must be worthy of trust." Nixon told his national audience that "the record is clear as to which side has gone the extra mile for peace. We have gone as far as we can or should go in opening the door to peace, now is the time for the other side to respond." Nixon forecasted that "the time was approaching when the South Vietnamese forces will be able to take over some of the fighting fronts now being manned by Americans."

The next day Hanoi issued a reply: "The plan of the Nixon administration is not to end the war but to replace the war of aggression fought by US troops with a war of aggression fought by the puppet army of the United States." In short, the North continued to hold its ground. After all, LBJ had halted the bombing many times and Kissinger had made several proposals, all in exchange for very little. The strategy of waiting seemed better and better.

Halfway through his first year in the White House, Nixon had yet to meet with the South Vietnamese leaders. President Thieu requested that a meeting be held in Washington, D.C., but Nixon, fearful of demonstrations, selected Honolulu, which the Vietnamese rejected because they did not want to meet on a U.S. resort island. Nixon next suggested the remote island of Midway for their first encounter on June 8—as in "mid-way between the U.S. and Vietnam," recalled Nha. Thieu reluctantly agreed. Thieu understood Nixon's political problems and had had plenty of time to think about what he would say at Midway. He knew he would be asked to buy into a phased withdrawal of troops that would be tied to a schedule giving the South Vietnamese enough time to assume sole responsibility for the war. Vietnamization was Nixon's only option, given his domestic critics. "I know that you are going to go, but before you go, you have to leave something for us as friends. Leave something to help me out," Thieu said. What else could he say?

Nixon thus won Thieu's public acquiescence for Vietnamization, which Thieu defined as the training of the South Vietnam Armed Forces and leaving behind adequate weapons and equipment for defense of their country. When Nixon proposed that secret or private contacts be started between the U.S. and Hanoi in an effort to secure a negotiated settlement, Thieu asked that he be kept fully informed on the details of these meetings and that he be consulted on any matters internal to South Vietnam. He received assurances that this would most certainly be the case.

Kissinger's memoir recalls that Thieu approved the secret talks at Midway and that "he was thoroughly briefed on my secret negotiations from the beginning." It is unclear whether Thieu believed these assurances, but he could soon have reason to suspect them. For years, critics have charged that Kissinger kept Thieu out of the loop, and indeed the record confirms these charges. After the meeting Thieu recalled the Vietnamese saying, "Dau xuoi duoi lot," ("if the head slides though easily, the tail will follow"). Thieu knew he was there to help solve Nixon's domestic political problems by accepting Vietnamization and that he had no recourse except to go along. But Thieu also had faith in Nixon and believed that the president would provide eight years of support for the South to survive.

By July 9, 1969, the first increment of American troops arrived home at McChord Air Force Base near Tacoma, Washington. In a visible signal that America was winding down its involvement, General William Westmoreland was present to greet this first contingent in the "de-Americanization" of the war.

But Hanoi had a plan of its own that overlapped with the Thieu-Nixon meeting on Midway. The NLF announced in Paris that a National Congress had met in a liberated area of South Vietnam and formed the Provisional Revolutionary Group—the PRG of South Vietnam. The next day, Tran Buu

Kiem announced that the PRG would take the NLF's place at the conference table in Paris. Mrs. Nguyen Thi Binh, Kiem's deputy, would serve as the PRG foreign minister and head the PRG delegation in Paris.

The creation of the PRG had important implications. President Ho Chi Minh and Premier Pham Van Dong sent telegrams that immediately recognized the PRG as "the legal government and the true representative of the people of South Vietnam." Almost immediately afterward, the Soviet Union recognized the PRG, dealing a blow to Nixon's hopes of using the Soviets to broker a peace.

The PRG would become a well-developed administrative structure from the national level down to the districts and villages it controlled. In its 1969 founding "Program of Action," the PRG identified as its first tasks "to force the U.S. Government to withdraw completely and unconditionally from South Vietnam the U.S. troops and those of foreign countries belonging to the U.S. camp with a view to bringing the war to an early end, restoring peace and enforcing the fundamental national rights of the Vietnamese people—independence, sovereignty, unity and territorial integrity—as recognized by the 1954 Geneva Agreements on Vietnam." It seemed noble, but the PRG was a puppet regime with no shred of independent legitimacy.

Shortly after their Midway meeting, President Thieu invited Nixon to Saigon. If Nixon had needed Thieu's support at Midway to shore up the American president's domestic standing, Thieu now needed Nixon in Saigon for the same reasons. The opportunity presented itself at the completion of President Nixon's around-the-world diplomatic tour in July. Nixon visited Saigon, where he was hosted at the Presidential Palace, the first American president to be accorded that reception.

On July 30 Thieu held a private reception for President Nixon. The declassified MEMCON provides new details on Nixon's thinking. Nixon wanted Thieu to know that the next move was up to Hanoi. "We can't have you nibbled away . . . that is something that we are not willing to permit." President Thieu warned Nixon that when all the American troops were gone, Hanoi would move in militarily. "He felt that they went to Paris to get concessions and to buy time; that by buying time in Paris they hope that the US position will continue to grow weaker." Kissinger interceded that "the position which the President had taken on the negotiations had put the doves in the U.S. on the defensive. The result is that if the enemy starts another offensive we are in a position to make a strong response."

Nixon then "wished to say something in utmost confidence and asked

President Thieu not to discuss this with any other individual. He said that he had in mind that it might be highly desirable to issue a *warning* in the near future to Hanoi about the course they were following, but he wanted President Thieu to know that this will be done in an unorthodox way. He wanted President Thieu to know that he was not discussing this at present with anyone in the U.S. Government, and that it should be held strictly between the President and President Thieu." Nixon told Thieu about the plans for Duck Hook—massive bombing strikes against the North.

Not a word was said that Kissinger was heading directly to Paris to meet secretly with the North Vietnamese for the first time in Sainteny's apartment. This would establish a pattern of exclusion for the next four years—Kissinger negotiating an American troop disengagement with the North Vietnamese while informing Thieu only after the fact. The U.S. entered the talks in 1969 seeking mutual withdrawal and no coalition government and ended the talks in 1973 accepting unilateral withdrawal of its own troops and no coalition, but a guarantee by Thieu to step down before the election. Throughout, the North refused to recognize the government in the South as legitimate and swore to destroy it. In the end, South Vietnam would be served a death warrant, and the North would be rewarded for stalling.

Before the first secret meeting with the North, Kissinger met with U.S. ambassador Henry Cabot Lodge in order to review the current situation. He explained, "The President's view is that we have made as many unilateral concessions as we are going to." Notes of the meeting add that Kissinger stated, "With regard to withdrawals, we must have a clear-cut assurance that once withdrawn, North Vietnamese are not coming back—an unambiguous verification process. A written document per se *is not* necessary. . . . Mr. Kissinger said that if they make it 'Nixon's War' he may try to win it. He does not want to see communist troops in Saigon."

Perhaps most interesting is Ambassador Lodge's comment that the North Vietnamese would never agree to free elections. Kissinger responded that "he did not expect to see elections either. There will be no winner-take-all solution."

The meeting ended with Phillip Habib saying, "We must convince them that the President can't hold still after November 1." Plans were already underway for the November "savage blow."

A plan for stepping up the war had begun months prior to Nixon's July meeting with Jean Sainteny. The plan's name was Duck Hook, from "all the 'ducks' of American power 'circling in' for the kill." Well before Ho's letter arrived in the White House, Kissinger was pushing Nixon "to make total mental commitment and really be prepared for the heat." Kissinger had little faith in Vietnamization: "I refuse to believe that a little fourth-rate power like North Vietnam does not have a breaking point. . . . It shall be the assignment of this group to examine the option of a savage, decisive blow against North Vietnam." At one time in this period, Roger Morris of the NSC staff was purportedly shown nuclear bombing plans.

Admiral Moorer, without informing Secretary of Defense Laird, undertook studies for a November attack, which his staff completed by July 20. Sometime in August, a team from the JCS went to Vietnam and developed plans for *Pruning Knife*, Duck Hook's code name in Saigon. This top-secret group mapped out all of the available military options, including mining Cambodian ports and a ground invasion across the DMZ. Led by Rear Admiral Frederic A. Bardshar, the exercise was intended to "develop a sound military concept of action needed to achieve U.S. objectives by force of arms." *Pruning Knife* included plans for aerial strikes against the North at a rate of 532 sorties a day.

At this time, Kissinger's doubts about Vietnamization were made clear to the president. In a memo dated September 10, Kissinger warned Nixon that if Vietnamization did not reduce American casualties, "the pressure of public opinion on you to resolve the war quickly will increase—and I believe increase greatly."

Recently declassified is the draft text of a Duck Hook speech for the president's review, as well as negotiating scenarios for meetings with the North Vietnamese following the "savage blow." A "Top Secret-Sensitive" "Vietnam Contingency Plans—Concept of Operations" paper dated September 16, 1969, uses November 1 as the day for action that would "apply whatever force is necessary to achieve basic U.S. objectives in Southeast Asia. Such operations will be designed to achieve maximum political, military, and psychological shock." The four-day attack included the mining of DRV and Cambodian ports and harbors, and air raids on twenty-nine military targets. A one-day pause would follow, allowing the North to ponder its options. If Hanoi remained intransigent to negotiations, then another four-day bombing salvo would commence. This pattern would continue until North Vietnam acquiesced and came to the table for serious negotiations. Contingency plans for escalating the pressure included blockading Sihanoukville, bombing Red River dikes, and invading across the DMZ.

Nixon even had a speech prepared on September 27. It reveals just how seriously the administration was contemplating the attack. It now stands as an interesting example of "what-if" history to which Nixon would frequently return: "It is my duty to tell you tonight of a major decision in our quest for an honorable peace in Vietnam. . . . Tonight after months of the most thorough study and deliberation, I must report to you that Hanoi has indeed made this tragic miscalculation of our will and clear warnings. They have refused to credit the word of the United States. Denouncing our every initiative as a fraud, they have treated negotiations as a forum for U.S. capitulation. . . . Thus, our course is clear. Continued bloodshed on the battlefield and Hanoi's rigidity at the peace table, have taught us that there is but one other choice. Our adversary will not heed our words because he refuses to believe we have the will to use our power. He cannot go on with this delusion. The United States has no choice but to take action to prove to Hanoi that we mean to have an honorable peace in Vietnam."

Most of the speech was predictable enough. Nixon planned to underscore America's resolve, while at the same time paradoxically insisting that "our aim is limited." He also inserted a "call once again upon the Soviet Union to help bring an end to this war by using its unique influence with Hanoi. If the leaders of the Soviet Union truly desire an era of negotiation rather than confrontation, let them begin with Vietnam." His final grasping at opposites involved a call "to our faithful allies in South Vietnam that our resolve to find an honorable settlement is stronger than ever before. Let us fortify our firmness in battle with a new spirit of compromise when genuine talks begin."

As late as September 30, in a meeting with Republican leaders, Nixon hinted at the November Duck Hook option: "I can't tell you everything that will be going on, because if there is to be any chance of success, it must be done in secret. All I can tell you is this: I am doing my damnedest to end the war. . . . I will not be the first President of the United States to lose the war." Why, then, did he abandon the plan?

Within the administration, the secretaries of state and defense both argued against Duck Hook. Melvin Laird maintained that air raids and blockades would fail to stop North Vietnam from carrying on the war. Duck Hook could prolong the conflict rather than bring it to an abrupt end on terms favorable to the United States. He also pointed out that B-52 and North Vietnamese civilian losses would be heavy, and so antiwar protest would skyrocket in intensity. Laird further noted that over 450,000 American troops still remained in Vietnam and that serious negotiations were not then underway, so the decision to start the raid at that time would send a signal that the United States was trying to win the war.

A national antiwar moratorium on October 15 played an important role in the cancellation of Duck Hook. With hundreds of thousands of demonstrators taking to the streets of Washington, D.C., it was apparent that Nixon's attack would face a groundswell of opposition. In the end, Nixon cancelled Duck Hook because it would have been very difficult to pursue an open military solution while the country was ostensibly beginning its disengagement from Vietnam. In short, American public opinion already had him over a barrel, and he knew it. On October 14 Radio Hanoi broadcast a letter from Premier Pham Van Dong to the American people in which Hanoi's premier applauded those "peace-and justice-loving American personages [who] are launching a broad and powerful offensive throughout the United States to demand that the Nixon administration put an end to the Vietnam aggressive war and immediately bring all American troops home." In his memoirs Nixon characterized Dong's letter as "a blatant intervention in our domestic affairs," which, of course, was Hanoi's intent.

The record shows that Nixon, Kissinger, and Haig later regretted not putting Duck Hook into action. If any of them could have foreseen that the war would still be going on in January 1973, they insist that Duck Hook would have been implemented. After the Paris Accords were signed, Kissinger casually remarked to Bill Safire, "We should have bombed the hell out of them the minute we got into office. . . . The North Vietnamese started an offensive in February 1969. We should have responded strongly. We should have taken on the doves right then—start bombing and mining the harbors. The war would have been over in 1970."

According to Haig, "I am absolutely, categorically convinced that, had we done in 1969 what we did in the end of 1972 that conflict would have been over and we would have gotten our prisoners out and our objectives would have been met. . . . We should have moved much more decisively in applying our power to the source of the problem. . . . I think in 1969, when the new President came in, had he immediately started to bomb Hanoi, mobilize our forces here at home, put the Soviet Union on notice . . . and done all the things that should have been done in the Johnson administration, that there never would have been those additional three years of conflict and that there would have been a negotiated settlement and withdrawal of North Vietnamese forces from South Vietnam, where they were the invader."

A recently released White House tape from June 1971 reveals the depth of Nixon's regret:

HALDEMAN   This war is immoral and more than most wars, more than any war we've ever fought, for the single reason that we have been un-willing to commit our resource to win it—

NIXON   Yeah, that's right. Let me say this, let me say this, because you, you don't think I mean what I'm saying, but I know this, that if we don't get the Soviet, if we don't get any Soviet breakthrough, if we don't get the Chinese, if we can't get that ensemble, we can't get any-thing on Vietnam, the situation is deteriorating, about November of this year, I'm going [unintelligible] to play [unintelligible] the god-damn [unintelligible], the hole card. As long as we've still got the air force—I'm not worried about bombing pauses, I'm, we're gonna take out the dikes, we're gonna take out the power plants, we're gonna take out Haiphong, we're gonna [pounding the table as he says:] level that goddamn country!—

KISSINGER   Mr. President, I think, I think the American people under-stand that.

NIXON   . . . support it, we'll see who they are. The point is, we're not gonna go out whimpering, and we're not gonna go out losing . . . That's what.

KISSINGER   Mr. President, I will enthusiastically support that, and I think it's the right thing to do.

* * *

On October 15, Nixon sat down to write a new speech for November 3. At the top of a pad he wrote, "Don't Get Rattled—Don't Waver—Don't React." Two days later he spoke with Sir Robert Thompson, the British ex-pert on guerrilla war, who grandiosely warned that "the future of Western civilization is at stake in the way you handle yourselves in Vietnam." Nixon's nationally televised November 3 address was given the title, "The President's Pursuit of Peace." Instead of any hint at the renewed use of force, the president merely reviewed the reasons for rejecting an immediate withdrawal of all American forces from Vietnam. "Precipitate withdrawal would thus be a disaster of immense magnitude. . . . It would not bring peace, it would bring more war."

The president then listed the steps that he was prepared to take in the pursuit of peace, which included the withdrawal of all American forces, a cease-fire under international supervision, and free elections under international supervision. "Anything is negotiable, except the right of the people of South Vietnam to determine their own future," he said.

During the talk President Nixon enlisted the support of a "Silent Majority" and blamed a "vocal minority" for dividing national support for the war effort. He also announced that North Vietnam would never be able to "defeat or humiliate the United States. . . . Only Americans can do that." Nixon also used his "Pursuit of Peace" speech to disclose the fact that he had secretly written to Ho Chi Minh, only to have been rebuffed. There was, of course, no mention of Kissinger's private meeting with Xuan Thuy, the Sainteny connection, or the plans for Duck Hook and Pruning Knife that were underway *before* Ho's reply arrived in the White House in late August 1969.

Nixon promised to bring all of America's combat troops home. Appealing for domestic support, he recalled, "I pledged in my campaign for the presidency to end the war in a way that we could win the peace. I have initiated a plan of action that will enable me to meet that pledge."

Instead of a show of force, the speech was a soft one of withdrawal. Yet Nixon remembered it as a triumph. "Very few speeches actually influence the course of history. The November 3 speech was one of them," Richard Nixon wrote in his memoirs. He was referring to the strength of support he quickly drew from the no-longer-silent majority. The president was so taken by the positive response that he wrote a note to himself: "Before November 3 a majority of the press expected RN to cave, and those who did not, expected him to have a violent reaction to the demonstrations. He surprised them by doing neither. The RN policy is to talk softly and to carry a big stick. That was the theme of November 3."

As 1969 drew to a close, the talks in Paris were at a standstill. These official negotiations had so far famously been all about the shape of the table. Hanoi believed that the talks were four way—involving the Democratic Republic of Vietnam, the National Liberation Front of South Vietnam, the United States and Saigon—and that all four delegations should be equal and independent. Hanoi thus had proposed a square table, with each delegation sitting on one side.

The United States, needing to justify its two-party conception between the United States and the DRV, at first proposed a rectangular table, with the United States and Saigon sitting on one side, the DRV and NLF on the other. Three other forms were then offered: two opposite though not separated arcs of a circle; two opposite and separated semicircles; and two opposite semicircles, with a gap separating them. At the end of the gap were to be two rectangular tables for secretaries. All of these proposals were rejected.

The United States then proposed a continuous round table, with two opposite parts reserved for secretaries, with parts lower than the rest of the table reserved half for the U.S. delegation and half for the communists. The Soviet ambassador to France made a recommendation for a round, flat table and two opposite rectangular tables off the round table for secretaries with no flags or plates for names. This way, the parties could speak of either a two- or four-sided conference, depending on their view. Even this was an ironic noncompromise. The United States would call the talks two-party; the communists would call them four-party. The United States called them the Paris Peace Talks, Hanoi the Paris Talks. For months, nobody spoke the same language.

CHAPTER THREE

"You Cannot Hide an Elephant with a Basket"

On New Year's Day 1970, Kissinger wrote a "Top Secret" memo to Major General Vernon Walters, the senior military attaché in the American embassy in Paris. Fluent in several languages and a man who kept secrets, Walters was perfect for the job Kissinger had in mind: to deliver a "top secret" message orally to either Xuan Thuy or Mai Van Bo on January 12. Kissinger instructed him that no "written message should be left with them." Nixon wanted the Vietnamese to know that the U.S. was ready to go beyond the framework of the plenary meetings at the Majestic Hotel. Kissinger could meet Xuan Thuy at a time and place of their choosing. Walters was instructed that after communicating this message, he should be clear that the United States preferred a weekend date "in order to limit speculation about my absence from Washington."

Walters was to make certain that the place for such a meeting was not the North Vietnam compound and that Kissinger's major requirements were for security and secrecy. Kissinger was hoping that Le Duc Tho would attend the meeting, instructing Walters that "if they suggest I meet with lesser-ranking representatives, you should emphasize our expectation that Xuan Thuy himself will participate in such a meeting. We would have no objection to Xuan Thuy's bringing along any other North Vietnamese representatives he wishes."

In order to maintain the level of secrecy Kissinger expected, Walters had to take careful steps when going to the communist suburb in order to deliver the message. Walters's car had diplomatic license plates, so in order to avoid attracting attention, he drove to a location several miles away, then took a bus, then walked to the location. In his memoirs Walters wrote that "most of the top-ranking North Vietnamese lived in the elegant 16th District of Paris. They even had a brothel there for their personnel, staffed entirely with women from North Vietnam. They always met, however, in a working class district." Walters delivered his message and went home. The back-channel talks were about to begin in earnest.

Days later Walters received a telephone call at his home from a North Vietnamese staff person requesting that he come to the DRV house at 78 Rue Jules Lagaisse in Choisy-le-Roi on Monday, February 16, for a meeting with Mai Van Bo.

After cordially greeting Walters, Mai Van Bo "took a piece of paper out of his pocket and read it to me," recalled Walters. The North Vietnamese agreed to meet on either February 20 or 21 at 11 rue Darthe in Choisy-le-Roi, a safe and discreet house where the North Vietnamese had received Averell Harriman for his private meetings with them. The date was a weekend; Hanoi wished to accommodate Kissinger's request. Walters then asked whether their "visitor" Le Duc Tho would still be in Paris at that time because "Dr. Kissinger would be willing to meet with him." Mai Van Bo said that he did not know whether Le Duc Tho would still be here, but if he were, he would take part in the meeting.

Tea was served. "Mai Van Bo asked me if I was studying Vietnamese and I said I was. He said that he was also trying to study English. Our countries would not always be at war and he might some day go to the United States. He said his people were fighting for what they thought was right and had taken a greater tonnage of bombs than any other people. I said that no one could challenge the courage of the Vietnamese people. As a soldier I took off my hat to them but we too were fighting for what we believed was right. My country four times this century had poured forth its blood for what it thought was right. He shook hands and poured me another cup of tea."

Kissinger, Nixon, and Walters have all described the elaborate physical and logistical planning arrangements for getting Kissinger in and out of Paris without notice. Recently declassified documents give even more detail. The pilot flying Kissinger needed a cover story, so he was ostensibly to operate a training mission to Rhein-Main Air Base, Germany, with one stop going and returning. All that was needed would be one set of boarding stairs and "special handling" through customs clearance. Walters later bragged that in all his fifteen trips in and out of France, Kissinger "never once saw a customs officer."

In the White House, Kissinger's assistant, Alexander Haig, had taken care of all arrangements for Kissinger's "weekend." The White House switchboard had been told that Kissinger was at Camp David with Tony Lake and secretary Dianne Matthews. Instead, the secret itinerary showed "Mr. Kissinger and Tony Lake to depart Ellipse by helicopter for Andrews, with cover story that we are departing for Camp David (Dianne will go by sedan directly to Andrews, with necessary supplies and equipment) and will be on board for take off as soon as helicopter arrives from Andrews."

Walters had a two-bedroom apartment in Neuilly. On his secret trips, Kissinger slept in Walters's bedroom, and his assistants in the other room. Walters slept on the couch in the living room. Walters's cook was told that the visitor was "Harold A. Kirschman," because Walters felt obliged to retain Kissinger's initials. Nixon characterized Kissinger's secret meeting as "full of cloak and dagger episodes, with Kissinger riding slouched down in the back seats of speeding Citroens, eluding inquisitive reporters, and putting curious embassy officials off the scent." The South Vietnamese soon referred to Kissinger as Midnight Diplomat or the King of Camouflage. Before the secret meetings were revealed to the American public in January 1972, code names were used for the principals: Kissinger was Luke, Xuan Thuy was Yul, Le Duc Tho was Michael, and General Vernon Walters was Xerxes.

The first meeting between Kissinger and Le Duc Tho occurred on February 21, 1970, in what Kissinger described as a "dingy living room" in Rue Darthe. Arriving late with Tony Lake and Vernon Walters, Kissinger was greeted by Xuan Thuy, who led the American team into a small drawing room beside the dining table. "It was a moment worth calling historical," wrote Luu Van Loi. "Kissinger met Le Duc Tho for the first time, two persons completely different in social origin, nature, and political ideals."

Kissinger later recalled in an interview with Stanley Karnow that "it was our misfortune that Le Duc Tho's assignment was to break the spirit of the American people for the war, and that he was engaged in a campaign of psychological warfare, so what he attempted to do to us was extremely painful. On the other hand, I had a very high regard for him. He was a man of enormous discipline. He never made any mistakes that I was aware of. . . . I don't look back to my meetings with him with any great joy, but I have to say he was a man of substance and discipline who defended the interest of the philosophy that he represented . . . with great dedication."

One of the most interesting descriptions of his relationship with Le Duc Tho came from Kissinger on March 17, 1975, during a White House meeting with a congressional delegation that had just returned from Vietnam. "It was my misfortune to negotiate with the North Vietnamese for four years. They are hard cases. I wish I could agree to get a political solution instead of a military solution. It was not possible to negotiate a political solution with them without a strong military solution. They are the most devoted, single-minded abrasive Communists I have ever seen. I once took Le Duc Tho to a museum in Hanoi, which he never visited himself. All of the artifacts reminded him of prisons where he had been. . . . He is a dedicated revolutionary. They are hard cases and in some ways rather admirable. Le Duc Tho and all the others have fought all their lives. They will not give up, unless they have to. They must run out. Look at the political options they put forward. For years they said they would not accept Thieu and then they did. Now they say they will not accept the government of Thieu again."

Kissinger began this first morning session by explaining that it seemed to the United States that "you want as a condition for negotiations to be guaranteed political predominance [a coalition government without Thieu] and that then we will rely on your good faith and self-restraint for the future. Perhaps to you, it seems that we are looking for military predominance and that we are asking you to rely on our good faith and self-restraint for the future." Raising for the first time the most serious of all points to Vietnamese from North and South, Kissinger then said, "We recognize you have a special problem in placing your troops in South Vietnam on the same legal basis as the American troops in South Vietnam. You do not recognize your troops in South Vietnam as foreign troops and instead you have never officially stated that you have troops in South Vietnam."

Kissinger insisted that any just political settlement must reflect the relation of existing political forces in the South, and neither side could be expected to give up at the negotiating table what it had not lost on the battlefield. Kissinger tabled the prospect of reconstruction assistance for North Vietnam because in his and Nixon's opinion, "an independent, prosperous, and self-confident Democratic Republic of Vietnam is appropriate to the national interest of the United States."

Kissinger said that because of their history, it was natural for the Vietnamese to think that all foreigners are treacherous to them. "As Vietnamese and as Marxists you are not too impressed by anything but objective factors. . . . For selfish reasons, I try to understand your position as well as I can." Kissinger noted that the consequence of all North Vietnamese proposals was to give political dominance to the NLF and for the United States then to rely on their good faith and self-restraint. "You do not say this is your intention, but it is the practical consequence of your position. At the same time, I can understand from your point of view, it may seem that what we are trying to do is get military predominance. . . . Since neither side wants to put itself at the mercy of the other, we have a problem. This is the problem I have come here to help start solving."

Kissinger apologized for speaking so long, "but as a professor at Harvard University, I always speak for 55 minutes."

Xuan Thuy spoke next, first by recalling that since their August 4 private meeting in Sainteny's apartment, the situation had deteriorated. Referring to Nixon's November 1 deadline, Thuy said, "The United States said it wanted to settle the problem before 1 November 1969 but it did not make any new proposal. . . . As for us, we have put forward two concrete proposals: first, the U.S. should rapidly withdraw its forces within 5 or 6 months, second, to set up a three-component coalition government."

Tony Lake's notes from the meeting include Xuan Thuy's questioning Kissinger on what he meant by a "logical political process" in South Vietnam. Kissinger joked that he "had read so many of your words that I am beginning to speak in paradoxical terms myself."

Kissinger and Xuan Thuy had taken up most of the morning, and it was then agreed that the parties would break for lunch and that Le Duc Tho would then speak. When that time arrived, Tho began as he would almost always, with a lengthy speech that traversed a range of subjects that might include U.S. public opinion, the Senate Foreign Relations Committee, Vietnamization, and a history of the struggle of the Vietnamese people against all oppressors.

Kissinger would later recall, "Le Duc Tho had a tendency to make the same speech every day, months on end, and it was sort of like a prayer session at the beginning of the meeting and it meant, what it symbolized was that they had all kinds of time, that we were going to have to collapse long before they would think of yielding. One of the lines in that speech was 'you make a big effort and we'll make a big effort.' One day I heard him say, 'you make a big effort, we'll make an effort.' I said, 'Mr. Special Adviser,' which was his title, 'have I noticed you've dropped an adjective here.' He said, 'you are absolutely right, because yesterday we made a big effort and you only made an effort. So today we reverse roles.'"

According to Tho, the United States would not win the war through Vietnamization, negotiations, or threats. Vietnamization would only prolong the war because the South would never be strong enough for the United

States to leave. No matter how progress was measured, Vietnamization would fail because the "puppet" government (as Tho always referred to the government in South Vietnam) would never be strong enough. The American goal for Vietnamization was for Asians to fight Asians.

Tho then made a bold prediction: "Although we have suffered great sacrifices and losses and undergone a great deal of hardship, we have won!"

"You have won the war?" Kissinger asked.

"We have won and you have failed. . . . Previously, with over one million U.S. and Saigon troops, you have failed. Now how can you win, if you let the South Vietnamese army fight alone and if you only give them military support? Only giving American support, how can you win? How can you win when you could not do it with 600,000 men? If our generation cannot win then our sons and nephews will continue. We will sacrifice everything, but we will not again have slavery. This is our iron will. We have been fighting for 25 years, the French and you. You wanted to quench our spirit with bombs and shells. But they cannot force us to submit."

Le Duc Tho then harkened back to Kissinger's August 4 threat to Xuan Thuy: "You threatened us. President Nixon also threatens us. But you have read our history. We fought against the French for nine years. We were empty handed. Myself, I participated in this resistance war against the French, without knowing military things. Yet we won victory . . . you cannot change the trend of the war. This is not a challenge. I am frank. We are a small people. We cannot challenge anybody. We have been under domination for many years." Tho finally warned Kissinger that putting maximum military pressure on the North would not work. "I am convinced we will win victory."

Kissinger's response was utterly deferential in tone: "I belong to those who since 1965 have tried to find a negotiated end to the war in Vietnam. I belong to those who believed that an end of the bombing would lead to productive negotiations. I have attempted to understand and study you very carefully. It is, of course, difficult for men who have shown your heroism and dedication to envision an end to the war, which doesn't guarantee all of your immediate objectives. It is not easy for us either, because we too have had over a period of time to adjust some of our thinking."

Regarding American public opinion, Kissinger tried to suggest that it was no business of Tho's. He argued that Nixon was a better judge of public opinion than those journalists or senators visiting Vietnam and that Tho should stay off the subject during these private sessions.

"We must take it into account," responded Le Duc Tho.

"That is our problem," said Kissinger.

"We have two ears and must listen," said Xuan Thuy.

"We will take care of U.S. public opinion, you take care of opinion in North Vietnam," Kissinger responded.

"Okay, but we must make an assessment of U.S. public opinion too," retorted Tho. Not a meeting would pass in which Tho did not offer his opinions on U.S. public opinion, dissent, or congressional actions aimed at curtailing the war effort. The antiwar movement was one of his strongest allies, and he knew it.

Lake's notes also include a revealing statement by Kissinger that although the United States would never dump Thieu, Kissinger guaranteed Le Duc Tho that Thieu would agree to whatever was negotiated. As Kissinger put it, "We do not ask about your making an agreement and the NLF's not agreeing. We assume you will use your influence. The same will be true with us."

Kissinger concluded by urging Le Duc Tho not to force a test of will because Nixon was not a man to be tested. This was, of course, exactly how Nixon wanted to be perceived. Ambassador Bill Sullivan called it Nixon's madman theory: "If he could make them believe that he was capable of becoming irrational and not under control, although he was a very cold, calculating man, he thought that that was a useful context, to give the appearance of being an uncontrollable man. And this was the way he wanted it done."

The two parties agreed to meet again in three weeks, on Monday, March 16, 1970.

Kissinger was afraid that his absence from Washington would be noticed and wanted to leave Saturday, not Sunday. "If I leave on Sunday, everyone will think I have a girl," he said.

"Leave the girl somewhere, and come here for the discussions. This is a suggestion of good will," remarked Xuan Thuy.

"As always, minister Xuan Thuy has left out the essential element. First I need a girl friend," replied Kissinger.

"Look for one. I am told you have many," replied Thuy.

And with that attempt at humor, the private channel was established. Many more would follow, and virtually everything of consequence would be discussed at them. These meetings would not be negotiations in the classic sense, however. "There wasn't the kind of give and take that you would have in a large labor negotiation or a business negotiation in the United

States, or for that matter in a normal international negotiation between governments," recalled Negroponte. "They tended both in public and in private, I should say, to follow a very set pattern—one side or the other would make a prepared statement and then the other side would reply with a prepared statement, and then we might adjourn for a break, and have tea and some refreshments and then there would be a little bit of give and take. But, since so little progress was being made, and since, until the latter part of 1972, the prospects of any settlement seemed so remote, they were not negotiations as you and I would normally think of them."

The records from these private meetings reveal that they were not parallel in substance to the plenary sessions being held at Avenue Kleber. Not only were they separate and secret; they were also sealed off from some key interested parties. President Thieu was never adequately briefed on the talks by Ambassador Ellsworth Bunker; Bunker received his information from Kissinger and did not always know the full score. The secretaries of state and defense, joint chiefs of staff, and other bureaucratic entities were also kept out of the loop, viewed by Kissinger and Nixon as untrustworthy and potential sources of leaks.

Kissinger reported to Nixon that this first seven hours with Le Duc Tho and Xuan Thuy "was a significant meeting. We had a frank exchange of views. They basically accepted our proposed procedure for future private meetings, dropped their preconditions for substantive negotiations, and gave the impression of being much more ready for business than before."

Kissinger characterized Tho's afternoon speech as "rather defensive" and Xuan Thuy's as "very perfunctory." Kissinger wrote Nixon that the private channel would continue. "It was also implicitly agreed that after we have discussed all the issues, and if we reach agreement, the other parties will be brought in to ratify it." Kissinger seems to have misjudged Le Duc Tho with respect to the important question of Hanoi's time horizons: "They know they cannot keep this channel going very long if they do not offer anything new. . . . They appear to be worried about Vietnamization, because if it succeeds they have lost and if it fails we may keep some forces there a long time."

It was Ambassador Ellsworth Bunker's task to keep President Thieu informed of the Kissinger-Tho meetings, but not until March 11 did Bunker provide what he described as "a comprehensive and detailed account" of Kissinger's meeting with "Michael, Yul and Nestor." In fact, the reports to Thieu were invariably sanitized. Bunker's briefings of Thieu would be from

one to two pages of talking points dealing with generalities and never revealing the substantive talks. Bunker informed Thieu that "the other side did not
balk at discussion of reciprocal withdrawal, did not argue over the need for
reciprocity in withdrawal, did not demand a change in Government of Vietnam as prerequisite to engaging in private talks, did not mention PRG."
Bunker assured Thieu that at the March 16 meeting in Paris, Kissinger would
continue to insist on mutual withdrawal and say nothing about the political
structure in South Vietnam, except to emphasize again that the U.S. would
not agree to the overthrow of the government of Vietnam.

Kissinger had good reason to keep Thieu in the dark. On March 13,
1970, Tony Lake of the NSC wrote to Kissinger that "it is almost certain
that the North Vietnamese will not agree to mutual withdrawal unless they
have a good idea about how the political future looks in South Vietnam."
Although Kissinger was not ready to admit it quite yet, Thieu's hold on
power would become a bargaining chip—with or without his consent.

* * *

By March, the next meeting with Le Duc Tho was fast approaching, and
Kissinger wanted to make certain that he and Nixon were in agreement on
how to proceed. In a memo entitled "How to Proceed in My Private Meeting with the North Vietnamese," Kissinger urged a break from past patterns, "where we have always been or appeared to be too eager for a
settlement, too anxious to show progress." Thus, "we have never forced
them to come up with really new formulations."

The United States made concessions on bombing; the North agreed only
to talk. Kissinger wrote: "My strategy at the meeting will be to gain their
agreement to the basic principle of *reciprocity* in the withdrawal of non–
South Vietnamese troops from South Vietnam (and foreign troops from
Cambodia and Laos)—or at least to smoke them out on this issue. Once they
accept this principle, we enter a different negotiation and have made the
basic breakthrough. The questions remaining would concern negotiating the
technical issues to implement an orderly and verifiable withdrawal.

"I will also seek to draw from them their proposals on a political settlement, without appearing too anxious to get into this subject. The record
should show that they, not we, pressed this issue, for the sake of our relations with the Government of Vietnam." Even without a political settlement, mutual withdrawal was in the United States and South Vietnam's
fundamental interests. "This will not be an opening bargaining position, but
a bottom line," stressed Kissinger.

In truth, this would be a shifting bottom line, and the veil of secrecy surrounding the talks meant that very few would be aware of the concessions being made in private. There was no precise negotiating position that had been agreed to within the United States government or even a general negotiating position agreed upon with the government of Vietnam. Kissinger fully understood the risks, telling Nixon that it "will require you to make decisions on our position which could, if later revealed, embroil us in difficulties with Saigon. This is risky, but I see no other way to proceed if we are to maintain momentum and secrecy."

Secrecy would be paramount throughout the process. Yet what did the U.S. gain by the secret negotiations? Momentum is hardly an appropriate description for the Kissinger-Tho negotiations. In the end, of course, the U.S. would get a troop withdrawal that retained Thieu in power with promises of air support. Soon after, Thieu would be betrayed by those promises. The costs of secrecy only compounded the betrayal.

At the March 16 meeting, Kissinger tried to establish mutual withdrawal as a non-negotiable U.S. position. He wrote in his memoirs that this recommendation was "contemptuously rejected with a pedantic lecture." As Tho put it, "According to your presentation, the complete withdrawal of U.S. and allied forces is a legal principle. The withdrawal of troops allegedly belonging to the North is not a legal principle, but a practical and technical question. However, when you speak about the withdrawal of the troops allegedly belonging to the North, you demand that these troops also be completely pulled out within the same time limit. In fact it is a demand of simultaneous and complete troop withdrawal."

As the meeting was drawing to a close, Kissinger showed some irritation: "Negotiation cannot be conducted in the way a teacher puts questions to his pupils to ascertain whether we have correctly understood your position." Beneath the condescension, however, the North's position was clear: it would not withdraw troops, whether or not the U.S. and Saigon claimed it was "supposed" to. Since Hanoi never formally acknowledged the presence of its troops in the South, Kissinger was forced to play along with this absurd semantic game. He would tell Thieu to take comfort in the fact that since the North Vietnamese said they had no troops in South Vietnam, after the agreement was signed, they could not claim a legal right to keep them there.

In a memo to Nixon immediately following the March 16 encounter, Kissinger described the four hours as "another important meeting."

Kissinger explained, "They went even further than last time in dropping pre-conditions for substantive talks, changing some of their traditional slogans, and they indicated very strongly that they want to preserve this channel and to work toward an overall settlement. . . . The atmosphere was even more free of unnecessary polemics and propaganda than at our last meeting. . . . Le Duc Tho gave an indication of flexibility when he said, 'So here each side can negotiate, change views, and come to an agreement.' They were very anxious to have another meeting."

It is difficult to explain just why Kissinger would offer Nixon such a disparate report from what had actually occurred at the meeting. Was the adviser clinging to a false hope that he could personally secure a settlement very soon? Even more puzzling is the account Kissinger related to Bunker for Thieu. After reading Kissinger's report, Bunker cabled Kissinger: "I am encouraged by report of your talk with Michael, Yul, and Nestor." Then he came to the heart of the problem: "We are in a somewhat delicate position here since we have always said that the GVN must participate in negotiations affecting the internal problems of South Vietnam. On the other hand, we told the other side that we are ready to discuss anything with them and, of course, we would have to keep Thieu informed of our discussion of political matters with Michael, Yul, and Nestor. With this caveat, I see no reason why we should not discuss matters relating to a political settlement."

Bunker echoed Kissinger's rosy report for Thieu and informed Thieu that when Kissinger presented a hypothetical mutual withdrawal covering sixteen months, "they asked some questions about it, but did not reject his statement that they have to withdraw also. They said this amounted to mutual withdrawal. Though they had always rejected this previously they did not do so this time. . . . They also said in effect that we should forget about the PRG 10 points which really resolved themselves into two questions, 'the military problem and the political problem,' which are linked." Bunker also reassured Thieu that "Mr. Kissinger has made it clear and will continue to make it clear that the demand of the other side for the overthrow of the GVN leadership is out of the question."

While Thieu "evinced great interest," he wanted Bunker and Kissinger to know that his own intelligence indicated that the Hanoi Politburo had reached a decision "to reduce the tempo of war in the South and to prolong it through guerrilla tactics; build their infrastructure in the South; and to restore the economy in North; this does not, however, in his view rule out their trying to make some progress in Paris. In the meantime, they will try to see what they can secure from us, will try to probe to find out what we want and may let us know what they want." Thieu warned Bunker that Hanoi's major objectives were still more psychological than military, attempting to influence U.S. and free world opinion. This was what happened at Dien Bien Phu prior to Geneva. Thieu described Hanoi's goal as securing only a "temporary peace."

Clearly President Thieu understood Hanoi's strategy better than the Americans did. Yet he was misled on mutual withdrawal and deceived with regard to the U.S. role in negotiating on the political context of internal Vietnamese politics. There is reason to believe that the only reason he went along with any of these proposals was the assurances he received that Hanoi was unlikely to accept them anyway.

For much of the next year, little would change as the North Vietnamese, reasonably enough, let time be their ally. They continued to insist on three conditions: the Thieu-Ky-Khiem government in South Vietnam would have to be removed; a three-component provisional government would be created composed of representatives of the PRG, a new (Thieu-less) Saigon government, and other political forces; and the U.S. would withdraw all of its troops, and a National Assembly would be chosen through elections to approve a new constitution and set up a coalition government. Only then would the fundamental national rights of the Vietnamese people be achieved through independence, sovereignty, unity, and territorial integrity.

These conditions were unacceptable to the United States because although Kissinger said he was prepared to negotiate on military and political issues, he did not intend to negotiate on replacing Thieu. "First, agreement should be reached on assessing the existing balance of forces and on the political process to be realized to reflect this balance of forces," Kissinger told Tho at an April 4 meeting. "Being Leninists, you should understand that theoretically a political process is never stable. Therefore, the United States would like to create a political process which would not exclude any result and which would allow all political groups to participate in the struggle about national political issues. We are trying to separate the military struggle from the political struggle. . . . The U.S. will not accept a solution imposed by military means. It is prepared to accept the results of a political process reflecting the aspirations of the people. . . . Our objection to your proposals is not to the objectives but to the fact that the political effect is to rule out a fair process. . . . They would pre-determine the political outcome by selecting those you define as peace-loving and smashing the organized political course of those who are opposed. . . . The mere act of discussing certain proposals changes the political reality."

Kissinger gave an illustration of his views. For instance, if the two parties discussed a change of Madame Binh, this would affect her morale. The Vietnamese side was demanding the change of certain leaders of the existing Saigon government as a premise to the political process. This demand was not acceptable to the United States.

And so it went, on and on, throughout 1970 and into 1971. Reading the transcripts of the meetings is like being transported into an Alice-in-Wonderland world. The United States had already accepted the principle of total withdrawal of American and allied forces, along with a precise schedule for this withdrawal. It had guaranteed that it was not committed to the maintenance of any political force in power *once a settlement was achieved*. Kissinger even tabled proposals and methods for consulting the will of the people. Kissinger told Le Duc Tho that he was prepared to discuss the relationship of elections to the elements of political power, the relationship of military to political authorities, the relationship of executive and legislative power, and how minorities are to be protected. It all sounded so noble.

Le Duc Tho had little interest in any of it. He believed that the U.S. was using military pressure to negotiate from a position of strength. Vietnamization merely pitted Vietnamese against Vietnamese in an American plan for retaining influence. He blamed the United States for orchestrating a coup against Sihanouk in Cambodia. To Tho, "through what has happened in Vietnam, Laos, and Cambodia, particularly your actions in Laos and Cambodia, I think that you are still actively carrying out the Vietnamization plan, prolonging the war and expanding it to the whole of Indochina. In Cambodia, it is wondered who has organized the coup to wipe out the independence and neutrality of that country and to rig up a reactionary group to power. No one other than the U.S. You said that it was not a threat to Vietnam, that you were not involved in Cambodia. This is completely contrary to the fact. As a Vietnamese saying goes, *'You cannot hide an elephant with a basket.'* Kissinger replied, 'I like this saying.'"

Le Duc Tho believed that the United States plan was to make gains on the battlefield while negotiations crept along. "But we think that it is mere illusion. You have not correctly assessed the strength of our entire people standing up to oppose you. Now you intend to extend the war to Cambodia and to fall again into an old rut. You think that after the overthrowing of Sihanouk by the reactionaries in the Cambodian army, everything will be over. This is too simple minded. . . . While you are failing in Vietnam and Laos, you cannot win in Cambodia. . . . You will reap what you have sowed. You have tried to incite national hatred between the Vietnamese and the Cambodian peoples, but the people of Vietnam, Cambodia, and Laos have got traditional cohesion in opposing the French during nine years and have long been associated together, you will not be able to break this cohesion. Today, the people of Vietnam, Cambodia, and Laos are still more determined to fight and will surely win victory. That is why, the peaceful solution of the problem of Vietnam, Laos, and Cambodia depends on you and not on us."

Kissinger's frustrations mounted. Eventually he accused Le Duc Tho of using his "dialectical talent" to prolong the talks indefinitely. In one exchange with Xuan Thuy, Kissinger remarked, "The Minister is of more difficult character than I am." Xuan Thuy responded, "I have got that difficult character since I met you. I have learned it from you." That particular meeting ended with Le Duc Tho observing, "The standpoints of the two parties are still far apart."

In July 1970 seventy-two-year-old David K. E. Bruce was appointed to head the American delegation in Paris. Bruce's appointment was widely praised because he was one of the most respected diplomats of the post–World War II period. Nixon called him out of retirement to assume his post. In his memoirs, Kissinger described Bruce as an honorable, distinguished, and nonpartisan individual dedicated to public service. "He was free of that insistence on seeing their views prevail through which lesser men turned public service into an exercise of their egos. . . . He saw man as uniquely capable of improvement through reason and tact in a world whose imperfections would yield—if only gradually to patience and good will." But all of this was before Bruce met Le Duc Tho and his colleagues.

Bruce's first plenary session was August 6, 1970, when Xuan Thuy and Madame Binh agreed to return to Paris after a ten-month lapse. In the United States, as a result of the U.S. invasion of Cambodia known as the Cambodian Incursion, antiwar sentiment was increasing on college campuses and within Congress, culminating with the tragic shootings at Kent State that touched off massive protests on college campuses across America. Two of Kissinger's top assistants, Tony Lake and Roger Morris, submitted their resignations on April 29. Two weeks later, Kissinger ordered wiretaps to be placed on Lake's telephones. In his memoirs Kissinger wrote that "historians rarely do justice to the psychological stress on a policymaker."

March and April 1970 had been months of "great tension" and, according to Kissinger, "what no document can reveal is the accumulated impact of accident, intangibles, fears, and hesitation." Kissinger's three closest aides were Lake, Morris, and Lord. "They had no great use for Nixon; emotionally, each would probably have preferred a Democratic President."

In a formal letter, the two aides explained that they were tendering their resignations from the NSC staff because "we have grave reservations about the value of using U.S. troops in Cambodia. We believe the costs and consequences of such an action far exceed any gains one can reasonably expect. But the reasons for our resignations, involving an increasing alienation from this Administration, also pre-date and go beyond the Cambodian problem. We wished to inform you now, before public reaction to our Cambodian policy, so that it will be clear that our decision was not made after the fact and as a result of those consequences. We have appreciated the opportunity to work for you. We hope to have an occasion to discuss with you at your convenience the considerations which have led us to resign. We certainly wish to minimize any embarrassment to you in this matter."

Then, in a personal and unofficial letter to Kissinger, Lake and Morris were more blunt about the reasons for their resignation:

In view of the closeness and apparent mutual respect of our working relations in the past, we naturally want to be completely honest in describing the reasons for our resignations. They involve some very strong feelings about this Administration. As we have said before, we sympathize with your difficult position and the pressures you are under, and do not intend this letter as an attack on you personally. But the strength of our feelings requires our writing this. . . . As we told you in February, we find ourselves increasingly alienated by the domestic and many of the foreign policies of this Administration. Because of our continuing personal loyalty to you and what you are trying to do, however, we have no desire for our resignations to become even a minor public issue. We do indeed believe . . . that a new era requires a new quality of leadership. It demands above all an understanding of urgent needs in America and abroad and a commitment to meet them. We have found neither. We have often heard courage equated with standing up to criticism. But it is not enough to dismiss the critics for their motives or manliness, nor to ridicule them with the catch phrases of the Right. We think real courage means recognizing the validity of the problems, however they are raised, and leading an effort to resolve them.

We think presidential politics should be the means to that end and not, as we see it practiced now, an end in itself through obsession with public relations.

Morris and Lake were also disturbed from listening to telephone conversations between Kissinger and an intoxicated commander in chief. Morris recorded that Nixon "drank exceptionally at night. There were many times when a cable would come in late and Henry would say, 'there's no sense waking him up—he'd be incoherent." Tom Wells reports that one Nixon aide overheard a drunk Nixon tell Kissinger, "Henry, we've got to nuke them." The invasion of Cambodia thus provided an exit, and both men warned Kissinger that "there would be blood in the streets" if the plans were implemented. Another staffer, William Watts, actually gave back to Kissinger his October 1969 memo that warned against Duck Hook, saying that "it still applies in spades" with respect to domestic unrest. On October 26 Watts refused to attend the NSC meeting on the Cambodian invasion and resigned on the spot. When Haig told him "he'd just had an order from your Commander-in-Chief and you can't refuse," Watts said, "Fuck you, Al. I just have and I've resigned."

America was in turmoil. Domestic dissent had produced two measures in the U.S. Congress that aimed to reduce America's military activity in Vietnam and all of Southeast Asia. Two Democratic senators, John Sherman Cooper and Frank Church, sponsored legislation that would halt all U.S. military activity in Cambodia as of July 1. And Senators George McGovern and Mark Hatfield proposed an amendment that would cut off all funding for the war by the end of 1970.

The Paris negotiations remained stalled, and on September 15, 1970, Ambassador Bunker visited President Thieu to present the outline of a major new diplomatic initiative comprising four interrelated components: an internationally supervised standstill cease-fire throughout all Indochina; an immediate, unconditional release of all prisoners of war held by both sides; an acceptance in principle that United States armed forces would be withdrawn from Vietnam; and an expanded international conference among interested parties to seek a negotiated settlement throughout Indochina.

Bunker emphasized to President Thieu that Nixon "does not regard cease-fire as an end in itself, but as leading to a larger, integrated effort to effect a just and honorable solution to the war." He explained that under conditions of a standstill cease-fire, there would be prohibitions against introducing reinforcements. This proposal would not affect the political side, which remained a matter for the South Vietnamese to determine. In other words, there would be no coalition government, no peace cabinet, or anything else that would betray him.

Thieu was caught off guard because it was evident that this "in-place" cease-fire had replaced mutual withdrawal of troops. He was full of questions about issues he believed had not been thought through. Thieu had served in the military and understood fully the implication of an "in-place" cease-fire. He also understood communist treachery and wondered who would monitor a standstill cease-fire. How would a supervisory group verify enemy units? What were the safeguards for infiltration and replacement of troops? Thieu believed that all of these concerns needed to be nailed down between allies before the plan was tabled for negotiations.

On September 18, Bunker cabled Secretary of State William Rogers that there were factors of the president's proposed initiative that needed to get worked out then, not later. "Specifically, we have assumed that a standstill cease-fire would be implemented as soon as there is agreement on the necessary conditions, with the other issues of a settlement left for negotiation at an international conference. This raises the question of whether there should be a time limit on the negotiations, since we all agree that an in-place ceasefire is inherently unstable and, over an extended period of time, could be exploited by the enemy. Thieu has stressed this point in our consultations, warning that the other side might seek to drag out negotiations on a settlement merely to take advantage of a stand-down in the fighting."

Bunker met privately with Thieu on September 20 and pressed Thieu to go along with the president's new initiative, requesting only that the president announce that it was done in coordination with the GVN.

On September 17 Madame Binh offered a new NLF eight-point peace plan significant for the fact that this was the first time the release of American prisoners of war was linked to a U.S. troop withdrawal. According to Madame Binh, if the U.S. agreed to withdraw all U.S. and foreign allied troops from South Vietnam by June 30, 1971, communist forces would "refrain from attacking" these "withdrawing" allied forces and immediately engage in discussions concerning the safety of the POWs and withdrawing troops. A cease-fire would follow, not precede, agreement on terms of a settlement.

The September 17 NLF proposal would have created a new coalition government, constituted by one member of the NLF, one from the anticommunists (excluding Thieu, Ky, and Khiem), and one from neutrals living abroad. According to Robert Brigham, the strategy was designed to harass the Thieu government because "although the United States remained faithful to Thieu and routinely rejected such proposals, Le Duc Tho's reports from his secret meetings with Henry Kissinger in Paris suggested that Washington was becoming more *flexible* in its responses to a non-communist government in Saigon." In private, Kissinger was already hinting at betrayal.

In his memoirs, Kissinger dismissed Madame Binh as a woman of insignificant stature. He felt that "her actual stature is reflected in the fact that after the North overran the South, she was relegated to the Ministry of Education and never heard from again." Most area experts drew a different conclusion. Nguyen Thi Binh came from a famous family. She was born in Saigon in 1927, the granddaughter of one of Vietnam's most celebrated patriots. As a student leader during the First French Indochina War, she was arrested by the French in 1950 and released after the Geneva Accords were signed. She was an important member of the southern intellectual resistance to the Diem regime. "Her background was legendary in revolutionary Vietnam. . . . With Ho's death, Binh was easily recognized as the communists' leading international figure by members of the European press and the peace movement in the United States," writes Brigham. In fact, she would be effective at chipping away American support of Thieu. (After the war, Binh rose to and remained vice president of the State of Vietnam into the 1990s, long after Kissinger had left government.)

Two days later, on September 19, Pham Van Dong was in Beijing for a meeting with Chou Enlai. Commenting on the secret talks, the Chinese premier now applauded the current status: "We see that comrade Nguyen Thi Binh is very sharp. We have also read the report of the meeting between comrades Huang Chen and Xuan Thuy on secret contacts between the latter and Kissinger."

The conversation between Dong and Chou focused on Nixon's Vietnamization plan. Dong believed that "Nixon's Vietnamization is still aimed at gaining a military victory in South Vietnam. It, however, does not mean that Nixon does not think about diplomacy. That they sent [Ambassador] Bruce to Paris is also aimed at deceiving the world. What should we do in facing Nixon's calculations?" The answer was to "step up the diplomatic struggle. . . . We have to influence the anti-war public opinion in the U.S. that includes not only the people at large, but also the political, business, academic, and clerical circles to ensure a stronger support by them. The world public opinion has been mobilized."

The NLF delegation was conducting a sophisticated diplomatic offense by demanding the unconditional withdrawal of American troops with a timetable as well as the removal of Thieu, Ky, and Khiem. "These points are not new," Dong told Chou, but "we want further to corner Nixon by influencing public opinion in the U.S. and the rest of the world. These points are also aimed at supporting the military and political struggles in the South. We do not have any illusion that they will bring about any results."

Throughout the entire negotiation, Hanoi would demonstrate a good grasp of American democratic politics. Clearly the North Vietnamese followed the antiwar movement closely; they brought it up again and again to a frustrated Kissinger. China too understood that time was on Hanoi's side.

As Mao would tell Dong, "Negotiations have been going on for two years. At first we were a little worried that you were trapped. We are no longer worried. . . . You are fighting well on the battlefield. Your policy for diplomatic struggle is correct." Finally, "The Americans still want to go to Beijing for talks. It is what they propose. . . . Kissinger is a stinking scholar. I have read the report about the meeting between comrade Xuan Thuy and Kissinger. The last part of it is very funny. Kissinger is a university professor who does not know anything about diplomacy. I think that he is not someone who can compete with Xuan Thuy, even though I have not met Xuan Thuy," said Mao.

By this point, the U.S. needed to reply to Madame Binh's proposal and feared that she and the NLF were just wasting time. Le Duc Tho was not expected to attend the September meeting, and Nixon was losing patience. Nixon wrote across Kissinger's planning memo, "I would only suggest that I would try to get sooner at the heart of the question. Do they mean business—or is this just another rehash."

On September 24, 1970, Bunker again conferred with Thieu and reported that Kissinger intended to "probe Madame Binh's eight point proposal to see whether there is any flexibility in it. He will try to draw them out on what ideas they may have on arrangements surrounding withdrawals, including how they will handle withdrawal of their forces and what their views may be on supervision/verification. We will continue to make clear that we will not accept their precondition of removal of the present GVN."

Kissinger was openly in Paris for meetings with Vice President Ky as well as to consult with Ambassador Bruce, but no one yet knew about the secret meetings with Xuan Thuy and Le Duc Tho. So the challenge was how to get Kissinger to the secret meeting in and around the very visible meetings with Ky and Bruce. Ambassador Dick Watson first took Kissinger for a ride in the country, and Kissinger then switched cars to head to the secret meeting. General Walters drove the second car since he was the only one who knew where the talks were being held—or even that they were being held. Despite these efforts, little progress was reported from the talks.

The biggest issue between South and North, and for that matter, between the South and its "ally" the United States, was and would remain the status of Northern forces in Southern territory. If everyone, including these troops, withdrew from the South, Thieu believed he had a fighting chance of survival. If the U.S. pulled out but the Northern fighters remained, Thieu believed there was little hope for his country's survival. As the Chinese sensed, and as Thieu and Hanoi knew all along, the U.S. did not have the stomach to force a Northern withdrawal. Why didn't Kissinger ever just say, "Mr. Special Adviser, if you do not admit you have troops in the South that must be removed, we have nothing to talk about"? Kissinger chose instead to insist that these forces were no threat to South Vietnam's survival.

Sure enough, on October 7, 1970, in a televised address to the nation, President Nixon offered a new peace initiative. For the first time the president said publicly that the United States would accept *a cease-fire in place,* thereby detaching the issue of a cease-fire entirely from the question of troop withdrawal. In his memoirs Kissinger confirms, "The decision to propose a standstill ceasefire in 1970 thus implied the solution of 1972. That North Vietnamese forces would remain in the South was implicit in the standstill proposal; no negotiations would be able to remove them if we had not been able to expel them with force of arms."

The JCS *History* noted that "at the conclusion of 1970, the two sides were no nearer a diplomatic settlement than in January 1969. The primary objective of the United States during the two years of negotiations had been the withdrawal of all external forces from South Vietnam and a political settlement decided by the South Vietnamese themselves free of outside interference." Now both objectives were set to be abandoned.

After two years of effort, despite new bombings and various displays of resolve at the negotiating table, Nixon was beating a steady retreat. He had come to rely on Vietnamization as the means to achieve his goal of an American withdrawal from Vietnam. He had given up on getting the Northern troops to leave South Vietnam. Frustrations were mounting. Congress passed the Cooper-Church Amendment on December 29, 1970, specifically denying the introduction of American ground forces into Cambodia or Laos. Within a month, sixty-four members of the House agreed to lobby against further use of American aerial and sea support for military activities in Cambodia. Senators George McGovern and Mark Hatfield reintroduced a modified Disengagement Act that would require the complete removal of all American troops by the end of 1971.

As the year drew to a close, White House counsel John Dean solicited the opinion of the chief justice of the Supreme Court on the legality of declaring martial law if a state of insurrection developed in the United States. The atmosphere in the Nixon White House was taking on its pre-Watergate mentality: wiretaps, surveillance of political enemies, opponents' lists. Meanwhile, Nixon was feeling the pressure to accelerate troop withdrawals from Vietnam, and he was getting desperate for a solution.

CHAPTER FOUR

McGovern's October Surprise

Senator George McGovern of South Dakota viewed the war in Vietnam as a terrible mistake. As a bomber pilot in World War II, he had witnessed first-hand the horrors of war. McGovern believed that the truth about Vietnam was that the United States was destroying the country it had gone to save.

On September 16, 1971, McGovern went to Vietnam as a presidential aspirant in search of a way to end a senseless war. Holding a press conference on his arrival in Saigon, McGovern declared, "Mr. Nixon's Vietnamization policy—like its predecessor policies—is a glaring failure. It is a bandage on a malignant cancer that is disrupting Vietnamese society, demoralizing the American army, and weakening America both at home and around the world. If American forces are not withdrawn quickly and our military operations ended, we shall see a further military, political, economic and moral debacle."

His visit was much publicized, but precisely what he accomplished, and tried to accomplish, has been mysterious. For four days McGovern engaged in around-the-clock meetings with the most knowledgeable and respected observers in Vietnam, Americans and Vietnamese. President Thieu, General Duong Van Minh, (known in South Vietnam as "Big Minh"), Ambassador Ellsworth Bunker, General Creighton Abrams, Gloria Emerson of the *New York Times,* and about fifty others including political prisoners and dissidents. They came away with a favorable view of McGovern and his views. "The Senator from South Dakota," Gloria Emerson later wrote, "was not pompous or confused, not seduced by the military and the helicopter rides, as were so many of the legislators who came whizzing through, wanting to know it all in a day and have a little sense of war."

McGovern's meetings in Saigon had been preceded by six hours of discussions outside Paris with representatives from Hanoi and the PRG. The meetings had been arranged by former Kennedy press secretary Pierre Salinger, who would play a prominent role in McGovern's presidential bid. McGovern was obsessed with bringing the war to conclusion and was intent on exploring every opportunity.

On September 11, accompanied by Frank Mankiewicz, Pierre Salinger, and a handful of trusted advisers, McGovern met secretly with Xuan Thuy, minister of the DRV delegation. Less than a month earlier, on August 16, Xuan Thuy had met secretly with Henry Kissinger in yet another mostly unproductive, secret meeting. But McGovern, like everyone else, was unaware of this and so unaware that his efforts were in certain ways redundant.

Two days prior to the August 16 meeting H. R. Haldeman had written in his diary, "Henry was in, discussing the problem of the [forthcoming] Vietnam election [scheduled for October] again, which does pose a serious problem. The P is strongly toying now with releasing the fact of our secret negotiations, blowing the channel, and forcing them to deal with us publicly, and then attacking the Senate opponents, saying they forced us to abandon our secret negotiations, and so on. K also got back on the line of what a real heartbreak the whole war situation is because we really won the war, and if we just had one more dry season, the opponents would break their backs." Haldeman thought Kissinger was sounding "like a broken record."

McGovern would attempt to extract a list of American POWs. Kissinger meanwhile was negotiating a comprehensive deal that would include release of all prisoners. The problem was that Hanoi found it easy to stall in both meetings. Kissinger's meeting on the sixteenth took place without Le Duc Tho. He elaborated a new eight-point framework that he said was an effort to combine the U.S. seven points and the Vietnamese nine points: The U.S. would withdraw all forces by August 1, 1972, provided that the final agreement was signed by November 1, 1971. The release of all prisoners would be carried out in tandem with the withdrawal of U.S. troops. The political future of South Vietnam would be left for the Vietnamese to decide for themselves, free from outside interference. The U.S. would declare that it supported no candidate and would remain completely neutral in the forthcoming South Vietnamese elections scheduled for October 3 and would abide by the outcome of the elections and any other political processes shaped by the South Vietnamese people themselves. The U.S. was also prepared to define its military and economic assistance relationship with any government that existed in South Vietnam, including setting limits on military assistance as part of an overall limitation on outside military assistance for both North and South Vietnam. Both sides would agree that the countries of Indochina should adopt a foreign policy of neutrality. Both sides would respect the 1954 Geneva Agreements on Indochina and those of 1962 on Laos.

Kissinger told Xuan Thuy that he was well aware that the Politburo had instructed him, since Le Duc Tho was not there, not to make progress. "It's a pity. The tragedy is that the war continues, in a year we shall be almost at the same point, and a day will come when the conditions we shall agree upon are more or less the same as those we are discussing at this moment." Kissinger added, "We will not thwart your plan if you win the political battle. Anyway this will come sooner or later. It's your task, but it is obvious that you are not ready to take it up. You want us to create a situation in which the Saigon administration will immediately and surely collapse. For our part, we should like to create a situation in which the replacement of the Saigon administration might occur, though we cannot guarantee it. The U.S. troops would stay 5 or 6 months more but keep reducing, making it all the more impossible for the U.S. to change the political situation in South Vietnam." His arguments were in vain; Xuan Thuy and North Vietnam preferred to wait.

"General Walters thinks you want to have dessert before taking soup," Kissinger told Xuan Thuy.

"Since you have been to China [a reference to Kissinger's recent planning trip to Peking], you should know people there eat dessert at the middle of the meal and go on to have the hot dishes!" countered Xuan Thuy.

Everyone laughed.

Kissinger hoped a final agreement would be signed before November 1, 1971. "If nothing happens from now to the elections in South Vietnam surely the present administration in Saigon will win the elections. If we can agree on the declaration of principle, there is the possibility that General Duong Van Minh will win the elections," Kissinger said. If Luu Van Loi's translation of Hanoi documents is accurate, Kissinger was offering Hanoi's acquiescence to this proposal as the carrot for leading to the replacement of Thieu by a more acceptable candidate to the communists, General Minh. Still, Kissinger was rebuffed by Xuan Thuy. It is apparent from the U.S. declassified record that Kissinger was much more inclined toward this type of outcome than Nixon, who felt more allegiance to Thieu. Moreover, Nixon and Kissinger must have known that a Minh victory would lead to a coalition government, and the record reveals that Kissinger was more prepared to accept that outcome than was Nixon.

In his August 16, 1971, memo to Nixon, Kissinger reported that his meeting with Xuan Thuy "was essentially a holding action, with Le Duc Tho still in Hanoi. They have apparently not yet made their decision about accepting our political formula, a decision which must be very anguishing for them."

McGovern was also unaware that inside the White House, Richard Nixon was losing faith in Kissinger's diplomatic skills with the North Vietnamese. On September 8, 1971, Haldeman recorded that Nixon "raised the question with me of his concern on Henry's delusions of grandeur as a peacemaker, in that he keeps hitting the P on the idea of his going to Hanoi secretly to try and settle Vietnam. The P doesn't want him to do it, first, because he doesn't think it'll work, and second, because he doesn't think it can be kept a secret. He's concerned that it would be a disaster to do it and fail; the risk is too great. . . . He wants me to have Haig tout Henry off of this. He feels that Henry doesn't realize that the communist method of working is to keep talking and to screw you behind your back while you're doing it. To them, talking is a tactic to win, not to work out an agreement, whereas Henry keeps trying to work out an agreement with them."

* * *

Against this hidden background, McGovern landed in Saigon. He came at the problem of U.S. POWs from a naive angle. McGovern assumed that if the United States agreed to a definite withdrawal date for its troops by the end of 1971 and a termination of all bombing, then Hanoi would return American POWs, and U.S. involvement in the war would be over. In private, of course, Hanoi had rejected the U.S. proposal of a complete withdrawal of American and allied forces within nine months of a settlement, so McGovern stood little chance of making any headway. Nonetheless, he tried—and in one of the most controversial twists in the story of the peace negotiations, he tried to use his position as senator to hint at a quid pro quo deal with the enemy. It was a deal that would have produced an October surprise for candidate McGovern in the form of a long-withheld list of American POWs.

McGovern's first meeting was with Dinh Ba Thi, deputy to Madame Binh of the PRG delegation in Paris. Madame Binh was in Warsaw, unable to meet McGovern. The meeting was held in PRG headquarters in the town of

Verrierres outside Paris in a house that sat on a small bluff overlooking a pond. Juice, hors d'oeuvres, and Dubonnet wine were followed with a toast to Senator McGovern's good health.

McGovern began the meeting by committing a slip of the tongue, which elicited an interesting response.

"Is Madame Binh in Saigon?" asked McGovern.

"Madame Binh is in Warsaw—in Poland," answered Thi.

"Excuse me, I didn't mean Saigon. I meant Vietnam. She's not welcome in Saigon," said an embarrassed McGovern.

"We are confident that the day when you will meet with Madame Binh in Saigon will come," said Thi.

McGovern began by asking Thi if he would identify the most important of the PRG's seven-points proposal that had recently tabled at the plenary sessions in Paris.

Thi ticked them off: "Mr. Nixon has to declare a terminal date for the withdrawal of all U.S. troops from South Vietnam within this year. The second point is that Mr. Nixon has to cease his support to Nguyen Van Thieu to allow the social, political and religious forces in Saigon to set up a government and a new administration favoring peace, independence, neutrality and democracy."

McGovern then asked a logical question, only to encounter the sort of doublespeak that Kissinger had so long endured: "Excuse me a moment. Are those points separable?" What if the president agreed to withdraw all troops by the end of the year? Was it not possible that if that happened, there could be a cease-fire and prisoner release and that the political settlement of Saigon could be left to some future date? "Could we proceed if we could agree on Point 1 and bring the killing and the fighting to an end and the release of all prisoners on both sides and leave the question of the political future of Saigon to some other date?" asked the senator.

But the communists would never give up their aim of winning the South. Peace was less important to them. When McGovern elaborated on his question by adding, "Let us assume the General Thieu wins the election in October. What is then the obligation of the United States if he wins an overwhelming majority of the vote? What do you expect us to do?" Thi responded that Thieu could not remain in power.

The best Thi could offer was that the PRG was on record as saying that if the U.S. declared a terminal date for the total withdrawal of all troops from Vietnam by the end of 1971, then the PRG would immediately discuss the return of American prisoners as well as guarantee the safety of the with-drawing troops. "This is the solemn statement of the PRG."

With no prospect of a comprehensive deal, McGovern moved on to his more immediate agenda. He explained that he and Senator Hatfield had sponsored an amendment that would set a date for American withdrawal. Congress could legislate the terminal date but could not go any further. "All it can do is set a date."

Thi, of course, knew all about the McGovern-Hatfield amendment, just as Hanoi knew the status of support for the antiwar cause more generally. He responded that if the U.S. set a terminal date for withdrawal of all its troops, "that is a big step forward to the solution of the problem of South Vietnam."

McGovern kept pressing. If a date was set and Thieu was still in power, would the American POWs be released? The answer was always the same. If that happened, discussions could begin on the modalities of prisoner re-lease. But there were no guarantees. "We have been fighting against aggres-sion for the last dozens of years. We are resolute in fighting against those who come to our country with guns in hands to invade our country. But at the same time, we understand deeply the anxiety of the American mothers and wives who have their sons or their husbands pushed to South Vietnam by successive U.S. administrations. I think it is exactly the same as the un-derstanding to the sufferings and mourning of the South Vietnamese people by the American peace fighters. Among these peace fighters, I think, there is Senator McGovern," said Thi.

McGovern tried one last time to come to an understanding about the Thieu regime. Would not the total withdrawal of all troops by December 31 demonstrate to the PRG that the U.S. no longer supported the Thieu gov-ernment? What further step would be needed?

Thi was quick to respond: "I think the total withdrawal of U.S. forces is one form to carry out the cessation of support. The fact that the U.S. ad-ministration leaves in South Vietnam tens of thousands of military advisors, administrative advisors, and even foreign forces to direct activities of the Thieu regime constitute a form of support rendered to the Thieu regime."

"I think I understand what you're saying," McGovern said. "You're not saying that the United States must create a new government in Saigon. You are simply saying that we must cut off all forms of support to the Thieu regime. Is that correct? In ending support, does that mean that we end not only military support but economic support? Supposing General Thieu wins this election, whether honest or not, but let's say he wins the election and the United States agrees to terminate all military operations, bombing, everything else. And we withdraw all our forces, but the Thieu regime remains in power. . . . Are we forbidden from providing economic support, technical support to that government, and medical support? We have helped to build up an army of a million men. Suppose we continue to put money into that Thieu regime in the form of financial and technical assistance. Does that mean, then, that the arrangements under Point 1 could not be implemented?"

"I think once the American government withdraws all its support to the Thieu regime, then this administration cannot be in power for a long period of time," said Thi. "Because Nguyen Van Thieu represents nobody in South Vietnam. Thieu remains in power, thanks not to the support of the South Vietnamese people, but thanks to the support of the U.S. Government." Thi told McGovern that all he needed to do was visit Saigon and look at "the defensive systems around the presidential palace in Saigon."

Since it was obvious that no agreement on Thieu was possible, McGovern returned to the subject of the POWs. Why had the PRG chosen not to release even a list of American prisoners? "You're an independent government and presumably a responsible government acting within the international community, and would it not be proper procedure to at least advise our government of the number of the prisoners you are holding and what their condition is—whether they're sick, alive or dead?"

Thi then went beyond the boundaries of the credible by telling McGovern that he and other friends in America need not worry because all captured men were being treated in a humanitarian way. "And we can state solemnly about this fact. We have a very clear definition between a man with guns in hand and participating in the invasion of our country with a man who was captured by our people. May I cite an example? The daily diet given to every U.S. captured military man in South Vietnam is better than the diet of the average colonels of our government. And we have given them due medical treatment. I think the most unsafe problems to them now are created by the U.S. side. Take for example the bombings by B-52s."

Thi now took the offensive. McGovern and "other friends" in the United States needed to exert as much pressure as possible on Nixon to fix a date for withdrawal of all American troops and the cessation of the Thieu regime. "Then all the other problems, including the question of the captured military men, will be easily settled."

McGovern finally offered, or at least suggested, his quid pro quo: "What I'm saying is that if you could some time in the near future supply me with a list of these prisoners, it would greatly strengthen my political ability to accomplish the kind of things I want to do, which is to bring about an end to the war. It would strengthen me politically—no question about it—because it would fortify the argument that I've made that we can deal with your government, that it is a humanitarian government, and that arrangements can be worked out. It would be one more sign of the reasonableness of your government. I don't deny for one minute what you say—that the best way to get the prisoners released is to end the war. I would like to have ended the war years ago. But it would strengthen those of us in the peace movement in the United States if in the near future we could release a full list of prisoners that you are holding."

The meeting closed with McGovern pushing for a list of prisoners being held by the communists and Thi stonewalling. Thi returned to the idea that the fundamental problem was that the American troops were the real prisoners of Nixon's war policy. "We know for a long time that the Senator has been fighting unremittingly against the American government's policy in South Vietnam. Our people have special sentiments toward the Senator, as well as to other American friends who are fighting for an end to the war."

The meeting ended when Senator McGovern proposed a toast to "a peaceful settlement of the war here today."

* * *

McGovern was not quite finished. He had one more chance to make his case, this time higher up the ladder when he met the next day with Xuan Thuy. McGovern would later characterize Thuy as possessing an appreciation for the relationship between "personal moral conduct and one's own sense of belonging to a community of free men where individual dignity is respected." In fact, the minutes of the meeting reveal that Thuy's greatest appreciation was for the scenarios of American domestic politics.

McGovern began by thanking Xuan Thuy for providing information to Senators William Fulbright, Edward Kennedy, and himself about downed American pilots. "It has put you in a stronger position with the American people." McGovern then asked whether Xuan Thuy was encouraged about the negotiating sessions in Paris. He meant, of course, only the public plenary sessions. "Do you think any progress is being made, or likely to be made in the near future?"

Thuy's response was blunt and honest. "Actually, I am encouraged by the general situation, but not encouraged by the negotiation situation," Xuan Thuy said with a straight face. "The general situation drives Mr. Nixon in more and more difficulties and creates more favorable circumstances for the just struggle of the Vietnamese people."

Thuy then shifted the discussion to American politics by telling McGovern that he appreciated the senator's "effort to bring forth the draft resolution to the U.S. Congress demanding that U.S. forces be withdrawn from South Vietnam by the end of 1971." Thuy reiterated that the PRG's seven points conformed to the aspirations of McGovern and other forces of democracy within the United States, without, of course, mentioning that the Nixon administration had already offered these same terms in private.

After a brief lecture on the failings of Nixon's Vietnamization policy, which played to its audience by claiming that Nixon seemed to want to prolong the war, Thuy again linked the prolonged troop withdrawals to a "refusal" to stop supporting Thieu. He dangled Nixon's reelection in front of him. "And so when he is reelected next year, then he will step up the implementation of this policy—that is to say, turn Indochina into a neo-colony and to jeopardize or to make pressure to constitute a menace to the DRV. But in my view, the more he goes down this path, the more he will meet with failure and he will meet with difficulty. Now, at the Paris conference, he tried to buy time to make believe that he desires also only the negotiations, but actually he doesn't."

McGovern responded, "Well, I think it's a fact what you say about Mr. Nixon's objectives. Unfortunately, he has convinced a lot of people that he is ending the war." McGovern lamented the gradual withdrawal of troops under Vietnamization that lent the impression that Nixon was ending the war when in reality he was expanding it.

Thuy observed, "Like in any other country at the beginning, the people don't understand, but later and later they will understand. I remember that in 1965 there was no anti-war movement in the United States at all. Neither in 1966, 1967. Gradually, the people realize that the statements made by the administration is not true. . . . If the Vietnamese people do not agree to the way of settlement proposed by Mr. Nixon, the war will go on."

McGovern again played his card, explaining that the McGovern-Hatfield proposal would require that the United States cease all military operations in Indochina by the end of 1971 and that no further funds would be allowed for military purposes in South Vietnam, Cambodia, or Laos. Skipping over Thieu, McGovern proposed that an American troop withdrawal be linked with the return of American POWs. The political future of South Vietnam could be settled at some future date between the Vietnamese, not the Americans. Kissinger had proposed the same deal on even better terms, but Xuan Thuy's response to McGovern was, "So far as we understand Mr. Nixon, Mr. Nixon is unwilling to act in the way proposed by you. What does Mr. Nixon want? He wanted to withdraw U.S. forces, but up to certain limits. He will leave behind some residual forces—50,000, 100,000 military advisors, military personnel. And then he still wanted to maintain an administration obedient to the United States to implement Mr. Nixon's policy. . . . As a result of that policy, what shall we have? If now there is an administration implementing Mr. Nixon's policy, then Vietnam is not independent."

Xuan Thuy repeated that none of this would be sufficient—that it would lead inexorably from economic support to advisers to providing air support to bringing back the GIs again, all to keep Thieu propped up. For America this was "a vicious, vicious circle." Only a complete withdrawal of all ground forces, naval forces, air forces, military advisers, war material, and military bases could lead to an end of the war and a return of prisoners.

McGovern now raised the question he had raised a day earlier with the PRG: "Well, supposing that the United States were to agree to the full withdrawal of all our military forces and an end to the bombing from whatever source, a cessation of all military activity, withdrawal of advisors, logistical forces? What if the Thieu regime continues this struggle under their own resources with perhaps some financial help from the United States, but no military?" Would the Vietnamese continue to release American prisoners if the Thieu regime continued to exist on its own even after the American forces were out?

Xuan Thuy rejected McGovern's premise as "not realistic" because "Mr. Nixon will not do that because he still wanted to maintain an administration obedient to the United States to implement his policy." Thieu was merely "a creation of the United States through fraudulent elections. Now, since the United States has established this administration, it has to change it. And then, the United States should let the South Vietnamese people settle themselves."

Thuy pointed to the forthcoming October 1971 elections in South Vietnam as ample evidence that the United States had been interfering in the electoral process in order to guarantee Thieu's election. How could Nixon affirm publicly that the U.S. was withdrawing forces and not interfering with the political situation in South Vietnam? "It is untrue," said Thuy. "Now, imagine that Nguyen Van Thieu has roughly one million troops, a huge police force, a great number of pacification teams. All these forces have been equipped by the United States and your American military advisors are present from the highest level to the lowest level of these forces. . . . And political advisors are present too, at all these levels. Moreover, the United States has a very advanced network of CIA agents in South Vietnam. And, in the meantime, sir, how can you say that the United States is not involved in this election?" In fact, Thieu was running unopposed in the election, and his own forces were more responsible for this than were the Americans.

Three candidates had originally declared for the October election: Nguyen Van Thieu, seeking a second term, Vice President Nguyen Cao Ky, and Big Minh, running as a peace candidate. On June 3, 1971, the National Assembly, at Thieu's urging, passed a bill establishing candidate eligibility laws. Each candidate would need at least 40 deputies and senators of the National Assembly or 100 members of the elected provincial councils to sign nominating papers. The overwhelming majority of Assembly members supported Thieu, so this new law gave the incumbent an extraordinary advantage. Only Big Minh secured enough signatures, getting 44 from the National Assembly. Vice President Ky was able to get 102 provincial council members, but many of those had already signed for Thieu. The issue of signature validity went to the Vietnamese Supreme Court, which ruled that Ky had not complied with the new election law, and he was disqualified. Thieu was embarrassed enough to ask the court to reconsider its decision on Ky's candidacy, and on August 21 it reversed itself by invalidating all of the signatures that Thieu secured from provincial council members. But Ky refused to accept the decision and refused even to vote in the election. "I cannot lend a hand to a dirty farce which would only make the people more desperate and disillusioned with the democratic system." Ambassador Bunker privately visited Ky and offered to finance a Ky campaign, because "a one man show will not be a good example for the rest of the world." Ky declined the offer. That left two candidates.

When Minh announced his candidacy in June, he promised that if elected, he would end the war through an immediate political settlement. He was acceptable to the PRG as a coalition candidate, and new evidence shows that at first the PRG provided him with encouragement and assistance in his candidacy but then changed strategy. On July 1, 1971, the NLF released its new peace program, which party strategists believed could influence events in the United States by linking Thieu's removal with the release of American prisoners of war and the withdrawal of troops. Robert Brigham's research shows that the NLF fully understood the implications of the McGovern-Hatfield amendment and the growing dissent in Congress that focused on placing a specific deadline for U.S. withdrawal.

Then, as Nixon's domestic crisis worsened, "the NLF persuaded Big Minh not to run in the rigged election." Brigham shows that PRG and NLF strategists believed that Nixon preferred Thieu over an open election and understood that a one-man election would create serious credibility issues in the United States. They could not have been more correct.

In Paris, George McGovern was more concerned about his own election. He tried to steer Thuy back to his amendment: If Nixon was forced by political pressure in the United States to withdraw all American forces and end the American involvement, would Hanoi turn over the POWs while Thieu remained in office? "Would you release the prisoners, even though General Thieu remains in power without our help?"

Xuan Thuy would not admit any legitimacy for Thieu. "I don't think what you have said is possible. Because if we think that this—your assumption—is possible, then we are fooled by Mr. Nixon. Since you are a Democrat, progressive American, anti-war American, we express our sympathy to you and the Vietnamese people who have been following your activities and the Vietnamese people show sympathy, deep sympathy for you."

Earlier, in a meeting with Kissinger, Le Duc Tho had made the ultimate proposal for "resolving" the Thieu question. Kissinger, he said, should simply arrange for his removal through a coup, or even assassination. Kissinger had rejected the idea out of hand, but hope is often eternal. To McGovern, Thuy now said, "I think that if Mr. Nixon changes Nguyen Van Thieu and recognizes the independence of Vietnam, the war can be ended. But if Mr. Nixon still persists in maintaining Thieu in power and still wants to retain residual forces in South Vietnam to support Nguyen Van Thieu, then the war will go on."

McGovern clearly had to shift the subject, so he returned to his October surprise idea. He noted that 42 of 100 senators had already signed the McGovern-Hatfield amendment that would accomplish what negotiations had failed to yield: an end of the war by December 31, 1971. McGovern explained that the amendment provided de facto acquiescence to Hanoi's demand that the United States set a firm date for withdrawal because it denied money for the war effort. But 42 Senate votes was not nearly enough, and one way to get the necessary votes for passage would be if Hanoi could promise that the POWs would be returned. He did not even ask for a list of names, merely a "promise" that the list would be released. Nixon would be forced to accept the will of Congress and the American people and remove all American troops from Vietnam, he said. McGovern-Hatfield could become American policy if there was a feeling that the prisoners of war would definitely be returned.

Thuy, as Kissinger knew, did not care about the POWs except as how they could be manipulated as a part of winning the war. "You have good will, but I doubt that what you say is possible," he remarked. "The Vietnamese people don't want to make a war with any other people. We have experienced two wars already. First, against the French then against the U.S. administration. And we can say that since World War II, generally speaking, the Vietnamese people have not known any period of peace. Therefore, we want an early restoration of peace. But not peace at any price." Thuy reiterated that Nixon wanted South Vietnam as a neo-colony, and Nixon feared both neutralization and reunification.

McGovern wanted the war to end; he also wanted to be the next president of the United States and thought that he would be strengthened politically if he could get an assurance on the prisoners. He could not promise passage of the McGovern-Hatfield amendment, but it seemed reasonable that momentum for it would increase if he could hold out the promise of a POW release, let alone that he would have demonstrated that the North Vietnamese were reasonable negotiators. As he had put it to Thi, a gesture on the POWs "would enable me and other people in the United States who are trying to end the war—it would give us another instrument with which to apply pressure. . . . If you at some time in the near future supply me with a list of these prisoners, it would greatly strengthen my political ability to accomplish the kinds of things I want to do, which is to bring about an end of the war. . . . It would strengthen me politically, no question about it, because it would fortify the argument—it would strengthen those of us in the peace movement in the United States."

But Thuy did not need McGovern in office in order to win the war, and McGovern apparently could not get rid of Thieu. There would be no October surprise. The two men adjourned to the adjoining dining room for lunch, described in McGovern's meeting notes as "a sumptuous feast" that began with won-ton soup, then a clear noodle dish with lobster and seafood, a delicious French quail stuffed with rice and tomatoes, and finally a white cake with a flowering tree icing, white wine, champagne, coffee, and tea.

"Now it is my turn to ask you some questions," Xuan Thuy said. What did McGovern think of the announcement that Nixon was going to Peking?

"I was surprised," said McGovern. "Mr. Nixon over the years has been so anti-Peking that I was surprised. I really don't have any opinion as to what he hopes to accomplish."

"How do you assess the situation in the United States and how do you think about Mr. Nixon's positions, ideas?" Xuan Thuy asked.

"I think much of what Mr. Nixon does is to create political effect in the United States," McGovern said. "He is a very difficult man to predict. He doesn't seem to operate from a consistent set of principles or philosophy. One of the reasons it's so hard to predict what he's going to do or analyze the meaning of any particular move he makes is that very frequently he is improvising from week to week to meet what he believes to be the current political pressures in the United States."

Xuan Thuy was also interested in getting McGovern's opinion of the new U.S. negotiator to the plenary sessions in Paris, William Porter, who was re-placing David Bruce. McGovern did not know him very well but thought that he would be personally amiable and honest, "although, of course, he would be following instructions from Nixon."

Xuan Thuy then offered to help Senator McGovern's electoral chances in any way possible, including not doing anything during negotiations that might help Nixon.

McGovern departed Paris for Saigon, but his six hours of discussion with representatives from Hanoi and the PRG led him to conclude that if Presi-dent Nixon would set the date of December 31, 1971, as the terminal date for total withdrawal of all U.S. military forces and operations in Vietnam, then simultaneously there would be a release of U.S. prisoners. No such promise had been made, but in a press conference on September 12, Mc-Govern said, "President Nixon holds the key to the jail cells in Hanoi."

Meeting with President Thieu at the Presidential Palace on September 15, McGovern started off bluntly by identifying himself as a critic of American involvement and noting that the upcoming presidential election had the ap-pearance of being a sham. "I'm wondering if you don't agree that it is dam-aging, both to your interests and your support in the United States to proceed with an election like that?" Thieu had not wanted to meet with Mc-Govern, but Ambassador Bunker insisted on Thieu's participation.

McGovern's handwritten notes said that "it took him about 10 minutes to say that it isn't his fault that nobody is running against him, the implication being that he would like to have some competition." Nha recalled that Thieu tried to explain the Vietnamese constitution to McGovern, but the senator had no interest in listening to why Thieu could not postpone the election. The forty-minute meeting covered a range of topics. McGovern had already spoken with Big Minh. He now reiterated that Thieu needed to understand that a one-man election was putting South Vietnam in a bad light with those who supported Thieu in America. McGovern told Thieu that since he was against American involvement, "you're not going to win my support," but there were other actions that could lead Thieu to "redeem or recover support" from others if only he would demonstrate compassion and release from jail his political opponents. "You don't really think they're a threat to society, do you?" McGovern asked Thieu. There was no real reply.

Did McGovern's intervention have any effect on the North Vietnamese? At first glance, the answer is probably no. But Hanoi seemed resolved to do nothing until after the October election, so it is hard to tell. Certainly relations with Kissinger turned feisty. At a meeting on September 13, Thuy challenged his authority: "If you speak on behalf of the White House I am willing to listen to you, if you speak on your own, I shall listen to you only partly," said Xuan Thuy. "Because I only listen to what you say on the instructions of the White House, and what I say is also for the White House to hear."

"Are you prepared to listen?" asked Kissinger.

"I am, if it is on behalf of the White House," said Xuan Thuy.

They broke off the talks for the time being. Xuan Thuy shouted at Kissinger, "You are speaking as if Vietnam were United States land, as if South Vietnam as well as North Vietnam both belonged to the USA. No! Vietnam belongs to the Vietnamese!"

Haldeman recorded on September 14, 1971, that "the North Vietnamese have called off the negotiations. . . . K wants to go to Moscow, his logic is that if we're going to pull out anyway, we might as well as try to get all the mileage out of it as we can."

Perhaps the biggest impact of McGovern's trip was on Nixon, who knew of the meeting but not the substance. McGovern and other congressional doves were driving Nixon crazy, and he knew that the sham October election would make things worse. On September 16, Bunker cabled Kissinger, "I feared that the political situation here, with Thieu as the only candidate and the outcome of the referendum a foregone conclusion, would lead the other side to dig in their heels. I think they must calculate that Thieu has weakened his position both domestically and abroad, hope that this may become increasingly evident with time, and so are inclined to wait. If, after October 3, Thieu comes to grips with and is able to overcome some of the political problems his miscalculations have created, the other side may change their views. Thieu will need to do this in any event if he is to govern successfully, despite the ability he has demonstrated in other areas and the very real progress evident in so many fields."

As Thieu's legitimacy waned and the antiwar movement gained steam, the lack of progress in negotiations frustrated Nixon. Time was not on his side, and he knew it. On September 17 Haldeman wrote, "Henry was in. . . . The P told him he thought it was important to give them [the North Vietnamese] a hard shot now to create in them the fear that the P may do more. So he ordered Henry to get a bombing attack going over the weekend. Said to handle it on a low key basis from a PR standpoint, . . . N wants to make the point that "the way we got into Vietnam was the overthrow of Diem, and the way to get out is not by throwing out Thieu." In a tape of a conversation between Nixon and Kissinger on September 17, the president said that "the way to get out of Vietnam is not be murdering Thieu."

On September 18, 1971, Kissinger wrote the president that recent events now forced the president to take a dispassionate look at where the U.S. stood in Vietnam and to evaluate the policy options for what Kissinger described as heading "into the terminal phase of our involvement." On the one hand, "At home, the need to close the conflict with dignity is perhaps even more compelling. . . . It is essential that we leave Vietnam as an act of governmental policy and with dignity, not as a response to pressures and in the form of a collapse." On the other hand, referring to McGovern's efforts, Kissinger warned the president that the political momentum for a rapid disengagement was building, and "we now face the real danger of congressional legislation setting a date for our withdrawals and perhaps limiting our assistance to South Vietnam. The clamor will rise for a straight deal of fixed withdrawals for release of prisoners." With a November announcement pending, Kissinger warned, "Should a total withdrawal be announced we will then be in a passive posture while Hanoi and our domestic political opposition slowly slice the salami."

On September 21, the United States carried out reprisal air strikes against air defense targets in lower North Vietnam. The Paris talks were deadlocked. The *New York Times* speculated that the administration had written off the talks and was turning to military power. Hanoi appeared to have concluded that Thieu would be weaker after the October election and that the United States would be forced to replace him and leave.

In a recently released White House tape, Nixon told Kissinger on September 20 that Thieu was the only person around whom a peace agreement could be built: "When you come down to it, what's the alternative to Thieu? There's no other leader. The only alternative is a Communist government, and that would mean slaughtering the poor sons of bitches. I'm really convinced that if we were to lose, our foreign policy would be in shambles. And domestically, it would kill us. If Saigon were to fall and murders were to occur, then, once it happened, they would say, 'You lost 50,000 Americans for what? And then lost the war!'"

On September 23, 1971, Alexander Haig was sent to Saigon for a meeting with Thieu at the Presidential Palace. Haig carried "President Nixon's personal outlook on the situation in Vietnam for the coming months." A newly declassified document sheds light on what transpired at this meeting, and it reflects the growing crunch of domestic American opinion. Haig first reassured Thieu that political stability, unity, and strength were paramount. "President Nixon believed that in times of increased tension it is all the more important that all parties not lose sight of the fundamental objective of the years of sacrifice which had characterized the contributions of both of our peoples during the conflict with the communists. Misjudgments at this juncture would be all the more tragic since success was so near at hand."

Nixon wanted Thieu to know that the only impasse remaining was his removal, which the U.S. would not do. The secret talks had been suspended, and "we have carefully reviewed the entire interplay of recent political trends both in Saigon and in the U.S. This review has confirmed that our most urgent task will be the need to maintain the necessary U.S. domestic support, which has been badly shaken by the evolution of events associated with the October 3 elections. A further complication will be the approaching U.S. political contest which cannot but increase domestic political overtones and further complicate the issue."

With all this and with the increasing possibility that Congress could severely cut back on legislative appropriations, Nixon had decided to submit a new negotiating proposal that Nixon "did not think Hanoi would accept, but public knowledge of it would silence domestic critics in the United States and Vietnam." The proposal would demonstrate to all that Thieu had gone the last mile in the interest of peace. Under Nixon's plan, Thieu would resign, and an electoral commission would oversee a new election. "For the U.S., we would have compiled a negotiating record with the other side which would be beyond reproach. If the proposal is rejected and subsequently made public by our side, both Congressional and other domestic critics would be largely defanged at the very time in our legislative process when their efforts would concert against us. For President Thieu the benefits are equally obvious—he will have placed peace above his personal position. It would discredit those critics who claim him to be the remaining obstacle to peace. Finally, the proposal, at least symbolically, meets Hanoi's demand that elections not be conducted by the GVN."

Nixon's plan was complicated. It assumed Hanoi would reject Thieu's resignation and a deal. Once rejected, the entire record of negotiations would be made public and this would lead to a continuation of congressional funding. Nixon offered Thieu a carrot; if he accepted the proposal, then Nixon would defer a dramatic troop withdrawal announcement until November. It was a classic Nixon maneuver—a complex game with layers of meaning—and it would soon haunt its creator.

By October 2, Kissinger and Haig were so fearful of a coup against Thieu that Kissinger cabled Bunker, "We are relying heavily on your leadership in insuring that there is no maneuvering which might have the effect of encouraging attempts to replace Thieu; keeping the most rigid discipline within the US country team on this subject because of the overriding importance of political stability between now and the turn of the year. The President wishes you to know that he is prepared to support you fully in relieving immediately any member of the country team who you might consider not to be fully supportive of this policy."

Kissinger buttressed the American ambassador, who was under unrelenting press criticism in Saigon, telling him that the president had the "fullest support" in Bunker and that "you must disregard all attacks in the press. The White House knows what the country owes you." Bunker cabled back, "I see no prospect of a coup, but more danger in possible attempt at assassination."

The October election was a referendum on Thieu, and not a real election contest. On October 3, 1971, 87 percent of the eligible 7 million voters went to the polls, and Thieu received 94 percent of the vote. "Ho Chi Minh couldn't have done better," observed Ky. "It was a ridiculous election, like a communist one." The historian for the JCS *History* wrote, "How could United States officials claim democracy and constitutional government were working in South Vietnam when there was only one candidate in the presidential race?" And McGovern characterized the election as "like a plebiscite in Nazi Germany and communist countries."

Right after the election, Haig met for over two hours with Thieu, reassuring him of continued U.S. support and gaining approval for a new negotiating initiative that would include his agreement not to be a candidate in the new presidential election that would follow a negotiated settlement under the plan that Kissinger proposed tabling with Le Duc Tho. But this meeting did not occur because Tho was "ill," and Kissinger refused to meet with only Xuan Thuy. What Thieu would not know is that the proposal was forwarded to Hanoi *without* Thieu's knowledge.

* * *

There was one final ironic twist to the McGovern story. In a letter to Xuan Thuy on October 4, the day after the South Vietnamese election, McGovern thanked Xuan Thuy for his hospitality: "The fine dinner and discussion were among the most useful and pleasurable portions of our journey." But his real reason for writing was more urgent. A dispute had erupted between the Nixon administration and McGovern with respect to the senator's account of what Xuan Thuy had said regarding the release of POWs. The White House had already requested transcripts of the meeting and was seeking to discredit McGovern's mission. McGovern needed the answer to just one question: Would a total U.S. withdrawal of military assistance to Thieu result in the release of POWs?

All Americans agreed on a single goal with equal intensity: the return of the American prisoners. "This fact has very important implications with respect to both the Congress and the White House. If the American people and members of Congress were truly convinced that this step would result in release of the prisoners, then I think there is a strong likelihood that the Congress would require withdrawal by adopting a proposal such as the one Senator Hatfield and I sponsored, and by refusing to make funds available for any purpose other than withdrawal by a certain date. We have already come within a few votes of adopting such legislation in the Senate, and I believe there is also a potential majority in the House of Representatives. On the other hand if neither the President nor the Congress responded to the people's wishes, I am convinced that the nominating processes and the elections next Fall would bring to the White House someone who is firmly committed to ending U.S. involvement in the war."

McGovern requested a partial prisoner release, particularly in the light of the fact that the Nixon administration had refused to set a firm withdrawal date. The biggest problem was that the Nixon administration had been able to discredit McGovern because he was reporting on the basis of private discussions that were inconsistent with what Hanoi and the PRG had stated were their conditions at the public plenary sessions. "It would, of course, remove a major obstacle to the peace forces in the United States if the issue could be made more explicit at that [plenary] forum."

McGovern needed a clear statement on American prisoners so that there would be increased confidence in the American people for the McGovern-Hatfield amendment. Indeed, whenever Hanoi released prisoners or provided a list of names of those held in North Vietnam, it "unquestionably strengthened the efforts of those of us in this country who are working for a complete U.S. withdrawal." A public statement at this time could have "a decisive impact in generating support for the withdrawal deadline and in getting such a deadline adopted."

McGovern concluded by noting, "It is, of course, impossible for me as an individual Senator to guarantee that any specific action by the United States would follow such a step. Based on our conversations in Paris, however, I thought you might be interested in my judgment on how a release of this kind would be greeted in the United States, and the effect it would have on my own efforts and those of many other people in this country to achieve an early American disengagement from Vietnam."

It was all for naught. The Nixon administration knew that Hanoi would not budge on POWs and would not even promise a cease-fire unless it was clear that they would win the South. To McGovern it looked as if the Nixon administration placed the survival of the Thieu regime ahead of a prisoner release. But the ultimate truth was not even that Nixon was playing McGovern for a patsy. Hanoi was playing both for fools. Vernon Walters was later asked why the North had never furnished a complete POW list. He responded, "Le Duc Tho looked at Kissinger [during the Paris talks] and said, 'I don't know why I'm negotiating with you. I have just spent six hours with Senator McGovern. Your anti-war movement will force you to give me what I want.'"

On October 25 McGovern received a letter from Dinh Ba Thi that praised the senator for condemning Vietnamization as well as the "October 3 election farce aimed at maintaining the dictatorial and warlike Nguyen Van Thieu in power." Thi urged McGovern and "all Americans of goodwill and the progressive American people" to do everything possible in pushing the Nixon administration to accept the seven-point peace plan of the PRG that "would rapidly end the war and result in the rapid return of all American servicemen, including those in captivity." Such was Thi's advice to the potential nominee.

Instead of an October surprise, Hanoi had engineered a waiting game. In retrospect, if Hanoi was serious about negotiations, all it had to do was say yes to McGovern's request for a POW list. Hanoi must have concluded that the balance of forces was still not in its favor—even with a complete American troop withdrawal under McGovern-Hatfield. Instead, the North would continue to plan for a large offensive and seek conditions more favorable to its long-term objectives.

CHAPTER FIVE

A Chess Match

**In a chess match, the winner and the loser must
be the players themselves, there is no other way.
We are independent in solving our problem.**

Le Duc Tho to Henry Kissinger,
July 26, 1971, private meeting.

Richard Nixon deserves a lot of credit for opening relations with China,
which culminated in his famous trip there in February 1972. As a matter of
cold war politics vis-à-vis the Soviet Union, certainly it was a major achievement. Sino-Soviet tensions grew enormously, leading Soviet military attention away from the West and toward the border stretching more than 1,000
miles with China. In much of the Third World, the once serious threat of an
international communist front devolved into a three-way struggle between
Soviet-and Western-backed regimes with a "non-aligned" movement often
supported by China.

But what effect did the China card have on Vietnam? Kissinger has argued that the opening of relations to China, which began in July 1971 when
he secretly flew to Beijing, put pressure on Hanoi. As Kissinger would put it
to Stanley Karnow, "I think the Chinese role towards the settlement was
again to contribute to the sense of isolation of Hanoi. The fact that Nixon
was received in Peking, that, obviously the Chinese were paying attention to
improving their relationship with the United States, and that they would set

a limit to the risks they were going to run." In other words, the China card hastened an agreement by adding pressure on the North. To Nixon and Kissinger, the China card and their Vietnamization policy fit together, forging an agreement by which the U.S. could withdraw and the South could remain standing. This was just how Nixon remembered Geneva in 1954.

The record supports this view in one sense. Hanoi *was* troubled by the opening of U.S.-Sino relations; to Hanoi's diehard communists, it was a betrayal of the cause. But the back-channel discussions between Beijing and Hanoi, coupled with the military evidence of the likely outcome of Vietnamization, had exactly the opposite effect from Nixon's intentions. Finally, now, the full story can be told.

The opening to China began in earnest when Henry Kissinger traveled secretly to Beijing for a clandestine meeting with Chou Enlai. After months of preparations, false starts, and great secrecy, it was arranged that Kissinger would visit Pakistan, where President Yahya directed a script that called for Kissinger to develop a stomachache at dinner. Yahya had Kissinger taken to the president's private estate in order to recover—but, of course, Kissinger was on his way to Peking with Yahya's trusted personal pilot. Meanwhile, the chubbiest member of Kissinger's security detail was selected to play Kissinger back at the private estate. Haldeman wrote in his diary for July 8 that "the P obviously is really cranked up about this whole Chinese thing. . . . P even lied to Billy Graham."

At the meetings of July 9–11, Kissinger tried to link China's interest in resolving the status of Taiwan to Washington's interest in resolving the Vietnam War. Kissinger told Chou that the U.S. sought an honorable peace in Vietnam and that following its withdrawal from Vietnam, the U.S. would withdraw two-thirds of its troops from Taiwan. Chou Enlai asked why the U.S. was so concerned with its honor and prestige in Vietnam when the greatest honor and glory could be achieved by withdrawal from Vietnam and all Indochina.

Kissinger brought along one of his top NSC aides, Dick Smyser, who recalled that "nothing was resolved [on Vietnam]. Chou Enlai said what we thought he would say, that the Vietnamese were fighting the war and it was up to them."

Chou went immediately to see Mao after his meeting with Kissinger. "The United States should make a new start and . . . let the domino fall, the United States must withdraw from Vietnam," said Mao. "We are in no hurry on the Taiwan issue because there is no fighting on Taiwan. But there is a war in Vietnam and people are dying there."

In his memoirs, Kissinger wrote, "Chou professed to be unaware" of his secret talks with Le Duc Tho. Throughout the delicate dance with America, however, Hanoi officials kept China fully informed and were reassured of its support. After Kissinger's trip, Chou Enlai immediately flew to Hanoi, where he briefed both Le Duc Tho and Pham Van Dong on his meeting with Kissinger. Chou emphasized that he had told Kissinger that American withdrawal from Vietnam was more important to the Chinese than was a seat at the United Nations or resolution of Taiwan's status.

Still, in fairness to Kissinger's version of events, as historian Qiang Zhai shows, "Despite Beijing's reassurances, the North Vietnamese had drawn the inescapable conclusion that China valued its relationship with the United States more than its revolutionary unity with the DRV. They believed that Beijing's opening to the United States undermined their interests and objectives. Specifically, they felt that the July 15 announcement of Kissinger's secret trip to China and Nixon's planned visit to Beijing significantly undercut their new peace offensive." By "new peace offensive" Zhai meant the PRG's seven-point proposal of July 1. Its promise to release prisoners in exchange for unconditional U.S. withdrawal by December 31, 1971 was intended to create ripples in U.S. domestic public opinion and Nixon's own approval ratings. Yet on July 15, China had publicly announced its willingness to receive a visit from President Nixon. China's announcement had a dramatic effect: Nixon's approval rating began to climb. Xuan Thuy thus called Nixon's opening to Beijing a "perfidious maneuver" and a "false peace offensive" designed to split the socialist world.

Back in March, Chou Enlai had extolled Hanoi's position and talents to Le Duan and Pham Van Dong. "Comrade Mao Zedong has said to comrades Le Duan and Pham Van Dong that the Vietnamese comrades knew how to fight and how to negotiate. I also told comrades Xuan Thuy and Nguyen Thi Binh that the negotiations went quite well. I gained some experience in negotiations before, but now I have to learn from you." He continued, "It is we who have to thank you and learn from you as far as the anti-American war is concerned. Not to support the revolution of the Vietnamese people is like betraying the revolution. At the same time, we are also prepared to render our sacrifices in case the enemy expands the war." Had everything now changed?

On July 12, 1971, Kissinger had a three-hour meeting with Le Duc Tho, later described by Kissinger as "more encouraging than ever seen before." Bunker cabled Kissinger, "Congratulations on rapid recovery from illness [a subtle reference to the stomachache], the operation was flawlessly performed and the cure a complete success. This will be recorded as a major achievement of the President's foreign policy. Your contribution has been magnificent."

Kissinger wrote in his memoirs that as he sat across from Le Duc Tho, everything was now different because of the Peking trip, "yet Le Duc Tho did not yet know this." This meeting accomplished little other than to reiterate that the North was obsessed with changing the Thieu regime. Still, Xuan Thuy asked whether the government of Nguyen Van Thieu would be replaced before the October election. "This administration should be changed," said Xuan Thuy. "You have supplied it with military machinery, a police force and an administrative apparatus for the repression of the people and its opponents. So practically you are maintaining the Thieu government. I should say that without changing it, there can be no peaceful solution to the Vietnam problem. . . . You say that you cannot do that; we think that you can but you are unwilling. The negotiation cannot bring about results and public opinion would think that the U.S. is reluctant to withdraw from South Vietnam. Your refusal to settle this question shows your lack of goodwill."

Le Duc Tho added, "Probably this is the greatest obstacle because the Thieu administration is very dictatorial and warlike. . . . As long as Thieu remains, there can be no peace. . . . It can be said that the change or the keeping of Thieu is the measure of your intention to restore peace or to continue the Vietnamization of the war. If you change Thieu, we are willing to settle the war quickly, not only in Vietnam but also in the whole of Indochina. We conducted negotiations in 1954 and 1962; you have seen how we had sensibly and reasonably settled the problem. Therefore, if you change Thieu, we shall make large and rapid steps satisfactory to all parties. What I tell you today is said with the greatest seriousness."

"You continually say that we should replace Thieu. What concretely do you want us to do?" asked Kissinger.

"You can replace him in many ways. For instance, you have brought him to power, now on the occasion of election you can swap him. The election is an opportunity. The press and public opinion and opposition forces in Saigon know that with your support Thieu will win the election; without your support, Thieu will lose," said Tho.

"There is a softer way," remarked Le Duc Tho. After the meeting, he suggested to Kissinger that "if you want to bring him down, ways are not lacking."

It was the day after this encounter that Chou Enlai visited Hanoi for a meeting with Le Duan in order to apprise the North Vietnamese of Kissinger's visit and Nixon's grand design. The negotiation stalemate was clear. The key question is, did China care about Northern victory over the South? Or was it more interested in its own maneuvering, come what may in Vietnam? Clearly China did not need to abandon its ally. First, Chou downplayed the Kissinger visit. "In the war of aggression against Vietnam, the U.S. goes from one surprise to another. Until the withdrawal of troops is completed, Nixon will be unable to expect what surprise is next. So the visit of Kissinger is designed to forestall these surprises," observed Le Duan. Then Chou informed Le Duan that when Kissinger was in Peking, the Chinese told him of their support for the seven points of the PRG and that the United States could not demand the withdrawal of North forces from South Vietnam. Le Duan responded that the secret meeting between Chou and Kissinger had produced "new complexities," which required that the North Vietnamese *not* move toward a quick settlement.

President Nixon announced on July 15 that he would visit Peking the following year. Haldeman wrote in his diary, "The general feeling of the group was that the North Vietnamese, when they find out about this, will undoubtedly be pushed even more strongly toward working out some negotiation with us, so that enhances the hope that something will develop there." Haldeman could not have been more incorrect. On July 17, 1971, Nguyen Duy Trinh sent a message to Le Duc Tho and Xuan Thuy saying, "For us the immediate period is not an opportune moment for settlement. The balance of forces was not yet right and settling too early would be as harmful as settling too late."

Kissinger did not know what messages China was giving to the North. He told Stanley Karnow, "We kept the Chinese generally informed on our negotiations with the North Vietnamese, but because we saw them less frequently during that period, we gave them somewhat fewer details, and they never told us what they did in Hanoi." In short, both China and North Vietnam knew that time was on Hanoi's side. The opening of Sino-U.S. relations did nothing to change that.

* * *

Nixon's Vietnamization policy, meanwhile, was only reinforcing Hanoi's self-confidence. Vietnamization came to mean very different things for the

Americans and the South Vietnamese. To the former, it was a simple code word for American withdrawal. The South feared it was an abandonment. Both wanted a test, a pilot program, to see how well the Vietnamese could do once the troops were gone. Lam Son 719, a ground incursion into Laos, code-named for a famous North Vietnam battlefield where the Vietnamese had defeated the invading Chinese army in 1427, was the pilot program.

On February 8, 1971, 16,000 South Vietnamese troops crossed into the Laotian panhandle to interdict the Ho Chi Minh Trail and attack North Vietnamese troops. American aerial and artillery support pounded the major supply route throughout February. The North Vietnamese used the first two plenary meetings on February 11 and 18 to protest the raid and then boycotted the Paris talks for two months. Lam Son 719 became a military test with no diplomatic distractions.

During a speech on February 17 reminiscent of the one he gave on Cambodia a year earlier, the president declared, "Tonight I can report that Vietnamization has succeeded." He went on to forecast that "the American involvement in Vietnam is coming to an end. The day the South Vietnamese can take over their defense is in sight."

But the truth actually was much different. Facing stronger resistance than expected, the Army of the Republic of Vietnam (ARVN) came under heavy fire, and the North Vietnamese, determined to protect its crucial Southern supply lines, sent 36,000 regular troops into battle. The North Vietnamese lost over 20,000 troops, but ARVN lost over half of its force. Furthermore, the U.S. lost 168 helicopters, with another 618 damaged. Fifty-five air crewmen were killed in action, 178 were wounded, and 34 were missing in action. The high number of aerial losses stemmed from the effective North Vietnamese use of antiaircraft artillery cannons. Bad weather and fierce North Vietnamese counterattacks combined to force the ARVN to withdraw in 60 days. "Lam Son destroyed the cream of the South Vietnam army and was far more serious and detrimental than was believed at the time. Our handling of that was very bad," observed Alexander Haig, who had been sent to Vietnam by Nixon in the middle of the operation.

Apart from his public portrayal of Lam Son as a success, Nixon needed to downplay it diplomatically. In his memoirs Nixon wrote, "I did my best to make sure that the Lam Son operation at the beginning of 1971 did not cut off this budding relationship as the Cambodian operation had threatened to do the year before. . . . I stressed that our intervention in Laos should not be interpreted as any threat to China."

The evidence of late July shows that Hanoi was now more confident that it would eventually prevail in the South. The July 26 meeting turned immediately to whether the United States was ready to set a definite date for withdrawal. Failure to set the date would prolong the negotiations. Xuan Thuy began by saying that some progress had been made between their nine points and the seven points of the United States, "but there remain two key points that you have said nothing about: the time limit for troop withdrawal linked with the release of prisoners of war and the administration in South Vietnam. We have clearly said that you should replace the Nguyen Van Thieu group. Your point 7 makes no mention of this question and you have not said anything about it, you said that we should agree on a framework, but this key point is the spinal column of the framework. If you do not refer to it, how can the framework take shape?"

Kissinger said, "Mr. Special Adviser is again engaging in creative writing."

"A framework without a backbone will collapse," said Tho, and then accused the United States of thinking that the Chinese would help them in Vietnam: "There is no miraculous way to settle the Vietnam problem other than seriously negotiating with us at the Paris conference on the basis of our proposals and yours. *In a chess match, the winner and the loser must be the players themselves, there is no other way.* We are independent in solving our problem."

Kissinger then responded with his critique of North Vietnam's strategy: "If I understand you correctly, your strategy is aimed at securing two results: that our forces be withdrawn as soon as possible and after the completion of withdrawal, you will overthrow the existing political structure in South Vietnam. Your demand is not a concession but a requirement that we offer to Hanoi the opportunity to reach your objectives. If you can secure them by yourselves, we shall respect the results, but probably you will not succeed in obtaining them at these negotiations. Of course, neither of us will sign an agreement to offer to the other side all the objectives it has set." Regarding the time limit for troop withdrawal, Kissinger said, "We are prepared to fix a date for the completion of the withdrawal of our forces and those of our allies within nine months of the signing of the agreement."

Kissinger concluded in frustration: "If you keep pursuing the tactics of stating your demands and then judging our replies, as if we were students taking an examination, I can tell you now that there will be no agreement. This proposition that we give you a deadline no matter what happens may impress the Special Advisor's friends at the *New York Times,* but . . . to retreat on a fixed deadline, we don't need agreement with you; we can do that on our own. And we will not settle the war just for prisoners. This is another point you should have no illusions about."

When the meeting came to an end, Kissinger would lay the foundation for an American deception of the North Vietnamese by insisting that "In 1954, Dulles wanted to have military bases, now you are negotiating with an administration that is not interested in military bases in South Vietnam. . . . For the United States, Vietnam is no longer a key problem. We know that you still have a great deal of suspicion. That is the tragedy!" Kissinger told Le Duc Tho that "it will be difficult to persuade Mr. Nixon to let me come here once again but I hope I will succeed."

When he returned from Paris, Kissinger told the president that "he had apparently a pretty good negotiating session with the Vietnamese, and they're in agreement now on eight of the nine points. The ninth point is that they insist that we agree to overthrow the Thieu government."

"What has been gained?" Kissinger rhetorically asked. "A superb public relations record of genuine willingness to compromise difference and to let the South Vietnamese people decide their future freely. We have conceded everything remotely reasonable, short of a coup against Thieu—neutrality, limitation on military aid, a withdrawal deadline, a large economic aid program. Also, a record of willingness to take steps and make efforts greater than those demanded by our domestic opposition. A commitment by the other side stated even more clearly today by Le Duc Tho to release our POWs in exchange for a date. Though this is not enough today we can return to it in the Fall. . . . I told them that we were prepared in the next 5 years to provide $7.5 billion in aid to Indochina, of which $2–2.5 billion could go to North Vietnam."

In other words, the U.S. had given in on almost everything. The question that remained was how to convince their ally that this was not a betrayal. This would be accomplished by promising Thieu just the opposite of what was being guaranteed to the North Vietnamese. That is, the United States would retain a military presence and be ready to use it when the communists violated the paper peace.

For months President Thieu had been concerned about the lack of information on Kissinger's private meetings with Le Duc Tho. These concerns started well before Kissinger's trip to Peking. In preparing for Kissinger's May 31 meeting with Tho, Bunker wondered, "How do we handle Thieu, including his likely reaction to the proposals? . . . You (Kissinger) indicated to Haig that we should test the other side's reaction before informing Thieu. This has obvious advantages and avoids possible problems such as shaking Thieu's morale when there are real doubts that the other side will negotiate seriously. On the other hand, failure to take Thieu into our confidence from the outset also has clear-cut pitfalls for our bilateral relationship. If we do go to him in advance how much detail should we give him? Do we seek his concurrence or do we in effect tell him what we are going to do in any event?"

Thieu sensed that he was being set up because of Nixon's domestic pressures. When he learned that the term *mutual withdrawal* had vanished, replaced by the requirement that the North halt infiltration into the South, he understood that the withdrawal of North Vietnamese troops was now a separate point to be solved by the Indochinese countries, not Kissinger. Winston Lord explained Thieu's dilemma: "We in effect adjusted our position from mutual withdrawal to in effect saying, well, on the subject of troops you all work this out among yourselves . . . but we would settle for a military settlement only or a cease-fire, withdrawal and the return of our prisoners. . . . In effect we split off the political from the military and we were on our way to a final agreement." Thieu was about to learn that the only guarantee he would get from a negotiation in which he did not participate was for American air power to keep the communists in line. If the China card had had any effect, it apparently was to increase the pace of American concessions.

CHAPTER SIX

Nixon Goes Public

My predecessor sent in 500,000 men into Vietnam, and I've taken 500,000 out. I will end American involvement—it's a matter of time.

President Nixon meeting with Chou Enlai
in China, February 22, 1972

In a nationally televised announcement on January 25, 1972, Richard Nixon disclosed to the world that Henry Kissinger had been engaged in private discussions with the North Vietnamese since August 1969 and that every reasonable American proposal to end the war had been rejected. Kissinger described the speech as "one of his most dramatic and impressive."

"Nothing is served by silence, when the other side exploits our good faith to divide America and to avoid the conference table. Nothing is served by silence when it misleads some Americans into accusing their own government of failing to do what it has already done," said the president. Twelve times, beginning on August 4, 1969, Kissinger had traveled to Paris for secret negotiations with the North Vietnamese. He had met seven times with Politburo member Le Duc Tho and five times with Xuan Thuy, but there had been no progress. Nixon provided the details of the October 11 secret proposal for a political settlement that included not only internationally supervised free elections with communist participation, but also President Thieu's resignation *before* that election.

"If the enemy wants peace it will have to recognize the important difference between settlement and surrender," President Nixon said. The North
Vietnamese had rejected the U.S. eight-point plan and offered instead its
own nine-point proposal; the PRG had offered its own seven-point version,
but always the bottom line was that the U.S. would have to drop its support
for the existing government in Saigon.

At a news conference in Washington on January 26, Kissinger added
more details to the president's speech. He said that North Vietnam's demand that the U.S. end all support to the South Vietnamese government was
one of two deal breakers it had advanced. The other was Hanoi's conception of the term *withdrawal,* which was interpreted to mean the removal of
all American equipment, economic aid, and arms from South Vietnam.
Since compliance with this request would mean the collapse of the Saigon
government, according to Kissinger, it was really a political proposal. "So
our attempt to negotiate the military issue separately was simply rejected,"
he declared.

Editorial reaction to Nixon's speech was full of praise for how far the
President had gone in private to secure peace. The *New York Times* opined
on January 26 that Nixon's efforts "represent a major advance over the Administration's previous public positions on ending the war. They merit support from all shades of American opinion and a positive response from the
other side. . . . By agreeing to set a fixed date for the withdrawal of American forces from South Vietnam in exchange for the return of prisoners of
war, the President has moved dramatically in the direction long advocated
by many members of Congress." The *Miami Herald* contended on January
27 that President Nixon's speech embodied "a brilliant performance as well
as a contribution to a fuller understanding of the issues. According to the
Chicago Tribune, "Whatever happens now, the exchange has cleared the air
of a good deal of rhetorical pollution and has unmasked Hanoi as the real
obstructionist all along."

* * *

Here is the real story of October 11, 1971 (and January 25, 1972). The only
problem with Nixon's speech was unknown to editorialists at the time: It
gave no indication of South Vietnam's interest in the U.S. proposals. It
could not have; Thieu was very upset at American duplicity in the preceding
months. In his memoirs Kissinger wrote that he had urged Nixon to autho-
rize the new October 11 proposal, "which would go to the limit of what was
compatible with our obligations, our sacrifices, and our honor." The pro-

posal shifted the focus from military to political solutions by proposing a presidential election in Vietnam within six months of a signed agreement. One month before the election, President Thieu would resign. "Nixon approved this offer on September 20. Haig left for Saigon on September 21. Thieu accepted it on September 23."

In his memoirs, Alexander Haig recalled that on September 21, 1971, Nixon had sent him to Saigon in order to get President Thieu's agreement on a new U.S. proposal to end the war: "The provisions of this early draft included a cease-fire; fixed withdrawal date for the U.S. and other foreign forces from South Vietnam; return of prisoners of war; elections five months after a formal peace settlement to be supervised by a mixed commission that would include Communists. Thieu would step down one month before the elections but would be entitled to run. I told Thieu that the United States considered it very unlikely that the enemy would accept the proposal," which is highly likely the reason that Thieu went along with it.

This message was transmitted on October 11 (after the South Vietnamese election) by General Vernon Walters to the North Vietnamese delegate-general in Paris with the request for another meeting with Le Duc Tho on November 20. There was only one problem: *No one had told President Thieu that the message had been transmitted to the other side.* Thieu did not find out until January 1972, when he was asked to go along with the president's January 25 announcement that would reveal the private talks as well as the October 11 offer. Nixon had intended to deliver this speech on January 18. As Kissinger wrote in his memoirs, there were some "touchy encounters in Saigon, because while Thieu had approved our offer, he had not known that we had in fact transmitted it to Hanoi before the projected meeting with Le Duc Tho on November 20. There was also some prickliness when Thieu realized that mutual withdrawal was being dropped from our public position." (Kissinger notes that Thieu's acquiescence in October to Haig's visit "was only a pretext; a year later, during our showdown over the final terms, Thieu was to tell us that he had been deeply offended by the basic proposal; he never gave us a hint of it at the time.")

The newly declassified files add much new evidence for this story that has never before been fully told.

Nixon had decided to deliver his speech on January 18. Nixon and Kissinger believed that by taking this public initiative, the North Vietnamese would have to respond to what Nixon said on January 18 rather than fall back on their private seven (or nine) points. At the time Kissinger cabled Bunker, "I think you are quite correct in assuming that they will not accept, given their failure to respond up to now, but putting the proposal forward publicly moves us over to the initiative." Bunker cabled back that all of this made sense except, "Thieu, of course, is unaware that the proposal has been passed to the other side."

On January 10, 1972, Bunker met privately with Thieu and asked if the president recalled the details of Haig's September 23 meeting and the proposal that was to have been tabled on November 20, until Kissinger cancelled that meeting due to Le Duc Tho's absence. Bunker now informed Thieu, for the first time, that although there was no meeting, the proposal had been passed on to Hanoi in order to prevent "losing weeks of time" in the negotiations. In other words, the North Vietnamese had been told on October 11, 1971, that President Thieu had agreed to step down one month before an election, although Thieu believed that since the proposal had not been forwarded then, in fact, he had not agreed to step down.

Thieu was furious. General Haig had assured him that nothing would be presented to the other side without his being informed. Bunker beseeched him to understand the critical domestic situation in the U.S. The president's position in Congress had deteriorated significantly since Haig's visit in September. With Congress convening on January 20, President Nixon wanted to give his speech on January 18 or 19, so that the pressure would be on Congress to keep the money flowing for equipment and support of Vietnamization. Thieu needed to understand the advantage of Nixon's January disclosure: "For the U.S. we would have compiled a negotiating record with the other side that would be beyond reproach. If the proposal is rejected . . . both Congressional and other domestic criticism would be largely diffused at the very time in our legislative process when their efforts could be expected to concert against us. For you, the benefits are equally obvious—you will have placed peace above your personal ambition. It would discredit those critics who claim you are the remaining obstacle to peace. For Hanoi, the proposal, at least symbolically, meets its demands that elections not be conducted by the GVN. Actually, however, you would remain in office as the modalities for the mixed commission, the supervisory body, and the election are largely developed."

Most important, this strategic approach would "cut the ground from under the critics both in the U.S. and Vietnam. It will demonstrate the reasonableness of our mutual policies and will greatly strengthen President Nixon's position in requesting adequate appropriations for both military and economic assistance which will be needed to make Vietnamization viable."

Characteristically, Thieu did not react initially to Bunker's news, opting to think about it overnight. The next day, January 15, Bunker wrote Kissinger that "for the first time, Thieu raised the question of the submission of the proposal to the other side without his being informed. He said that he had been very disappointed to learn this, since he had understood from General Haig that he would be consulted before this was done." Bunker summarized Thieu's principal concerns: "That the Vietnamese people may fear that the withdrawal of U.S. and allied forces may take place independently of a settlement of the other elements of the proposal . . . that the withdrawal will take place before the elections are held." Kissinger cabled Bunker on January 15 that "we believe it is essential that we have mutual understanding with Thieu and a coordinated *public line* before proceeding. Division between us would, of course, have grave impact in Vietnam and here, and seriously undermine our common purpose."

Bunker now told Thieu that "the President would give his address on the evening of January 18. . . . He will emphasize that not only this proposal but the whole negotiating process was worked out in close consultation with you throughout. He would emphasize your extremely forthcoming posture on negotiations." But Thieu wondered, what if he was queried? "We could say that after getting your concurrence to the proposal, we passed It to the other side in Paris in advance of the meeting which they subsequently aborted?"

Thieu took the unusual step of writing a memorandum on January 14 from Saigon that detailed the Nixon administration's subtle deception. He wanted the record to show that on January 10, Bunker had given him a document purporting to be a draft of a new peace initiative that Nixon planned to make public on January 18. Upon closer examination, however, this was the full text of a "statement of principles" that the United States had passed on to the other side without telling Thieu. "I am not even informed of the date when this statement was forwarded to the other side."

Moreover, this was the first time that Thieu had seen a document that involved shaping the peace and the political future of South Vietnam. It was a text of principles that would lead to a treaty. No one had asked him for a list of principles for his country's future. Thieu demanded to know who was to sign this statement of principles and who would sign the final agreement. Who, he wanted to know, had defined such concepts as a foreign policy of neutrality? Why was there no prescription for the withdrawal of communist armed forces from South Vietnam? How were they to be removed before any elections could occur? Did Kissinger or Nixon believe that free elections could be held in the South while Northern troops were still present?

Thieu warned Nixon that unless his concerns were addressed, "I will not be able to jointly release the full text of the 'statement of principles.' On the contrary, on that day, I will only tell the people of Vietnam that I have another peace initiative. . . . What in essence I am going to say is the reiteration of the points of my July 11, 1969 proposal, and develop and complement it by new peace initiatives on the reelection of the President and Vice President after the problems related to the end of the war, such as cease-fire, international control, withdrawal of forces, exchange of prisoners, etc. have been satisfactorily solved."

The White House was so concerned with Thieu's response that Nixon delayed his speech until January 25 because, as Bunker explained to Thieu, "the President feels it is important that we should develop together a coordinated public line. . . . The delay would allow time to 'work out our mutual problems.' But there could be no delay beyond January 25, and "absolute secrecy is essential if the speech is to have the impact we expect from it. Any premature disclosure would be disastrous."

Bunker tried to mend fences with Thieu by admitting that "the President and Dr. Kissinger agree that you are entitled to express disappointment. We recognize that we erred. . . . I want to make sure that you realize there was no intent to deceive or proceed without your full and complete accord. President Nixon feels that we have a long record of mutual trust and cooperation under his Administration and we certainly would not want this incident to mar that record."

Bunker needed Thieu to know that going public now would neutralize the increasing opposition to the war, help maintain domestic support, and prevent the passage of disabling legislation by Congress that would impair the viability of Vietnamization. Congress was reconvening, and the administration wanted to preempt "damaging resolutions which could force the US out of the war." The central purpose of going public on January 25 was "to take the offensive so that, barring a negotiated agreement we can continue to do what we wish in order to support your government and you yourself. If we make this proposal after an enemy offensive has begun, it will look like a sign of collapse. By moving first with it, it makes the other side look unreasonable if they launch an offensive and any response by us will appear fully justified. As you know, we could have reached agreement last summer by agreeing to overthrow you. Our refusal to do so—which we will maintain firmly in any event—was the only stumbling block to a settlement."

Bunker emphasized again that the joint proposal allowed the U.S. and

Saigon to take the offensive in an election year and would greatly strengthen the U.S. ability to maintain the necessary material support. "We are under no illusions that the other side is likely to agree to our proposal and frankly believe they will not. Our surfacing it at this time, however, could prove to be the essential factor in allowing us to continue our support for the GVN."

When Thieu saw a draft of Nixon's January 25 speech, he told Bunker that "since the President mentions that the proposal was transmitted to the other side October 11," he wanted it made clear that he too was in possession of the proposal on that date. As late as January 24, Thieu fought for the insertion of the words "with the full knowledge and approval of President Thieu." He asked that the words "National Liberation Front" replace "Vietcong" because Thieu never used the term VC. Thieu fought for one other change in wording, from "We make this offer as part of the peace plan," to "I and President Thieu," because "we" translated into Vietnamese is equivalent to the polite form of "I." Finally, Thieu wanted to know whether "withdrawal of all U.S. forces" applied to U.S. forces in Thailand or to the Seventh Fleet. He was told it did not.

The North Vietnamese responded to Nixon's January speech by releasing their secret nine-point peace plan that had been tabled by Le Duc Tho on June 21, 1971, in Paris. This plan had two more points than the one that had been tabled in Paris, and when Kissinger asked Tho what the two additional elaborations actually elaborated, he was told the truth: nothing. It was merely an attempt by the North Vietnamese to have something "new" in response to Nixon's public revelations.

Did the Nixon speech of January 25 really catch North Vietnam off guard? President Thieu and Hoang Duc Nha believed the October 11 proposal actually moved the U.S. to the North Vietnamese position. North Vietnam's nine points and its elaborations were aimed at gaining additional concessions and dividing Thieu from the U.S. On January 25, Nixon said that the United States *would* withdraw its troops from South Vietnam *before* the North Vietnamese removed their troops and that President Thieu would step down *before* an election. Who had been caught off guard? The United States abandoned mutual withdrawal, thereby allowing the Northern troops to stay in place. From the North Vietnamese perspective, there was no serious need to consider any U.S. proposal; in fact, Hanoi was already making plans for a new military offensive aimed at altering the balance of forces in the South in order to push its cause even further.

A few weeks after public criticisms of Nixon's January 25 peace proposal surfaced in the press, H. R. Haldeman had a television interview with Barbara Walters on NBC's *Today* show. During the interview, his first on television, Haldeman accused war dissenters, including U.S. senators, of "consciously aiding and abetting the enemy of the United States" and of being "in favor of putting a Communist government in South Vietnam, and insisting that it be done." Although Haldeman's statements inflamed Democrats by suggesting that war dissent was treason, the White House proclaimed that the comments were "his own personal point of view" and that he was "not a spokesman for the President."

Nixon quickly backed his top aide, however, saying that criticisms of his peace initiatives by Democratic presidential rivals "might give the enemy an incentive to prolong the war until after the November election." In a February 9 radio address, Nixon declared that he was not questioning the sincerity or patriotism of his war critics, but whereas "there should always be free debate and criticism," such criticism should not deter the search for an "honorable peace." He reminded his Democratic rivals that "we have only one President at a time, and only the President can negotiate an end to the war." In a news conference the following day, Nixon reiterated that although his opponents had a right to suggest proposals "that would overthrow the government of South Vietnam, or some other proposal that would satisfy the enemy," as a consequence "the responsibility for the enemy's failing to negotiate may have to be borne by those who encourage the enemy to wait until after the election."

Nixon soon left on his historic trip to China, full of hopes that he could use the Chinese (and later the Soviets) to help him end the war and join him in the construction "of a new international order." Before departing for China, Nixon guaranteed Thieu that there would be "no secret deals" with the Chinese involving Vietnam.

Two days before leaving, on February 15, Nixon made hand-written notes on what he intended to tell Chou Enlai about Vietnam:

1) We are ending our involvement-
2) We had hoped you would help—but now it doesn't matter
3) We must end it honorably—+will.

James Mann recently unearthed new archival evidence that on February 6, 1972, "Nixon and Kissinger launched a last, unsuccessful foreign policy initiative, one that was kept secret at the time and wasn't mentioned in their memoirs." They asked for a meeting on Chinese soil with Le Duc Tho during Nixon's trip.

Thieu was unaware of this offer, but he confided to Hoang Duc Nha that "America has been looking for a better mistress and now Nixon has discovered China. He does not want to have the old mistress hanging around. Vietnam has become old and ugly." While Kissinger and Nixon met with Chou Enlai, Bunker went to see Thieu on February 21 to report that "Michael and Yul" had asked for a private meeting with Kissinger. Thieu was suspicious of Nixon's meetings in China and even asked if Le Duc Tho was going to be in China at the same time. Bunker cabled Haig that "Thieu speculated further as to whether Michael [Le Duc Tho] would be in Peking during the President's visit. I said that we had no information to that effect, that I doubt he would be wanted there at this time."

China rebuked the offer of a private meeting, forcing Nixon to the realization that while many benefits would flow from the new relationship with China, he would not get it to broker a peace in Vietnam. Vietnam was, however, the subject of several conversations in private talks between Nixon, Kissinger, Mao, and Chou Enlai. On February 22 in the Great Hall of the People, Chou Enlai told Nixon that "the Geneva agreement was a mistake because it led the U.S. into a quagmire. . . . Dulles did . . . have America sink in. . . . Ho would have won the elections and relations with the U.S. would have been better. . . . The most pressing question now is Indochina, which the whole world is watching."

When Chou asked for Nixon's views on Vietnam, the president was ready: Nixon reiterated that the Americans wanted to leave Vietnam and that their military presence was now below 100,000; in April, more will be gone. In two to three months America's role "will be finished, unless, of course, the problem of our prisoners is still outstanding." Nixon said that if he were sitting across the table from the North Vietnamese, he would negotiate a ceasefire, get U.S. prisoners back, and be out in six months, but he would not dump Thieu. "We have offered to withdraw all Americans, with no 'tail' behind—to use the Prime Minister's expression—and to have a ceasefire throughout Indochina provided we get our prisoners back." Nixon expressed frustration that even this was not enough for the North Vietnamese, who insisted that the U.S. also impose a political solution. "The only gainer in having the war continue is the Soviet Union," Nixon observed. "They want the U.S. tied down. They, of course, want to get more and more influence in North Vietnam as a result. From all the intelligence we get they may even be egging on the North Vietnamese to hold out and not settle."

Nixon wanted the Chinese to understand that "the negotiating track is open, and as I indicated, we are willing to negotiate a settlement on military issues alone, if they are willing. To negotiate a general political settlement in which Thieu would resign and an impartial commission would run the elections. If, in answer to our proposals, North Vietnam chooses to step up the fighting, I have no choice and the action I take is apt to be very strong. This is my record, and that is what's going to be so that other nations in the world know that the U.S. will react strongly if tested." Nixon stressed that, "the U.S. is prepared, just in conclusion, to provide a very heavy economic assistance to Cambodia, Laos and North Vietnam for rehabilitation, and to South Vietnam in the event a settlement is made. We don't want to leave a tail behind. We don't want bases. We would accept a neutralized area. On the other hand, it takes two to make a deal."

Kissinger chimed in to repeat that "the People's Republic wants the war to end and the Soviet Union wants the war to continue." "Yes," "Yes," responded Nixon and Chou.

Chou wondered how it was that Nixon could say that the United States could not cast aside friends like Thieu. He seemed to agree with Le Duc Tho. They had discarded other friends in the past, and all of this was getting in the way of other global issues. "That is still your saying—you don't want to cast aside old friends. But you have already cast aside many old friends. . . . As for Vietnam, you went there by accident. Why not give this up? . . . Diem and his brother went to see God. These fellows are not reliable. If the United States really wants to create a good impression in the world, you don't need these so-called good friends." What Chou did not know was that, for Nixon, Thieu was needed for the guaranteed return of American air power. Anyone else, especially Big Minh, was likely to move toward a coalition government and would reject B-52s. Nixon needed Thieu in order to prevent South Vietnam from moving into the neutralist camp—a slippery slope toward communist control.

In another meeting, this one on February 24 in the Great Hall, discussion moved to China's political support of Vietnam. Chou made it very clear that China supported the seven points of the PRG as well as the two points of elaboration and that it would continue its support for Vietnam and all of Indochina, whether the Americans were there or had withdrawn. "It would not be beneficial to you or for the honor of the United States to leave behind a tail. . . . The tail means American forces," observed Chou.

Nixon asked whether the tail meant "bases." He assured the Chinese that the U.S. had no intention of leaving behind this sort of tail. But, "we are not going to engage in unilateral withdrawal without accomplishing the objective of our policy there." Chou concluded, "The channel of negotiations should not be closed. We can only go so far. We cannot meddle into their affairs."

Nixon responded by saying something a bit curious: "I think I can understand this, although I oppose it. I can understand North Vietnamese going into the South; it's all Vietnam. But North Vietnam has no business going into Cambodia."

Even with Chou Enlai's frank admission that the Chinese could not meddle in Vietnamese affairs, the Sino-U.S. summit rekindled Hanoi's memories of the 1954 Geneva Conference. Chou Enlai was in Hanoi by March 4, just days after Nixon's departure, to reassure the North Vietnamese that there had been no sell-out. Kissinger would soon be in Saigon to assure the South Vietnamese of the same thing. Neither side would believe it.

While in China, Kissinger received a message from Vernon Walters that the North Vietnamese wanted Kissinger to come for a luncheon meeting in Paris immediately after the president's China trip. "Henry was particularly ecstatic because they said it would be for lunch. They have never had any American official for any meal before in all of Henry's meetings with them. . . . He thinks this is a significant time. . . . It could lead to a breakthrough," Haldeman wrote in his diary.

CHAPTER SEVEN

The Easter Offensive

**Most important—the President must not lose
the war!**

John Connally, May 1972

By January 1972 the U.S. had conceded on almost every major point, including, at least implicitly, that any cease-fire would be a "cease-fire in place," that is, North Vietnamese troops would stay in the South if they were already there. What came next was predictable: The North could not get the U.S. to get rid of Thieu for them. They did not intend to stop fighting until they regained the South. Thus, they had one obvious strategy: stall the peace, pour forces into the South, and strike a deal only once a cease-fire in place was nearly a "victory in place." For months, Le Duc Tho kept Kissinger's hopes alive that more serious talks were about to begin, but it was all a ruse. On Easter Sunday, March 30, 1972, North Vietnam launched the largest attack of the entire Vietnam War. It was a conventional military attack designed to inflict a crippling blow against ARVN forces and would last six months.

To lead the offensive, General Giap selected his favorite general, Van Tien Dung, a veteran of the 320th Division who had fought against the French in the Red River delta. North Vietnamese strategy during the Easter Offensive deviated sharply from its previous unconventional style. Giap hoped to use massive waves of troops to capture and hold territory, including major South Vietnamese cities such as Hue and Da Nang. The attacks were launched from North Vietnamese sanctuaries in Laos and Cambodia.

Captured documents and interrogations of North Vietnamese Army (NVA) POWs revealed that Giap wanted to destroy as much of the ARVN as possible. Capturing major populated areas would allow the NVA to attack Saigon itself. This was a radical departure from small-scale hit-and-run tactics employed in the past. Giap hoped to bring about the collapse of the Thieu government. Nixon believed that the enemy had committed itself to a make-or-break campaign.

The attack occurred during the planning stages for an upcoming summit with Soviet leader Brezhnev. Kissinger was scheduled to visit Moscow secretly from April 20–25 to make arrangements. On April 1 Nixon responded by ordering the bombing of North Vietnam within 25 miles of the DMZ. By April 14 he ordered air strikes up to the 20th parallel. The Paris talks were again suspended.

Four days into the attack, Haldeman recorded, "The P's massing a huge attack force. . . . B-52s (Freedom Train) for the first time against North Vietnam. . . . He feels that this will give us a fairly good chance of negotiations, which he has never really felt we've had up to now, but thinks they're doing this as a desperation move and then will have to negotiate. Henry has the same view."

But was the North desperate, or was it pressing an advantage? By April 6, Haldeman recorded that "the P was very upset with the military. . . . He made the dramatic point of the fact that this may very well be the last battle that will be fought by the United States air force . . . and that it would be a tragic thing if this great service would end its active battle participation in a disgraceful operation that this Vietnam operation is turning out to be."

Several days later, Haldeman recorded the thrust of another conversation with Nixon: "He feels very strongly that we've got to make an all-out effort now, and that it's really a do or die proposition. The North Vietnamese have committed all of their resources to the current attack and the South Vietnamese have pretty much committed all of theirs to the defense. We're doing virtually everything we can do, short of putting American troops in, which we won't do. The P has moved the bombing activity up to a very high level and intends to maintain it there . . . to give the South Vietnamese a chance to win this one. . . . It's apparent that we have the potential at least to break the North Vietnamese back, but the question is whether or not the South Vietnamese will be able to hold. If they can, the P comes out in extremely good shape, because it would be almost inevitable that we'd move immediately from this attack to the conference table within the next few months, and that we might get something settled by summer." It was a test of American bombing against intensely motivated enemy ground troops. It would not be the last such test in a distant land.

On April 12, 1972, just weeks after Nixon's visit, Chou Enlai confided in Nguyen Tien, the Vietnamese chargé d'affaires in China, that "the United States is to expand bombardment and use warships to shell the territory of the DRV. It tries to use expanding bombing and expanding fronts to prevent its defeat. This certainly will not work. The people in Indochina are standing together and fighting together. No matter where the United States will bring the war to, it will suffer from heavy strikes. China firmly supports the serious stand of the DRV government, and will try its best to support the Vietnamese people to carry out the anti-American patriotic war to its end."

On April 16 a new operation, Freedom Train, sent five B-52s to attack North Vietnam in the Hanoi-Haiphong area. Four Soviet ships were hit by mistake, but the Soviets chose do nothing—sending a clear signal that they did not intend to risk the summit.

On April 20 Kissinger secretly departed for Moscow, where the reception he received was exceptionally cordial. The Soviets told him they wished to assist in a Vietnam settlement and eliminate any obstacle to the summit. Kissinger promised Brezhnev that the U.S. would accept a cease-fire in place, as well as the presence of North Vietnamese troops in South Vietnam—even those troops that had entered after the offensive. Kissinger asked Moscow to pass this message on to Hanoi. Now it was official.

In a cable to Bunker on April 24, Kissinger wanted the ambassador to instruct Thieu not to make any mention of Kissinger's Moscow trip since the Soviets did not want it known that Vietnam was discussed. The official White House announcement said only that between April 20 and April 24, Kissinger was in Moscow to confer with Gromyko on important international problems as well as with bilateral matters preparatory to talks between Nixon and Soviet leaders in May. The Soviets had told Kissinger that "they want to help in a settlement," so the U.S. had agreed to attend the plenary session scheduled for April 27. The other side had agreed to May 2 for a private meeting. "We believe that this will give us a chance to test out Soviet intentions and their influence with the other side and also see whether the other side is serious about private talks. If the May 2 meeting fails to take place or if the other side gives no indication of willingness to negotiate seriously, we will engage in a massive air campaign against North Vietnam and would cancel the Paris sessions again." Not a word was said about the Northern troops remaining in the South.

Facing an invasion from the North spearheaded by Soviet tanks, Thieu wondered how the U.S. could return to public forums. He was dumbfounded when told that Nixon planned to announce the withdrawal of another 20,000 troops by July 1, bringing the total U.S. force level to 49,000. Thieu was told that this would increase public confidence in Vietnamization.

At just about the same time, Konstantin Katushev, head of the Soviet Central Committee Foreign Relations Commission, flew to Hanoi with a personal message from Richard Nixon. Katushev told Premier Dong that "the United States would not tolerate drawn-out negotiations in a Presidential election year." The war would be expanded to North Vietnam if Hanoi refused to compromise. Dong became livid: "Who allows them to threaten us? We have to let them understand that Vietnamization will surely fail, that the puppets will undoubtedly be swept away, that there is no way to revive them."

Meanwhile, on May 1, Kissinger reported that General Abrams had just cabled the bad news that Quang Tri was lost and a fierce battle was being waged at Hue. "Highway of Terror" was the name given to the coastal route south from Quang Tri, as it was bombed by both North Vietnamese and American military. Abrams warned Kissinger that the ARVN may have lost their will to fight and that "the whole thing may be lost." Nixon recorded in his diary that this was the period that he gave serious thought to stepping down, but Kissinger told him that "the North Vietnamese should not be allowed to ruin two presidents." Haldeman recorded, "He's obviously facing the very real possibility now that we have had it in Vietnam, and he's going to have to deal with that situation. . . . Both he and Henry agree that no matter what happens now, we'll be finished with the war by August. Either we will have broken them or they will have broken us, and the fighting will be over. There still seems to be some possibility of negotiation or a cease fire because it's quite possible, maybe even probable, that the North Vietnamese are hurting even worse than the South Vietnamese, and that both sides may be ready to fold."

The atmosphere for the May 2 meeting was heavy and tense. Luu Van Loi wrote that on May 2, Kissinger "no longer had the appearance of a university professor making long speeches and continually joking, but a man speaking sparingly, seemingly embarrassed and thoughtful." Kissinger described the meeting with Tho as "brutal," because Tho now sensed a complete South Vietnamese collapse. Le Duc Tho was buoyed by reports of victories on the battlefield: Quang Tri had fallen, and Pleiku and An Loc appeared to be next.

Kissinger began the meeting by saying that "the President would not have sent me across the ocean three times unless he knew that a rapid and fair solution to the war could be achieved. . . . After the U.S. withdrawal, the Vietnamese still remain. The solution must therefore meet the interest of Vietnam . . . The U.S. is now prepared to reach such a solution. . . . But Vietnam is requested not to misunderstand. The U.S. will not negotiate at gunpoint. There is no reason to discuss a future agreement if the North Vietnamese 'invading forces' are encroaching on our side."

Kissinger spoke directly and bluntly, filled with a controlled anger, reflecting what must have been months of frustration in dealing with an adversary whom he felt did not want to negotiate seriously. "Over recent months, Vietnam has eluded a negotiated solution. . . . We no longer want to accept this trick, we request you to end the offensives; to abide by the 1968 understanding; to negotiate seriously, concretely, constructively to end the war."

For Le Duc Tho, however, everything was going his way, and there was little reason to flinch. Still not ready to negotiate, he responded that "after 7–8 months meeting each other, I expected you to tackle the question of solution immediately, but to my chagrin, you did not say anything new. I traveled a longer distance than you to come to Paris. . . . You, and no one else, have used military pressure in negotiations to impose your conditions on us. That is why the people in both zones of Vietnam have to oppose your attacks. That is something natural. Senator Fulbright has admitted this fact."

Kissinger interrupted Le Duc Tho: "I don't want to discuss the internal situation of the U.S."

"I said so to point out the fact that we are not alone in saying this. Americans also do," retorted Le Duc Tho.

"Discussion of U.S. affairs is our concern," said Kissinger.

Le Duc Tho rubbed it in: "I'm giving an example to prove that Americans share our views. On 8 April, Senator Fulbright said the intensified military activities of the patriotic armed forces were but a natural response to the U.S. policy of undermining the 1954 Geneva Agreements."

Kissinger said, "I am aware of that, you need not tell me."

"I just briefly mention it to you," said Tho.

"I have heard," said Kissinger.

Le Duc Tho continued, "This truth is pointed out not only by us. It is also the view of Americans who have a minimum of conscience. Therefore, your statement that we are invading South Vietnam is an absurdity." Tho then moved on to the *Pentagon Papers,* which he believed documented to the world "evidence of the U.S. process of intervention and aggression."

Kissinger refocused the conversation to what he believed was a reasonable solution—one that at a minimum would be taken seriously as a point of departure for serious negotiations. Both sides would return to the situation prior to March 29, the day the offensive started, the United States would withdraw the reinforcements it had brought into the region and stop bombing. Thereafter negotiations could start.

In response, Xuan Thuy, as he so often did, ignored what had just been said, launching into other issues: "You are ignoring the realities and arguing only for your advantage. You carry out what is advantageous and you do nothing that is not. You take for granted your expansion of the war to all Indochina and now you demand that the Vietnamese stop their opposition to your aggression."

Tho now jumped in: "There are two questions: a definite date should be fixed for the completion of troop withdrawal. The United States has proposed 6 months after the signing of the agreement. It is still too long. For the political issues, the United States proposed Thieu would resign one month before the election. We insist on Thieu's immediate resignation and the change of policies by the remaining members of the administration ."

"All other members, except Thieu, can remain in the administration [government], can't they?" asked Kissinger.

"They can remain but they have to change their policies," said Xuan Thuy.

"What does a change of policies mean?" Kissinger persisted.

"It means the abandonment of all repression and oppression of the people and the real enforcement of all democratic freedoms," responded Le Duc Tho.

"Then how will it be ascertained that policies have been changed?" Kissinger asked.

"A statement about a change of policies is not enough, action must be taken to this effect," said Tho.

"For instance, the established concentration camps should be dismantled, the political prisoners released, and the publication of forbidden newspapers allowed," was Xuan Thuy's answer.

"Will Thieu resign immediately after an agreement is reached or right now?" queried Kissinger.

"Immediate resignation is one with no delay. Tomorrow is best," said Xuan Thuy.

Kissinger asked about what he had conveyed through the Soviet Union. "Through your allies, we have put forward issues to be discussed, and your allies have conveyed them to you. I am surprised that you make no comments on these questions."

Le Duc Tho did not respond to this question. "We have on many occasions said that if you have any question you should directly talk to us, and we shall directly talk to you. We don't speak through a third person. If you have anything to say now, we are prepared to discuss it with you."

The meeting adjourned with no new date set.

Kissinger later wrote that "Le Duc Tho was not even stalling. Our views had become irrelevant; he was laying down terms." Using words like *insolent* and *unbearable* to describe his adversary, Kissinger wrote to Nixon, "I spent three hours today with Le Duc Tho and Xuan Thuy in a session that was thoroughly unproductive on substance but served to bolster further our negotiating record. . . . They made very clear that they were not prepared either to deescalate the fighting or offer anything new concerning a settlement."

Kissinger later recalled, "The most impossible sessions I had with Le Duc Tho were after they had, after the North Vietnamese had taken Quang Tri. We had a meeting in May of 1972, which we had negotiated to arrange for months. When I arrived there all he did was read newspaper accounts to me. When I said I didn't have to come thousands of miles and negotiate for five months for a meeting to hear newspaper accounts, he said 'If they're true what difference does it make.'"

Bunker told Thieu that Le Duc Tho refused to discuss the end of their offensive, refused to discuss separating political and military issues, insisted on a final troop withdrawal date, and insisted on overthrowing the current regime. As a result, Ambassador Porter would be instructed to walk out of the plenary sessions.

Nixon's mind was made up. He recorded in his diary for May 2, "That was Hanoi's last chance. I decided now it was essential to defeat North Vietnam's invasion."

The next day on the yacht *Sequoia,* Kissinger told Nixon that Hanoi believed it was close to victory. Nixon would now follow his own instincts. "We know from experience, based on their record in 1968, that they will break every understanding." Nixon asked Kissinger and Haldeman to visit with Treasury Secretary John Connally, a close confidant of the president. Connally emphatically said, "Most important—the President must not lose the war! And he should not cancel the summit. He's got to show his guts and leadership on this one. Caution be damned—if they cancel, and I don't think they will, we'll ram it down their throats."

The president next met with Kissinger, Haig, Connally, and Haldeman. "As far as I'm concerned, the only real mistakes I've made were the times when I didn't follow my own instincts." Nixon gave examples: the war would be over if only he had bombed North Vietnam at the time of the Cambodian invasion. "Whatever else happens we cannot lose this war," declared Nixon.

On May 8, President Nixon convened a three-hour meeting of the NSC, where he described plans for mining Haiphong harbor and renewing the bombing of Hanoi-Haiphong. He planned to announce his decision in a televised speech that evening. This was the moment that Nixon had prepared for since abandoning Duck Hook in November 1969, although Duck Hook did not include B-52s. Secretaries Laird and Rogers were both against the plan. Secretary Rogers spoke so equivocally that Kissinger passed Haig a note that read, "If it works, I'm for it; if it fails, I'm against it." Vice President Agnew and Alexander Haig were solidly behind the plan.

Following the NSC meeting, Nixon assembled his cabinet, where he stated frankly, "We've crossed the Rubicon." As Nixon would put it to Kissinger the next day, he wanted to "go for broke" and "go to the brink" to "destroy the enemy's war-making capacity." He wanted to avoid previous mistakes of "letting up" on the bombing that he and Johnson had made in the past. "I have the will in spades," he declared. Nixon was determined not to repeat LBJ's mistake.

Between the NSC meeting and his evening speech, Nixon convened a meeting with the joint congressional leadership in the Roosevelt Room of the White House. Nixon wrote in his memoirs that no one interrupted or asked even a single question. "There was complete silence as I rose and left the room." Haig described the reaction: "Both Democrats and Republicans received his words in stony silence. It was a chilling and revealing moment." Admiral Moorer recalled the reactions of Senators Fulbright and Mansfield:

"I did observe Senators Fulbright and Mansfield shaking their heads quite a bit over the thought that this would widen the war, and that the Soviets would immediately dash down to the Tonkin Gulf and sweep the mines."

Speaking to the nation that evening, the president outlined the steps he was taking militarily: "There is only one way to stop the killing. That is to keep the weapons of war out of the hands of the international outlaws of North Vietnam. I have ordered the following measures, which are all being implemented as I am speaking to you. All entrances to North Vietnamese ports will be mined to prevent access to these ports and North Vietnamese naval operations from these ports. United States forces have been directed to take appropriate measures within the internal and claimed territorial waters of North Vietnam to interdict the delivery of any supplies. Rail and all other communications will be cut off to the maximum extent possible. Air and naval strikes against military targets in North Vietnam will continue."

Nixon went on to present a new peace proposal, which he later claimed became the reference point for the terms of the final settlement the following January: the return of all POWs and an internationally supervised cease-fire throughout Indochina to be followed by a complete withdrawal of all American forces within four months. In his television address, Nixon concluded that "there are only two issues left for us in this war. First, in the face of a massive invasion do we stand by, jeopardize the lives of 60,000 Americans, and leave the South Vietnamese to a long night of terror? This will not happen. We shall do whatever is required to safeguard lives and American honor. Second, in the face of complete intransigence at the conference table do we join with our enemy to install a communist government in South Vietnam? This, too, will not happen. We will not cross the line from generosity to treachery."

On that day, United States Navy planes dropped mines into the port of Haiphong and six other harbors of North Vietnam to block the arrival or departure of North Vietnamese and foreign ships. In a statement distributed by the official news agency *Tass*, the Soviet Union called on the United States to stop its mining of Vietnam, declaring that the bombing and mining "were fraught with serious consequences for international peace and security." On May 9 the Chinese agreed to send a team of navy commanders immediately to assist in mine-clearing operations. Later that month, a Chinese mine investigation team arrived in Haiphong.

Nixon told JCS chairman Thomas Moorer that he wanted the Soviets and North Vietnamese to get a clear message of United States intent to use force, *whatever* force was necessary. The military was to "exercise maximum aggressiveness in the use of air power." Moorer then wrote to his field commanders, "We do not expect to lose this one, consequently, we must bring as much air and naval forces to bear as possible in order to give the enemy a severe jolt. . . . We have received increased authorities and must make full use of them at every opportunity. Our objectives are: to ensure that the North Vietnamese do not endanger remaining U.S. forces, to provide maximum assistance to the South Vietnamese in their efforts to destroy the invader and to prevent the North Vietnamese from interfering with Vietnamization plans." Moorer told his field commanders "how intensely the President is in this operation, how determined he is that the enemy does not succeed in their objectives, and how forthcoming he is when presented with requests for authorities and additional resources."

"Those bastards are going to be bombed like they've never been bombed before," gloated Nixon. What followed was the most successful use of airpower during the Vietnam War, and one of the largest aerial bombardments in world history, known as Operation Linebacker. Targeting roads, bridges, rail lines, troop bases, and supply depots, the attack was the first large-scale use of precision-guided laser bombs in modern aerial warfare.

"I intend to stop at nothing to bring the enemy to its knees," Nixon told Kissinger. But Nixon was disturbed by what he described as the "reticence" of the military planners. It seemed to him that the Pentagon was holding back and was not "going for broke," as he intended. He wrote Kissinger, "I am totally unsatisfied at this time at the plans the military have suggested as far as air activities are concerned. . . . Our greatest failure now would be to do too little too late. It is far more important to do too much at a time that we will have maximum public support for what we do. What all of us must have in mind is that we must *punish* the enemy in ways that he will really hurt at this time." Nixon railed against the Defense and State Department bureaucracies, telling Kissinger to get them off their "backside" and give him an action plan that would allow the United States to "destroy his warmaking capacity." Drawing a comparison between himself and his predecessor, Nixon wrote that "what distinguishes me from Johnson is that I have the *will* in spades."

In his masterful study of airpower during the Vietnam War, Mark Clodfelter calculated that "from April through October 1972, 155,548 tons of bombs fell on North Vietnam"—and with remarkable success. Linebacker seriously disrupted and damaged North Vietnam's lines of communication.

Most significant, Nixon employed Linebacker in support of very limited objectives. As Clodfelter concluded, "Unlike Johnson, who used air power to help establish an independent, stable, non-communist South Vietnam, Nixon applied air power only to guarantee America's continued withdrawal and to assure that the South did not face imminent collapse after the United States departure."

Opinion polls conducted immediately after the initiation of the bombing campaign revealed that the American public approved of the bombing by wide margins. The Silent Majority spoke loudly. Nixon was also correct in his assessment that the Soviets would not risk détente over the May 8 decisions, and in any event, "the summit isn't worth a damn if the price for it is losing South Vietnam. My instinct tells me that it can take losing the summit but it can't take losing the war."

Both sides claimed victory from the Easter Offensive. In the short term, the offensive was clearly a military defeat for the North Vietnamese and would cost General Giap his job. By spreading its troops across three disparate fronts and attacking in massive waves, the North Vietnamese were spread too thin and proved unable to pour enough firepower on any one point to win major territory. Many North Vietnamese units were annihilated and some battalions were reduced to 50 men. The North Vietnamese forces were vulnerable to air attack in logistical resupply for gasoline, tanks, trucks, and rail. Hanoi's casualties from its conventional offensive were staggering, losing over half of the 200,000 troops committed to the fighting. The Linebacker campaign also had made headway in reducing the supplies funneled along the Ho Chi Minh Trail, although the trail was not crucial because of the nature of the conventional attack.

Although Hanoi never retained control over a provincial capital, the North Vietnamese did gain ground along the Cambodian and Laotian borders and the area south of the DMZ. Hanoi remained in control of this territory for the rest of the war, and in 1975 it would use this territory to launch a successful attack on Saigon. As with the war as a whole, then, the story for the North was one of massive sacrifices yet eventual success. According to a State Department document, "One of Hanoi's objectives was to force the GVN to deploy all of its combat resources to meet the major mainforce thrusts. This, Hanoi calculated, would permit NVA/VC forces to return to former strongholds in the South Vietnamese countryside and thus regain a source of manpower and supply in the South." This they succeeded in accomplishing.

For South Vietnam, the Easter Offensive was a hollow victory. Stiffened by U.S. airpower, the offensive was proof that Vietnamization was working—at least better than it had a year earlier in Lam Son 719. In his study of the Easter Offensive, Dale Andrade concluded that "despite Vietnamization, the South Vietnamese Army exhibited many of the same problems in 1972 as it had ten years earlier, a fact made painfully clear during the Easter Offensive. . . . The Easter Offensive showed that this partnership [U.S.-ARVN] could work, but only so long as American firepower remained abundantly available." This lesson would be an important one for Nixon when it came to trying to convince his ally that the piece of paper to be signed in Paris meant very little.

There was also a crucial irony to the Linebacker support, which most certainly caused Hanoi to reconsider its negotiating strategy and led to significant concessions. As Mark Clodfelter has cogently noted, "While it contributed to Hanoi's negotiating concessions, Linebacker did not achieve the 'honorable peace' Nixon desired. Paradoxically, while the campaign contributed to Hanoi's willingness to settle on Nixon's terms, it also stiffened Thieu's opposition to an agreement by convincing him that he could gain total victory. Viewing the concessions that Linebacker helped extract from Hanoi, the South Vietnamese president reasoned that continued strikes could win the war, and he was skeptical that Kissinger's accord could produce lasting peace."

Nonetheless, there was one clear immediate result to Linebacker. The disappointing results of their Spring Offensive forced Hanoi to return to negotiations. It also now appeared likely that Nixon was destined to win reelection in November because on May 15, George Wallace was shot at a rally in Maryland. With Wallace in the race, the outcome was anything but certain for Nixon. Wallace had won Democratic primaries in Florida, Tennessee, North Carolina, Maryland, and Michigan and had strong second-place finishes in Wisconsin, Indiana, and Pennsylvania. If denied the Democratic party nomination, Wallace posed a significant threat to Nixon as a third-party independent. With Wallace out of the race and with George McGovern's nomination seemingly assured, Nixon no longer had to be concerned with electoral constraints.

On the same day that Wallace was shot, Bunker informed Thieu that Nixon had received a private note from Soviet leader Brezhnev urging Nixon to announce, before their forthcoming summit, that the U.S. would

return to the plenary sessions in early June. If Nixon took that step, the Soviets would then pressure the North Vietnamese to meet "without preconditions." Thieu reacted vehemently to the idea of any collusion with the
Soviets. He asked Bunker why Nixon had not first received a Soviet guarantee of change in Hanoi's position. Thieu's protest was to no avail.

On May 20, Nixon would be off to Moscow. After they were airborne,
Kissinger came into the president's cabin and exuberantly said, "This has to
be one of the great diplomatic coups of all times!" The summit went off as
scheduled on May 22, where several meetings were held on the subject of
Vietnam, the most significant being when Kissinger said that the U.S. would
accept a three-part electoral commission in South Vietnam encompassing
the Saigon government, the Vietcong, and neutrals. Not surprisingly, Thieu
was told only that "the talks on Vietnam were extended and sometimes
heated. The President set forth our positions on military measures and negotiations. He made it clear that the North Vietnamese actions had left us
no choice but to act decisively." Once again a concession had been made,
and Thieu had been kept in the dark.

Thieu kept asking for more and more information about what Nixon and
Brezhnev had discussed. On June 17, Bunker gave Thieu a special message
from Nixon: "President Nixon wishes me to repeat again to you that we
have not made the great sacrifices that the recent enemy offensive has in-
curred merely to concede at the negotiating table what he has been unable
to achieve on the battlefield. President Nixon wants me to assure you that
he continues to support you fully. At the same time, he is able to enlist the
maximum domestic support through continuing a blend of forceful action
on the battlefield combined with demonstrated flexibility on the negotiating
front." Whether from Soviet pressure or not, Hanoi now indicated that they
were ready to renew the private talks.

On June 17, 1972, five men were arrested breaking into the Democratic
National Committee headquarters in the Watergate complex in Washington, D.C. Little could anyone imagine that by August 9, 1974, the president
would resign. As it would turn out, however, Watergate destroyed the secret
assurances that Nixon was about to make to Thieu. Vietnam did a great deal
to trigger Watergate, for Nixon's "plumbers" were first set up to haunt
Daniel Ellsberg and to recover copies of the *Pentagon Papers* and even perhaps to find out if Ellsberg had even more information that might be in-
criminating to Nixon's 1968 dealings with Thieu over the bombing halt. In

return, Watergate would destroy Nixon's plans for Vietnam by destroying his public support, and thus all chance for him to continue bombing after a peace agreement was signed.

* * *

Before the next meeting with Kissinger and Le Duc Tho, Tho went to Beijing on July 12, 1972, for another meeting with Chou Enlai. The Easter Offensive was by now even more evidently a failure, and Chou pressed Tho to move toward Kissinger's latest concessions. "We do not recognize Nguyen Van Thieu as he is a puppet of the U.S. Yet we can recognize him as a representative of one of the three forces in the coalition government. The coalition government will negotiate the basic principles for it to observe and control the situation after the U.S. withdrawal of troops. The U.S. will see that Thieu is sharing power in that government, and therefore, find it easier to accept a political solution. In case negotiations among the three forces fail, we will fight again," said Chou Enlai.

"But we still think of a government without Thieu," said Tho.

Chou asked Le Duc Tho to consider the possibility of dropping the demand for Thieu's ouster because sometimes it is necessary to talk to the "chief, not his advisors." However, "if we hint that Thieu can be accepted, the U.S. will be surprised because they do not expect that. Of course, Thieu cannot be a representative of a government. But in negotiations, surprise is necessary."

Tho held firm: "We are asking Thieu to resign. If he does not, we will not talk with the Saigon government."

Chou then asked who else would be acceptable. Tho responded that they were prepared to talk with anyone, but Chou tried again by warning that this could be even more dangerous: "It is Thieu's policy without him." Chou then cut to the chase: "A coalition government could be established, but we later have to resume fighting. The question is to play for time with a view of letting North Vietnam recover, thus getting stronger while the enemy is getting weaker." Although Tho was not yet ready to accept Thieu's presence even under these conditions, Chou Enlai had put his finger on the truth. Thieu or no Thieu, the Chinese and the North Vietnamese believed that once the Americans were gone, South Vietnam would eventually fall.

Finally, on July 19, negotiations resumed between Kissinger and Le Duc Tho. At first, in one of the most amusing episodes of the entire talks, they discussed Jimmy Hoffa. The former teamster boss wanted to go to North Vietnam and secure the release of American POWs. Ever since Nixon had become president, there had been pressure to pardon Hoffa. Nixon finally commuted Hoffa's sentence on December 23, after hundreds of thousands of dollars had been contributed to the Nixon campaign and after Hoffa guaranteed Teamster support to Nixon in the 1972 election.

Prior to the July meeting, Kissinger met with William Taub, Hoffa's lawyer, in San Clemente after Taub had returned from giving the pope and Le Duc Tho a letter from his client. In it, Hoffa had offered himself as a replacement for Kissinger! He did so, he said, because Le Duc Tho had agreed to release American POWs to Hoffa. Kissinger asked Taub, "If we give a pardon to Hoffa, what will he do in Hanoi?" Taub answered that he would go to Hanoi and negotiate privately and bring back the first prisoners on September 8, 1972. Kissinger did not believe a word of it.

Yet at the July 19 meeting, Tho immediately brought it up. Kissinger told Tho, "He is a convict, he has just been in a penitentiary and is on probation. Therefore he is still under sentence. I cannot believe you would have us release a convict in order to release prisoners to him. He says he has documents you gave him. . . . We would have to pardon him for him to go to Hanoi. He is not a political activist. It is not political. He is in prison for stealing money. We would let him go to Hanoi only if you said you would release prisoners to him. And then it would be an interesting question why you would release prisoners to someone who is under sentence in the United States."

Le Duc Tho laughed and responded, "We don't know the curriculum vitae of Mr. Hoffa. We know only that he is a trade unionist."

"He may go to Hanoi—but that is up to you," said Kissinger. "We were only concerned about prisoners. I understand the prisoner issue. He was put in prison by Robert Kennedy, not by us. As long as Mr. Hoffa doesn't concern prisoners, Mr. Hoffa doesn't concern me." In September, Hoffa would begin, then quickly abort, a trip to North Vietnam. Secretary of State William Rogers later revoked his travel clearance. It was never made clear just what the North Vietnamese had promised him, but it seems entirely unlikely that they intended to release POWs at that point of the negotiations.

Moving on to more substantive issues, Kissinger told Le Duc Tho that he carried with him yet another proposal, reaffirming that the United States wanted to put an end to the war. "Vietnam still misunderstands the objective of the U.S. . . . It is true that the U.S. has so far tried to separate the military issues from the political ones, but not for the purpose of returning to Vietnam or prolonging the war. The purpose is to separate the U.S. direct involvement in Vietnam from the political outcome so that later the solution of political problems in Vietnam will depend on Vietnamese conditions, and not on U.S. actions. The U.S. is doing this in good faith and not because of our desire to return to Vietnam."

Kissinger reiterated that it was his belief that North Vietnam had missed an opportunity in 1971 and on May 2, when the military situation was "better" for the North—this despite the fact that Hanoi now had more troops in the South than ever before. Kissinger reassured Tho that "in a period when the U.S. is reducing its presence in Asia, there is no reason for it to keep forces and bases and political dominance in such a corner of Asia as Vietnam. When the U.S. can accept non pro-U.S. governments in larger countries, why should it insist on a pro-U.S. government in Saigon? The U.S. can coexist with Beijing and Moscow, so it can do the same with Hanoi. The U.S. will not be a threat to Vietnam in the future. . . . We are not attached to any particular personality or any particular political orientation in SVN. We are willing to let events in South Vietnam take their natural evolution without our presence or our predominant influence." Le Duc Tho must have sensed that this was a dishonest statement of Nixon's intent.

Finally, Kissinger warned Le Duc Tho that any effort to take advantage of the negotiations to influence the election in the United States would only delay the solution. Since it had been Nixon and McGovern who tried to influence their own campaigns in the past, and Hanoi that had stonewalled, this was a vividly ironic—and impotent—warning.

Afterward, Kissinger cabled Bunker with his assessment. "The 6 1/2 hour session with Le Duc Tho and Xuan Thuy was the longest we have ever had. . . . The contrast with their strident belligerency at last May 2 was striking. Their positions contained fresh nuances that could either presage progress by them toward a settlement or a holding action to probe for our concessions and to keep the talks going pending developments on the battlefield and the American political scene. They probably do not yet know themselves."

The next meeting was fixed for August 1, where, as Kissinger later described it, "Le Duc Tho continued the retreat that he had begun on July 19." Kissinger described the August 1 meeting as "the most interesting session we have ever had." Kissinger spoke first and put forward a new twelve-point plan. "We agree to solving military and political issues at the same time."

Xuan Thuy laughed and said, "Last time you had 5 points, you now have added 7 points."

Le Duc Tho added, "Numerically speaking, you have made great progress."

Kissinger read out point after point. Arriving at point 6 and seeing Le Duc Tho and Xuan Thuy speaking together, Kissinger joked, "It seems that you are arguing with each other. We think that if Mr. Adviser and Mr. Minister had an argument it would be an indication of eventual settlement."

"But I think that this cannot happen before election day," said Tho.

After reading point 7, Kissinger stopped and said, "Probably you are accustomed to these ideas because they are similar to yours."

After point 12, Kissinger handed a text to the North Vietnamese and noted that in this proposal, the United States had agreed to the complete withdrawal of allied forces, as well as equipment and the dismantling of all bases. The United States had also shortened the time of withdrawal to four months, meaning that if a settlement was reached before September 1, "the last U.S. soldier will have left Vietnam by the end of this year." Kissinger also noted that the United States would "solemnly declare our respect for the result of the political process. The only thing the United States will not do is decide this result beforehand in Paris." The United States was giving de facto recognition to any new government in South Vietnam, he added. President Thieu had stated that he would resign two months before the election, and the timing of Thieu's resignation might also be more flexible.

Still Hanoi stalled. After yet another inconclusive meeting on August 14, Kissinger wrote to Nixon that "the North Vietnamese will be watching the polls in our country and the developments in South Vietnam and deciding whether to compromise before November. They have an agonizing choice. They can make a deal with an Administration that will give them a fair chance to jockey for power in the South, but refuses to guarantee their victory. Or they can hold out, knowing that this course almost certainly means they will face the same Administration with a fresh four-year mandate that reflects the American people's refusal to cap ten years of sacrifice with ignominy. During this process we have gotten closer to a negotiated settlement than ever before; our negotiating record is becoming impeccable; and we still have a chance to make an honorable peace." It was admirable spin. In truth, Hanoi knew that as time went by, the North would have more and more troops in the South, and America would be less and less willing to support Thieu. Thieu knew that the end game had arrived.

CHAPTER EIGHT

"They Have Concluded They Cannot Defeat You"

By late summer 1972, George McGovern had failed to make any headway. In fact, Nixon's prospects for reelection already looked quite good. Unlike 1968, when the U.S. was sinking deeper into Vietnam and LBJ already was closely identified with the U.S. commitment and losses, Nixon in mid-1972 was generally perceived as working toward peace. His mining of the harbors and stepped-up bombing had pulled Hanoi back to the table; American troops were slowly but surely coming home. Nixon could still have been hurt by a massive military defeat, but after the failed Easter Offensive and with Vietnamization almost complete, that seemed unlikely. A peace agreement would have been a coup and would have sealed McGovern's fate in November, but it wasn't absolutely necessary.

For Kissinger, the situation was somewhat different. Buoyed by success in China and the Soviet Union and becoming more of an international celebrity, he yearned more than ever before to secure a peace treaty in Paris before the election. Kissinger wrote in his memoirs that while Nixon thought it very unlikely that an agreement could be achieved before the election "and probably did not even desire it," he believed that "our election would serve as an unchangeable deadline for Hanoi, the equivalent of an ultimatum." Certainly Hanoi would fear that after reelection, Nixon the hawk or even the "madman" would stop at nothing to secure his terms with Hanoi. Kissinger also believed that the United States would be worse off after the election because all available polls showed that the new Congress would likely terminate the war by legislation, although Nixon certainly planned on vetoing any such measures, and Congress (before a Watergate crisis) would have been unable to muster the two-thirds vote required to override the veto.

In the weeks before the election, Kissinger and Alexander Haig would negotiate furiously with President Thieu and his two trusted assistants, Nguyen Phu Duc and Hoang Duc Nha. Nha was the closest of Thieu's immediate staff; he held the titles of private secretary and press secretary to the president. Born in 1942 in Thieu's home village near Phan Rang, Nha was a second cousin to Thieu, like a younger brother. Nha stayed at Thieu's home for two years while attending high school in Dalat. After graduating high school, Nha attended Oklahoma State, graduating in 1964 with a bachelor of engineering (electrical) degree. In 1967 he studied management at the University of Pittsburgh.

Describing himself as a "technologist," he was a technically trained official with broad interests and a creative streak. Nha spoke English well, translating public statements and writing speeches for President Thieu. He served as Thieu's right-hand man in many matters relating to the business of running government and brought some of his friends from high school into Thieu's regime. He also traveled to Washington several times to act as Thieu's unofficial eyes and ears in foreign affairs. He often came to conclusions independent of other South Vietnamese administrators, including even the minister of information. Nha was particularly critical of U.S. foreign policy during the Nixon years and especially distrusted Henry Kissinger

Like Nha, Nguyen Phu Duc, Thieu's special assistant for foreign affairs, was educated in the both Vietnam and the United States, earning a doctorate of law from both Harvard and the University of Hanoi. Unlike Nha, Duc was born in the North. A career diplomat, he possessed a legalistic mind and was described as fastidious about language. He became centrally involved with the Paris negotiations, for which he helped devise negotiating strategy and positions. Yet he often was eclipsed in power by Nha due to the latter's closeness to President Thieu. Both Nha and Duc understood America and knew its public opinion. Both knew that Kissinger was anxious to make a deal, but both were unsure just how far Kissinger was prepared to go. From August to October, Kissinger scrambled to close the deal. He almost pulled it off.

On August 17, Kissinger, Bunker, and Lord went to the Presidential Palace in Saigon for a meeting with Thieu, Nha, and Duc. Having spent the previous day in Switzerland celebrating his parents' fiftieth wedding anniversary, Kissinger arrived in Saigon "teeming with rumors that I had come to impose peace." Kissinger arrived with a proposal that he believed Hanoi might accept; he planned to submit it on September 15. The proposal spelled out the composition of a joint electoral commission, a tripartite formula that now had a name: Committee of National Reconciliation (CNR), which eventually evolved into the National Council of National Reconciliation and Concord (NCRC). Kissinger told Thieu that the CNR would put an end to any ideas the communists may have harbored about a coalition government because each side would appoint half of the third segment. No decision could be made without unanimity, so in effect, "Saigon had a double veto: in the composition of the committee and in its operation." Moreover, the only function of the council would be to oversee the election. "I was rather proud of this scheme," wrote Kissinger. "I thought it put to rest once and for all the idea of a coalition government, yet gave us a defensible position at home if Hanoi turned down our proposal."

Predictably, Thieu rejected any proposal that would include a CNR because he insisted that this was the first step toward a coalition. Kissinger tried to reassure Thieu and play an election card. "They have concluded that they cannot defeat you. Their only hope is that we overthrow you," Kissinger told Thieu. "For you it is essential that this administration survive, because we will never overthrow you directly or indirectly. The only way you can get us to do this is to keep the war going on—they would rather pay the military price here. That's why they do not give the prisoners or agree to a cease-fire. They are in a real dilemma. If there is no cease-fire, their military situation deteriorates, and they don't give back the prisoners, we keep bombing them. So long as they talk to me, this confirms negotiations. I know you think a ceasefire might come soon. I have that impression." In short, he admitted that Hanoi could just as soon fight, but claimed that its military situation was deteriorating. Thieu knew, of course, that more Northern troops were penetrating the South with each passing month.

Perhaps most revealing is Nixon's memoir account of this period: "I sympathized with Thieu's position. Almost the entire North Vietnamese army— an estimated 120,000 troops that had poured across the DMZ during the spring invasion—were still in South Vietnam, and he was naturally skeptical of any plan that would lead to an American withdrawal without requiring a corresponding North Vietnamese withdrawal. I shared his view that the Communists' motives were entirely cynical." Yet Nixon would never instruct Kissinger to demand from Le Duc Tho the removal of communist troops. Instead, he sent Thieu a personal message: "I give you my firm assurance that there will be no settlement arrived at, the provisions of which have not been discussed personally with you beforehand." It was a meaningless communication.

While Kissinger thought there would eventually be a cease-fire, he told Thieu that he did not believe it would happen because Hanoi was not ready. "We want to go to the absolute limit of what is and looks reasonable but defend the principle that the U.S. will not end the war in which it lost 45,000 men by joining our enemy against our friend, or destroying a government allied with us for 400 prisoners of war, or even to win an election, we would rather not win the election on that basis. *The history books will last longer than the election.*"

To Thieu, these were just words. He demanded to know what had happened to the presumption of a mutual withdrawal of troops. Kissinger told him that he could not get the Russians to agree. Kissinger then raised the possibility of a raid into North Vietnam, which Nha derided as meaningless. "I think they are keeping the prisoners as blackmail," Kissinger told Thieu. "We will raise this issue *brutally* after November if they don't return them. They won't release them. They have made no proposal. If they accept our May 8 proposal for a cease-fire and prisoners, then we must withdraw. That is our official position and we can't change that. But they won't accept it. There is no possibility."

Thieu asked what would happen if Hanoi proposed a cease-fire in exchange for the POWs. Kissinger admitted, "I will be honest. If they propose this during the election campaign, we will be in a very difficult position."

The next morning at 10:00 A.M., Kissinger was back in the Presidential Palace to tell Thieu, "I thought at first it would be best to have a cease-fire as soon as possible because of our election. But upon reflection I have decided that it is easier if we keep up the bombing through the elections, unless in your view your military situation requires a cease-fire. You see, our strategy is that we are prepared to step up the military pressure on the DRV immediately and drastically and brutally one or two weeks after our election. We want to be in a position that they have rejected our reasonable proposals. After that we will put everything on the prisoner of war question. They think that they can use the prisoners of war to overthrow you. If we can move quickly after the elections, we can destroy so much that they will not be in a position to come back and harm you for a long time to come."

Kissinger reiterated that there would not be a cease-fire in the near future; "in fact I prefer that they don't return the prisoners of war and that there be no cease-fire before the election," he said. If Le Duc Tho proposed a cease-fire at their next meeting on September 15, Kissinger would insist on such detailed supervision requirements that it would all have to be worked out during the Paris public sessions at Kleber. "It is inconceivable that we will make any additional concessions after the election." It was, tough talk, but he belied himself by repeating that "at some point we may have to accept the prisoners of war for an ending of the bombing. But if so, it will be at a point when we have severely weakened them. At some point we may have to stop the bombing for this. Maybe in the second half of next year."

To Thieu, a cease-fire in place must have sounded more and more likely, with all it implied about future trouble from North Vietnamese troops. Kissinger later understood that Thieu had treated him in the same manner as Le Duc Tho: "He simply sought to grind us down by keeping his agreement ever tantalizing close, but always out of reach. I should have recognized the methods from Le Duc Tho." Kissinger left Saigon believing that he and Thieu had reached a meeting of minds. "In fact, he and I had engaged in a minuet, stately in its colorful avoidance of the real issues, courtly in its pretense of continued partnership, inherently inconclusive in confining itself to traditional, now irrelevant, patterns." This was because Kissinger believed that Thieu was not ready for a negotiated peace. "They had a few vague ideas that amounted to an unconditional surrender by Hanoi. They were not satisfied with survival; they wanted a guarantee that they would prevail. They preferred to continue the military contest rather than face a political struggle." Nha later told me that Kissinger's historical recollection was a "very preposterous point of view." All President Thieu wanted was for the North Vietnamese troops to go home, and then an election based on the principle one man, one vote could be held. The NCRC could organize the election but could have no governing authority.

On August 19 Kissinger cabled Bunker with a lengthy response to the GVN comments on the peace proposal that Kissinger planned to table on September 15. "I cannot emphasize too strongly the point I made repeatedly to Thieu that we must keep our eye on the main issue and not get hung up on minor legal technicalities." Here again, is evidence that the two allies had not even settled on the major issues.

The Republicans held their nominating convention in Miami on August 22. In accepting renomination, Nixon said, "Standing in this convention hall four years ago, I pledged to seek an honorable end to the war in Vietnam. We have made great progress toward that end."

Returning to Paris, Kissinger stopped in Oahu, where Ambassador Bunker was there to meet with Nixon and the new Japanese prime minister. Bunker told Nixon and Kissinger that Thieu viewed the proposed CNR as a disguised form of a coalition government or at least an entering wedge for it. Bunker also believed that South Vietnam "was not yet ready for a political confrontation with the communists, that the nationalist side is not well enough organized, despite an overwhelming majority, to compete with the tough, highly disciplined communists." They realized that they were in danger of alienating Thieu utterly, and if America seemed to be betraying its ally, it would not look good. Kissinger expressed that he was worried about a break with Thieu and its effect on the 1972 election. "We haven't sacrificed all these years in order to sell out now. If you think this is unreasonable, we'll change it. And we'll pay whatever price we have to," Kissinger said about the proposed CNR. Then, in a remarkable private admission, Bunker said that the idea of a referendum was horrible because "if it is held with the government in power, it will be rigged just as the presidential election of last October was—unnecessarily rigged."

Kissinger found consolation in the fact that delay was inevitable. "If all this works, with all of these elaborate forums, the process will last at least through November. We can then say it's a mess; we can go back to the proposal for the military issues alone. We can say, give us the prisoners and a cease-fire; we're getting out. . . . But we cannot have a confrontation now. It will be their death, and our death. We have positioned ourselves domestically so that a confrontation would prove McGovern's case. It would be the biggest boost for McGovern. They can't have the President go through the whole election without their help and then have a confrontation with the North Vietnamese in November as we plan."

Kissinger now dictated to his assistant, Peter Rodman, a letter to Thieu (for Nixon's signature) that said, "It is essential for us to have a position from which we can demonstrate to the American people that the only obstacle is the communists' insistence on our putting them in power. Once we do this, we can survive a stalemate and have a basis for returning to the May 8th position—settling the military issues alone." In other words, airpower, more specifically Linebacker-type punishment, could sustain South Vietnam indefinitely if the North Vietnamese (and South Vietnam) refused compromise on political issues.

But Kissinger caught himself, "We have to survive if the letter surfaces. Don't say the May 8th position. Say that it will show world opinion the lengths to which we are willing to go, and provide a basis for handling the consequences if it fails. Their suspiciousness is unbelievable."

Bunker responded, "This is Thieu's defect."

"But it's true of Le Duc Tho, too. They'll never accept this. Our plan is this, to be precise: If there is no settlement by November 7th we plan to walk out by November 9th. If Thieu wants to do a heroic landing operation, let him do it." Kissinger complained that he felt like "the headmaster of a reform school" because he was facing unruly behavior in Saigon and Paris. "Tell Thieu his only friends are the President and I."

Kissinger ended with the thought that even if Thieu "should tearfully say, 'Let's sign it' we wouldn't be able to sign it right away. If we table this on September 15, it will take through October. I will take personal charge of confusing who offered what. We will be able to say to McGovern that the only thing we haven't offered is a communist government. I don't see why Thieu is so obtuse."

The letter from Nixon to Thieu that resulted, dated August 31, did little more than try to rally him. Nixon promised that the U.S. would never betray an ally and would not sell out South Vietnam for an easy peace. "We will not do now what we have refused to do in the preceding three and a half years. The American people know that the United States cannot purchase peace or honor or redeem its sacrifices at the price of deserting a brave ally. This I will not do and will never do . . . but for us to succeed on this last leg of a long journey, we must trust each other fully. We must not hand the enemy through our discord what we have prevented through our unity."

It must have been cold comfort to Thieu, who knew that a deal between the U.S. and Hanoi was getting nearer. The September 15 meeting with the North Vietnamese lasted six hours. Kissinger wrote Nixon it "was in many respects the most interesting we have ever had. They were defensive; they professed eagerness to set the earliest possible deadline for an over-all settlement; and they have never been so eager to have early and frequent meetings. They repeatedly and almost plaintively asked how quickly we wished to settle and there was none of their usual bravado about how the U.S. and world opinion were stacked against them. For the first time in the history of these talks I sensed that they were groping for their next move and their tack was devoid of any apparent, clear-cut strategy."

Kissinger tabled the new proposal with its tripartite CNR to supervise the presidential elections. Kissinger cabled Nixon that this was done "without complete Saigon agreement." But he hastened to reassure his boss that

Hanoi would be unlikely to settle now because a settlement would only help Nixon's domestic situation without in any way restricting U.S. military flexibility. "My surmise is that they are deeply concerned about your re-election and its implications for them but, with their collective leadership, they may be having deep difficulties coming to grips with the very political concessions they will have to make to move the talks off dead center. They continue to pose unacceptable demands, perhaps because they lack imagination, perhaps because they wish to defer the necessary concessions to the last possible moment."

Kissinger informed Nixon that he "made it clear that the time to settle is short and that the President will have a new mandate in two months. I read them polls on the hawkish mood of the American people." Still, Kissinger warned that "this plan is still far from acceptable because elements like Thieu's immediate resignation upon signature of an overall agreement and the continued presence of the North Vietnamese army in the South, would all but ensure the psychological demoralization and political deterioration of the GVN. But from Hanoi's perspective it represents major movement. . . . It remains clear that the North Vietnamese want a settlement if at all possible before our elections give the Administration a fresh mandate. The central question is, of course, whether they want it badly enough to accept terms that we and Thieu can also accept."

On September 16, 1972, Bunker reported to Kissinger that Thieu's main concern remained the CNR, which he still saw as a formula that would lead to a coalition government. Bunker tried telling Thieu that the North Vietnamese had never seemed so anxious to negotiate and that when Kissinger told them that their political proposal was unacceptable, they had responded that it could all be negotiated and reconsidered. In fact, he said, Le Duc Tho had requested a two-day meeting and wanted it earlier than even Kissinger proposed: "Dr. Kissinger wants to make it clear that we intend to follow the strategy we have outlined, we will not accept the other side's plan, and we will not undermine our objectives or our friends in the homestretch. We propose to make no new proposals. Dr. Kissinger emphasizes that it is of the greatest importance now that we carry out the tactics we have outlined. The whole orientation and direction of our policy is being challenged by our critics and we both, the GVN and the U.S., have a big stake in it." Lost in all this was Thieu's offer to step aside prior to any new election—once the other issues were satisfactorily resolved—such as the withdrawal of North Vietnamese troops.

There was only one problem: Thieu had decided to go on a public relations campaign against the CNR. On September 21 Kissinger cabled Bunker
that "we have become increasingly concerned about the tenor of Thieu's recent public remarks on negotiations." Kissinger cabled Bunker again on
September 23 that "it is essential that Thieu stay close to us so that we
demonstrate solidarity to Hanoi." But Thieu was already off the reservation. Thieu's public remarks, as Kissinger knew, were having an effect in the
United States. Furthermore, Thieu's recent decrees suspending elections in
hamlets and placing restrictions on the press had been widely criticized.
"Coming before our elections, these measures also have played into the
hands of the critics of the U.S. administration and its Vietnam policy,"
Kissinger said.

Prior to his next meeting with Le Duc Tho, Kissinger received a memorandum from President Thieu on the communist proposals. "The communist September 15 proposals are even more arrogant than their August 1
proposals. The September 15 proposals show clearly the intention of the
communists who simply seek to force us to surrender unconditionally. Further, they reveal the communists' dark schemes."

As Hanoi requested, there would now be a two-day meeting on September 26 and 27; the location was switched to the suburbs of Paris in a house
that had belonged to the painter Fernand Leger, a member of the French
Communist party, who offered it to the party at the time of his death. Le
Duc Tho began by saying, "I should like to ask you in a very frank and serious manner whether the United States wants to prolong the negotiations
until after the election or does it want to settle the war by signing a comprehensive agreement before October 15? Whichever way you choose, we are
ready. . . . If you choose the second way, not much time is left." Kissinger
reaffirmed his desire for an early settlement and he was willing to remain in
Paris as long as necessary.

Yet after eleven hours with Le Duc Tho on September 26 and 27, there
was no significant progress, and no agreements of any kind were reached.
Tho proposed a variation of the CNR, a "Provisional Government of National Concord," that excluded Thieu entirely. In Kissinger's view the communist plan was still unacceptable, but slowly the communists were moving
closer to the U.S. position. Kissinger anticipated that the next meetings,
scheduled for October 8, would be decisive in arriving at a settlement or
produce a new military round.

Yet this is not what Thieu was told. "Looking to the immediate future, we see practically no possibility of a settlement between now and November unless Hanoi totally reverses its position," Bunker told Thieu. "What we must look to now is how best to insure that we keep the situation under control and position ourselves for post-November strategy along the lines Dr. Kissinger discussed with you when last in Saigon."

President Thieu continued his public relations battle, deriding the communists for offering a trick solution. The Republic of Vietnam was a constitutional and legal government. Thieu was its elected president. What right did the United States and Hanoi have to formulate political solutions for the future of South Vietnam? Speaking at Saigon University on September 29, Thieu characterized the new proposals as "more vicious and stubborn than before" and stressed that a coalition government with the communists would result in South Vietnam's losing the political war. Thieu railed against the "third force" in Vietnamese politics that was supposed to be a balance between the GVN and PRG in a tripartite government. In a speech at Hue, he characterized this third segment as "a small number of political speculators, lackeys, and exiles who call themselves a Third Force in South Vietnam." Thieu believed that this group would be pro-communist.

Within South Vietnam Thieu's rhetoric enhanced his image as a nationalist leader who was resisting foreign pressure and interference. The rhetoric also boosted morale among the armed forces. In America it had a different effect, as even long-time supporters of the president's policy wondered why Thieu seemed to oppose the negotiated peace terms. "Appreciation for services rendered is not a Vietnamese trait," wrote Kissinger in his memoirs.

Nixon had to rein Thieu in, and he dispatched General Haig to Vietnam with the tasks of both briefing Thieu on Kissinger's upcoming October 8 meeting with Le Duc Tho as well as getting Thieu to tone down his public rhetoric. Haig felt a special bond with Thieu borne of mutual respect for military careers. "Kissinger couldn't handle Thieu. I was a soldier; I had fought in the war. They knew me; I was a quasi-hero in their minds. Thieu thought Henry was a little duplicitous—too quick to advocate Hanoi's line. And in fairness to Thieu, he was right," recalled Haig.

At 11 A.M. on Monday, October 2, Haig and Bunker arrived at the Presidential Palace, where they were met by President Thieu and Hoang Duc Nha. General Haig informed President Thieu that President Nixon had asked him to meet initially in private so that Haig could convey a message that "Mr. Nixon hoped to confine to President Thieu's ears alone."

President Thieu asked both Nha and Bunker to wait in the adjoining conference room. Haig dispensed with diplomatic niceties and talked soldier to soldier: "President Nixon is concerned that President Thieu be genuinely aware of President Nixon's innermost thinking at this current juncture of the war. This is particularly important in the current atmosphere when routine diplomatic reporting and inaccurate and speculative press accounts can lead to disastrous misunderstandings between the two leaders." Haig then outlined a series of proposals that Kissinger intended to table with Le Duc Tho on October 8. As usual, Thieu listened, asked questions, and showed no sign of being upset. In fact, Haig even cabled Kissinger that Thieu's frame of mind "was as constructive as we could have hoped for and he will be inclined to be more cooperative than otherwise would have been the case." They were to meet the next day to discuss details and options. Haig was then scheduled to depart for Paris, where he would join Kissinger for the very first time at the negotiating table.

But the next day's meeting was cancelled, without explanation or note.

Before leaving for Paris the following day, October 4, accompanied by John Negroponte and Ambassador Bunker, Haig went to the Presidential Palace for a second meeting with President Thieu, this time with his entire National Security Council. Already hanging from the wall were key parts of the text from Hanoi's September 26 proposal and the current U.S. proposal for October 8. Nha, standing in front of the chalkboard, provided translations to the Vietnamese-language texts. Thieu accused Kissinger of being "ambushed" by the communists' proposals. The CNR, while not a government, was in essence the same thing because it was composed of the same three components of a government.

Vice President Huong outlined the numerous concessions that the communists had already gotten from the United States: "They got the U.S. to agree to accept the NLF as a party to the talks, thus giving them recognition as a political entity. The communists have demanded U.S. withdrawal while North Vietnam has obligated itself to do nothing in return, thus depicting the U.S. as the invader. It follows that it is the duty of the Vietnamese to drive out the U.S. Thus North Vietnam poses as the big brother who will settle the problems between the other two elements." Huong said that the communists could not be believed; "they have done nothing in return for the cessation of bombing [Linebacker]."

Haig responded that "our purpose has been to avoid being put in a position in which our critics in the U.S. can accuse us of being unwilling to accept a settlement." The GVN needed to understand that the U.S. would do nothing that involved the discontinuance of the GVN—"that it will be in control of the realities of power." He continued, "Up to now, the DRV has played into our hands in their demands for the resignation of President Thieu and the dismantlement of the GVN. There has, however, been a slow evolution of the communist position. They have made some concessions, moving away from outright demand for the overthrow of the GVN." The U.S. therefore had no alternative but to negotiate, because failure to do so would lead to even greater domestic political pressure. "The issue is whether we are going to be able to continue our policy of military assistance and of bombing and mining the North until Hanoi comes forward with reasonable proposals. If President Nixon has to be informed that we cannot agree on our counter-proposals, we will be faced with a crisis which can only hurt both our governments." Haig emphasized the need to harmonize their views in order to carry on the war effort. He argued that the North was "hurting" but that the U.S. needed to talk about political, and not just military, solutions. "We must not put the other side in a position to say that we are opposed to any solution other than a military one. President Nixon has laid our position on the line at great personal risk and we must go ahead together."

Thieu accused Kissinger of double-dealing the South Vietnamese. He had submitted his own lengthy counterproposal on September 13, but on September 26 Kissinger tabled a proposal that bore little resemblance to it. Haig responded that "in the judgment of both President Nixon and Dr. Kissinger, the GVN's counter-proposal in all probability would have broken up the talks. . . . Had the talks in fact broken up we would now face a degree of turmoil in the United States which would be serious for both of us. President Nixon is trying to use the strength he presently has to maintain our posture of support. If he now has to report that President Thieu is holding to his September 13 position, we will be faced with very great difficulties." In other words, Thieu's attempt to return to an insistence on mutual withdrawal was now a deal breaker.

Thieu spoke derisively of the absent Kissinger, who "does not deign to accept GVN views, but wants to go his own way." Thieu asked Haig, "How many concessions do we have to follow?" Prime Minister Tran Thien Khiem asked Haig if he understood the motive of the military in 1963 when overthrowing Diem. One of the underlying causes had been the circulation of rumors, just like now, that he was considering entering into a pact with the communists. The same was true of General Duong Van Minh when he was dealing with de Gaulle between 1945 and 1947. The one thing Thieu had always feared was a coup.

Khiem said that under the current proposal, the government "would be looked upon as a lackey of the U.S. and would have little power. The NLF, on the other hand, would become a power—like the poor man who won a sweepstakes. The GVN would, in fact, be a non-existent government— what the communists all along have wanted. In Paris the GVN has been accused by the communists of being a tool of the U.S.; if we accept their proposal, it will be confirmation of what they have said."

Thieu then declared his wish to be an independent party in the talks. So long as Kissinger played the role of middleman, "he will be confirming that the GVN is a lackey of the U.S. Moreover, in working out the technical aspects of the proposal, a stalemate would probably result and this would permit the communists to throw all the blame on the Americans. The road on which we have engaged is one with no end in sight. On the other hand, if the U.S. tells the DRV, once and for all, that the U.S. and the DRV can solve the military problems but that only if the DRV and the GVN talk together can there be a solution of the political deadlock and progress can be made."

Haig turned to Thieu and asked, "What shall I tell President Nixon?"

Finally, Thieu backed down. He reiterated a point that he thought needed no further expansion: The United States and North Vietnam could not settle the affairs of South Vietnam. Kissinger and Tho could not negotiate the sovereignty of his country! He told Haig that the U.S. could do whatever it wanted, but "it should not be caught trying to solve the internal problems of South Vietnam."

Haig responded by cutting to the chase: "If we are going to insist on total surrender we are in for an indefinite conflict and the will of the American people might not sustain such a conflict." Thieu dared Haig to make the proposals public: "We should not fear to make them public. . . . We should not have the erroneous concept that we must save face for the DRV or that we should make them lose face." Haig said, "We are apparently on a divergent course. We are not trying to save face for the other side, but want to find out whether they are in the mood to make concessions. We will both have to reconsider our positions." Thieu spoke of being "at the edge of the abyss" and questioned whether the U.S. still wanted to defend Southeast

Asia. "No one demands that anyone in the DRV step down," he finished plaintively.

* * *

Haldeman recorded in his diary for that night, October 4, 1972, "We had a big flap with Henry last night and carrying on today . . . complete tantrum. . . . Henry actually believes still, even though Thieu has completely refused to go along with anything Haig has proposed that we still have a 50–50 chance of pulling something off with the North Vietnamese this weekend and he's scared to death that the P will louse it up." The president did not think there was any chance to settle and "that's probably OK because they would be charged with selling out for the election. . . . I think he'll (K) use anything that comes up as an excuse if the thing blows, so it works out pretty well for him."

Haig had returned to Washington, although Nixon believed he should have stayed in Saigon to "work over Thieu." On October 5, Bunker again went to see Thieu for a "cold turkey" talk: "President Nixon wishes me to say that he is extraordinarily disappointed by your reaction to our negotiating proposals and strategy. The position which you and other members of your government have taken in opposition to these proposals has made immensely more difficult our joint effort to move in negotiations in a way that would ensure a non-communist structure in South Vietnam."

Bunker reiterated that Nixon's actions had nothing whatsoever to do with the November election; instead, the administration was concerned "with building a platform creating a position—which will enable us to take the kind of action we want in the post-election period. If there is a public confrontation with us now it will make it absolutely impossible even to maintain the present level of our military action after the election, much less to step it up. Such a development could only result in negating ten years of effort and the lives of thousands which have been devoted to securing the future we have both sought."

On October 6 Nixon sent Thieu a warning that there could be no public confrontation between them, threatening that if this were to occur "our only option in that event would be a unilateral disengagement." Nixon had to be bluffing when he raised the possibility of a coup: "I would urge you to take every measure to avoid the development of an atmosphere which could lead to events similar to those which we abhorred in 1963 and which I personally opposed so vehemently in 1968."

Finally, on October 9 (after a one-day delay because Haig was detained in Saigon), the fateful meeting arrived. Kissinger sat down in Paris, again in secret, with Le Duc Tho. It had taken over 18 months of talks and tens of thousands of lives to reach a point that might have been conceded from the beginning: the U.S. had neither the ability nor the will to force all Northern troops out of the South. Nor did Kissinger care all that much about the fate of the weak and myopic government of the South. He was there to get agreement on terms for a political battle between the Vietnamese, but the battlefield would be an uneven one, and the terms in contention were Le Duc Tho's. Kissinger accepted that this was all America could hope to achieve from the negotiations. Richard Nixon, however, expected more from Kissinger and from Thieu. He intended for South Vietnam to receive the backing of American airpower through 1976, the end of his second term as president. He preferred that there be no deal before the election because he would then be free of McGovern and would be able to punish Hanoi in the manner of May 1972. He could go for broke. Despite these differences, however, both Nixon and Kissinger needed Thieu to understand that it was time to deal.

The first thing Kissinger did was apologize for having put off the meeting for one day and then joked that he was sorry that Xuan Thuy could not be able to attend church, since they were now meeting on a Sunday.

"If your soul is not saved, we are to blame for it," said Kissinger.

"Today, the weather is fine, and we have to come here to work for peace, we together apologize to God," Xuan Thuy responded.

"God also wants peace and not war," said Le Duc Tho.

Kissinger immediately offered his new proposal: "Regarding the political issues, we recognize that actually there are two armies, two administrations [governments], and three political forces in South Vietnam. The United States' proposal clearly reflects this conception. We also adhere to another basic principle, that is the establishment of a three-component organ which will play the role of intermediary and adviser to both parties and may contribute to the implementation of the signed agreements."

Kissinger emphasized that this proposal was a big concession on the part of the United States, making clear that he still did not have Saigon's approval on the question of the election of the National Assembly and the election of the president. He reiterated that the three component organs would be a temporary body. It was not a government because its tasks were not those of a government. If the term *committee* was not agreeable, Kissinger was willing to call it a *commission*.

The United States was willing to accept some Vietnamese armed forces in South Vietnam, but Kissinger requested that Hanoi provide a list of the precise location of their troops in South Vietnam and asked that Hanoi remove the units that had been used in the Spring Offensive. He also made it clear that no document would be signed in which the United States took responsibility for war reparations, "but was willing to participate in a large-scale reconstruction plan throughout Indochina and to write this intention in a unilateral statement."

When Le Duc Tho's turn came to speak, he quickly said that "to rapidly end the war and restore peace, to show our goodwill we are proposing something new today both in content and in the practical and simple way to conduct the negotiations:" an *Agreement on Ending the War and Restoring Peace in Vietnam* that would settle military questions involving troop withdrawal and the release of POWs, a cease-fire in Vietnam with international supervision and control, and what Le Duc Tho called healing "the wounds of war and to rehabilitate the economy in North Vietnam."

"After the signing of this agreement, the cease-fire will become effective at once."

Kissinger had dreamed of this moment for four years.

"While making these new proposals, we do not want to let the political issues of South Vietnam, which are the most difficult, to prolong our negotiations; we wish to rapidly end the war, in response to the peaceful aspirations of the people of both countries. At the same time we have paid attention to the questions of your greatest concern," concluded Le Duc Tho.

Luu Van Loi, who was present at these meetings, wrote that Kissinger and his assistants had been taking notes, but Kissinger now interrupted Tho and asked: "Would you give us your proposal, will you spare us taking notes?"

"We shall give you the text of our proposal," Tho answered. "In this proposal, we do not demand the setting up of an Administration of National Reconciliation before the cease-fire. We will let the two South Vietnamese parties set it up within three months after the cease-fire at the latest." This was the key. Thieu's resignation was no longer a requirement, although Tho was unaware that Thieu had offered to resign before that session.

John Negroponte described the moment. "I remember this rather vividly. Le Duc Tho took the proposal out of his pocket. He handed it to our side, he said, 'I'm sure you are in a hurry to bring the war to a conclusion.' And we nodded. And he said, 'Well, here is a plan—a comprehensive plan—to end the war and restore peace in Vietnam.' We of course were rather excited by this document, because it was the first time a proposal had been put to us in the framework of an agreement—it was not a five point plan, or a four point plan, or a three point proposal. It was an actual text of a treaty to end the war. And we, of course, immediately took a break to go outdoors in the garden there at the safe house and consult each other and have an opportunity to read the agreement . . . and Dr. Kissinger's immediate reaction was that this document really did contain the seeds for a breakthrough."

Hanoi had finally separated military and political questions and no longer demanded Thieu's head as a precondition of peace. "For nearly four years we had longed for this day," wrote Kissinger. "We have done it!" declared Haig. Kissinger described the moment as the most thrilling in all his years of public service.

Le Duc Tho proposed that the time limit for the withdrawal of U.S. forces should be 60 days; there was still a difference of 15 days in the proposals of the two sides. "If you agree, we can divide these 15 days in two," said Tho.

"I had the same idea as you, I intended to propose 67 days and half," joked Kissinger.

"I said 60 days only. For us a few days is of no importance. You have remained in our country for over ten years and we still have enough force to cope with you, if you stay 7 days more it doesn't matter," said Tho.

When Le Duc Tho finished, Kissinger said, "Mr. Special Adviser, Mr. Minister, first of all I should say that I fully share the ideas that Mr. Special Adviser has just expressed. Our two countries will achieve peace, and peace will open a new relationship between them. This relationship will change the hostile relations that have existed for many years now. On the basis of your ideas and your way of presentation, I think you have opened a new page in the history of our negotiations and we can possibly reach an early settlement."

In fact, Hanoi's proposal was a reiteration, under different wording, of its major points combined with the concessions already made by the United States, such as the nonwithdrawal of North Vietnamese troops. It still had the NCR described in a manner that would lead inexorably to a coalition government, and this would become a major issue in Kissinger's forthcoming meetings in Saigon.

Kissinger and his team spent most of the night reviewing and expanding on the North Vietnamese proposal, confident that an agreement could be reached. Negroponte recalled, "We adjourned the meeting that day, streaked back to the Embassy in Paris, where we had also set up our offices. And Dr. Kissinger had us sit up virtually the entire night to draft what was in effect a counterproposal to the Vietnamese document."

The Vietnamese proposal and the United States counterproposal represented concessions by both sides. The North Vietnamese no longer insisted as a precondition for a cease-fire a settlement on the political question of the Thieu government. The United States, on its own part, would settle for a cease-fire in place (including the Easter Offensive troops) in return for its POWs and the removal of its military combat forces and equipment.

Kissinger envisioned a timetable that would complete the agreement by October 11, 1972; he would return to Washington and be back in Saigon on October 15, 16, 17, and 18 for discussions. If Thieu went along, Kissinger would go to Hanoi on October 19 and return to Washington by October 21. The president would be able to announce the agreement by October 22 at the latest. The signing could occur by October 25 or 26, two weeks before the election.

The mood was so jovial that Kissinger said that after the war, he would like to visit the Ho Chi Minh Trail. "I will go with you and visit the Ho Chi Minh trail, but I am afraid that you are not strong enough to climb up the hills," joked Tho. When Tho said that crossing the Red River was possible only via a floating bridge, he told Kissinger "Maybe you will have to get down by parachute."

* * *

The following days were consumed with details, but hardly insignificant ones. Tho rejected repeated attempts by Kissinger to insert the words "North Vietnamese forces" in discussing disposition of forces. "This is a matter of principle for us," said Tho. "I have been telling you so for four years now, therefore I cannot accept this sentence. This approach is incorrect and too one-sided, while you have been building the South Vietnamese army to over ten divisions and they remain intact!"

Kissinger put forward an important question regarding the release of detained and arrested persons who were now political prisoners. Kissinger proposed separating the question of civilian prisoners from American POWs, saying, "The question of other Vietnamese personnel should be settled by the South Vietnamese parties." This question of political prisoners was "resolved" in provision 8c of the final accord and became one of the most contentious of the negotiations. To the North Vietnamese, the question of detainees was a very important matter because over the years, the Thieu regime had arrested and detained a great number of cadres and workers of the PRG and the NLF. When the war ended, Le Duc Tho did not want these detainees rotting away in jail. "When the cease-fire is installed, all of these persons must be released," demanded Le Duc Tho. "The same measures were taken after the Geneva Agreements of 1954 on Vietnam and 1962 on Laos." Eventually he would be betrayed by Kissinger on this point.

The meeting on October 11, 1972, was the longest of all private meetings, lasting 16 hours. Much of the morning session was occupied by Le Duc Tho's maneuvering for reparations ("healings of war") to be paid by the United States. When the discussion finally focused on point-by-point provisions of a cease-fire in place, the North Vietnamese wrote, "The armed forces of both sides shall remain in place within their zone of control." But Kissinger was reluctant to accept the term "zone of control" until Xuan Thuy clarified that there would be three zones: one under the control of the PRG, one under the control of Saigon, and one in contention. Kissinger accepted these terms and later that day cabled Bunker "to request Thieu to exert the greatest efforts to encroach on the PRG controlled areas, as much as possible." The more land he could capture before the cease-fire went into effect, the more he would control under the terms of the cease-fire in place. Kissinger also agreed that the United States would remove and deactivate the mines and destroy all the mines in the ports and waterways of North Vietnam.

Le Duc Tho and Kissinger expressed satisfaction with the agreement. Kissinger proposed a new timetable that would have the treaty signed by October 31, and both sides left jubilant about the accord. The Vietnamese delegation sent a letter of self-congratulations to the Politburo in Hanoi: "We have achieved four objectives (end of U.S. military involvement, cease-fire in SVN and NVN, withdrawal of U.S. forces, recognition of the existence of two administrations, two armies, two zones of control, recognition of the democratic liberties in SVN—moreover U.S. acceptance of the responsibility for post war reconstruction)." Nevertheless, the Vietnamese delegation expressed reservation that Nixon may not want to sign until after the presidential election and that they were remaining alert for a "public offensive."

On October 12, 1972, Haig and Kissinger returned to Washington.

Haldeman had already gone home, but Nixon abruptly called him back for dinner at the White House. Kissinger told Nixon that night, "Well you've got 3 for 3," implying that problems in China, the Soviet Union, and Vietnam were now settled. Kissinger told Nixon that Le Duc Tho had finally said, "After 4 years of negotiating, it is time to make peace." Nixon, sitting in his easy chair, appeared "incredulous" at first and started questioning Kissinger. Becoming nervous, Kissinger pulled out his secret red folder and "made the point over and over that we got a much better deal by far than we had expected. The net effect is that it leaves Thieu in office. We get a stand-in-place cease-fire on October 30 or 31." The cease-fire would be followed by a complete withdrawal of troops within 60 days and the return of POWs. "We'd have everything done by the end of the year," Kissinger concluded. Nixon found the idea of economic aid to Vietnam to be significant since it was a rejection of "communist principles." He told the group, "This gives us leverage on them."

Nixon was apparently satisfied, though a few days later he would send Haig to confer with Haldeman about Kissinger's projection. As Haldeman recorded Haig's conversation, "He shares the Ps view that Henry is strongly motivated in all this by a desire for personally being the one to bring about the final peace settlement. Al feels that this poses a major problem in that it's causing him to push harder for a settlement and to accept a less favorable thing than he might if he didn't have this push. . . . Haig urges us that while Henry is gone we give every possible evidence to him that we can of total support so that we won't feel that he has to prove anything."

On October 12, however, Nixon seemed mostly celebratory ("cranked up," according to Haldeman). He ordered the opening of a 1957 bottle of Lafite-Rothschild, "usually just served to the President and the rest of us have some California beaulieu Vineyard stuff. . . . Overall it boils down to a super-historic night if it all holds together, and Henry is now convinced that it will," wrote Haldeman. "The real basic problem boils down to the question of whether Thieu can be sold on it."

CHAPTER NINE

Thieu Kills the Deal

In the week that remained before the U.S. election, Thieu would do everything possible to kill the deal, apparently in the false belief that he could get better terms later. Kissinger would fail to achieve his preelection coup de grace, though it would have no ill effect on the November vote or on his job. The chief lesson that emerged was that the U.S.'s greatest challenge now lay in spinning its ally, not in negotiating with its enemy. Kissinger's task was to get his ally to agree to the deal.

On October 13 Bunker cabled Kissinger that there might be a repeat of 1968 in process because President Thieu might again hold out for better terms after the election. "I have been refreshing my memory by reading over some of the memoranda covering the period November/December 1968 and have been fearful that we may be heading into a similar situation; what we see now has a somewhat ominous tone of history repeating itself." Apparently Thieu might have thought that a reelected Nixon would be tougher on the North than candidate Nixon could afford.

Nevertheless, Kissinger certainly believed that October 31 was a realistic date for settlement. He cabled Bunker that the time had arrived to get the ambassador's "best estimate of what we may be able to get Thieu to do with respect to the estimated 30,000 political prisoners he holds in South Vietnam. . . . Obviously a major problem for Hanoi involves Thieu's willingness to release at least a portion of the political prisoners in conjunction with a cease-fire."

Kissinger also told Bunker that Thieu "must understand that the period ahead is not parallel to the 1968 period either for him or for us." The U.S. would never drop Thieu, but that if Hanoi accepted the proposals, the president would move ahead with or without him. "We will not sell him out. But he must be under no illusions that he can stare us down." How would it be possible to bomb Hanoi for not abiding by the terms of the accord if America's ally had not agreed to the terms as well?

In order to put Thieu at ease, Nixon ordered expedited shipments of additional military equipment to South Vietnam to arrive no later than November 1. On October 14, Ambassador Bunker came to the Presidential Palace to meet with Thieu. Bunker explained that in order to get ready for an in-place cease-fire there was "the need for our side to regain as much territory as possible." Thieu assured Bunker that he was moving aggressively in this area. "He had instructed General Vien, the South Vietnamese JCS head, to clean out the enemy quickly and brutally." There was little hint of disagreement between the two countries.

Yet, it became increasingly apparent that President Thieu was having serious qualms. Haldeman recorded, "Both the P and Henry are realizing in the cold gray light of dawn today that they still have a plan that can fall apart, mainly the problem of getting Thieu on board." In another candid diary entry Haldeman wrote, "The settlement he's got is the best Thieu is ever going to get and unlike '68 when Thieu screwed Johnson, he had Nixon as an alternative. Now he has McGovern as an alternative which would be a disaster for him, even worse than the worst possible thing that Nixon could do to him."

In Saigon, President Thieu was bracing for the bad news of the specifics of the agreement. John Negroponte had already told Kissinger and others on the negotiating team that when Thieu saw the proposed text, he would view it as a betrayal. Kissinger considered sending Thieu an earlier draft with even worse terms, hoping that Thieu would then jump to sign the current proposal. There was a fateful delay of four days, until October 18, before Kissinger would share it with him. Meanwhile, a letter from Nixon on October 16 told Thieu that he needed to understand that the most important feature of the proposed treaty was that his government, armed forces, and political institutions would remain intact.

History loves to thumb its nose at the best-laid plans, sometimes with the oddest of coincidences. On October 17 Thieu received a captured enemy document found in an underground bunker in a remote VC district in Quang Tin Province. Titled "General Instructions for a Cease-Fire," Thieu now realized that "communist cadres in an isolated province of Central Vietnam knew more about the details of the Paris talks than he did." Prospects for a peace settlement were suddenly nil. Not only was a draft text apparently circulating, a draft he had not yet seen, but the communists were already devising a strategy for furthering their advantage by occupying as much territory as possible in anticipation of the "stand-still" or "in-place" peace. Suspicious for some time that he was being shut out of the talks, this information confirmed his worst fears. Thieu would now formulate a counteroffensive.

That very day, meanwhile, Kissinger was giving both sides even more reason for suspicion, though Thieu could not have known it and Tho did not realize it. Kissinger and his North Vietnamese counterparts were meeting again, discussing the 30,000 political detainees. Kissinger restated the problem, first admitting that "we will have left Vietnam by the time the consequences of these provisions are apparent. The difficulty we now face is that you are first asking that all of your forces can stay in the South—the second is that on top of this you are then asking Saigon to release some 30,000 individuals whom they consider to likely engage in military activities against Saigon." Then he fudged: "So we have looked for a formula in which we did not have to settle this issue now, but at the same time, retain the possibility of using our maximum influence to bring about a favorable result with our ally after a settlement is arranged."

Kissinger was walking on thin ice in this deception of both Le Duc Tho and the South Vietnamese. As he framed it to Tho, "So the choice is not between no one being released and everyone being released. The choice is about some substantial number being released initially and the remainder being released over a two-month period. . . . So we can do one of two things. We can either stick with what we have, shorten it to two months with an undertaking by us to you that we would certainly bring about a very substantial release—and give you that number before the agreement goes into effect—during the period of the withdrawals. And a second undertaking from us that we would use our maximum influence to bring about a satisfactory resolution during the two months for the remainder. Or we can write down one of the versions of the Geneva Agreement and take it to Saigon, with the possibility of meeting here again at this time next week if we run into major difficulties—which I am certain we shall. I recognize that this is a profound human problem for you. So I am approaching it not without sympathy for your point of view but from a desire to find a practical resolution, in order to bring a more rapid end to the war."

Much seemed to hang on the vague promise to wield "maximum influence" with the South to get the majority of the detainees released after the treaty went into effect, but nothing concrete was guaranteed on that score.

Kissinger concluded the meeting by telling Tho, "I believe that the US proposals will be accepted by Saigon." According to Luu Van Loi's notes from the meeting, Xuan Thuy said, "We want to end the war, the hostility and hatred among the South Vietnamese people, but after the cease-fire and the signing of the agreement, if the Saigon administration continues to keep a number of persons in detention, the PRG also will not release all the prisoners, even some U.S. personnel." Despite this threat, Kissinger would almost immediately tell Thieu, amazingly, that he should *hold on* to the detainees and use them for leverage in getting the North's troops out of the South. Thieu viewed this as a ploy by Kissinger to bargain with the North because the South had no interest in releasing the prisoners until their own prisoners were released.

On the evening of October 18, Kissinger flew directly from Paris to Saigon to brief President Thieu on the peace agreement. The October 19 meeting lasted nearly two hours (11:00 A.M.–1:00 P.M.) in the military operations room adjoining Thieu's presidential office in Independence Palace. After patiently listening to Kissinger's presentation, Thieu asked for a copy of the text. He was handed the English text, missing a new timetable that included an accelerated date for signing of October 31, which Kissinger and Tho had worked out.

Everything about the meeting went badly. First, Nha was given the text in English only. He responded indignantly: "We cannot negotiate the fate of our country in a foreign language!" He was outraged and demanded the Vietnamese version. Nha challenged Kissinger by asking if the North Vietnamese had given Kissinger an English or Vietnamese text. Kissinger conceded that it was a Vietnamese text and that his staff had then translated it into English. Nha demanded to see the Vietnamese text—the one given to Kissinger by the communists. As Nha recalls the exchange, Kissinger said, "Oh, we forgot. I said, what do you mean, you forgot?" Nha mocked the entire process, telling Kissinger, "You mean to tell me an American could understand Vietnamese better than a Vietnamese? We want to see the Vietnamese text. . . . Send your linguist back to school." But Kissinger did not have the text with him, and it would only later be sent by courier to the South Vietnamese. It was then that Nha recognized that the South Vietnamese were being asked to sign an agreement that was tantamount to surrender.

Since Kissinger did not have the document with him, all he could do was summarize the deal in a 45-minute talk. Nha recalled, "He said, well, this new settlement is a complete deterioration of the North Vietnamese position, and [that] even Mr. Le Duc Tho embraced me [Kissinger] and wept, at which time, I stared at him in complete disbelief. I said, Le Duc Tho? An old communist hand? Weeping? And I made the joke, which he didn't like. [I said:] Be careful of the crocodile tears."

Afterward, Thieu told Nha, "I wanted to punch Kissinger in the mouth."

John Negroponte recalled the exchange in somewhat more diplomatic terms:

I do not believe that the Saigon government was sufficiently aware of the evolution of our own thinking in this regard [on the question of troop withdrawals]. And this is the reason why, when we went to Saigon with those fateful negotiating sessions with the South Vietnamese, that they raised the issue of North Vietnamese troop withdrawal, and asked why that had not been dealt with in our document? And they insisted that we go back to the Vietnamese and raise this issue. Now, most of us on the delegation knew that this would not likely do any good. And would not likely meet with any success on the part of the North Vietnamese. . . . The atmosphere in Saigon when we brought to Saigon a draft of the treaty we had negotiated with the North Vietnamese was very tense and very unpleasant. And this I ascribed to the fact that it came pretty much as a complete surprise to the South Vietnamese. They had been briefed in very general terms in the preceding weeks and months, but no one had ever been so explicit as to show them significant drafts of treaty language. And now here we were arriving in October of 1972 with a complete treaty to end the war, which had a direct bearing—in fact, an almost total bearing on their existence as a state in the future. And we were asking them to sign on the bottom line. So the atmosphere was very tense, and President Thieu reacted very badly to the draft agreement. And I think felt cornered. He wasn't certain he knew what to do about it. But the one thing he was sure of was that he wanted to find a way to delay.

In fact, as the record shows, Thieu had been briefed on the troop disposition—but Negroponte is right that he so hated the idea he could not yet accept it.

The South Vietnamese sensed betrayal, and a working group convened for lunch at Le Cave in order to discuss the provisions that Kissinger had just outlined, although they still did not have a copy of the Vietnamese text.

At 5 P.M. that same day, Nha briefed Thieu on the preliminary findings of the working group and identified 64 clarifications that Thieu would need from Kissinger. President Thieu agreed with the strategy as outlined by Nha.

Nha stayed up late into the night reading the American translation of the text. For the first time, the South Vietnamese learned if not the general nature of concessions to Le Duc Tho, certainly their depth and consequences. Nha discovered that there were points in the text that "we completely had rejected during the previous secret negotiations, and we thought that the American side had agreed with us to not raise the issues anymore, and now we see that those matters are being brought up again by the Communists in one form or another."

From their point of view, Le Duc Tho had apparently won the negotiating war. The text referred to the three nations of Indochina: Laos, Cambodia, and Vietnam. Thus, right at the beginning Vietnam was described as one country, not two. How could its own troops be removed from one country? Nha asked Kissinger what happened to the "four states." Kissinger assured him it was a typographical error. Nha laughed. "I said I know how you guys work, and the word, the number 'three' is not written in there, the word 'three' is not a number, it's three, T-H-R-E-E, so that was one thing that we didn't like."

As Tran Van Don recalled, there was another issue with country tallies that contradicted this one: "The draft mentioned the 'three nations of Indochina' and three Vietnams. However, since 1954, four countries had existed on the Indochinese peninsula, not just *de facto* but *de jure,* as sanctioned by the Geneva Convention and through diplomatic recognition by many nations on every continent. These four nations were North Vietnam, South Vietnam, Laos, and Cambodia. Conversely, there could in no way be discussion of 'Three Vietnams' since the National Liberation Front as a puppet of Hanoi could not pretend to represent a second state south of the 17th parallel."

Next, Nha surmised that the so-called National Council of Reconciliation and Concord (NCRC) was de facto a "disguised coalition because the Communists had been a little bit smarter than the United States." The English text referred to that council as an "administrative structure," while the Vietnamese text said that it was "co cau chanh guyen," which should be translated as governmental structure, thus implying a structure from the top to the bottom and covering the whole government—executive, legislative, and judicial branches and functions. This became a major issue for the South Vietnamese.

Finally, Nha noticed that the disposition of North Vietnamese forces had not been made clear, and the question of the DMZ was completely erased, in violation of the 1962 Laotian accords. By the time he was done, Nha came up with 64 points that needed elaboration before any agreement could be reached.

After Nha's night of study, at 10:00 A.M. on October 20, the working group met with Kissinger at the home of Tram Van Lam on Hop Thap Tu Street. Tram Van Lam, a Catholic, offered the opening prayer: "May God bless this meeting between the representatives of the Republic of South Vietnam and Dr. Kissinger." Nha then demanded the 64 clarifications from Kissinger, of which Kissinger considered no fewer than 8 important. The meeting was extremely contentious, but the South Vietnamese held their ground. Nha left to warn President Thieu that Kissinger had come to Saigon to betray South Vietnam, that this was a matter of life and death, and that the president needed to develop a strategy for dealing with Kissinger.

Nha convinced Thieu to cancel a meeting with Kissinger later that day. Kissinger was furious, telling Nha, "I am the Special Envoy of the President of the United States of America. You know I cannot be treated as an errand boy. I insist on seeing president Thieu tonight." Nha's response was firm: "Don't take offense, I never considered you an errand boy. The president cannot see you and it truly is because of the meeting with the military chiefs. It will last four hours." Actually, two meetings were being held simultaneously. The first was Thieu's meeting with the military province chiefs, convened to brief them on the Kissinger plan but also to warn them of communist plans that had been found in the bunker. As Thieu met with his military chiefs, Nha and the working group briefed the National Security Council in the vice president's residence.

Kissinger was especially upset because he had just learned that Arnaud de Borchgrave, a *Newsweek* senior correspondent who had been in Hanoi to conduct an interview with Prime Minister Pham Van Dong, was about to release a damaging story. Dong's interview would reveal that an accord had been reached, with the signing scheduled for Paris on October 31. It reported the main American issues: the POWs were coming home, the U.S. was withdrawing, and a coalition government without Thieu would be constituted. Dong referred to a "coalition of transition," and when de Borchgrave asked whether Thieu could be part of a coalition, Dong replied, "Thieu has been overtaken by events. And events are now following their own course." De Borchgrave, like most other observers, was unaware that

Hanoi had dropped its demand for a coalition government in the secret ne-gotiations. Kissinger had wanted to warn Thieu personally because this story was everything that Nha and Thieu feared. The NCRC was now pub-licly identified as a coalition government, and the press was about to report that following an American troop withdrawal, Thieu might not even be part of the government.

Kissinger must have realized by now that Thieu would refuse to sign. Nonetheless, he left Saigon for Cambodia, where he and Premier Lon Nol toasted "peace in Vietnam." Bunker cabled Haig that "Lon Nol's reaction to our proposal, like Souvanna and Thanom, had been extremely favorable." While in Phnom Penh, Kissinger left Lon Nol with the impression that Thieu had endorsed the accords. When Thieu learned what happened, he grew more and more outraged at Kissinger's audacity.

Peace was still a long way off. On October 21 Kissinger returned from Phnom Penh and went directly to see Thieu, who by now had fully digested the Vietnamese-language text. Four people were present at this confronta-tion: Kissinger, Bunker, Thieu, and Nha. Thieu, in a "tense and highly emo-tional state," thought the proposed agreement was even worse than the 1954 agreements: "I have a right to expect that the U.S. has connived with the Soviets and China. Now that you recognize the presence of North Viet-namese here, the South Vietnamese people will assume that we have been sold out by the United States and that North Vietnam has won the war."

He continued, "Dr. Kissinger said the other day that Le Duc Tho had burst into tears, but I can assure him the South Vietnamese people are the ones who deserve to cry, and the one who should cry is I. . . . If the U.S. wants to abandon the South Vietnamese people, that is their right!" Thieu harkened back to an earlier period. "Ever since the U.S. asked me to resign and bargained with me on the time of my resignation, had I not been a good soldier I would have resigned, because I see that those whom I regard as friends have failed me. However great the personal humiliation for me I shall continue to fight. My greatest satisfaction will be when I can sign a peace agreement. I have not told anyone that the Americans asked me to re-sign, since they would share my humiliation, but have made it appear vol-untary on my part."

Kissinger expressed amazement that Thieu could have suspected he and Haig of spreading rumors and conniving against Thieu. Notes of the meet-ing record Kissinger's response: "Never had he, as a representative of the president, been subjected to such treatment as he had experienced here in the last four days—nor had the Ambassador experienced in the last month." Kissinger added, "We have fought for 4 years, have mortgaged our whole foreign policy to the defense of one country. What you have said has been a very bitter thing to hear."

Kissinger tried to assure Thieu that he had never been cut out or not consulted. The disagreements between them now threatened everything; all the sacrifices and achievements to date were about to be undone. The president had risked everything for Thieu:

> When we talked with the Soviets and Chinese, it was to pressure them to exert pressure on Hanoi. We genuinely believed that the proposed agreement preserved South Viet-Nam's freedom—our principles have been the same as yours and we have defended them. You have only one problem. President Nixon has many. Your conviction that we have undermined you will be understood by no American, least of all by President Nixon. We have not recognized the right of North Viet-Nam to be in the South. We have used the language of the Geneva Accords, since we thought this the best way to work out a practical solution. Had we wanted to sell you out, there have been many easier ways by which we could have accomplished this. We do not regard the Agreement as embodying a coalition government, but as a major communist defeat. With respect to the DMZ we may be able to add another sentence, which would clarify this point. We are faced with a practical problem. Concerning the immediate situation, it is imperative not to have a confrontation. Should the U.S. withdraw, it will affect all of your neighbors. The longer-term problem is what happens to our relationship. I do not see how the U.S. can justify to the Congress what it is we are fighting for. We have not destroyed your government; we have obtained better terms than any American would have believed possible. Concerning your resignation, we think that the January 25 speech got us through this Congressional period and enabled us to get appropriations in an election year. It is impossible to say that President Nixon who risked the summit meeting with the Soviets could conceivably undermine you. It is clear now that we cannot continue with the present negotiations. I would like to know how you view that we should proceed from here.

President Thieu responded that despite all that had happened, he was grateful to President Nixon for all that he had done for South Vietnam. He knew that Nixon had to act in his own interests and the interests of his peo-

ple. He too would have to act in the interests of the South Vietnamese people. "I have been the subject of organized slander in the U.S. press and pictured as an obstruction to peace."

Still, Thieu was not prepared to give in on the points of clarification. Indeed, he never believed these reassurances because he was firmly convinced
that Kissinger was merely grasping at the pole the North Vietnamese gave
him and was intended to pressure the South—nothing more. "The omis-
sions and language in the agreement were telltale signs of the U.S. abandoning all our previous positions," recalled Nha. Kissinger had abandoned all
mutually agreed-on positions with America's ally and, in Thieu's view, had
taken on the role of selling the North Vietnam plan to the South.

The deal was far from done, and Kissinger cancelled his return trip to
Hanoi. He cajoled, telling Thieu that the course he was following would be
suicidal. He could not understand, nor could Nixon, why Thieu was behaving this way. Thieu retorted by noting that there were 200,000 to 300,000
Northern troops in the South and that the NCRC had three segments. "If
we accept the document as it stands, we will commit suicide—and I will be
committing suicide."

Kissinger again reassured Thieu that the United States would never sacrifice
a trusted friend, and Thieu needed to understand that no one, least of all
Kissinger and Haig, took the NCRC seriously and that the phrase had no
meaning in English. "In the United States the NCRC would be considered an
absurdity, a tremendous defeat for Hanoi." In a last desperate attempt to sway
Thieu, Kissinger told him that in six months, American congressional funding
would be cut off. Despite Kissinger's pleas, Thieu still refused to sign.

Kissinger said to Nha, "The President has chosen to act the martyr, but he
hasn't got what it takes! If we have to, the United States can sign a separate
peace treaty with Hanoi. As for me, I'll never set foot in Saigon again. Not
after this. This is the worst failure of my diplomatic career!"

"We are so sorry," added Nha, "but you must remember that we have a
country to defend!"

Thieu asked Kissinger to communicate his fears to Nixon. He pointed at
the maps and said, "What does it matter to the United Sates to lose a small
country like South Vietnam? We're scarcely more than a dot on the map of
the world to you. If you want to give up the struggle, we will fight on alone
until our resources are gone, and then we will die. The United States' world
policy dictates that you dance lightly with Moscow and Peking, that you
make different choices to follow your new strategies. But for us, the choice

is between life and death. For us to put our signatures to an accord, which is tantamount to surrender would be accepting a death sentence, because life without liberty is death. No it's worse than death!"

Kissinger warned Thieu that the media, the press, and intellectuals all had a vested interest in the United States defeat. When he returned to the United States, he promised to hold a press conference and give the impression that progress was being made, that a war that had lasted ten years could not be settled in a week. Finally, he noted that the next round would only be worse: "It is hardly conceivable that Congressional support can continue. Unfortunately, we are in the position now of having to make concessions. We thought we had achieved victory, but obviously were mistaken."

At the end of this meeting Thieu told Kissinger that he saw no reason for them to meet again and asked Kissinger to convey the South Vietnamese position to President Nixon. But Kissinger requested that the meetings continue so as to give the impression that the talks were still going on and were not deadlocked. As Nha recalled, "President Thieu and I grinned at that request and agreed to another meeting the following day."

It was then that Kissinger made a last attempt to convince Thieu, but to no avail. Kissinger cabled Haig on October 22, "It is hard to exaggerate the toughness of Thieu's position. His demands verge on insanity." At 8:00 A.M. on Monday, October 23, Kissinger returned to the palace. He assured Thieu that "there never have been talk or communications with the other side which have not been communicated to you. You have been apprised fully of every development as it has occurred and have been consulted on every move we have made with the single exception of the meeting on September 15 when we believed it necessary to move before we had heard from you." He continued, "You must understand how it seems to an individual who has stood against 300,000 demonstrators, against bureaucratic and Congressional opposition, against public opinion and the press—this is why I took the liberty of speaking as I did. Both your present and former Ambassadors will tell you who stood for you and who against. As I mentioned yesterday, I believe the course you are following is suicidal."

Changing tactics, Kissinger reassuringly told Thieu that there was no need for him to worry because President Nixon was certain to be reelected. "Please sign the accord. If they violate it, we will launch an operation into North Vietnam."

"But where?" Thieu queried. "A landing or an invasion through the 17th parallel?"

Kissinger replied: "In the region just north of the DMZ."

Thieu disagreed with Kissinger, saying, "To be effective, the landing should be in the vicinity of Vinh."

Kissinger pleaded with Thieu that he not reveal the tone and content of their discussions to the media. Nha reminded Kissinger that "leaks always come from the U.S. side through 'deep backgrounders' and that at the first sign of such backgrounders, the South Vietnamese would reveal everything.

Kissinger returned to Washington, D.C., on October 23, full of despair.

* * *

On October 24 President Thieu addressed the people of Vietnam on radio and television in a two-hour speech concerning the possible settlement of the war. He sought not to be preempted by Kissinger, who was going to manipulate the U.S. process and accuse the South Vietnamese of blocking the prospects to peace. "We also had to keep our promise not to reveal what our two sides had discussed in the last four days," Nha recalled. "Thus I came up with a ploy to tell our countrymen about the substance of the peace agreement without referring to the draft. For that I used the NLF September 11 declaration and proceeded to compile details of the most dangerous clauses. Thieu and I prepared that speech without telling anybody in our government because we suspected word would get back to the Vietnamese Embassy. That is why the speech was such a surprise to the Embassy."

Instead of his customary style of reading polished and literary text in a monotone, Thieu extemporized in an informal and folksy manner. He used colloquialisms and adopted a noticeable southern slur in an attempt to connect with the working and farming classes. He paused twice to take out a handkerchief and wipe perspiration from his face.

Thieu reviewed the history of past GVN peace initiatives and then focused on the communists' September 11, 1972, proposal for a tripartite government. He disparaged the "third force" as lackeys of the communists. He pulled out the captured documents explaining secret instructions to their cadres on how to violate the cease-fire and liberation zones. Thieu said that the only reason the communists wanted a cease-fire was to drive all the Americans out in order to facilitate their conquest of the South. Their troops remained in place. Thieu appealed to Vietnamese nationalism in order to save their country from a false peace. The future of seventeen and a half million people of South Vietnam was at stake, and President Thieu wanted his countrymen to know that he would never stand in the way of a truly lasting peace and that he was willing to step down once peace had been guaranteed. Thieu closed by warning that a coalition government would lead to bloodletting in the South; he predicted that as many as 5 million people would be massacred.

Kissinger returned to Washington where on October 26 (October 25 evening in Vietnam) he held a press conference on the status of the Vietnam negotiations. Kissinger began with a response to both North and South Vietnam's versions of what had transpired during the fateful weeks of October: "Ladies and gentlemen, we have now heard from both Vietnams, and it is obvious that a war that has been raging for ten years is drawing to a conclusion, and that this is a traumatic experience for all of the participants. The President thought that it might be helpful if I came out here and spoke to you about what we have been doing, where we stand, and to put the various allegations and charges into perspective. . . . We believe that *peace is at hand*. We believe that an agreement is within sight, based upon the May 8 proposal of the President and some adaptation of our January 25th proposal, which is just to all parties. It is inevitable that in a war of such complexity that there should be occasional difficulties in reaching a final solution, but we believe that by far the longest part of the road has been traversed, and what stands in the way of an agreement now are issues that are relatively less important than those that have already been settled."

Kissinger later recalled,

The peace is at hand press conference was not something that we had planned to do. It was something that was *imposed* on us by the North Vietnamese. We woke up on the morning of October 26 with the news that the North Vietnamese had published the preliminary understandings we had negotiated with them two weeks earlier in Paris and in this period between October 8 and October 26 there had been exhausting and long negotiations with the North Vietnamese followed by equally exhausting and long and frustrating negotiations with the South Vietnamese so when we woke up to that news our basic concern was two-fold. One, not to let the North Vietnamese stampede us into something that Saigon was not yet ready to do but on the other hand, not to give Hanoi the impression that we were overthrowing the agreement and the phrase "peace at hand" was chosen to indicate that we were sticking to the fundamentals of the agreement, but at the same time that something still remained to be done was a warning to Saigon that we were not going to be driven off our course, a signal to Hanoi that we were sticking to the main lines of the agreement, and the fact that still some things remained to be done. Had we had three days to

prepare for it we might have chosen a happier phrase and one that lent itself less to later second guessing, but we only had an hour or two to prepare for it.

Hoang Duc Nha later laughed when recalling Kissinger's remark that
peace is at hand: "I don't know what Mr. Kissinger meant, but I still see war
around the corner. That was my oblique answer to a seemingly, how should
I say, what I saw as a deliberate part of Mr. Kissinger to think that peace is
right near, and that the South Vietnamese were still obstructing it."
John Negroponte offered the following assessment:

I think it would be very unfair to blame President Thieu alone for delaying
the agreement. He had not been previously familiar with the text; it severely impacted on the fate of his own country, and he wanted time to reflect on the provisions of the agreement, and also wanted the opportunity
to perhaps secure some changes in it. So in effect, what Thieu did was to
ask for time. Under these circumstances President Nixon and Dr. Kissinger
felt they had no choice but to delay the timetable that had been tentatively
agreed to earlier, with the North Vietnamese, and therein lies the explanation for the delay in concluding the agreement. . . . My explanation of
[peace is at hand] had always been my feeling that Dr. Kissinger wanted to
reassure the North Vietnamese that we in fact intended as soon as we
could to go through the agreement in the form in which it had been
agreed, because, for a moment put yourself in the North Vietnamese
shoes. They had gone through this entire negotiating process, they had
reached agreement with us. They had even begun giving instructions to
their cadre to prepare for a cease-fire, and some of their cadre had, in fact,
exposed themselves to the South Vietnamese security forces at the time
that they thought the cease-fire was to go into effect. So, some of the
North Vietnamese leaders might have begun to think that they were, they
had been victims in the biggest con job in history and that we had simply
led them down the garden path of a negotiating process sufficiently close
to our own elections and then we were gong to welsh on the deal. . . . Dr.
Kissinger's statement to the effect that peace is at hand, I have always construed to mean a reassurance to the Vietnamese that we were very close to
an agreement, that we would do our best to conclude one.

Several years later, during a private luncheon on February 21, 1975, in
the secretary of state's dining room, Kissinger confided to McGovern that

he had made his "peace is at hand" speech not to hurt McGovern but rather to nail down General Thieu and his own colleagues in the administration so they would not back away from the negotiations once the election was over. Kissinger needed to commit hawks in his own administration publicly in this way too, he claimed. "It was the only way I could consolidate the understanding we had with Hanoi to reassure them that we saw the obstacles to peace as few and small, not as complicated and overriding." Kissinger told McGovern that it was Haldeman who was most opposed to signing off on the agreement before the election, since the election was already won and the administration needed to protect itself from the charge that it had sold out to Asia. Yet the hawks by 1972 were few and far between—and surely McGovern would not have picked up any votes from anyone who thought the United States had sold out South Vietnam.

On October 28, 1972, Bunker cabled Kissinger with disturbing news. We had learned that Thieu was in possession of intelligence intercepts of Hanoi's and NLF instructions to cadres in South Vietnam from October 21 and 25. These intercepts reported communist strategy as follows: "Our army and government will remain in South Vietnam. The cease-fire in place will be very profitable to us because it allows us to maintain a tooth comb or leopard skin posture in South Vietnam." By this metaphor, Bunker understood each side was going to be able to buttress their positions prior to the cease-fire and the U.S. was moving vast amounts of equipment into South Vietnam as part of the accelerated equipment shipments named Enhance and Enhance Plus. Bunker recognized that "there is thus a serious discrepancy between our position as explained to Thieu by our side and the alleged American position as reflected in the enemy's documents."

Kissinger's response offers the first clue to Nixon's view on the fate of the South. Nixon believed that the American people would support the administration if the U.S. renewed bombing the North *if* the communists first broke the truce. Since 150,000 troops were in the South, it was patently obvious that they would break the treaty and attack, even though Kissinger insisted that just the opposite would happen: they would go home once they realized that they could not move and could not reinforce.

Thus, Nixon was trying to sign a peace agreement merely in order to enable him to continue the war without American troops. Kissinger cabled Bunker that "Thieu must understand that in dealing with the subject the likelihood of the North Vietnamese treachery is an essential facet of our assessments. One reason we are trying to do our utmost to maintain a common front with Saigon is to enable us to continue support after our withdrawal in the event of violations by the other side." Kissinger continued, "The initial leopard spot situation [i.e., spots of Northern control throughout Southern territory] should be manageable. More importantly, however, if the U.S. and GVN have moved with good will and unity in the effort to achieve peace, we will be able to respond to violations by the North with the essential basis of U.S. domestic support." Whether Kissinger really believed, with Nixon, that America would ever support renewed bombing is a different question.

On October 30, 1972, Nixon wrote a lengthy personal letter to President Thieu.

"Dr. Kissinger's press conference was conducted on my detailed instructions. He was doing his utmost to prevent you from being portrayed as the obstacle to peace with an inevitable cut-off by Congress of U.S. funds to the government of South Vietnam and the creation of unmanageable impediments to continued U.S. support for you and your government. Constant criticism from Saigon can only undercut this effort. . . . I cannot fail to call to your attention the dangerous course your government is now pursuing. . . . You can be assured that my decisions as to the final character of a peace settlement are in no way influenced by the election in the United States, and you should harbor no illusions that my policy with respect to the desirability of achieving an early peace will change after the election. . . . I urge you, Mr. President, to maintain the essential unity which has characterized our relations over these past difficult four years and which has proven to be the essential ingredient in the success we have achieved thus far. Disunity will strip me of the ability to maintain the essential base of support which your Government and your people must have in the days ahead, and which I am determined to provide. Willingness to cooperate will mean that we will achieve peace on the basis of what I consider to be a workable agreement—especially with the amendments, which we are certain to obtain. From this basis, we can move with confidence and unity to achieve our mutual objectives of peace and unity for the heroic people of South Vietnam."

Nixon's words would fall on deaf ears. At his press conference, Kissinger had said that only "small details" were left to be resolved. But for the South Vietnamese, these were main principles: the DMZ, North Vietnamese troops in the South, and a coalition government. Thieu believed that Hanoi had gotten just about everything it sought from the negotiations except his elimination; he found little consolation in Nixon's letter because he realized that the future of South Vietnam could not depend on retractions and amendments to a treaty draft. It would be better to go on fighting for years than to accept these conditions for peace.

* * *

When Le Duc Tho dropped his demand for Thieu's ouster as well as the immediate creation of a coalition government, it reflected the Politburo's acceptance of the extraordinary hardships that Nixon's military policies had inflicted. The president's May 8 decision to bomb and mine and Hanoi's corresponding return to negotiations had reestablished a degree of public confidence, and Nixon was running way ahead of Senator George McGovern in opinion polls. The North Vietnamese were hurting as a direct result of the Linebacker raids.

New research in the Hanoi archives reveals that Le Duc Tho's concession came as a complete surprise to NLF leaders, who since 1968 had insisted on Thieu's removal. "Kissinger, the White House, and Le Duc Tho had seriously underestimated the response of the two southern protagonists," writes Brigham. The NLF objected to "the lack of a guarantee that civilian prisoners would be released and the fact that Thieu would be left in control of the political apparatus in Saigon." The NLF formally protested to Lao Dong officials. Madame Binh met personally with Le Duc Tho and Xuan Thuy, and "the northerners assured Madame Binh that the freedom of American POWs was tied to the liberation of civilians in the south and that Thieu would be only a figurehead until elections were held."

This issue of political prisoners was central to the NLF because so many of their members had been jailed by Thieu. Now Hanoi appeared to be insensitive to the concerns of its Southern comrades. Le Duc Tho had compromised on October 16 by no longer linking the POWs with political detainees. When Kissinger announced that "peace was at hand," NLF officials complained that Hanoi had gone too far. According to one NLF official, "Hanoi's message was clear. It cared more about the American prisoners of war, those who had fought against us, than it did for its southern comrades." In fact, the NLF was in no hurry for peace, while the Northerners wanted it badly. As Brigham observed, "Many southerners, communists and non-communists alike, simply could not understand Lao Dong's haste to reach an agreement on its policies towards the south." This would have significant consequences in December, when Hanoi endured the next wave of Linebacker bombings because the NLF had exerted such pressure for new concessions in Paris. Many Northerners never forgave their Southern communist brothers for making them endure such punishment.

* * *

Meanwhile, once Kissinger told Thieu about the proposed terms on October 19, he was free to share them with the military. Critical questions of implementation would now be addressed or at least planned for. Between October 8 and 18, not even the most senior American officials in Saigon were told what had taken place in Paris. After that, the work of the Joint Military Commission (JMC) would begin in earnest, despite the fact that Thieu was all but certain to kill the deal.

The record reveals that President Thieu was scheduled to discuss a paper on "cease-fire instructions" on October 21 that described the cease-fire plan as "a leopard's spot" variety rather than the withdrawal of forces to specific areas. This would necessitate a number of actions, which included that "all GVN operating bases would be abandoned in order that most troops would be available in a mobile role. All persons suspected of communist leanings would be rounded up and 'put in a safe place.' Elected village councils would be queried for names of individuals thought to be 'dangerous.' All houses would have flags available [i.e. to identify their allegiance]."

Among the Americans, General Fred Weyand was instructed to form a small planning group, but no written papers were to be exchanged. The South Vietnamese contact to Weyand would be General Cao Van Vien, the general chief of staff. Weyand was to provide a brief outline of his concept for a cease-fire and the role of a military commission by November 3, 1972. He believed, however, that as things now stood in Paris, the political dimensions of ending the conflict were far too intermingled with the military dimensions to permit a purely military commission to accomplish much.

General Weyand's main concern was that the specifics of what was to be accomplished under the October draft were not set forth in any detail. Why was the entire burden of translating ambiguous phrases being left to military planners? The official historian for the JMC concluded that Weyand "suspected that matters unsuccessfully negotiated in Paris over a 4-year period would have no better chance of successful resolution in South Vietnam in the middle of the combat zone."

Weyand set up a two-man planning group under Chief of Staff Major General Gilbert H. Woodward of the Military Assistance Command Vietnam (MACV). Woodward had extensive experience negotiating with communists, having been staff secretary to the Berlin Command in 1953 and senior member of the United Nations Command Armistice Commission in Korea in 1968–1969. As a young lieutenant colonel, he had confronted the Russians, and as a general officer at Panmunjom had negotiated the release of the crew of the U.S.S. *Pueblo.* The two members of the planning group were Colonel George T. Balzer, U.S. Marine Corps, and Major Paul L. Miles, U.S. Army, both from MACV's Plans and Operations Division. Miles had served in the Pentagon as aide-de-camp to General Westmoreland. He had graduated from West Point in 1960 and had studied modern history at Oxford as a Rhodes scholar. Balzer was a senior and experienced Marine combat officer.

Miles and Balzer were instructed to work in total secrecy under the supervision of Woodward and with access to Weyand. Their first task was to meet the Kissinger deadline of November 3 for "An Understanding for the Foundation of the 4- Party Joint Military Commission." Miles and Balzer gave careful consideration to what the communists might insist on organizationally; thus, they studied the communist demands during the Korean armistice and the French experience in Indochina. Miles and Balzer focused on the essential requirements for an effective cease-fire from a military viewpoint. This included the status of opposing forces, the question of territorial limits of areas controlled by belligerents, the need to forestall last-minute military operations outside areas of control, the means to police and enforce the cease-fire, and the means for replacing armaments, munitions, and other war material.

There were, however, many sensitive political issues, such as territorial control, which could be decided only by the governments concerned. For example, there was a provision calling for the commanders to meet in order to determine control of territory. This was the type of issue that should have been negotiated in Paris between the South Vietnamese and the Vietcong, but Kissinger insisted that this was not going to happen.

At a meeting at Ambassador Bunker's residence, General Weyand detailed the essential requirements for an effective cease-fire. Weyand's major concern was the same one President Thieu had voiced when he first heard that mutual withdrawal had been replaced: how to fix the status of opposing forces on the effective date of the cease-fire. Paul Miles recalled, "One of the points he [Weyand] stressed the most was that of freezing the status of the opposing forces—locations, strengths, etc—and preventing the establishment of new bases and a buildup of material."

Weyand warned Kissinger and his staff that in any true standstill cease-fire, no side should be permitted to improve its military situation and that an effective cease-fire would be possible only if the location and strength of opposing forces were fixed at the outset. Understandings on base locations, troop identification, troop size, and replacements were necessary to implement the military terms of the peace. Kissinger appeared to assume that the commission could settle what were essentially political questions, particularly the issue of who controlled what territory. It was not practical for a military commission to provide a formula for the ultimate political settlement. If the commission were charged with the task of determining who exerted political control over what territory, the chance of accomplishing the more immediate objective of a cessation of hostilities was likely to be jeopardized.

At this point, General John Wickham, Jr., also was brought into the process. An infantry officer who had served in Berlin in the early 1950s and earned an international relations degree from Harvard, he later served in Korea along the DMZ and held high-level staff assignments in Washington and troop command assignments in Vietnam and Germany. In October 1973 he was assigned to the MACV staff as director of economic affairs. He would soon become Woodward's deputy chief of the U.S. delegation.

Wickham and others believed, with Kissinger and Thieu, that the communists were unlikely to abide by the conditions of the cease-fire, so it was essential that the planning mechanism be effective. Just what *was* a cease-fire in place? It was the question that would determine South Vietnam's fate—and the reason that Thieu would not now sign the agreement. Yet the declassified military records (at least the documents that are not under Kissinger's personal control) detail a total disinterest at the highest levels in any of the details for securing the peace on the part of Kissinger and Nixon. The most plausible explanation is that Kissinger and Nixon did not expect anything from the JMC except to guarantee the return of the American POWs. This was what they and the American public expected most from the Paris negotiations. They had another plan for saving South Vietnam from the communist violations, and it had nothing to do with the work of Miles, Balzer, and others on the JMC: They planned to continue a ceasefire war.

CHAPTER TEN

Peace Is at the End of a Pen

On November 7, Richard Nixon was reelected by beating George McGovern in 49 of 50 states. "If anyone had told me [in 1968] that the war would be waging four years later, with the architects of that war victorious in 49 of 50 states, I would have said he was crazy," McGovern later said. There were many reasons for the lopsided vote. As a whole the country felt that Nixon had brought some of the worst problems under control, including Vietnam, even if peace was not yet finally at hand. American involvement in the war certainly seemed to be winding down at last.

Nixon's second term would, of course, be dominated by a scandal that was just beginning to unfold. Watergate would provide Nixon, Kissinger, and others with an unanswerable and one of the most powerful of Vietnam's what-ifs: What if Nixon had no Watergate and he had been in a strong position when the peace was finally signed? Would he have bombed the communists rather than let them seize Saigon? Although the record offers many hints of an answer—that Nixon fully intended to do so, but Kissinger did not think the public would ever support it—no one can ever fully answer a what-if like this one. What we can say is that every month Thieu stalled and delayed the peace, Watergate's momentum brought *both* Nixon's and more certainly his own downfall.

Through November 1972, relations frayed between Nixon and Thieu, between Le Duc Tho and Kissinger, between the NLF and Politburo, and even between Kissinger and Nixon. Thieu was livid that Kissinger at his October press conference had given the impression that only "details" rather than "principles" remained to be resolved, and he demanded that an unequivocal statement be added to the treaty on the withdrawal of the North Vietnamese army from South Vietnam. He also wanted a clear articulation of the DMZ as separating the two Vietnams. Finally, he wanted it clear that the political problems of South Vietnam were to be resolved by the forces and groups within South Vietnam.

Thieu believed that Kissinger had made major concessions to the communists and he was being asked to ratify concessions that would result in a coalition government, which would lead to the eventual reunification of Vietnam. Thieu viewed the absence of a provision for the withdrawal of North Vietnamese forces as a major concession to the other side. He believed that the lack of a reference to the DMZ would allow for the continuing infiltration of men and supplies, as well as the dilution of South Vietnam as an independent country. He believed that the coalition structure would give the NLF equal weight with his government, something that was outrageous since it had not happened at the polls. The differences between the English and Vietnamese texts only reinforced his suspicions.

Thieu also understood that these concessions would have disastrous effects on the morale of the military and civilian populations within South Vietnam. The South Vietnamese people began to see contradictions between what was said about the future of their country in Hanoi and Washington. Thieu had little choice but to use the South's fear of communists, distrust of Americans, and apprehensions for the future to unite political and religious groups against all enemies, which now included their erstwhile ally, the United States.

Nixon, meanwhile, thought he had the luxury of more time with the election behind him. He did not want to give away unnecessary inches to the communists. It was time to turn hawkish to whatever extent possible. For the next round of talks with Thieu, he sent not Kissinger but Haig, a decision that reflected Haig's ascendancy during the period. In Nixon's mind, the decision to bomb on May 8 had been the turning point in the Vietnam negotiations. As Haig recalled, "Remember, that was a very important sequence of events, that bombing and mining, because here at home, with the single exception of Al Haig and John Connally, everyone told the President that if you do this, you are going to blow the summit with the Soviets."

Nonetheless, Kissinger would stay involved. Haig arrived on November 9, but Ambassador Bunker actually went first to Presidential Palace to inform Thieu that Kissinger was now scheduled to meet Le Duc Tho next on November 15. At that session, Kissinger planned to offer "changed and improved language with respect to the NCRC so that it is clearly evident that we are *not* talking in the agreement about a coalition government. Elimination of the inadvertent reference to the 'three countries of Indochina.' The de facto removal of some North Vietnamese troops from the South. We do not believe that we can get agreement on the removal of all North Vietnamese troops. However, we shall do our best in this respect."

Bunker appraised Thieu of General Weyand's work with General Vien on plans for the supervision of a cease-fire. Kissinger had hoped that this type of planning would stiffen Thieu's confidence in the agreement, though Kissinger knew it to be a ruse. Thieu warned Bunker that a cease-fire in place would present many difficulties, and if it was to be effective, a large number of joint teams would be necessary. Supervisory teams would have to be present in every district of every province of the country. "The VC will try to extend their area of control over as many hamlets and people as possible in preparation for a political solution." Thieu warned that there would be a "half-light, half-dark period between the actual declaration of a cease-fire and the establishment of full control. It was during this period that the VC would put soldiers in civilian clothes and even in ARVN uniforms as a method of concealment for expansion of control." Thieu wanted the joint commission and supervisory control commission to be formed before the cease-fire was put into effect because the VC would be preparing for the political contest and hence would seek to expand their control over the countryside immediately.

Meanwhile, as the commission did its work on implementation plans, it was clear that Thieu's concerns were difficult to assuage. Kissinger told Weyand that he doubted that freezing or accounting for enemy units in place would be possible since the North refused to admit that they had these units there in the first place—the very terms that Kissinger had already accepted. It was now apparent to members of the commission that Kissinger would give only scant consideration to the major concerns of Weyand's group. The official MACV historian of these events concluded that "Weyand's suspicions that the burden of negotiating the critical details of the workable peace would be transferred from Paris to Saigon were confirmed."

The implications of Kissinger's attitude are crucial for understanding what he and Nixon expected from the agreement. The commission and MACV were on record with reservations concerning any prospect for ensuring a cease-fire in place, yet Kissinger refused to address these details. There could be only two reasons: (1) that Nixon and Kissinger had their own ideas about compliance (sending the bombers back in) or (2) that they did not care if the North violated the agreement.

Prior to Haig's meeting with President Thieu, Ambassador Phuong and Nha met with him and submitted a prepared set of "talking points" on the shortcomings of the peace agreement. Drafted by Nha, the document raised all of South Vietnam's major concerns. First, it asked, with respect to the cease-fire, why there was a one-month gap between the cease-fire in Vietnam and the cease-fire in Laos and Cambodia. This would allow the North Vietnamese troops to launch an offensive and gain more territories in those countries while South Vietnam's troops would be "completely petrified." Second, what would happen when the cease-fire became effective and there was no two-party JMC ready to police? The communist troops would try to capture as much territory as possible, and the South Vietnamese certainly would not stay idle. How did Haig visualize the organization of the International Control Commission (ICC), and how long after the cease-fire would it actually operate in South Vietnam?

The ICC would be responsible for monitoring adherence to the agreement throughout Vietnam. ICC teams from Canada, Poland, Hungary, and Indonesia would be located at over 48 subregional and entry-point sites. Nha feared that the ICC "is unbalanced and will work to our disadvantage." The communist side would be assured of automatic support from two ICC members (Poland and Hungary), while the South could not be absolutely certain of its friends (Canada and Indonesia). "We suggest that the two Communist members should be replaced by two other non-aligned countries," he wrote. Finally, with regard to an international conference planned for Indochina after the signing, Nha asked, "What would you think of the eventual participation of Japan in the International Conference? Japan has been asked to contribute to the reconstruction efforts of both North and South Vietnam and as a big Pacific power she has at least as much right as France and Great Britain to be one of the big power guarantors." Nha would be unsuccessful in all of these efforts.

Haig would try to answer many of these questions during his visit, but the first order of business was to deliver a letter from Nixon. That letter is worth reproducing at length to show how far apart the "allies" had moved.

Dear Mr. President:

On this day after my reelection I wish to reopen our dialogue about the draft agreement to end the war. I must first of all express my deep disappointment over what I consider to be a dangerous drift in the relationship between our two countries, a tendency which can only undercut our mutual objectives and benefit the enemy. Your continuing distortions of the agreement and attacks upon it were unfair and self defeating. These have persisted despite our numerous representations, including my October 29 letter to you. They have been disconcerting and highly embarrassing to me.

In my previous communications, and in the presentations of Dr. Kissinger and Ambassador Bunker, we have repeatedly explained why we consider the draft agreement to be sound; we continue to believe that it reflects major concessions by the other side, protects the independence of South Vietnam, and leaves the political future to the South Vietnamese people themselves. You are fully informed as well about the massive re-supply movement that is under way to strengthen your forces before a ceasefire. I have repeatedly given firm guarantees against the possibility that the agreement is violated. I have offered to meet with you soon after the agreement is signed to symbolize our continuing support. I will not recount here the numerous arguments, explanations, and undertakings that have been made. They all remain valid. In the light of the record, the charges by some of your associates are becoming more and more incomprehensible. . . .

It seems to me you have two essential choices. You could use the public support your recent actions have mobilized to claim the military victory the agreement reflects and to work in unity with your strongest ally to bring about a political victory for which the conditions exist. You could take the political and psychological initiative by hailing the settlement and carrying out its provisions in a positive fashion. In this case I repeat my invitation to meet with you shortly after the signature of the agreement, in order to underline our continued close cooperation.

The other alternative would be for you to pursue what appears to be your present course. In my view this would play into the hands of the enemy and would have extremely grave consequences for both our peoples and it would be a disaster for yours.

Mr. President, I would like you to tell General Haig if we can confidentially proceed on this basis. We are at the point where I need to know unambiguously whether you will join us in the effort General Haig is going to outline or whether we must contemplate alternative courses of action which I believe would be detrimental to the interest of both of our countries.

I hope that you and your government are prepared to cooperate with us. There is a great deal of preparatory work that needs to be done and we believe joint US-GVN task forces should begin working together so that we will be in the best possible position to implement the settlement.

It is my firm conviction that your people, your armed forces, and you have achieved a major victory, which the draft agreement would ratify. It is my intention to build on these accomplishments. I would like to work with you and your government in my second term to defend freedom in South Vietnam—in peacetime as we have worked during my first term to defend it in conflict.

In four years you and I have been close personal and military allies. Our alliance has brought us to a position where the enemy is agreeing to conditions, which any objective observer said were impossible four years ago. Our alliance and its achievements have been based on mutual trust. If you will give me continued trust, together we shall succeed.

But to Thieu, the victory at hand was something different. "You, General Haig, are a general. I am a general," Thieu told Haig on November 11. "Have you ever seen any peace accord in the history of the world in which the invaders had been permitted to stay in the territories they had invaded? Would you permit Russian troops to stay in the United States and say you have reached a peace accord with Russia?"

Haig had no answer. He told Nixon the next day that "we are dealing with a razor's edge situation." He tried explaining to Thieu that the newly elected U.S. Senate was even more dovish than its predecessor and that if Thieu was seen as an obstacle to peace, it was a certainty that Congress would cut off all funds to South Vietnam.

That evening President Thieu replied to Nixon's letter. Congratulating Nixon on his election victory, which Thieu portrayed as a validation of the president's policy in Vietnam, Thieu argued that it was wrong of Nixon to accuse Thieu of making distortions of the draft agreement because he merely called attention to the facts. Thieu asked Nixon to reconsider and readjust his position because there could never be a free election in South Vietnam so long as the North Vietnam army was in place in the South. "But I completely share your views that, much as we desire and need peace, the peace that we are actually searching for should be an honorable and just peace. For the peace to meet this criterion, I firmly believe that a peace settlement should indicate unambiguously that North Vietnam has no right to invade South Vietnam, and therefore should withdraw its forces back into North Vietnam, pending the discussions between South Vietnam and North Vietnam for the settlement by peaceful means of the problems between North Vietnam and South Vietnam. If a settlement allows North Vietnam to maintain its forces in South Vietnam, then our struggle and the sacrifices we made during so many years would have been purposeless."

He also reiterated that the NCRC must not be construed as having governmental authority. To make this clear, Thieu suggested that "co cau chinh-quyen" ("governmental structure"), used by the communists, should be substituted by "co quan hanh-chanh dac-trach bau cu" ("administrative organ in charge of elections"), which indicates more clearly that the role of the Council of National Reconciliation and Concord was only in organizing and supervising the elections.

On November 12, Haig flew from Saigon to Cambodia, where he met with Lon Nol at the private residence of the president of the Khmer Republic. "The [Saigon] talks were very cordial and constructive. There are some differences between us and President Thieu on the provision of the draft agreement but these differences are narrowing and we are narrowing them even more," Haig told Nol. "The only serious difference is the question of North Vietnamese armed forces in South Vietnam. As a result of our discussions yesterday, we found a means of exploring this issue, which will give us the means to jointly explore this question at the next meeting with the DRV." Haig was hopeful that an agreement could still be reached by December. He told Lon Nol that Nixon had asked him to communicate the news that "we plan to keep a massive air and naval presence in the area and once an agreement has been reached on Vietnam make it even more at your disposition. I want to reassure you that once an agreement is reached the President intends to guarantee its enforcement."

While Haig was in Cambodia, Bunker cabled Kissinger with an update on Haig's meeting with President Thieu: "The one fundamental difference remaining between us is that of the withdrawal of NVA troops from South Vietnam. This, I think, has always been Thieu's major concern. As long as NVA troops remain in South Vietnam, he sees 'real peace' as impossible to attain, rather a continuing state of turmoil, a fact which he feels is confirmed by the intelligence we are getting on the other side's intentions; he believes that as long as the NVA remain in the South, the NLF will be compelled to do their will, and that this will prevent a solution which he is convinced could be readily worked out between the GVN and the NLF. He believes that if it is just and correct that the U.S. and other allies are compelled to withdraw troops from South Vietnam, those who have invaded the country should likewise be compelled to withdraw."

Three days later, Nixon wrote another letter to President Thieu responding to Thieu's letter of November 11. "You can be sure that we will pursue the proposed changes in the draft agreement that General Haig discussed with you with the utmost firmness." Concerning the status of the North Vietnamese forces that were currently in South Vietnam, Nixon thought it important that President Thieu understand that the supervisory mechanism was not nearly as important as the United States' firm determination to ensure that the agreement worked and "our vigilance with respect to the prospect of its violation." This is more evidence that Nixon, at least, firmly expected the North to go back on the offensive—as any realist would have admitted. But did he really think the American public would let him resume the bombing?

To Thieu at least, Nixon said so twice in the same letter that Thieu accepted as pledges of honor between two allied leaders: "Above all, we must bear in mind what will really maintain the agreement. It is not any particular clause in the agreement but our joint willingness to maintain its clauses. I repeat my personal assurances to you that the United States will react very strongly and rapidly to any violation of the agreement. But in order to do this effectively it is essential that I have public support and that your Government does not emerge as the obstacle to a peace which American public opinion now universally desires. It is for this reason that I am pressing for the acceptance of an agreement which I am convinced is honorable and fair and which can be made essentially secure by our joint determination."

Bunker delivered Nixon's letter to Thieu on November 15. Thieu read the letter carefully and made notes, but offered no comment. Bunker gave yet a third assurance that "the ultimate protection for the GVN is our ability to enforce and protect the agreement, and that the President has given written assurance of our intention to do so. This means that if the agreement is not observed, that if the cease-fire is violated, we will react promptly and effectively in support of the GVN."

Thieu may or may not have believed them, but he could not accept the draft peace deal. The South Vietnamese submitted new modifications that they wanted incorporated during Kissinger's forthcoming meeting with Le Duc Tho. Nixon wrote in his diary on November 20 that Kissinger was more concerned with establishing a good record with Thieu, whereas Nixon was more interested in saving South Vietnam. "As I told Henry when he began to rumble around to the effect that we have a very good record in this instance, I said, Henry, we're not concerned about being right on the record. What we are concerned about is to save South Vietnam and that's why we had to temporize with Thieu as much as we did, because our interest is in getting South Vietnam to survive and Thieu at present seems to be the only leader who could lead them in that direction."

One needs to ask, How is it that the president could believe that only Thieu, and no one else, could enable South Vietnam to survive? Could it be that Nixon still believed he owed Thieu for 1968? Was Thieu a synonym for American airpower after the POWs were home? That was the deal Nixon was about to make, and he was quite right that Thieu, and only Thieu, even with his own grave doubts, would accept. What choice did he have after all these years?

* * *

Tensions between Nixon and Kissinger now began to emerge: the President was furious at Kissinger because of an interview he had recently given to Italian journalist Oriana Fallaci in which he apparently took credit for all of the administration's foreign policy initiatives. Describing himself akin to a "lone cowboy," Kissinger was more critical of Thieu's intransigence than of Le Duc Tho's. In describing "the mechanics of my success," Kissinger told Fallaci, "I have acted alone. The Americans love this immensely. The Americans love the cowboy, who leads the convoy, alone on his horse, the cowboy who comes into town all alone on his horse, and nothing else. Perhaps not even with a gun, because he does not shoot. He acts, and that is enough, being in the right place, at the right time. In sum, a Western. This romantic and surprising character suits me because being alone has always been part of my style, or, if you wish, of my technique."

"We've got to stop paying the price for K[Kissinger]," Nixon told Haldeman in frustration.

Kissinger arrived in Paris on November 19, a Sunday. Haldeman recalled that although he had the day off, Nixon kept calling. "He later told me I should let Henry know that obviously the EOP (Executive Office of the President) and the Oval Office and the Lincoln Room have all been recorded for protection, so the P has a complete record of all your conversations, which of course you can carry when you write your book."

Haldeman and Nixon believed that Kissinger, feeling that he had lost Nixon's confidence, was manifesting signs of depression. The South Vietnamese disdained him. Among the large Vietnamese community living in Paris, rumors began circulating that Kissinger was living with the North Vietnamese—eating their food, drinking their wine, and agreeing to their demands.

In a November 20 diary entry, Haldeman wrote that Nixon was "very depressed with the K interview, which gave away the moral ground in Vietnam, plus praising Le Duc Tho and knocking Thieu, which was bad. He wants to set up a situation for a social engagement with General and Mrs. Haig as a cover and he wants to talk to Haig candidly. He wants me to knock off K's going to China before the inaugural, which Henry wants to do. He wants to be sure that I get from K's office all the memoranda from and to the P and get them into the P's files, especially all of his handwritten stuff, the originals, physically move it into the P's files now." By the next day, Nixon was fretting that Kissinger would be named *Time*'s Man of the Year. Nixon told Haldeman "he can't tolerate Henry's increasing problems," and Haldeman had better "bring him back to earth."

To make matters worse for Kissinger, because the negotiations were no longer secret, the eyes of the world were focused on his next meeting in Paris. Media towers had been constructed at the site of the private meetings. Kissinger's and Le Duc Tho's every move was watched, which irked Nixon because photos were taken with Kissinger and Le Duc Tho smiling. Nixon sent instructions that Kissinger was not to smile in public with Le Duc Tho.

At least the meetings themselves were still closed to the press. The meeting on November 20 began amicably enough, with Kissinger inviting Le Duc Tho to give lectures at Harvard University, maybe as early as that spring. But by the time Kissinger was through presenting Thieu's 64 proposed text changes, Le Duc Tho's anger swelled to the surface: "We have been deceived by the French, the Japanese and the Americans, but the deception has never been so flagrant as now. . . . You told us this [was a done deal] and you swallowed your words. What kind of person must we think you to be?"

Kissinger remained calm. He joked that he had contributed to the unity of the two zones of Vietnam because "both North and South Vietnam hate me now." In his memoirs, Kissinger admitted that presenting these proposed changes had been a tactical mistake, which he regretted. He described the changes as "preposterous." At the time, according to Ambassador Bunker's notes, "In the informal conversation which took place during the luncheon break Dr. Kissinger impressed upon Le Duc Tho the importance which the GVN attaches to the question of North Vietnamese troops in South Vietnam and indicated that in our judgment a resolution of this problem which would conform to the principles we have previously stated was the central issue that we foresaw in these current negotiations." Kissinger maintained that a settlement was still possible—that it was natural after years of fighting that new complexities would arise as the settlement approached. According to Luu Van Loi's account, Kissinger insisted that "we keep to the agreed principles and the substantive issues achieved in October. We firmly believe that we shall settle the problem in the coming weeks. We are sure that a great part of the text of the agreement may be finalized this week. After agreement is reached this week, we will request no other changes."

That afternoon, Kissinger presented the most important modifications that had been requested in Saigon. First was the deletion of the name "PRG of the Republic of South Vietnam" in the preamble to the agreement. He did not want to recognize the existence of two governments in South Vietnam. Next, he raised the complete withdrawal of all non–South Vietnamese troops from Vietnam. He did not want to recognize the presence of the two armies south of the 17th parallel. He also demanded that the demobilization of soldiers be on an equal number basis and that demobilized soldiers return to their native homes. What he wanted, he said, was the "practical removal" of these armed forces—not something that had to be written in the agreement. Kissinger also reiterated that the return at the earliest date of U.S. prisoners of war was not to be linked in any way to the return of political prisoners. Furthermore, Kissinger wanted to reconsider, if not totally abandon, the three components of the NCRC, the lower levels of that committee, and the function of that committee in promoting the implementation of the agreement by the two administrations. He also wanted the question of the DMZ addressed by a conference in Geneva and not in Paris.

Finally, Kissinger rejected any written reference to reparations, because "my President believes that this way of writing will make the United States appear like a culprit. . . . We are prepared to accept the obligation to respect the independence, the sovereignty . . . of Vietnam, but we are unable to sign an agreement in which we consider ourselves criminals." Instead, Kissinger proposed that "the independence, the unity, the sovereignty of Vietnam must be recognized by all countries."

Luu Van Loi observed, "Generally speaking, the United States demanded amendments to almost all the chapters of the agreement, especially those regarding the cease-fire, troop withdrawal and internal political issues of South Vietnam. Those issues included the following substantive questions: withdrawal of North Vietnamese troops, non-recognition of the PRG, diminishing the role of the Committee for National Reconciliation and Concord, keeping South Vietnam as a separated state, reduction of United States responsibility. . . . All these amendments were aimed at enhancing the political and legal strength of the Saigon administration and weakening the prestige of the revolution in SVN."

Kissinger later wrote in his memoirs that the list of 69 amendments was "so unreasonable and went so far beyond all that we had envisaged in both public and private negotiations that it undoubtedly strengthened the already firm position of Hanoi to stick to its positions and to wait until we were in a stranglehold by the deadline fixed by Congress. I had presented these demands; it was because I did not want to be accused of neglecting the interests of Saigon and because I thought it would facilitate Thieu's acceptance of the agreement."

After hearing Kissinger's presentation, Le Duc Tho could only say, "If these are your last, unchangeable proposals, settlement is impossible."

Kissinger responded, "These are our last proposals, but not an ultimatum."

On the next day, November 21, Le Duc Tho arrived with his own intransigent attitude, asking Kissinger what Vice President Spiro Agnew had meant on October 29, 1972, when he said that there were only a few phrasings left for clarification, that no substantive matters were outstanding. "We should have dismissed the person who drafted that speech," said Kissinger jokingly. Le Duc Tho belittled most of Kissinger's points from the previous day, beginning with the United States' demand that all mention of the PRG be deleted from the treaty. He reminded Kissinger that the PRG had been recognized by over 60 countries.

Tho next turned to Kissinger's demand that the area under PRG control be wiped out, something that neither the United States nor Saigon troops had been able to accomplish. Tho insisted that the final treaty include three areas under control: one by Saigon, one by the PRG, the third in contention. Tho flat out rejected the demand of the withdrawal of North Vietnamese forces.

Under pressure from the NLF, Tho now retracted his agreement from October on political prisoners and demanded that the release of all civilian personnel still in detention be carried out within the same period as the withdrawal of United States forces. Tho stressed that this was the responsibility of the United States, and not Saigon. To support his argument, Tho quoted a report of the House of Representatives investigating committee and said the Congress had affirmed that the United States had spent money to build jails for Thieu.

Using virtually the same language that President Thieu had just used with General Haig and Kissinger, Tho wanted to know, "Have you ever seen any war in the world in which one party returns all captured persons to the other at the end of the war and the other party refused to return the prisoners? If one party retains the prisoners, the other will do the same. This is just and reasonable. . . . If this question is not solved, not only the Vietnamese people but the people the world over will be indignant."

By now Kissinger understood that the agreement was dead: Saigon would never accept North Vietnamese forces remaining in South Vietnam. The meeting broke, though both sides agreed to meet the next day, November 23. President Nixon asked Haldeman "to call Haig in Paris and dictate a cable to Kissinger, saying the President is very disappointed in the lack of progress in the negotiations to date, under the circumstances, unless the other side shows the same willingness to be reasonable that we are showing, I am directing you to discontinue the talks and we shall then have to resume military activities until the other side is ready to negotiate. They must be disabused of the idea they seem to have that we have no other choice but to settle on their terms. You should inform them directly, without equivocation, that we do have another choice, and if they were surprised that I would take the strong action I did prior to the Moscow Summit, and prior to the election they will find that now with the election behind us, I will take whatever action I consider necessary to protect United States interests."

Kissinger wrote that "relations between Nixon and me now were wary and strained. . . . Ensconced at Camp David, surrounded only by public relations experts, Nixon was still deep in the bog of the resentments that had produced the darkest and perhaps most malevolent frame of mind of his presidency." Kissinger kept getting cables from both Nixon and Haldeman to get tough and stop smiling in public for photos with Le Duc Tho. "Smiles in Paris were frowned on in Camp David," Kissinger later wrote in his memoirs.

Nixon was prepared to get tough. But against whom? On November 23 Nixon sent Thieu a "Top Secret-Sensitive" letter delivered personally by Bunker, threatening to proceed "at whatever the cost." Nixon wrote, "I am increasingly dismayed and apprehensive over the press campaign emanating from Saigon. . . . The unfounded attacks on the draft agreement have continued with increasing frequency. . . . I am struck by the dilatory tactics which we are experiencing from your side in Paris. . . . As I told you in my letters of November 8, 14, and 18, I will proceed promptly to a final solution if an acceptable final agreement is arrived at in Paris this week. . . . Any further delay from your side can only be interpreted as an effort to scuttle the agreement. This would have a disastrous effect on our ability to support you and your government."

President Thieu chose not to respond directly to Nixon's letter. Instead, he instructed Nha to write Ambassador Bunker with a point-by-point rebuttal to Nixon's charges. He indirectly denied any public relations offensive against the peace treaty or Kissinger, though not very convincingly, and he claimed not to be foot dragging. Yet once again he insisted that Northern troops could not be allowed to stay in the South.

On November 23 Kissinger and Haig tried to threaten Tho and Thuy. Kissinger read a message from Nixon that Kissinger stressed was not in official diplomatic language: "I am disappointed at the tone as well as the substance of the last meeting. Under such circumstances, unless the other side shows its willingness to take into account our reasonable concern, I direct you to discontinue the talks and we shall have to resume military activities until the other side is willing to negotiate on honorable terms. They must be disabused of the idea they seem to have that we have no choice but to settle on present terms. You should inform them directly that we do have now a choice, and if they were surprised that the President would take this strong action as he did prior to the Moscow summit and prior to the elections they will find now that we will take whatever action we consider necessary to protect the U.S. interests."

Threatening Le Duc Tho had little impact, however. He would not sign an agreement in which there was a clause to the effect that North Vietnamese forces would be withdrawn from South Vietnam: "President Nixon speaks about U.S. honor. We have ours too. You have brought your troops for aggression against our country. Now that you are to withdraw, you demand that we, the fighters against aggression, shall also withdraw. If such a clause is found in the agreement, how can our people bear it? How can we sign an agreement while tens of thousands of our people are still in detention?" Le Duc Tho scoffed at Nixon's threats: "Threats have no effect on us! We have been fighting against you for ten years and negotiating with you for several years, therefore now is the moment to adopt an attitude, which will lead to a settlement. Threatening is a futile effort!"

Le Duc Tho told Kissinger that Hanoi had already conceded as much as it could. "Imagine an agreement implying the presence of North Vietnamese forces, continuing to retain the detainees, refusing to set up a three-component government, maintain Thieu in place and foreseeing further discussion on the Council. How could we sign such an agreement! I agree with you that it now is the moment of truth—we can either peacefully settle the problem or continue the war, there is no alternative. We do want peace, but there are limits to our goodwill. Excessive concession is but a disguised surrender. Our people will never give up."

Of all things, the two sides still could not even agree on which parties should join the agreement, Tho insisted on the enumeration of the official names of the four governments signing the agreement, as in the 1954 Geneva Agreements on Indochina and the 1962 Geneva Agreement on Laos. "The PRG will not sign the agreement if its official name is not mentioned." Tho then wryly asked Kissinger, "For the United States, is there any sentence saying that the U.S. troops must remain within the borders of the United States? You are haunted by the Ho Chi Minh trail and we are continuously thinking about what will become of your forces in Thailand, the Philippines and your naval forces in the Pacific." Finally Tho said, "This is our last effort. If you refuse to settle, the negotiations can be said to have come to a deadlock. There is no other way. Peace or war entirely depends on you."

"Is that an ultimatum?" Kissinger responded.

Le Duc Tho pounded on the table: "The words we have proposed cannot be changed: three components, councils at various levels, the name of the Council. We'll make no concessions on these points!"

Following the meeting, Kissinger cabled Nixon; "Haig and I have met with Le Duc Tho and Xuan Thuy for an hour and 20 minutes this morning and I covered your message of November 22 in detail. There is no question that it sobered him considerably." Kissinger reported that Tho railed about being threatened and passed along Tho's argument. "How, he asked, could he now be expected to leave thousands of their people languishing in South Vietnamese jails and agree to specific language with respect to North Vietnamese troops in the South?"

* * *

Both Hanoi and the Nixon administration knew that time was running out for the South. For months now, Kissinger and Nixon had tacitly accepted a cease-fire in place. Thieu was losing the support of his ally, no matter what. Congress was getting closer to cutting off all funding for Vietnam operations.

Later that day, Kissinger presented the brutal facts to the South Vietnamese delegation to the plenary talks. Meeting in the library at the private residence of the American ambassador, Kissinger told the Vietnamese that Le Duc Tho had reacted very sternly to the numerous amendments. Kissinger was going to request a postponement in their private meetings. "If there is a breakdown, the consequences for your government will be disastrous, and you will bear full responsibility." Kissinger also told them that

for four years, by maneuvering and manipulation, we have managed to keep the Congress from passing resolutions requiring United States withdrawal in exchange for our POWs. This was my nightmare. On October 8 I thought that their acceptance of our proposal plus your enthusiastic support would make the American people so proud of what we had achieved that they would enable us to support your government. Imagine now the attitude of a Midwesterner who reads every day that we are accused of betrayal. If it is portrayed as a worthless agreement, how can the American people support it? What is your protection? *Your protection is our unity. Your protection is our enthusiastic support. You won't be able to wave a document at them, whatever is in it. The North Vietnamese fear is whether the B-52s may come again; if we convince them of this, the agreement will be kept. If we can't convince them of this, all your 69 changes mean nothing. We think we are watching a suicide.* You are losing your public support. Why did we want an agreement in October, in November and now? The election meant nothing. If we got it now it would be our success. If it happens next March, every liberal newspaper in the country would think it had brought it about.

Kissinger read a letter from Nixon concerning congressional sentiment that was intended as a wake-up call: "I have checked today as to the attitude of the leading Democrats and Republicans who support us in the Senate on Vietnam. In preparing them for the consultation which must take place once agreement is reached we have informed them of the key elements of the October 8 agreement: the return of our POWs, a ceasefire, and a formula under which Thieu remains in power and all South Vietnamese have an opportunity to participate in a free election to determine what government they want for the future. The result of this check indicates that they were not only unanimous but vehement in stating their conclusions that if Saigon is the only roadblock for reaching agreement on this basis they will personally lead the fight when the new Congress reconvenes on January 3 to cut off all military and economic assistance to Saigon. My evaluation is that the date of the cut-off would be February 1. They further believe that under such circumstances we have no choice but to go it alone and to make a separate deal with North Vietnam for the return of our POWs and for our withdrawal."

Nixon's personal instructions to Kissinger on how to deliver this message to the South Vietnamese contained some of the strongest possible terms:

The fat is in the fire. It is time to fish or cut bait. We do not want to go it alone. I personally want to stand by Thieu and the South Vietnamese government but as I have told him in three separate messages, what really counts is not the agreement but my determination to take massive action against North Vietnam in the event they break the agreement. The North Vietnamese troops in the South mean absolutely nothing in that eventuality. If they had no forces there at all and I refused to order air retaliation on the North when infiltration started to begin, the war would be resumed and the outcome would be very much in doubt.

You must tell Thieu that I feel we have now reached the crossroads. Either he trusts me and signs what I have determined is the best agreement we can get or we have to go it alone and end our own involvement in the war on the best terms we can get. I do not give him this very tough option by personal desire, but because of the political reality in the United States it is not possible for me, even with the massive mandate I personally received in the election, to get the support from a hostile Congress to continue the war when the North Vietnamese on October 8 offered an agreement which was far better than both the House and the Senate by resolution and directive to the President indicated they thought we ought to accept during this last session.

Tell Thieu that I cannot keep the lid on his strong supporters in the House and Senate much longer. They are terribly disturbed by what they read and hear out of Saigon. It is time for us to decide to go forward together or to go our separate ways. If we go separate ways, all that we fought for, for so many years, will be lost in my opinion. If, on the other hand, he will join us in going forward together on the course I have laid out we can, over the long pull, win a very significant victory.

The third option of our trying to continue to go forward together on the basis of continuing the war is simply not open. The door has been slammed shut hard and fast by the longtime supporters of the hard line in Vietnam in the House and Senate who control the purse strings.

Kissinger told the South Vietnamese that many leaders in Congress had lost their offices and had been defeated "because they supported you. . . .

We kept the war going by always keeping North Vietnam in the position of appearing unreasonable on issues that Americans could understand, like overthrowing an ally. But even that would not last beyond next year."

Ambassador Sullivan then raised the historical analogy of South Korea: "In 1953 Syngman Rhee did not like the agreement and did not trust us. But we have kept every commitment to South Korea, and today South Korea is in the strongest position."

Kissinger threatened that Nixon was prepared to make a unilateral deal with Hanoi: a complete U.S. military withdrawal in return for prisoners of war. When Nguyen Phu Duc turned to the question of North Vietnamese troops and that North Vietnam had violated previous agreements on Laos, Ambassador Sullivan told him that it was only "a piece of paper." The ink on the paper was not nearly as important as the steel and power of the American B-52s.

The meeting ended with little indication of movement from the South. A total public blow-up with Saigon now loomed. Nixon could either try to ram the draft down Thieu's throat or take another military step. Kissinger told Haldeman that Nixon needed to get "tough with both the South and North—giving them, threatening them both with extreme ultimatums."

At the end of the month, Nguyen Phu Duc flew to Washington for face-to-face meetings with Nixon and Kissinger. The South Vietnamese did not trust that Kissinger or Haig had told the whole truth about the South Vietnamese position to Nixon. Duc's instructions were to convey Thieu's position and to make certain that he did not flinch when Kissinger and Haig threatened to cut off their ally. Neither Thieu, Nha, nor Duc took that option seriously. Extensive documentation available on these meetings offers much new detail on the state of thinking in the Nixon White House.

Nguyen Phu Duc arrived in Washington carrying a 24-page letter from President Thieu, drafted by Nha and Duc, with additional instructions to make an urgent appeal for changes and delay in the Vietnam peace agreement. In a background memorandum for the president, Kissinger explained that the purpose of the "crucial" meeting "is to convince an almost pathologically-distrustful Thieu through a key member of his palace inner circle, to close ranks with us this week on the Paris agreement." Kissinger noted that President Thieu "remains intransigent. Rather than joining us, he has rallied personal support with his tough independent stance, and fought valiantly in public and private for changes and delays. The performance of this shrewd, paranoiac mandarin probably reflects a blend of genuine opposition to aspects of the agreement; distrust of us, as well as the communists;

fear of peace and political struggle after years of war; patriotism; personal ambition; domestic politics; and bluff. Thus, you will have to combine brutality with reassurance in your approach to one of the few Palace guards to whom Thieu listens."

Kissinger urged Nixon to take the following steps: "You must ruthlessly convince Duc that the GVN must decide this week to accept (1) the agreement, with whatever further changes we can get in the December 4 round, and (2) the unalterable schedule leading to a signature three weeks from now. Thieu must realize that the alternative is a Congressional cutoff of funds within weeks and suicide for South Vietnam." At the same time, it was essential that Thieu and the GVN approach the settlement with confidence in its abilities and U.S. backing. "We must reassure the South Vietnamese that they have the assets to prevail under the terms of the settlement, and most importantly, that you will do whatever is required to ensure that the agreement is observed by the communists."

Nixon wrote across the top of this memorandum that, "if not settled, aid is cut." Most relevant, however, was Nixon's notation, "agreement meets our realities" and "I need support for aid—for massive retaliation."

Arriving in the Oval Office at 3:05 P.M. on November 29, Nguyen Phu Duc delivered President Thieu's letter. President Nixon read it, marking key portions with his fountain pen. It again dissected the draft agreement and warned that this was not an honorable settlement for the people of South Vietnam. Indeed, Thieu asserted, the 17 million South Vietnamese would soon be living under communist tyranny at some interval after the American departure. "I have been informed that in the event that we cannot accept the absurd demands of the communists, the United States would seek a separate arrangement with North Vietnam for the withdrawal of U.S. forces and the return of American prisoners of war. If indeed the question of the prisoners of war is an important question for you, I believe there are still ways to obtain their release other than jeopardizing the fate of the 17.5 million South Vietnamese. . . . No one can deny that South Vietnam is the victim of a blatant aggression committed by North Vietnam. Therefore, any suggestion that our people and their elected leaders are an obstacle to peace for refusing the terms imposed by the aggressions is a most cruel irony."

In the conclusion of his lengthy letter, President Thieu called on President Nixon to use his forceful persuasive leadership with the U.S. Congress: "You can gain support for what needs to be done to safeguard freedom and the long range security of the free world."

President Nixon began the discussion by telling Duc how important it was for the U.S. and South Vietnam to go forward as allies. Nixon even agreed with much of President Thieu's letter. As notes of the meeting report Nixon's words, "No one was more suspicious of the communists. The President had known the misery that has been imposed on the people of North Vietnam. He observed it first-hand in 1956. The traffic in this respect has been all one-way."

What concerned President Nixon most was President Thieu's fear that the proposed political settlement was a coalition in disguise. The declassified conversation notes quote Nixon at length:

> He noted that President Thieu understood that Hanoi had abandoned its demand for President Thieu to be replaced. The Council of Reconciliation thus "had no effect on the government of South Vietnam." In addition, "the commission meant nothing without the agreement of both sides. While there was some psychological impact, in reality, with the continued U.S. aid—military and political—and, most importantly, with firm presidential assurances, the problem was manageable.
>
> Nixon told Duc that it was essential that the United States get a signed agreement because otherwise the United States "would not even have the power to police the agreement. More important than any other factor was not the language of an Agreement, or a piece of paper, but the United States' commitment to enforce the agreement. That commitment was being made at this meeting. If Saigon accepted the Agreement, the United States would then be justified in asking for continued funds. As Mr. Duc was aware, the United States had shipped in vast amounts of additional military supplies. Thus, a satisfactory agreement would enable us to go to the Congress and provide adequate military and economic aid in the future. Further, the United States would maintain military assets in Thailand, offshore, and in other adjacent locations, which would ensure its ability to react if Hanoi violated the Agreement. The President of the United States would then be able to stand firmly with President Thieu, and say so publicly, and form a united front against all potential enemies. . . . Thus, with continued military and economic power, and a credible U.S. threat to resume military operations without hesitation, should a violation occur, the prospects were optimum.

Here, in plain language, was Nixon's strategy. Both popular and congressional opinion would change upon a peace accord that the public would see as an honorable end to American involvement. When—not if—

the communists violated it, somehow Nixon would muster the public support to bring American air back to the nearly lost cause. Nixon told Duc that President Thieu's failure to go along would deprive the United States of what it needed to secure continuing congressional funding. Nixon had already been told by friendly Senate leaders, including John Stennis, Barry Goldwater, and Gerald Ford, that if Saigon refused to go along, a congressional resolution offering U.S. POWs for a total U.S. withdrawal and a cut-off of aid would pass the House by a two-to-one margin. Without U.S. aid, Saigon could not survive. President Nixon needed President Thieu to see the situation from Nixon's perspective. Nixon had complete sympathy with the South Vietnamese people. "No one could be more strongly behind the survival of the GVN," said Nixon. Haig urged Thieu to sign the agreement so that the United States could remain permanently involved in Vietnam.

Nixon explained to Duc that if Hanoi were aware of these political divisions, "it would be impossible to get them to negotiate" (though as we have seen, Hanoi was very well aware of them). Nixon's next words to Duc, as recorded in the official declassified transcript, are worth quoting:

> These realities had crystallized, not because the United States had moved too fast, but in fact, it had managed to stay just one step ahead of the sheriff. Dr. Kissinger's visits to Paris helped in this process. But if at this point no agreement was reached, in view of all of the above, then Washington and Saigon had failed. President Thieu must understand this reality. Exchanges of letters were no longer adequate. The fact was, the President stressed, that President Thieu and President Nixon were of the same mind in wanting to prevent the collapse of South Vietnam. Communists did not respect paper. They understood bombs, and mines and the U.S.'s resolve. President Nixon frequently referred to this issue in terms of hardware and software. President Johnson stopped bombing in 1963 and it was a grave mistake. Now the situation was different. Hanoi had observed U.S. actions in Cambodia and Laos, and the bombing and mining on May 8th. The credibility of our resolve had been established. The American people recognize that if the President supported the Agreement they would have to do the same. Why did Korea survive today? Partially because of U.S. aid, but primarily because North Korea knew that if they violated the DMZ a violent reaction would ensue. The situation was the same in Vietnam. If North Vietnam infiltrated again they would run a mortal risk.

Duc listened carefully to President Nixon. He replied, however, that the only way that the agreement could succeed would be if the North Vietnamese troops were required to leave the South. South Vietnam had fought off an invasion. Hanoi had no right to keep its troops in the South, and the current treaty ratified victory to the invaders. Following the settlement, there would be a political contest. Duc believed that with the North Vietnamese in the South, "the people could not express their choice in freedom."

President Nixon responded that the timing of the election was up to the people and up to President Thieu. Kissinger chimed in that "without a North Vietnamese withdrawal there was no reason to risk the political solution." In other words, elections could be put off until the North's troops were removed. Thieu need not hold elections, release prisoners, or do anything else if it looked as if the political solution would not go his way.

Kissinger noted "that he has observed President Nixon carefully. He has always reacted strongly to communist threats. On May 8, only one key adviser [Haig] was in favor of the action that was taken. How could President Nixon now, after all of the sacrifices that have been made, permit Hanoi to overrun South Vietnam?"

President Nixon added, "It won't be necessary to haggle over proof. The simple fact was if Hanoi reinforced, the U.S. would react. . . . He had no confidence in the U.N. and the International Control Commission or any other vehicle that might try to police. The problem was to watch unilaterally and react in the face of violation."

Duc now raised a fundamentally important point. Would it not be better, and simpler, if there were something specific in the agreement that the United States could invoke to justify a retaliatory action? If this was how Nixon felt, why not put it in writing and establish a legal basis for reentering the war? Otherwise, it would be seen as a nonbinding moral obligation without legal standing. The president said there was already "plenty of justification." He went on to state more precisely what he saw as a necessary distinction of separating hardware from software: "Hardware was steel and bombs. This was far preferable to a paper war. Saigon's point was a good one, but in reality the United States would interpret the Agreement in this way in any event, and when President Thieu and President Nixon met, the message would be sent directly to the North through strong public statements. It would also be quite evident to the world and most importantly to the people of South Vietnam. However, if the meeting occurred before Saigon and Washington agreed and there was to be another haggling session, we would have a repeat of past summit failures in other areas. Leaders must not attend summits unless they knew beforehand that they would succeed, so the meeting should be after agreement between Saigon and Washington."

Beneath all the arguments, Nixon must have known that Congress would not accept the very terms he was promoting. He was counting on the American public to rally around the flag for a fait accompli rather than expecting an up-front commitment to send bombers back to Vietnam. The meeting concluded with more of the same arguments from both sides. Duc still refused to accept the disposition of Northern troops. Nixon reminded him that "the Department of State had wanted to flush President Thieu and the President had refused."

Duc would get little time to reflect on his meeting with Nixon because almost immediately he was ushered into another meeting in Kissinger's private office with Kissinger, Haig, and Winston Lord. "You have made so many public demands that you have given the North Vietnamese a victory. Making your demands in private is one thing, but publicly insisting upon them, we now have this problem," Kissinger told Duc. *"What is most important is the commitments which the President made to you, which we will put on record in our files, commitments from the President of the United States"* (emphasis added). In fact, there were no records in the files, nor would the U.S. lift a finger to stop the North's takeover of Saigon. Kissinger would even insist during the final weeks of South Vietnam's life that he and Nixon never claimed there was a legal commitment made to South Vietnam, only a moral commitment. They had dodged this with Duc, but not with history.

Kissinger then went a step further in the private meeting with Duc by raising the issue of detainees, and he plainly contradicted his promise to Hanoi to use influence to secure their release. Kissinger now told Duc, "I think you would make a terrible mistake to release the prisoners. The prisoners are something concrete in your hands that they want. The troops I can understand, though you made it a huge affair out of all proportion. The Council [NCRC] you should treat with total contempt."

In order to make a deal and get the U.S. out, Kissinger was willing to tell one side one thing and the other the opposite, leaving them to sort things out later. This may well be evidence that Kissinger never believed the U.S. would bomb again, aggression or no aggression. If the North was going to finish off the South anyway, then the detainees would cease to be an issue. If, on the other hand, the U.S. was supposed to police all conflict, then the fact of the detainees was an instrument of conflict that America certainly would not have wanted.

On the morning of November 30, the president met with the Joint Chiefs of Staff, and Kissinger was to brief them with respect to details of the draft agreement. The president "noted that he had spoken to General Westmoreland several weeks ago, and that General Abrams, like General Westmoreland, had long agonized over the war." Westmoreland felt a total withdrawal should be insisted on and that all of Thieu's political concerns must be met. "But the fact is," the president continued, "that the U.S. has stayed one step ahead of the sheriff, just missing fund cutoffs."

Nixon recalled for the JCS that on May 8, he had laid down three conditions for peace: a cease-fire, return of American prisoners of war and an accounting of the missing in action, and assurance that the people of South Vietnam would have the right to determine their future without the imposition of a communist government or communist coalition. "The proposal made by Hanoi on October 8 meets these requirements but now Saigon and some in the U.S. say this is not enough. The facts are, however, that if the American people knew all the details of what has been offered, they would never continue to support a prolongation of the war."

The president told the JCS that he wanted this meeting to focus on contingencies for Vietnam—specifically, "it should encompass two contingencies: The first is if the talks break off. What military action should be taken? The second is if the talks succeed but the agreement is subsequently violated. What actions should be taken?"

After Kissinger briefed the JCS of the details of the agreement, Nixon interjected that "what counts is the knowledge that Saigon is getting U.S. support and that Washington is intent on enforcing the paper commitments. . . . Unfortunately, Thieu is now hung up on the language cosmetics." Kissinger added that there were currently thirty-eight thousand political prisoners in Saigon's jails. "This is Thieu's main asset in getting North Vietnamese troops out of the South." With respect to the Northern troops in the South, Nixon and Kissinger continued their somewhat tortuous logic that "Hanoi has painted itself into a corner. Since they say there are no troops in the South they have no right to be there." Kissinger said that "the agreement does not legalize the presence of North Vietnamese troops in the South. They claim they have none there. This is a lie, of course, but contrary to some misunderstandings there is no legal basis for their being there. Therefore, we can retaliate strongly if they move troops in." President Nixon

added that "he had told Thieu through Duc that there is a sound basis of retaliation if the agreement is violated." Kissinger concluded that "the basis is
far better than it was as a result of the '54 Accords because we are now part
of the agreement. . . . Hanoi cannot keep its army in the South. It must either attack or withdraw."

Nixon now cut to the bottom line: Hanoi would have to decide if violating the agreement was worth the cost of resumption of fighting and massive
U.S. retaliation. Admiral Moorer had prepared contingency plans for three-
and six-day strikes against the North. Nixon asked that the JCS strengthen
the plan to include "the resumption of mining and the use of B-52s over
Hanoi. If Hanoi violates the agreement, the U.S. response must be all out.
We must maintain force in the area to do the job. It cannot be a weak response but rather must be a massive and effective one. Above all, the B-52s
must be targeted at Hanoi."

As Admiral Elmo Zumwalt recalled the meeting, it was then that he recognized the depths of Nixon's deception: "The President's discussion of the
status of the cease-fire increased my sense of being on a strange planet. . . . It
was perfectly obvious to all of us at the time that the promise of massive
American assistance to South Vietnam and of prompt U.S. retaliation to serious truce violations were the critical elements in securing the cease-fire
and that the fulfillment of these promises would be the critical element in
maintaining the cease-fire. Yet the administration never really let the American people—or Congress—in on this non-secret, apparently on the assumption that the critical element in persuading Americans to accept the
terms of the cease-fire was to allow them to believe that it meant the end of
any kind of American involvement in Vietnam no matter what happened
there after the cease-fire was agreed to. Not even the JCS were informed
that written commitments were made to Thieu. There are at least two
words no one can use to characterize the outcome of that two-faced policy.
One is 'peace.' The other is 'honor.'"

Later that day Nixon had his second and final meeting with Duc. The
president got to the point quickly. Kissinger had just informed the president
that Saigon had made a recommendation that very morning that the United
States proceed bilaterally with Hanoi in order to achieve a military solution.
It appeared that Saigon now wanted to go its own way, alone.

Duc told President Nixon that President Thieu believed that this was a
matter of vital national concern, and that if no additional changes were
made to the treaty, "President Thieu would prefer that the United States ex-

plore a bilateral termination of its participation in the conflict directly with Hanoi, and leave Saigon to continue the struggle." Duc then told President Nixon that "President Thieu felt it would be preferable to die now than to die bit by bit."

Thieu wished Nixon well in finding a formula that would allow the exchange of U.S. prisoners of war in return for a cessation of U.S. mining and bombing together with a cease-fire. "President Thieu recognized this would be a very severe setback for him, and that the bombing and mining were an essential adjunct of the current campaign. Nevertheless, President Thieu would prefer this route rather than to abandon the three vital principles."

President Nixon now told Duc about his two-hour meeting with the JCS: "The Joint Chiefs were unanimous—especially General Abrams—in agreeing that there was an irrefutable basis for direct U.S. retaliation. . . . Secondly, the Joint Chiefs had contingency plans in being for air and other responses beyond anything that has ever been undertaken should a violation occur." The minutes go on to say that "the President said he would not provide the precise details of these plans, but wished to emphasize that Hanoi would not get off lightly. Thirdly, Secretary Laird, who was a great friend of South Vietnam's, and a U.S. domestic political expert, had just met with the key members with the Armed Services Committees. These were essentially hawk-orientated. They confirmed, to a man, that if an agreement were achieved and if the provisions of the Agreement became public, and Thieu were the only obstacle, then they would have no alternative but to vote against continuing U.S. aid to South Vietnam."

Nixon ended the discussion by saying that he was willing to meet with President Thieu again at Midway, not to discuss or negotiate the pros and cons of the agreement but to give his personal assurances to President Thieu of continued aid and prompt enforcement. (Thieu would later insist that the meeting be held in the United States.) The JCS *History* notes that on November 30, Nixon instructed the Chiefs to develop contingency military plans in the event that talks were broken off. "It was a contingency plan for intensive air and naval operations throughout North Vietnam, called Priming Charge . . . designed to impose maximum damage to the enemy's war making capability" while producing a "mass shock effect in a psychological context." This included 58 targets in North Vietnam, naval gunfire, and mine reseeding in deepwater ports. The plan was to be ready for execution within 48 hours.

Zumwalt's notes from the JCS meeting with the president illustrate the state of the president's thinking: "If we fought for 2 more years, we might get a marginally better deal. . . . The President insisted that he must have JCS support. . . . Thieu should crow—he gets continued US economic and military support. The President then said, we need to make the point that no paper is worth a damn, what really matters is the economic and military support and will. . . . He urged that we not worry about the words, we will keep the agreement if it serves us—their interests require them to obey."

Nixon was thus deceiving the public, but perhaps also himself. It seemed obvious to Zumwalt that America would never go back to bombing. Nixon was prepared to take that chance and try to rally the silent majority around the signed agreement. Whether Kissinger was in accord with Nixon's plans is hard to say, but clearly the whole situation was getting to him. The president suspected Kissinger was keeping a private diary to protect himself if the plan fell apart. On November 29, Haldeman, at the president's request, met with Haig, who "expressed great concern about K's mental health. Henry, in his view, is completely paranoid—was in absolutely terrible shape in Paris last week and handled things very badly because of it. And that he was even in worse shape in Vietnam before that. And basically the screw up was Henry's fault, in that he committed to final negotiation and settlement before he really should have, which really screwed things up with the North Vietnamese and South Vietnamese." It would be a while before Kissinger would reveal his innermost thoughts.

CHAPTER ELEVEN

Linebacker II

Richard Nixon's diary entry for December 4, 1972, is revealing. "We enter a very tough week and a very crucial one," he wrote, "but in some way I think it's got to come out because the great forces of history—what is really right—are moving us in these directions. Only the insanity and irrationality of some leaders may move us in other directions."

When do statesmen think in terms of maneuverability and when in terms of inevitability? It would be too simple to suggest that they credit victories to their strategy and defeats to impersonal forces of history—but surely that is a temptation. Richard Nixon was a strategist par excellence. As the Watergate tapes reveal, he had so much confidence in his ability to outstrategize any opponent that it got him in trouble. Indeed, he rarely talked in terms of the forces of history; if anything, he would speak of conspiracies of his enemies. "We're up against an enemy, a conspiracy. They're using any means. We are going to use any means."

Here, however, just as Thieu was threatening to split with the U.S., leaving Nixon in the position of abandoning an ally to certain destruction in order to get out with American POWs before the Congress forced his hand, he spoke of the forces of history. Why not attack the doves in Congress? Why not blame the communists for stalling in the talks? Why speak of impersonal forces when he had a plan to go back in and resume bombing after the deal was struck? Perhaps part of him knew that resumed bombing was a long shot. Perhaps he knew the troubled political waters that awaited him because of the Watergate mess. Maybe it was about to unravel his presidency and force the abandonment of an ally and the loss of South Vietnam to the communists.

As December's events would reveal, these "forces of history" would not resolve themselves easily. It would take more diplomacy *and* more bombing before a deal could be struck.

On the same day, December 4, Bunker cabled Kissinger that "Thieu's preferred position, of course, would be to go on fighting for another two or three years with our support in the hope that the points on which he is insisting now would be attained. My judgment is that two years from now the situation would be quite similar to that presently obtaining, the NVA would still be in South Vietnam and the fighting would continue."

Nixon had already decided that the United States would not go on fighting on the ground for another two years. He was not going to be bogged down in Vietnam during his second term. One way or another, Nixon was going to get back America's POWs and withdraw all troops. The state of Nixon's thinking was captured in a diary notation by Haldeman: "The P had E [for Ehrlichman] and me over at 8:15 and we met in the Aspen living room, by the fire with the lights low on a cold night, and the P was slumped down in his chair and sort of went through the whole thing with John." Nixon was concerned about Kissinger, Congress, and South Vietnam: "The key issue is the POWs; if we start bombing, do we get them back in a month or July; will Congress continue its support and what about public expectations. He feels Kissinger's approach now is not very rational. . . . He said we have to recognize that the North Vietnamese are evaluating K, personally, too."

Haldeman's notes were full of numerous entries about Nixon's having lost faith in Kissinger, whom he believed was obsessed with cutting any possible deal. On December 7 Haldeman recorded in his diary that the president was fixating on Kissinger's psychological makeup. "The P is convinced that if K came back without an agreement, he would resign." On December 4, Haldeman wrote: "P doesn't think K is in touch with reality."

This assessment came on the very day that Kissinger was in Paris to begin what Nixon hoped would be the final round of negotiations with Le Duc Tho—but Tho had not come to Paris for compromise or concessions. The meetings were totally unproductive. Not only was Tho uncompromising, but he kept raising new conditions, making new demands in areas on which they had already reached agreement. Kissinger cabled Nixon that the North Vietnamese were more intransigent than ever before. The NLF had been pressing publicly and privately for linking the release of American POWs with political detainees, and Tho was beginning to raise the point. At a press conference on December 8, Madame Binh declared that "there is no reason why we should free American prisoners while our compatriots remain in jail." This position created a great tension within the Northern Lao Dong. According to Brigham, "The NLF's intransigence destroyed any chance for peace." As one party member put it, "We had come very close to reaching an agreement when southerners sabotaged the entire plan."

A bitter Kissinger returned to Paris for a meeting with the Vietnamese delegation at the home of U.S. ambassador. Kissinger brought bad news: There had been no compromises regarding the disposition of North Vietnamese troops. "It is a total absolute impossibility. To insist on it is to guarantee that there will be no agreement."

Kissinger told the South Vietnamese that he was unable to get mention of the PRG deleted from the entire accord because Le Duc Tho insisted that the preamble refer specifically to the PRG.

"Nothing is resolved," said Kissinger.

"Mr. Duc was hoping that you would succeed to not mention the PRG anywhere," said Ambassador Phuong.

Finally, Kissinger vented his frustration: "I know you gentlemen will be elated when this breaks down, and Mr. Nha will have a celebration for a month. . . . I must say, as a result of all this leaking they have taken back all of the concessions they made. For example, the DMZ. Because of the leaks for every concession they made we make one."

Kissinger reported that he and Le Duc Tho had spent over an hour on Articles 8c and 8d. "They have broken it out: they have one section on military personnel, one on foreign civilian personnel, one on Vietnamese civilian personnel, and one on missing in action. But the terms are the same as their old ones. That's a concession to us, because I told them we did not want American military men linked with civilians! In the one you have, the one paragraph for all detained people is now broken out into three paragraphs. But the obligations are the same.

"You are a time-consuming race. So frankly this is where we are. There is nothing new to report. If it stays in this position tomorrow, I will return home Friday. And we will put Senator [Charles] Percy [of the Senate Foreign Relations Committee] in charge of the negotiations. Since we have a meeting tomorrow afternoon, would it be possible to have a morning session as non-contentious as possible?"

Ambassador Porter interceded: "Peu de contention, et aussi court que possible."

"I don't want any trouble tomorrow," said Kissinger.

When the discussion turned to whether Kissinger would be able to interject the term "non–South Vietnamese forces," in Article 3 of the text, Kissinger shot back, "In Saigon you think that I am the enemy."

"No," said Ambassador Phuong.

"No, let me finish," said Kissinger. "You think if I agree to raise it, it is as good as if Le Duc Tho agreed to it. Then Duc asks for a consequent one."

"You promised you would make an effort," said Ambassador Phuong.

"We have had a rough week, and we spent it defending your views. Our views are essentially expressed in our October draft," said Kissinger.

"What about the Vietnamese text?" asked Pham Dang Lam, chief of the GVN delegation to the peace talks.

"We have no text, no agreement yet. If we get any agreement you will get the text. . . . One thing puzzled me. For my own education. If I understood President Thieu's letter to President Nixon, it was suggested that we should make a separate deal with the North. . . . It was that we should make a separate deal for a cease-fire. You would release some prisoners, and you would respect the cease-fire. By that agreement, all their troops would remain in the South, and there would be no prohibition with respect to Laos and Cambodia and the DMZ. How do you think you would survive under that agreement?" asked Kissinger.

Ambassador Phuong ducked the question, though Thieu himself had already answered it by saying that he would rather die quickly now than more slowly later. Instead, humorously, Phuong told Kissinger that Mr. Duc was a bit hard of hearing, so he asked that Kissinger talk slowly and loudly to be understood. Kissinger was incredulous: "Now you tell me! One could draw a profound conclusion from the fact that your President sends someone to our President who can speak but not hear."

Ambassador Lam then asked about Le Duc Tho: "Is he sure of himself?"

"Yes. You are giving him problems with your constant propaganda. This is good in the short term, but in the long term. . . . the damage done is done. We have explained to you the consequences of a failure to agree. If there is no agreement, we will have to fight the war in a different framework," said Kissinger.

As the meeting broke up, Kissinger explained that the treaty actually guaranteed the survival of South Vietnam—if only the GVN leaders would listen. "Haig and I, who have saved you before, are in despair about you. We don't want anything from you any more, frankly, because if there is no agreement, the war will end in six months or so with a deal between us and Hanoi on withdrawal for prisoners. There will be no link between us and

Indochina. This agreement provides a link to Indochina—provided you do one thing: your President should thank our President for having accomplished a significant thing, so the American people can have some pride. Even the October agreement if accepted enthusiastically or even willingly— its primary use to you is not this or that clause but that it ties us legally to your survival, to the stability of Indochina." Then he cut to the chase: "Do you think I believe Le Duc Tho? Of course they will cheat. But if they use the Ho Chi Minh Trail and we bomb the Ho Chi Minh Trail, we have a legally strong position. If the war ends the other way, there is no way we can do that. Within a year, all our aid will be cut off, that is why we who support you despair of your shortsightedness. You have missed the real issues. The key is whether the American people know they have achieved something. No one knows what the Korean Armistice Agreement says. But the people know they have achieved something and if the North Koreans violate it, the President can defend it. . . . The major use of the agreement to you is it links us legally to you on a long-term basis for an indefinite period."

Kissinger's suggestion that the words, details, and clauses did not really matter needs to be analyzed in the context of the previous three years. This was indeed exactly how he had conducted his negotiations with Le Duc Tho. And *if* the U.S. would have bombed the North again after a deal, the specifics of that deal would hardly have been final and dispositive. They still mattered, of course; the release of prisoners or withdrawal of troops is never to be skipped over lightly in hopes of a better military situation in the future. More likely, then, is the interpretation that Kissinger just wanted a deal, any deal, that got the U.S. out. So while Kissinger kept reassuring Thieu that he need not be concerned with phrases or clauses having to do with the disposition of the North Vietnamese troops in the South, the mention of the PRG, the characterization of the DMZ, and the composition of the NCRC, Thieu knew otherwise. Nixon was expecting to rally the American people through a deception akin to the events in 1964 at Tonkin Gulf that had committed America to the war.

Kissinger had come to Paris with instructions from Nixon to settle. "Le Duc Tho kept me there ten days, our longest negotiating session ever, and each day we seemed farther away from an agreement," Kissinger wrote in his memoirs. John Negroponte characterized Hanoi's tactics in the December round of negotiations as "clumsy, blatant, and essentially contemptuous of the United States, tawdry, petty, and at times transparently childish."

The records of these meetings from both sides confirm Kissinger's observation that Le Duc Tho was unprepared to settle. The meeting began with another lecture from Tho: "In the past two years of war, we have known all of the atrocities of war. Particularly under the Nixon administration, the atrocity has been to the extreme. We also understand that without a settlement the war will be merciless. You may bring B-52s to raze Hanoi and Haiphong. You say your President is determined: we know he is determined to invade and devastate our country. We have not misunderstood him. We have undergone tens of millions of tons of bombs and shells, equaling 500–600 atomic bombs, but we are not afraid. We are determined to oppose you. We will not submit, we cannot accept being slaves. That is why your threats and breach of promises prove that you are not yet really serious about negotiation."

In vain, Kissinger tried to raise the series of issues for insertion that he had promised the South Vietnamese delegation he would attempt: "Regarding the preamble, the U.S. is not willing to sign an agreement in which in the preamble the name of the PRG is explicitly mentioned." Tho didn't budge. From here the session went downhill as discussion ranged from the DMZ, to troop demobilization, to the word for administrative structure, to the disposition of political detainees.

Kissinger was of the view that Tho was raising the stakes on a number of issues. Tho answered that the U.S. put forward changes and then withdrew them, claiming they were concessions. Le Duc Tho admitted that "I have been harshly criticized" in Hanoi by the Politburo for exceeding instructions.

On December 10 Haldeman wrote: "The P made the point strongly to Al that the problem is that we pushed so hard on the settlement before the election that that put us in a bad spot. We're still trying to dig out from that. Haig agreed. Haig is very much concerned about maintaining the cease-fire. He feels we want to be prepared to react hard if they violate it, and he's sure they will. That means bombing the North. The P then took a very strong position on violations. It should be clear that it will not be on a tit-for-tat basis. It'll be all out, regardless of potential civilian casualties, if we have a provocation."

On December 12, Thieu was scheduled to give a speech to a joint session of the National Assembly. Ambassador Bunker was asked by President Nixon to meet with Thieu prior to this address to say that the president "hopes that in what you plan to say concerning the negotiations that you will not refer to conflicting negotiating positions. At this delicate stage of the talks, this could only serve to make much more difficult the complicated situation we are both in."

Thieu paid little attention to Nixon's warning. In his one-hour address, he reaffirmed his position regarding the Indochina peace settlement. He repeated his demand that there must be a complete withdrawal of all NVA troops from South Vietnam and told the Assembly that the National Council of Reconciliation was in fact a disguised coalition. Thieu went on to tell the Assembly that Hanoi must accept the principle of four separate Indochinese states and commit itself not to launch aggression against any of the three other states. Thieu repeated that the GVN would never accept any demand for a general election that would aim at replacing its constitution and government structure.

In a three-hour briefing the same day to his country's leading politicians, Thieu said that the GVN demands for revisions had not been met and predicted that "the communists would eventually expand their influence in the South to the point where they could win an election." Thieu used the number "300,000 NVA in South Vietnam" as the great danger facing South Vietnam, and he called the draft agreement "too high a price to pay for the release of 600 U.S. POWs." Ever the realist, Thieu admitted that if he failed to sign, "the U.S. Congress would cut off aid within two months and the GVN would be finished anyway." Thieu used a Vietnamese slang term to describe his situation: "I would be asphyxiated."

Thieu exhibited the strongest skepticism about whether the U.S. would honor its pledge to intervene militarily if the communists violated the treaty. He acknowledged that although the U.S. had promised retaliation, "Who can know for sure?" With great pride Thieu said that he had been the first chief of state "to stand up to Mr. Nixon." Thieu ended the meeting by saying that he was still undecided as to whether he would sign the cease-fire agreement.

On December 13, Kissinger cabled Nixon that the previous day's meeting with Le Duc Tho followed the same pattern as the last three days, "just more ludicrous and insolent in form." Kissinger separately summed up the state of the negotiations in a memo to Nixon: "Hanoi is almost disdainful of us because we have no effective leverage left, while Saigon in its short-sighted devices to sabotage the agreement knocks out from under us the few remaining props. We will soon have no means of leverage at all while pressures will build domestically if we fail to reach an agreement nor be able to preserve Saigon. We now have two essential strategic choices. The first one is to turn hard on Hanoi and increase enormously through bombing and other means. This would include measures like reseeding the mines, massive 2 day strikes against the power plants this weekend, and a couple of B-52 efforts. This would make clear that they paid something for the past 10 days. Concurrently, we would try to line up Saigon and at least prevent Thieu from making further unilateral proposals. Pressures on Saigon would be essential so that Thieu does not think he has faced us down, and we can demonstrate that we will not put up with our ally's intransigence any more than we will do so with our enemy."

From Washington, Alexander Haig dispatched a "Sensitive Exclusively Eyes Only" memo to Winston Lord in Paris for Kissinger's attention. Haig wanted Kissinger to understand the pressures that Nixon was now facing. He also wanted Kissinger to know Haig's position: "1) I believe time has come to initiate massive military pressure against Hanoi and Vietnam. No other course of action will meet the present need, despite the severe domestic risks which this course of action will entail; 2) it is our own failure to keep sight of this fact that has brought us into this current dilemma; 3) I do not share yours [sic] or the President's view that the American people, the Congress, and whoever else is asked to support the action will not ultimately do so. There will, of course, be a lot of White House discomfort, but the simple facts are that the American people understand Hanoi's treachery and would never understand abandoning Thieu because of his failure to accept the presence of North Vietnamese troops in the South. This has always been my view. It is inconceivable to me that the Congress could cut-off funds to Thieu while Hanoi held our prisoners or refused to meet reasonable demands associated with the peace settlement."

Haig informed Kissinger that he would be at the airfield to meet Kissinger upon his return from Paris, so that the next morning a decisive recommendation could be made regarding a new bombing campaign, dubbed Linebacker II.

On December 14 Kissinger cabled Bunker to secure an immediate appointment with Thieu and not allow "the palace to deflect you." "For your information, and you may hint to Thieu, the President is considering forceful military actions in response to the North Vietnamese stalling tactics in Paris. . . . You should also make it crystal clear to President Thieu that the President is increasingly impatient with President Thieu's stand with regard to the negotiations. If at this juncture his totally negative attitude continues, it cannot but threaten the fundamental character of our future relationship.

He should be under no illusion about the fact that the President is at the point of reconsidering our whole relationship."

* * *

The peace talks collapsed on December 13, and the next day Nixon ordered a resumption of the bombing. This time, he had only one goal: to bring Hanoi back to the negotiating table. On December 18, Linebacker II, often characterized as the "Christmas bombing," began with B-52 bomber sorties and fighter bomber sorties striking the Hanoi-Haiphong area.

Just prior to the Easter bombing in May, President Nixon had said, "The bastards have never been bombed like they're going to be bombed this time." Now, the day before the Christmas bombing began, Nixon told Admiral Moorer, "I don't want any more of this crap about the fact that we couldn't hit this target or that one. This is your chance to use military power effectively to win this war, and if you don't, I'll consider you responsible." Admiral Moorer issued the order to execute expanded air attacks with an objective of "maximum destruction of selected military targets in the vicinity of Hanoi/Haiphong." Moorer ordered that all resources be used and that B-52s carry maximum ordnance with preapproved restrikes of targets. Kissinger later wrote, "The North Vietnamese committed a cardinal error in dealing with Nixon, they cornered him." The B-52s were his last roll of the dice.

Nixon rejected Kissinger's advice that he should announce this escalation in a nationally televised address. Instead, he instructed Kissinger to conduct a press conference on December 16 in which he would blame the stalemated negotiations on communist intransigence. Kissinger was advised to hint that sterner measures were being contemplated.

The Linebacker II operation contingency plan called for three days of all-weather around-the-clock bombing that would give maximum effort against the most lucrative and valuable targets in Vietnam. "While seeking to avoid civilian casualties, air chiefs complied with Nixon's desires and designed Linebacker II to inflict the utmost civilian distress," wrote historian Mark Clodfelter. "I want the people of Hanoi to hear the bombs," said Admiral Moorer.

Nixon intended for Linebacker II to inflict maximum physical damage on the North Vietnamese. Whereas Linebacker I in May 1972 sought to destroy North Vietnam's war-making capacity, Nixon intended Linebacker II to destroy the North's will to fight, as well as to demonstrate to the South Vietnamese that he was a man of steel. In his masterful account of the air war in Vietnam, Mark Clodfelter explained that "the B-52, with its massive conventional bomb load, and all-weather capability, was air power's best tool to disrupt the enemy psychologically." Vietcong Minister of Justice Truong Nhu Tang recalled, "The first few times I experienced a B-52 attack, it seemed as I strained to press myself into the bunker floor, that I had been caught in the Apocalypse. The terror was complete. One lost control of bodily functions as the mind screamed incomprehensible orders to get out." Bui Tin recalled that the Christmas bombing was "like living through a typhoon with trees crashing down and lightning transforming night into day."

Hanoi was rendered defenseless by the Linebacker assault, but the United States sustained serious losses as well. According to the JCS *History,* "overall, Linebacker II caused serious damage in North Vietnam, and both military assessments and press reports revealed 'very heavy' destruction in target areas. But, if the United States inflicted considerable damage in Linebacker II, it also received the same in terms of losses of aircraft and personnel. During the 12-day campaign (11 days, a day pause on Christmas, and another day of bombing), the enemy downed 13 U.S. tactical aircraft. More significantly, however, was the enemy destruction of B-52s. Heretofore, only one B-52 had been lost to enemy action in the Southeast Asian operations of November 1972, but during Linebacker II, enemy SAMs downed 15 of the strategic bombers. In addition, United States aircrew casualties during the expanded bombing of December amounted to 93 missing with 31 reported captured."

The American prisoners of war were buoyed by Linebacker II. Commander James B. Stockdale recalled, "When the ground shook and when the plaster fell from the ceiling. . . . the guards cowered in the lee of the walls, cheeks so ashen you could detect it from the fiery sky. . . ."

* * *

Linebacker II was also intended as a clear message to President Thieu, but Nixon wanted to make certain that Thieu did not draw the wrong lesson, and on December 19 Haig traveled again to the Presidential Palace in Saigon, where, joined by Ambassador Ellsworth Bunker, he met with President Thieu and press secretary Nha. Nixon had asked Haig to go to Saigon and explain the situation in Paris and "future U.S. intentions." Haig carried a personal letter to President Thieu, the contents of which had been seen only by Haig, Kissinger, and the president. No copies had been distributed within the U.S. bureaucracy. "President Thieu should understand that President Nixon had written this letter only after the most careful and painful reappraisal in Southeast Asia, the current state of negotiations, and especially President Thieu's attitude with respect to them. The President is confident that President Thieu will treat this letter with the greatest secrecy," Haig explained.

Haig then handed the letter to Thieu, who read it carefully, "obviously somewhat shaken by its contents." The letter prepared Thieu for Linebacker II but warned him that there was little reason to be buoyed by the campaign. This was it: When Hanoi returned to the table Thieu was expected to be on board as well. The bombing was a sort of insurance policy for Thieu. If South Vietnam's life was threatened, the policy would be executed. Haig elaborated that Hanoi, encouraged by the growing drift between Washington and Saigon, now believed that time was on its side. "It is obvious that they may have concluded that the longer they delay, the wider the gap will become, and the greater the possibility that time will accomplish for them what they have been unable to achieve on the battlefield or at the negotiating table."

The declassified records show that Haig told Thieu that "it is the general impression in Washington, however, that President Thieu has been the main cause for the turn in Hanoi's attitude." President Nixon had made the decision to renew the air war "at a scale heretofore never contemplated." Haig briefed Thieu on the specifics of Linebacker II and told him that "President Nixon was determined to continue these strikes at a maximum intensity. . . . It was designed to again convey to Hanoi that they could not trifle with President Nixon. More importantly, however, the action, which was now underway would underline to Hanoi the determination of the President to enforce the provisions of any political settlement that might be arrived at. President Thieu also should draw appropriate conclusions from the President's actions."

Haig expressed the hope that Hanoi might immediately return to the negotiating table and be ready to settle. Should Hanoi wish to settle, it could be done very quickly. Therefore, he stressed, President Thieu should take no comfort from the bombing raids over Hanoi-Haiphong because this would only lead to greater domestic pressure on President Nixon to end the war. Haig now pushed his major point:

Unless the U.S. finds an entirely new basis to justify the sacrifices that the American people have been asked to bear, there is no hope that the American Congress will be willing to continue to do so. Thus, it is not that we are naïve and expect that peace will automatically follow the agreement;

rather, precisely the opposite motivations underlay President Nixon's desire to have President Thieu's concurrence in the proposal. It is the President's view and one shared by Dr. Kissinger and General Haig, that if we have an agreement, then those elements in the U.S. who have long-supported the war effort and President Thieu will be able to claim, with obvious justification, that they have been right all along, and that continued support for Thieu has finally brought Hanoi to the peace table. With this agreement, the anti-communist elements in America will have a sense of pride in what has been done up until now, and, more importantly, the American people can rally behind an agreement, which has been achieved through the President's persistence in doing the right thing. With this renewed sense of pride, *the American people will be willing to make whatever sacrifices are necessary to ensure that the agreement succeeds.* Thus, continued support, economic and military, for South Vietnam will be assured. But even more importantly, *should Hanoi violate the agreement, then the legal, psychological, and patriotic basis will exist for brutal U.S. retaliation.*

In other words, Nixon was bombing the North in order to pressure the South, yet happy that the American public would believe he had succeeded in pressuring the North. The official meeting notes record that "General Haig concluded by again emphasizing the absolute essentiality of changing the fundamental character of the conflict in such a way that a whole new basis can be found for U.S. support." Thieu would later tell his NSC that "if Kissinger had the power to bomb the Independence Palace to force me to sign the agreement, he would not hesitate to do so."

Following his meeting with President Thieu, Haig traveled to Phnom Penh for a meeting with Prime Minister Lon Nol and then to Bangkok for a meeting with Field Marshal Thanom. In both meetings, Haig continued to maintain that if the agreement was finalized, "the U.S. will have the legal, moral, and political basis to provide assistance to our friends in all of Southeast Asia, and to intervene in the likely event that the communists violate it. . . . We plan to remain engaged in Southeast Asia to the full extent permitted under the agreement. . . . We plan to keep substantial forces in Southeast Asia for hair-trigger response to violations. The actions the President has taken this week against the North are a demonstration of a firm resolve. They are meant to show Hanoi that they will face the same response in the event that they cheat or abrogate the agreement. And they should be a demonstration to you of the President's determination to police and guarantee this agreement once we have the right kind of settlement. In other words, the whole purpose of this agreement from the President's point of view is that it provides the indispensable foundation for continued American involvement in Indochina, not for American political disengagement. For four years we have said that we will not betray our friends; we seek this agreement because it meets our terms and provides the best basis—given our domestic situation—for providing the support for our friends that is the central principle of the Nixon doctrine."

* * *

After the initial seven days of bombing, Nixon ordered a Christmas pause. On December 26, he renewed the attacks, and almost immediately, Hanoi agreed to resume negotiations. The post–December 26 attacks were massive in scale. Ten targets from fifteen directions received the brunt of the attack. It was classic cause and effect. Linebacker II was terminated on December 29. On December 28 Kissinger had informed Bunker that "we have asked the North Vietnamese to meet with me in Paris on January 3. . . . We have no answer from them at this time, but there is an outside possibility that they will accept." Hanoi did.

Nixon understood that the use of B-52s in Linebacker II would be met with a public outcry, especially just a few weeks after Kissinger had said, "peace is at hand." A December 28 *Washington Post* editorial asked, "How did we get in a few short weeks from a prospect for peace that 'you can bank on,' to the most savage and senseless act of war ever visited, over a scant ten days, by one sovereign people over another?" The *New York Times*'s Tom Wicker described the Linebacker II raids as "shame on earth." In Congress, Senator William Saxbe of Ohio said that Nixon had "taken leave of his senses." Senate majority leader Mike Mansfield described the bombing as "a stone-age tactic." Yet it worked, on both the North *and* (perhaps more important) the South.

One of the most interesting accounts of the bombing and its consequences was offered by Neil Sheehan in *After the War Was Over.* Sheehan returned to Bach Mai hospital, which had been hit by a B-52 during the Christmas bombing. At the time of the attacks, physical destruction of populated areas was exaggerated, but Bach Mai became a focal point for the world's attention. The B-52 had been trying to hit a small French airfield about a half-mile away, but Bach Mai became "collateral damage." It took eleven years to rebuild Bach Mai, which was finally opened on December

22, 1983. Sheehan also asked to be taken to three adjoining houses on Cam Thien Street, just south of the Hanoi railroad station. Here again B-52s had accidentally obliterated three homes, killing more people than had been killed at Bach Mai. "In honor of the dead, the houses had not been rebuilt. There was an iron grill fence in front of the missing homes with their numbers on a gate: 47-49-51. Behind the gate was a statue of a young woman carrying a child in her arms, a memorial to a Vietnamese mother who perished with her family in one of the houses."

Sheehan recounted his visit to the Army Museum in Hanoi:

As a visitor worked his way forward through the exhibits of the American war, he gradually found himself in the midst of the battle of the B-52s. The initial encounter was a pile of wreckage in the museum yard, the remains of one of the bombers shot down on December 18, 1972, the first night of the raids. Nearby was a torn section of fuselage from another B-52 with the emblem of the Strategic Air Command, a bolt of lightning grasped in a fist, painted on it. Inside the main room of the museum the battle unfolded. There was a large photograph of Nixon discussing strategy with Kissinger, pictures of B-52s in flight, streams of bombs falling from the bomb bays, the rubble at Bach Mai and Khan Thien Street, and then one photograph after another of Vietnamese in flak jackets and helmets firing antiaircraft guns, tracking bombers on radar, launching missiles. They had to defeat the planes. . . . Nevertheless, the Vietnamese looked at the results, and the results convinced them that they had won a triumph grand enough to justify, once the war was over, renaming an avenue in Hanoi "Duong Chien Thang B 52"—Avenue of the Victory over the B-52s.

CHAPTER TWELVE

Nixon's Peace with Honor

In Washington D.C., on January 2, 1973, the House Democratic caucus voted 154 to 75 to cut off all funds to Indochina, subject only to the safe return of American POWs and the withdrawal of all United States military personnel. "The Congress," Kissinger later wrote, "was threatening to abandon all our allies in Indochina." The 93rd Congress was scheduled to convene the next day, and passage of a resolution soon after forcing the American president to terminate all military activity in South Vietnam was likely. On January 4, the Senate's Democratic caucus passed a resolution similar to the House's by a 36 to 12 vote. Legislation to terminate the war was speeding its way to the floor.

The *New York Times* reported that Le Duc Tho was en route to Paris, but he was actually making a stop in Beijing to consult with Premier Chou Enlai. The secret meeting with Le Duc Tho began by Chou's observing that Nixon's effort "to exert pressure through bombing has failed. Nixon is facing many international and domestic problems. It seems that he intends to retreat from Vietnam and Indochina. During the negotiations, you should adhere to principles and show necessary flexibility. Let the Americans leave as quickly as possible. In half a year or one year the situation will change."

On January 3, Haldeman recorded in his diary that the president seemed preoccupied and was having trouble focusing on his State of the Union speech. "I think until he gets Vietnam settled, everything else is going to pretty much stay in the background and there won't be much concentration going on."

From Paris, William Sullivan, a member of the negotiating team, cabled Kissinger that the technical experts had met and that his North Vietnamese counterparts acted "hang dog," reflecting the effects of the bombing on their morale. "I remember coming back on New Year's Day," Sullivan later recalled. "The senior members of the Vietnamese delegation had been back in Hanoi during the bombing. In fact, I was informed . . . that one string of bombs had fallen very close to Le Duc Tho's house. So they had absorbed the full impact of the bombing, and they were aware that it was a serious effort. . . . It was a very somber meeting, no joking as usually went on, and whenever points were pressed, and we seemed to be at a point of suggesting that our patience was wearing thin, they either made a concession there or moved rapidly on to something else, and set that aside."

With President Nixon's inauguration just two weeks away, President Thieu wrote Nixon a lengthy letter that sought to address his gravest concerns: "I do not think we should be resigned to accept that the question of withdrawal of North Vietnamese troops cannot be solved satisfactorily just because the North Vietnamese side used to oppose this reasonable demand from our side." Thieu reiterated the points made in his previous letter, dated December 20, 1972. For the South Vietnamese, the concessions were issues of life and death: "I value very highly your assurance of continued assistance in the post-settlement period and that you will respond with full force should the settlement be violated by North Vietnam. For this, however, I believe that the settlement should be based on sound principles. Any concessions we shall make to the Communists will be theirs forever, while they consider any compromises they would make as only temporary."

With Kissinger about to leave for Paris, Nixon summoned his aide to Camp David for final instructions and strategy. Kissinger later wrote that Nixon "urged me to settle on whatever terms were available." Nixon recorded in his diary that there were now only two options available. The first was that "we would agree to an immediate settlement on the best terms we could negotiate." The other was an immediate break with President Thieu, to be followed by massive bombing until the North released the POWs in return for an immediate and complete American withdrawal. Nixon told Kissinger to settle, because "a poor settlement on Option One was better for us than Option two at its best would be." As Kissinger said his good-byes at the door of Birch Lodge at Camp David, Nixon said, "Well, one way or another, this is it."

As soon as Kissinger left Camp David, the president (according to Haldeman's diary) "raised his concern about the K[issinger] papers—and all the P[resident']s papers on national security—that K is holding, including Henry's phone calls and conversation memos and cables and so on, which he wants to be sure we get a hold of and stay on top of as much as possible." Nixon feared that Kissinger would either take all the credit for a successful outcome or pass the blame for an unsuccessful negotiation. In fact, a day earlier Nixon had instructed Charles Colson to make certain that Kissinger's telephone logs were all checked, suspecting that Kissinger was leaking information to *New York Times* writer James Reston or Max Frankel. Nixon suspected it was Frankel, since "Henry is compulsive on Frankel. He's Jewish."

Recently released transcripts of Nixon's private Oval Office conversations further reveal that the president told Haldeman, "I want Henry's phones logged. Now, can you do that? Will the telephone company do that without—I mean, the point is, we've got to look in terms of leaks."

Upon arrival in Paris on January 6, Le Duc Tho spoke of the indignation of the entire Vietnamese nation as a result of the recent U.S. bombings. Characterizing the attacks as "the most barbarous and inhuman ones ever seen in the history of war," Tho described a trail of death and destruction "when our compatriots were sleeping, attacking indiscriminately, hospitals, schools, factories, and dwelling-houses, all considered as military targets." Referring to the meetings that were about to start between the two sides, Tho warned the U.S. not to keep "demanding unreasonable changes bearing upon the principles and content of the agreed agreement."

* * *

The first meeting of the final round of negotiations took place on January 8 at the house in Gif-sur-Yvette. Unlike the previous meetings, the Vietnamese delegation did not greet Kissinger at the gate, and he received a cool reception upon entering. Le Duc Tho opened by criticizing the 12 days of bombing. "Under the pretext of interrupted negotiations, you resumed the bombing of North Vietnam, just at the moment when I reached home. You have 'greeted' my arrival in Hanoi in a very 'courteous' manner! Your action, I can say, is flagrant and gross. You thought that by doing so, you could submit us. You were mistaken. . . . You and no one else made the negotiations difficult," said an angry Le Duc Tho.

Tho was so angry that he slammed the table over and over, uttering the words "Ngu Xuan" while looking at Kissinger. "Stupid, Stupid, Stupid" was the translation that no one wanted to give Kissinger. "I have heard many adjectives in your comments, I propose that you should not use them!" said Kissinger.

Le Duc Tho replied: "I have used these adjectives with a great deal of restraint already. The world public opinion, the United States press and United States political personalities have used harsher words."

Kissinger responded that the number of outstanding issues was very small and that "if this time they cannot be settled, I am sure they will remain insoluble the subsequent times. . . . I hope that at the end of this round of talks, we will have brought peace to Vietnam and Indochina." In hearings before the Senate Select Committee on POW/MIA Affairs, Kissinger said, "When I met Le Duc Tho after the B-52 bombing, I thought he had discovered a physical relationship with me. He couldn't keep his hands off of me."

Nothing was accomplished at this first meeting, but Kissinger reassured Nixon that "it would probably not be realistic to expect the communists to give in or give up on the first day back after the bombing." At the next meeting, on January 9, Kissinger and Tho addressed the explicit understanding that the return of all U.S. military and civilian prisoners be guaranteed unconditionally and would not be linked in any way with a settlement by the South Vietnam parties of the question of civilian detainees in South Vietnam. Le Duc Tho told Kissinger, "Here I would like to say that American prisoners have been covered by Article 8a, and I have been telling you they are not linked to the question of civilian detainees. But the American prisoners belong to the category of military captives, military prisoners of war. We will discuss this in the protocols. We don't propose linking the question of political detainees with military detainees."

Dr. Kissinger interjected, "Or civilian American detainees."

Tho responded, "American civilians are also covered by 8(a)."

Kissinger added, "So it is our understanding that 8(a) is separated from 8(c) and not linked to it."

Le Duc Tho replied, "Agreed. But here you said about 'throughout Indochina.' Regarding Laos, it is a separate understanding. This should not be done."

Dr. Kissinger agreed, "All right, we will say 'Vietnam.'"

Tho then asked, "So we have agreed with that. Why is such an understanding necessary then?"

Kissinger answered quickly, "For our own domestic opinion."

Tho retorted, "I have answered to you this."

Kissinger replied, "All right. I understand and I will consider in the light of your answer whether we need a formal understanding."

Tho then said, "It is not necessary. Please remember my statement. I will honor it."

Kissinger asked, "How about Madame Binh?"

Tho explained, "Madame Binh also does not link the question of American prisoners with civilian detainees. But it is the result of a long and perseverant persuasion of mine over Madame Binh. This is a fact."

Kissinger stated, "I believe it! Now then, on my list we have the questions of civilian detainees in South Vietnam and U.S. technical personnel in Vietnam. Now with respect to civilian detainees in South Vietnam, we have given you a proposal, but in the light of our discussion this morning I would like to rewrite it tonight to make it somewhat more specific along the lines of our previous discussion. And I will bring it with me tomorrow morning."

Tho added, "Let me add one sentence regarding the question of American prisoners. We have settled this question in a very adequate way, and we take into account of your views and I am fair in this. Therefore I would suggest that you should consider the question of political detainees in a very positive way and in a very good way."

Kissinger responded, "Well, this is why I am not discussing the proposal we gave you last time and why I will see if we can make it somewhat more specific. And somewhat more consistent with the Minister's selective recollection [laughter]."

Kissinger clearly believed the treaty was going to be signed, cabling the president on January 9, "We celebrated the President's birthday today by making a major breakthrough in the negotiations. In sum, we settled all the outstanding questions in the text of the agreement." The president described the news by saying (according to Haldeman and Kissinger), "This was the best birthday present he's had in sixty years."

Bunker now cabled from Saigon with news that the proposed procedure for signing was likely to give President Thieu another opportunity to engage in delaying tactics through a new range of negotiations, "a procedure which he considers has been highly successful so far." Bunker believed the GVN would prefer one document in which the preamble did not list the titles of the governments but would refer simply to "the parties participating in the Paris conference on Vietnam." Otherwise Thieu would say that the signing publicly assigned the major roles to the U.S. and the DRV, leaving the Republic of Vietnam in a subsidiary position. If the U.S. and the DRV jointly signed in a public ceremony with the four parties signing in a private ceremony, the GVN would likely feel that this procedure derogated from its sovereignty and made it appear subservient to the United States. Bunker recommended as an offsetting measure "that the GVN would sign a document which would not contain anywhere the title of the PRG" because "I believe this can carry weight with them."

On January 11, both sides concentrated on the question of procedures for signing the agreement. Kissinger proposed a two-party signing and a four-party signing, but the text signed by the four parties would contain different sheets for the signing of each party. These four sheets would be included in the agreement; the functions of the signatories would be mentioned. Tho agreed to separate signings—a two-party signing and a four-party signing. The place of signing would be the International Conference Center on Avenue Kleber.

By the afternoon of January 12, the major issues were resolved. Le Duc Tho and Kissinger gave the experts instructions to work on the completion of the protocols regarding the cease-fire, the JMC, the ICC, and the return of the captured and detained personnel. Now, with virtually all of the issues that had divided them for the past three years resolved, Kissinger said to Tho, "I have one consolation, my successor eight years from now will have to meet with the Special Advisor and try to understand what we agreed to here. . . . I pity my poor successor." The declassified notes record "laughter" at the comment.

The final meeting was held on January 13 at Saint-Nom-La-Breteche. Le Duc Tho and Kissinger discussed the U.S. contribution to the reconstruction of North Vietnam, approved two understandings on the political prisoners and the stationing of U.S. aircraft carriers, and finalized other issues. Kissinger proposed that there be no speech at the signing ceremony, only congratulations outside it. He said that it would be a solemn day in the United States and all the more so in Vietnam. Le Duc Tho agreed. "No doubt, you would not use the term 'victory over the United States war of aggression'!" remarked Kissinger.

At lunch, Le Duc Tho raised his glass to toast peace: "So today we have completed the negotiations. We have obtained the first result; though initial they are very important and fundamental results to restore peace in Vietnam. . . . I agree with you not to change anything in the text of the agreement and the timetable. We shall act strictly as agreed. That is our commitment. And we are confident that in a few days time, peace will be restored in Vietnam."

Kissinger replied: "I consider the Agreement, the understandings, and the protocols completed. I assert that our side will make no change whatsoever and I firmly believe that peace will return to Indochina and to our two peoples on January 27, the day of the signing of the Agreement; we shall respect the Agreement. The Agreement must be one that marks the beginning of genuine peace. The best guarantee for that genuine peace is the improvement of the relations between the two countries. We have experienced many long years of sufferings. I should like to tell you that we will do our utmost to improve the relations between our two peoples."

"We shall not forget this day."

"Both of us shall not forget it."

* * *

And so, finally, Northern troops were allowed to stay in place. Thieu had still not agreed to sign, however, and the president instructed Haig to tell him that the United States was ready to go alone. "The only diplomacy that Haig should exercise is to trick Thieu, if it looks like he's not going with us in regard to shooting his mouth off before the Inaugural. He's got to work out some way to stop him from doing that. If he takes on K or the agreement, he takes on the P personally and he's got to understand that," Haldeman recorded.

There was so much uncertainty that the president instructed Kissinger to draft two speeches—one if Thieu went along, the other if not. Haldeman wrote in his diary for January 13 of "the Thieu problem, which he's still sweating out, because he hasn't heard from Haig yet. The question now is whether Thieu will go along."

On January 15, 1973, Nha, in a letter to Ambassador Ellsworth Bunker, said, "I must draw your attention to the fact that in the latest draft of the Agreement which Ambassador Bunker gave me last Saturday, I have noticed that Hanoi continues to be very stubborn in refusing to withdraw its forces from South Vietnam, even after the GVN has made a major concession on the political solution. . . . On the particular question of the content of the draft agreement I look forward to my meeting with General Haig tomorrow to have further clarification. In the meantime, I suggest that an announcement on 'significant progress' in the negotiations with Hanoi be postponed until such clarification has been made.'"

On January 18 it was jointly announced in Washington and Hanoi that the Paris negotiations would resume on January 23 "for the purpose of completing the text of an agreement." In his memoirs, Nixon wrote, "We anxiously awaited further word from Saigon." He added, "In the meantime, Haig had traveled to Bangkok and Seoul. The Thai leaders and President Park had no confidence that the North Vietnamese intended to abide by the agreement. But they understand the political realities of the American scene, and they agreed to support the settlement publicly and privately to urge Thieu to sign it."

A memorandum of conversation between Haig and Prime Minister Souvanna Phouma at the prime minister's residence in Vientiane was recently declassified. As a summary of the state of affairs, it bears quoting at length. It shows, once again, Nixon's plan to use the peace agreement as a pretext for continued American involvement in the war. Haig began the meeting by telling Souvanna Phouma, "President Nixon asked me to bring you abreast of the current negotiations and generally tell you of the plans as we see them for the future. You will recall that when I was here last, we were having great difficulties with the Vietnamese—we started using B-52s in the Haiphong area, even though at that time there were only small differences to settle with Hanoi. On the text it was clear they were not going to settle. I am very pleased to inform you that as a result of the bombing they returned to Paris with a much more flexible attitude. As a result, we have arrived at an agreement. . . . When I say that, I mean that we have agreed on the terms of a settlement and the broad principles of the protocols. . . . We feel the Agreement is substantially better than the Agreement we originally had in October in certain respects. I will just touch on the main improvements. First, there is a clear and precise statement on the obligations of the parties to respect the DMZ. Second, there are provisions throughout the Agreement, which establish the sovereignty of South Vietnam. Actually, it is cited in four different parts of the accord. Third, we are pleased to have completed all the protocols, including the ICCS, the joint military commissions, and the ceasefire.

> There are also many other improvements. The Agreement is more balanced and not accusatory of South Vietnam or the United States. We have not gotten what President Thieu wants regarding the North Vietnamese in South Vietnam, except for demobilization and we have no more finite formulation on the withdrawal of the NVA. But we are convinced that this problem is manageable for the following reasons. First, because there is a specific requirement for withdrawal from Laos and Cambodia. Second, because there is a prohibition against infiltration of men and material into South Vietnam. Third, because we believe that enemy forces in the South are fighting weak now. And fourth, because we do have recognition of the DMZ and sovereignty of South Vietnam, which theoretically means they do not have the right to be there.

President Thieu has two means to assert leverage to solve the NVA problem. First, he maintains 40,000 political prisoners, which North Vietnam wants released and he can trade their withdrawal for demobilization and release of prisoners. He will also be able to control progress in the political area. The PRG must talk to him and he can control the pace of political progress in relation to the degree of withdrawal. We had presented this plan to President Thieu the day before yesterday and gave him some elaboration yesterday. I will return to Saturday and I am hopeful that he will accept this peace plan.

I would like to explain why we are so concerned that President Thieu join us. He has opposed this plan valiantly for subjective reasons of his own. Through his opposition we have bought much time for him. He is better prepared for a ceasefire. There is an improved situation on the ground in South Vietnam. We improved the document and the bombing of the North weakened North Vietnam and served to convince Hanoi that in the event of future violations we have the capability to send B-52s.

So we, and President Thieu are better prepared than in October but this time it has been at the expense of President Nixon's flexibility at home. We have consumed all of the goodwill in Congress, and even our traditional friends Goldwater, Hebert, and Stennis have told President Nixon it is time to settle. So President Nixon recognizes that if there is no settlement upon which to build a new basis for support in Southeast Asia, then Congress will cut off funds. This would be a tragedy. President Nixon recognizes the risks in this settlement but he also recognizes that the only way a basis can be formed for friends at home to support Southeast Asia is through this Agreement. The President is not naïve regarding Hanoi's intentions. He knows they do not want to abandon the struggle to political insurgency. . . . For all these reasons President Thieu must join with us and as a realistic soldier I am optimistic. If President Thieu's representatives get in touch with you in the next few days and seek your guidance on the situation, I would hope that you urge him to settle.

Phouma asked, "Why can't you reach agreement with Hanoi on the withdrawal of the NVA?" In response, he received Haig's assurance that the United States would "keep our air" until the withdrawal of North Vietnamese.

Phouma then asked, "Won't you have difficulties with your Congress?"

Haig answered, "We will get more Congressional support after a ceasefire in Vietnam. All who have favored continuing the Indochina war correctly will have more support because of the Agreement."

Phouma stated, "It would be much simpler if we told the North Vietnamese that we signed in 1962 and withdrew and they should do the same thing. Why should they withdraw if we stop the bombing before then?"

Haig responded, "We believe that our experience shows that we must maintain our ability to punish them until they abide by the terms of the Agreement. We will keep the paramilitary forces and the air."

The next day Haig traveled to Bangkok to deliver a similar message to Field Marshal Thanom Kittikachorn and his unofficial cabinet. Repeating much of what he told Souvanna Phuoma the previous day, Haig expounded on a few important points:

We believe the issue of North Vietnamese troops in the South is manageable. . . . President Thieu has available leverage, which he can use to secure NVN troop withdrawals. First, there are the civilian prisoners of war. As I mentioned to you the last time, President Thieu will control the timing of the release of political prisoners in South Vietnam and he can do that in the context of North Vietnamese troop withdrawals. His second lever is the political process itself. He can govern the progress of the settlement of political issues. President Thieu is still quite concerned about this issue. On the other hand, he thinks it is manageable. The enemy is weak, he has improved the situation in South Vietnam and psychologically the South Vietnamese are better prepared for a ceasefire. President Thieu has not, however, yet given us his answer. . . . President Nixon does not think this is a perfect agreement. But as we have delayed, we have also consumed a great deal of Legislative goodwill. And if we do not get a new basis for support, Congress will cut off the necessary funds. If we have an agreement, then Congress will be able to provide continued support. Moreover, Hanoi has given more than we have. They have abandoned their demand for a coalition government. They have abandoned their demand that we dismantle the GVN and they have abandoned their objectives in Laos and Cambodia. It is essential that we proceed even with the risks involved. Otherwise we are faced with the prospect of a reaction from Congress.

Haig emphasized that he believed President Thieu was a good soldier and that in the end he would accept the agreement in order to obtain the necessary aid. "It is possible that the GVN will contact your government and ask for your views as to how to proceed. I would hope that you encourage them to accept, because it is only in this way that United States support can be assured.

Then the case in the United States becomes one of reinforcing a peace settlement rather than continuing an endless war. With a settlement, which the American people can look to with pride, then we can get the funds we need for all of our friends here. This is the practical reality of the situation. We do not think this is a perfect agreement. We are not naïve. Hanoi did not settle in December. Then we used the B-52s and they met our major demands. To demand NVA withdrawals would delay the settlement indefinitely."

Thanom asked, "I wonder why Congress is so much more worried about your enemies than your friends."

Haig replied, "That is a good question and President Nixon worries about the same problem. . . . I have talked to President Thieu and in the current situation there are very few areas where the enemy is in control. If there is a ceasefire, President Thieu believes he can manage because he has so many forces of his own. What he is concerned about is not the reality of the NVA but the principle. I think the situation is greatly improved in the present document because it refers to the sovereignty of South Vietnam four times so we can claim that the North Vietnamese have no right to be in South Vietnam. In addition, President Nixon intends to reaffirm support for the GVN."

Thanom stated, "Regarding Congress, if President Nixon has a treaty but keeps his Air Force here and the 7th Fleet in the South China sea, what do you think the prospects are for Congressional support?"

Haig responded, "We think that with a settlement the United States people will support the need to enforce it. There will be some Fulbrights and Mansfields but we have always had them. But getting funds is going to be much easier. . . . With a peace settlement, it will be different."

Haig then moved to a discussion of NVA troops. He noted that Thieu was, of course, unhappy "because of the issue of NVA troops but everything else is manageable. If he does not accept, then he will deprive us of our ability to provide support. No provision of the Agreement is going to prevent the enemy from violations, except their determination and ability to keep the peace."

President Thieu was still resisting the schedule as well as the terms. He complained that he and his advisers had not seen any of the latest text, and he was suspicious of a replay of October. Now, in a final attempt to win Thieu's acquiescence, Nixon wrote a letter to him. Coming directly to the point, Nixon stated that the United States was going to sign the agreement and the situation was one of "extreme gravity" for South Vietnam. "We have made innumerable attempts to achieve the very provisions you have proposed with respect to North Vietnamese forces, both in the text of the Agreement and in formal understandings. We have concluded that the course we have chosen is the best obtainable: While there is no specific provision in the text, there are so many collateral clauses with an impact on this question that the continued presence of North Vietnamese troops could only be based on illegal acts and the introduction of new forces could only be done in violation of the Agreement. . . . This Agreement, I assure you again, will represent the beginning of a new period of close collaboration and strong mutual support between the Republic of Viet-Nam and the United States. You and I will work together in peacetime to protect the independence and freedom of your country as we have done in war. If we close ranks now and proceed together, we will prevail."

On January 23, on instructions from President Thieu, both Nha and Nguyen Phu Duc telephoned Ambassador Bunker with the long-hoped-for news that Thieu was willing to sign. Their only concern was over the plan to publish the text on January 24. They presented several reasons for a later release, including the transparently silly one that the only person in the GVN authorized to release text international agreements was the foreign minister, and he would not be able to do this until January 27. The acting foreign minister was unfamiliar with the text and therefore could not answer questions. Nha and Duc told Bunker that it was not customary to publish texts of agreements before they are signed.

Bunker tried to point out that once the text was initialed, there would be enormous pressure to release the terms of the agreement. If the text was not made public, distorted versions could be published, and the danger of leaks would be very great. Bunker cabled Kissinger, "I did not give Nha or Duc any encouragement, but it seemed evident from the tone of their conversation that Thieu has some deep concern about the release of the text before the signing. I think this is probably because he fears that with its release, concerns about some of the provisions will be aroused here and he would like to give the people an opportunity to get used to the fact that an agreement was imminent before springing it upon them." There were also rumors that Thieu would rather sign the agreement after Tet because "Thieu's astrologer [whom he regularly consulted] advised him not to enter into any new agreements before the new year, and perhaps he feels that by going through the motions he will be in the clear." Thieu had finally given up the struggle.

The text was going to be released no matter what. Bunker wrote to Nha that it was impossible to keep it secret during the three-day hiatus between the initialing and signing. "There is no way to keep these provisions secret, given the number of people who are now privy to them. We would run the great risk of selective or distorted revelations. The U.S. Congress and the press would be merciless in ferreting out the information. Under the procedure as now set, we can immediately take the initiative in presenting the Agreement in positive fashion, which we believe should benefit both the GVN and the USG. I believe that with the complete and thorough knowledge which both you and Mr. Duc have of the texts and the course of negotiations you will be able to respond to questions with competence and skill."

On the morning of January 23, Le Duc Tho and Xuan Thuy met Henry Kissinger again in the Kleber conference room with all their experts. The atmosphere was full of enthusiasm. Kissinger asked Le Duc Tho about the place for the return of the United States prisoners of war. Tho told him that the United States pilots captured in North Vietnam would be handed over to the United States in Hanoi; those captured in South Vietnam would also be returned in North Vietnam, but for those captured in Laos, Vietnam would exchange views with its friends in Laos.

After initialing the agreement, Kissinger handed the pen he had just used to Tho and said: "I am offering you this pen for the lasting remembrance of this historical day."

Tho accepted the pen joyfully and gave Kissinger the pen he had just used: "In return I offer you this pen, but you should keep your words!"

President Richard Nixon told the world that "the people of South Vietnam have been guaranteed the right to determine their own future, without outside interference." He declared that the treaty had achieved America's objectives of "peace with honor" and that the accord had "the full support" of South Vietnam's President Thieu. Nixon also told the American public, "Now that we have achieved an honorable agreement, let us be proud that America did not settle for a peace that would have betrayed our allies, that would have abandoned our prisoners of war, or that would have ended the war for us, but would have continued the war for the 50 million people of Indochina."

Listening to the speech, Nguyen Cao Ky, South Vietnam's vice president, described Nixon's use of "peace with honor" as "a sanctimonious passage which I could not stomach, so nauseating was its hypocrisy and self-delusion." Ky described the agreement as a "sellout." Ambassador Bui Diem recalled, "They said they wanted an honorable solution, but really they wanted to wash their hands of the whole business and run. But while they were washing their hands and scuttling, they did not want to be accused by the Vietnamese and the world of abandoning us. That was their difficulty."

Two decades later Nixon told Monica Crowley that "looking back, I think that the biggest flaw with the Paris Peace Accords of 1973 was that the cease-fire provisions allowed North Vietnamese forces to stay in some South Vietnamese territory captured in the '72 invasion." It was late in the day for the admission.

At a January 24 press conference, Kissinger was asked "if the peace treaty is violated and if the ICC proves ineffective, will the United States ever again send troops into Vietnam?" Kissinger's answer was disingenuous: "I don't want to speculate on hypothetical situations that we don't expect ever to arise." In truth, Kissinger expected the violations to occur almost immediately. There was nothing hypothetical about South Vietnam's threat of extinction under the agreement.

President Thieu vowed a new phase of resistance and said there would never be a coalition in the South. In his forty-minute radio address to the nation announcing the initialing of the cease-fire agreement, Thieu stated that the communists, after imposing eighteen years of suffering and war on the South Vietnamese, had been defeated militarily and forced to sign the cease-fire agreement. He warned that in the four days before signing the agreement, the communists would be attempting to seize control of territory and population, and he appealed to all of the people and the armed forces to maintain a state of high alert in order to foil this plot. Regarding withdrawal of NVA troops, Thieu said that the GVN could not be forced to accept the right of the NVA to remain in South Vietnam. As long as the NVA remained within the territory of South Vietnam, he said, the people of the South could not exercise their right of national self-determination in a free and democratic fashion; hence no elections needed to be held. President Thieu concluded his national address by appealing to the national population to fly the national flag beginning at noon on January 24 "and to defend it against communist efforts to tear it down."

The mechanism for signing the agreement illustrated the practical realities of securing peace at the end of a pen. On Saturday, January 27, Secretary of State William Rogers, on behalf of the United States, signed the agreement, bringing the cease-fire and protocols into effect. In the morning, Secretary Rogers signed a document involving four parties, and in the afternoon he signed a document between the United States and the Democratic Republic of Vietnam. The documents were identical, except that the preamble of each differed. The reason for the separate signing was that although the agreement explicitly directed and identified the two South Vietnamese parties to settle their disputes in an atmosphere of national reconciliation and concord, neither side was yet ready to recognize each other's existence.

Thus, after four years of negotiations, it was still necessary to write a document in which neither side was mentioned by name. A reader of the four-party document would have no idea to whom it applied until the final signature page. The document itself referred only to the parties participating in the Paris Conference, which all knew but all refused to acknowledge. Moreover, the document was signed on two separate pages, with the United States and GVN on one and the DRV and PRG on the other.

In the afternoon, the secretary of state and the foreign minister of the DRV signed the second document. The preamble introduced the parties to the agreement as the United States, with the concurrence of the Republic of Vietnam, and the DRV, with the concurrence of the PRG. This document was not signed by either Saigon or the PRG. Thus, all obligations to the treaty were derived from the four-party document signed in the morning. If any more evidence had been needed that North and South Vietnam were not prepared for peace, this was it.

Editorial reactions to the president's peace agreement applauded Nixon's "peace with honor" over a "peace with expediency" (*Portland Press Herald*). "Nixon's War Becomes Nixon's Peace," wrote Holmes Alexander of the *Fort Worth Star-Telegram*. From the *Milwaukee Sentinel* came this: "President Nixon's courage, astuteness, patience, and firmness of purpose have paid off with an agreement to end the Vietnam War that, all things considered, appears to be about as good as all sides could reasonably expect." From the *Washington Post*: "He has honored a substantial part of his pledge to 'end the war' in four years. We are deeply grateful that he has." From the *Boston Herald-Traveler*: "It is certainly far better than the abject capitulation that some Americans have demanded and or have been willing to settle for . . . the American people owe Mr. Nixon a debt of gratitude for refusing to abandon our allies, or forsake our commitments, or abandon our prisoners, and for holding out for an agreement that promises a just and lasting peace." From the *Wall Street Journal*: "One can quarrel with his pace, but not with the fact that he has got 550,000 men out of Vietnam and the POWs back without causing the defeat of the Saigon regime. . . . It was our enemies that came to understand best that the spine of the man in the White House was made of steel. It was the steel that brought the agreement while the jackals yelled and the hyenas howled." From the *Cleveland Plain Dealer:* "The cease-fire finally is a tribute to Mr. Nixon. His global poker game has paid off in the face of pressures of all kinds from home and abroad. For our thirty-seventh president, this has been his finest hour."

Haldeman recorded in his diary for January 27, 1973, that the president felt that most editorials were missing the point. Nixon was a man of character, and he had toughed this through. "K, at Congress, didn't make the point regarding the character of the man, how he toughed it through. We should quit worrying about defending the agreement; it either works or it doesn't, and it doesn't matter, but K just can't go through the details. Why not say that without the P's courage we couldn't have had this. The basic line here is the character, the lonely man in the White House, with little support from government, active opposition from the Senate and some House members, overwhelming opposition from media and opinion leaders, including religious, education, and business but strong support from labor. The P alone held on and pulled it out. . . . The missing link now is the Profile in Courage."

The president, he wrote, was upset at Kissinger's briefings because he "hardly mentions P. . . . K is feeding the separation idea by his failure to build the P. Can you imagine Sorenson, Schlesinger, McNamara, or Rusk handling things this way with Kennedy? The rift between Henry and the P is not created by leaks, it's fed by Henry's own nuances, because the press want to think there's a rift. We have to have Henry build the P."

* * *

With the news of peace came one of the war's final ironies. Lyndon Baines Johnson had died of a heart attack just hours before the news of peace was made public. The front page of the January 25, 1973, *Washington Post* bore witness to the war's coincidence. The headline, "Terms of Peace Detailed," was accompanied by a photo of a smiling Henry Kissinger talking of a lasting peace, not a temporary armistice, in Vietnam. In the bottom corner of the front page was another photo, this one of President Nixon and Mrs. Johnson watching as the casket carrying the lifeless body of the nation's thirty-sixth president approached the Capitol.

Nixon returned to the White House residence and went to the Lincoln sitting room, where he ate dinner alone, played several records, and sat by the fire. Before retiring for the night, he wrote a short note to Lady Bird Johnson: "Dear Lady Bird, I only wish Lyndon could have lived to hear my announcement of the Vietnam peace settlement tonight. I know what abuse he took—particularly from members of his own party—in standing firm for peace with honor. Now that we have a settlement, we shall do everything we can to make it last so that he and other brave men who sacrificed their lives for this cause will not have died in vain."

During an Oval Office meeting with former Japanese prime minister Eisaku Sato on January 31, Nixon told Sato that Johnson "did know. I told him on the 2nd of January that talks were going to begin. On January 15, when Henry returned to Paris, I had Henry call and tell him there was a breakthrough and we had halted the bombing. Two days later we sent him some papers of the agreements, so he knew before he died."

"So he died in peace," said Sato.

"In fact, his widow put out a statement he was so appreciative that he had been told, he was drafting a statement of support," said Kissinger.

"We are relieved that he knew," concluded Sato.

Nixon then spoke to Sato about how the bombing had allowed the United States to end the war in an honorable way. He told Sato that "the problem which many friends in the world did not recognize was that it was essential for the U.S. to the end the war in an honorable way. Many in this country thought that when I came into office that I, as a political act, would let South Vietnam go down the drain, and blame Kennedy and Johnson, who started it." Nixon told Sato that while "peace elements" in other countries would have welcomed that type of "bug out" in 1969, leaders like Sato "have seen that how the U.S. stood by a small ally would show the U.S. could be relied upon by a great ally, like Japan. . . . The people who had the greatest stake in the outcome were our allies in the world. If our allies saw we were undependable to a small ally, big allies would lose confidence in us. That is why it was essential that we show that strength and dependability."

A Vietnam's speakers' kit assembled within the White House distilled the president's announcement as "vindication of the wisdom of the President's policy in holding out for an honorable peace—and his refusal to accept a disguised and dishonorable defeat. Had it not been for the President's courage—during four years of unprecedented vilification and attack—the United States would not today be honorably ending her involvement in the war, but would be suffering the consequences of dishonor and defeat. . . .

The difference between what the President has achieved and what his opponents wanted, is the difference between peace with honor, and the false peace of an American surrender."

A Vietnam White Paper drafted in the White House for distribution to members of Congress offered the following perspective:

> For four agonizing years, Richard Nixon has stood virtually alone in the Nation's capital while little, petty men flayed him over American involvement in Indochina. For four years, he has been the victim of the most vicious personal attacks. Day and night, America's predominantly liberal national media hammered at Mr. Nixon, slicing from all sides, attacking, hitting, and cutting. The intellectual establishment—those whose writings entered America into the Vietnam war—pompously postured from their ivy hideaways, using their inordinate power to influence public opinion. . . . And over all those years, there were the incessant attacks from the United States Congress—the low-motivated partisan thrusts from many who envied the President's office and many more who cynically molted their hawk's feathers for those of the dove.
>
> No President has been under more constant and unremitting harassment by men who should drop to their knees each night to thank the Almighty that they do not have to make the same decisions that Richard Nixon did. Standing with the President in all those years were a handful of reporters and number of newspapers—nearly all outside of Washington. There were also the courageous men of Congress who would stand firm beside the President. But most importantly there were the millions upon millions of quite ordinary Americans—the great Silent Majority of citizens—who saw our country through a period where the shock troops of leftist public opinion daily propagandized against the President of the United States. They were people of character and steel.

Thus, the crude surgery of the president's spin doctor.

* * *

The term *peace with honor* had a precedent. In 1938, British prime minister Neville Chamberlain returned in triumph from Munich. John Colville, then a junior official in the Foreign Office with one year's standing, described the scene in his memoir, *Footprints in Time:* "While the returning Prime Minister's car was surging through hysterical crowds, a French window opened beside me and the Deputy Under Secretary, Sir Orme Sargent, stepped on to the balcony. He surveyed the scene below with dislike and disdain. 'You might think,' he said to me, 'that we had won a major victory instead of betraying a minor country.' Then, after a pause, as the window opposite opened and it was clear that Chamberlain was expected to say a few words, Sargent added, 'I can bear almost anything provided he doesn't say it is Peace with Honour.'

"Meanwhile, as I subsequently learned, Chamberlain was greeted by his loyal and elated staff at the end of the long red carpeted passage which runs from the front door of No. 10 to the cabinet Room, and he said that in response to the clamour outside he must go up to the first floor window—Dizzy's bedroom—and say a few words. It was then that Mrs. Chamberlain put the words into his mouth: 'Tell them,' she said, 'that you have brought back peace, but not just peace—peace with honour.'"

CHAPTER THIRTEEN

The Jabberwocky Agreement

We bombed them into accepting our concessions.

John Negroponte

Signed at the International Conference Center in Paris on Saturday morning, January 27, 1973, the essential elements of the Agreement on Ending the War and Restoring Peace on Vietnam included the cessation of hostilities and the withdrawal of American troops. The United States would halt all air and naval actions against North Vietnam and dismantle or deactivate all mines in North Vietnam's waters. Within 60 days after the signing of the agreement, all United States forces, as well as all forces of foreign nations allied with the United States, would withdraw from Vietnam. The United States was prohibited from reintroducing new war materials or supplies into Vietnam and was required to dismantle all military bases in South Vietnam. The armed forces of the two South Vietnamese parties were permitted to remain in place, but the cease-fire prohibited accepting the introduction of troops, military advisers, and military personnel, including technical military personnel, armaments, munitions, and war materiel from the North or anywhere else. The disposition of Vietnamese armed forces in South Vietnam would be settled by the two South Vietnamese parties in a spirit of "national reconciliation and concord." The two South Vietnamese parties were permitted to make periodic replacement of armaments, munitions, and war material that had been destroyed, damaged, or used up on a one-for-one basis under international supervision and control.

The agreement further called for the return of all captured military personnel and foreign civilians during this same 60-day period. The return of Vietnamese civilians would be left to the two South Vietnamese parties. The United States and North Vietnam pledged to respect the principles of self-determination for the South Vietnamese people, including free and democratic elections under international supervision. To this end, the two South Vietnamese parties would create the National Council for National Reconciliation and Concord. The United States was prohibited from intervening in the internal affairs of South Vietnam.

In spite of this, there was not supposed to be a coalition government in South Vietnam. The existing government in Saigon would remain in office. Yet no national boundary would formally separate North and South Vietnam, meaning that two governments were running one country. The agreement identified the military demarcation line between the two zones, the 17th parallel, as "only provisional and not a political or territorial boundary." Both North and South Vietnam were required to respect the DMZ on both sides of the Provisional Military Demarcation Line.

If that was not extraordinary enough, for implementing and monitoring compliance with the provisions on withdrawal, cease-fire, base dismantling, return of POWs, and exchange of information on those missing in action, the treaty provided for the Four-Party Joint Military Commission to be constituted by the four signatories. An International Commission of Control and Supervision (ICCS), composed of representatives from Canada, Hungary, Indonesia, and Poland, would oversee the agreement and report violations. A Two-Party Joint Military Commission, consisting of representatives from the two South Vietnamese parties, would be responsible for overseeing the implementation of provisions specific to the two parties, such as determining the areas controlled by each party, modalities of stationing, and the return of civilian detainees. This Two-Party JMC would continue operations after the 60-day period.

"The Jabberwocky" is the strange, nonsense poem of gibberish from Lewis Carroll's *Through a Looking Glass and What Alice Found There*. It contains words of nonsense, or as Alice put it, "It seems very pretty, but it is rather hard to understand. Somehow it seems to fill my head with ideas—only I don't know what they are! However, somebody killed something; that's clear, at any rate." The peace treaty written in Paris was indeed a Jabberwocky agreement.

Not a moment of peace ever came to Vietnam. Hoping to establish the province city of Tay Ninh as their new capital, the Vietcong immediately launched an assault to capture the city. Two separate communist delegations to the Two-Party JMC, one arriving from Hanoi and the other from Paris, looked out their airplane windows in hopes of seeing PRG flags flying over that city. Sir Robert Thompson reported that Vietcong delegates "flying by Air France from Paris asked to be diverted over Tay Ninh on their way to Saigon so that they could admire the PRG flag flying over their new capital. But they were disappointed to find the town firmly in Government hands and South Vietnamese flags waving strongly in the wind."

When the first delegation arrived at Tan Son Nhut, they were presented with debarkation cards by the South Vietnamese and instructed to fill out name, rank, and signature. An almost routine procedure, commonly required in international travel, was quickly elevated to a principle of national pride and sovereignty. The North Vietnamese believed that they were in their country. The delegation's spokesman, Colonel Luu Van Loi, accused the United States of violating the Paris agreement, alleging that the Vietcong had received assurances from the United States that they would be exempt from such processing. Loi had sat with Le Duc Tho at the private meetings with Kissinger and had dealt with the French in 1954. He was not to be taken lightly.

The delegation refused to sign the cards and staged a one-night sit-in on the aircraft. Tempers flared when the South Vietnamese would not allow the delegates to leave the plane for food or toilet. MACV finally provided food and milk, but the delegates, many of whom drank the milk too quickly, now encountered stomach disorders, and still the South Vietnamese authorities refused to allow anyone off the plane. The communist delegation sent an urgent message to the U.S. delegation. With meetings scheduled for the next morning, it would be necessary to shift the location of these negotiating sessions to the aircraft, which now smelled like a public restroom. The next morning, President Thieu, under pressure from Ambassador Bunker, agreed that the delegates should be permitted to leave the aircraft without filling out the cards, but only under condition that all future arrivals from Hanoi would be expected to comply with the procedure.

In his address to the nation marking the beginning of the cease-fire, President Thieu urged his countrymen not to let down in their vigilance against the communist enemy. He warned that the current atmosphere of international détente should not lead to a false sense that citizens were safe from communists in their midst. Thieu described the agreement as "a ceasefire in place, no more, no less, which would develop into a true and lasting peace depending on four factors: (1) The degree to which the communists respect the ceasefire in the coming months; (2) The sincerity of the communists in the coming talks with the GVN: specifically, whether or not the communists would use the talks as a delaying tactic behind which they would make preparations for a renewal of the war; (3) The attitude shown by the communists, particularly whether or not they remained in South Vietnam and threatened the freedom necessary to ensure the right of self-determination for South Vietnamese people by engaging in violence and assassinations; (4) The attitude of the communists toward the results of an election in which they might achieve only a minority."

A day earlier Thieu was quoted in *Le Monde* as saying, "If the communists dare put a foot in our zones, we will kill them." This warning was consistent with the instructions that were being distributed to South Vietnamese on how to implement the agreement. These guidebooks were questions and answers on the significance of the Paris Agreement—for example:

Q. "What to do if we see the enemy putting up flags, carrying out counter-propaganda, or exhorting people to demonstrate while we are performing our duty?"

A "Under the terms of the agreement, loyalists were advised to "arrest them immediately, and if they offer resistance we may kill them."

Q. "But what if the communists cite Article II of the agreement, which specifically deals with basic freedoms, ending of hatred and enmity, saying they are visiting their families in the South?"

A. Again, the answer was clear: "You are authorized to forbid and arrest them. Because it is a cease-fire in spot, they cannot move. GVN laws still pertain in the spot of GVN territorial control."

Q. "And what about serious violations?"

A. "Our Allies, especially the United States, have pledged their continuing support to us for the preservation of peace, and will react very strongly in case of a brazen violation of the agreement by the communists. We must keep in mind that the United States 7th Fleet is still stationed in the Pacific area."

Q. "Do North Vietnamese soldiers have the right to stay in South Vietnam?"

A. "No. In the agreement there is no provision calling for the withdrawal of North Vietnamese troops from the South as there is no provision saying that they have the right to stay there. It was US Vice President Spiro Agnew himself who stated that the United States did not recognize the right of any foreign army to station on the RVN territory on his last visit to the RVN in Saigon on 30 and 31 January 1973. The confirmation by the United States has proven once more the collapse of the communist position in their demand for maintaining their troops in South Vietnam."

Days before the cease-fire, the blue and red NLF flag was erected in areas of communist control, and the red-striped yellow flag of the RVN was displayed in areas of their control. The RVN flag was painted on rooftops and houses and on every car and motorbike. Troops were given flags and told to wave them wherever they went. All of this made it virtually impossible for the ICC to determine who controlled an area and who initiated a violation. There was frenzied competition by both sides to remove enemy flags and plant their own.

Donald Kirk reported walking with Don Tate of Scripps Howard through the borderline between the liberated zone of the PRG territory and territory controlled by the ARVN. Virtually all of the hooches had flags flying at the top of bamboo polls: "a minimal sign of loyalty to one side or another." Some had signs scribbled in Vietnamese, "Peace and welcome." Yet as soon as the GVN spotted VC flags, they came and burned down those hooches. "Across the road, South Vietnamese troops fan out toward another tree line over which hang several more VC flags. Suddenly a woman screams uncontrollably, 'My home is destroyed. Ten people in my hamlet have been killed. Peace, peace, they promised us peace.'"

In a private meeting with French president Pompidou on the day of the signing, Secretary of State William Rogers was asked "if the U.S. had a commitment from North Vietnam on the withdrawal of their forces from the South." Secretary Rogers duly responded that "there was no specific commitment in the agreement itself and that it would have been difficult to obtain because Hanoi refused to admit that North Vietnamese troops were in the South." Meanwhile, violence continued.

* * *

Article 1 of the Paris agreement was, to the Vietnamese, what the essence of the war was all about: "The United States and all other countries respect the independence, sovereignty, unity, and territorial integrity of Vietnam as recognized by the 1954 Geneva Agreements on Vietnam." This wording, as Thieu understood all too well, was virtually identical to the NLF's Ten Points of May 1969: "The U.S. must respect the Vietnamese people's fundamental national rights, i.e. independence, sovereignty, unity, and territorial integrity, as recognized by the 1954 Geneva Agreements."

Throughout October, November, and December, President Thieu had fought for better and more improved language to soften Article 1. He wanted language that would guarantee Saigon's sovereignty over South Vietnam, since there really were two countries in Vietnam, not one. To the extent that there was only one, Thieu knew it would be controlled by Hanoi. He wanted the 17th parallel to be recognized as an international political boundary. Thieu knew that if he could get these additions, the DRV and PRG would be defeated diplomatically.

In the end, Kissinger was able to mollify Thieu with references in the agreement (Articles 14, 18(e), and 20) regarding "respect for the sovereignty of South Vietnam" pending reunification, but because the agreement specifically stipulated "two South Vietnamese parties" as governments, Thieu could not claim sole sovereignty there. The agreement left two rival parties in the South to contest political power. Nonetheless, President Nixon publicly stated that "the United States will continue to recognize the Government of the Republic of Vietnam as the sole legitimate government in Vietnam." For the same reason, the DRV and PRG delegation to the Four-Party JMC had refused to fill out Saigon forms before debarking from their planes.

The status of the DMZ and the 17th parallel was also a victory for the communists. According to the Paris agreement, pending reunification, "the military demarcation line between the two zones at the 17th parallel is only provisional and not a political or territorial boundary, as provided for in paragraph 6 of the Final Declaration of the 1954 Geneva Conference." Compare this with the almost identical wording of the NLF's ten points of May 1969: "The military demarcation line between the two zones at the 17th parallel, as provided for by the 1954 Geneva Agreements, is only of a provisional character and does not constitute in any way a political or territorial boundary."

Finally, the North Vietnamese troops would remain in the South. The agreement provided only for future discussions between the two South Vietnamese parties on the subject of demobilization. General Cao Van Vien and Lieutenant General Dong Van Khuyen in their monograph, *Reflections on the Vietnam War,* concluded that "the Paris Agreement of January 1973 served only the immediate purposes of the United States and North Vietnamese." The Paris agreement "offered North Vietnam the favorable conditions to pursue its conquest of South Vietnam with success. . . . In South Vietnam, the NLF was given a legitimate national status. It now had an official government, an army, and a national territory of its own. In all respects, the NLF had become a political entity equal in power to the GVN. . . . Never since 1954 had the communists enjoyed such a strong political and military posture."

Comparing the NLF's ten-point program of 1969 and the 1973 final agreement, it is striking how much of the former remained intact in the latter; in fact, the wording is almost identical on key points. Articles 9, 10, and 11 of the Paris agreement are the actual text of the NLF proposal with respect to the political components of the agreement. The National Council, while not a coalition government, was everything that President Thieu feared it would be. Its functions, as specified by the Paris agreement, were to implement the agreement; prohibit all acts of reprisal and discrimination against individuals or organizations that had collaborated with one side or the other; ensure democratic liberties; decide the procedures and modalities of these general elections; and organize the free and democratic general elections. It was hardly the "joke" that Haig and Kissinger presented it as to Thieu and the South Vietnamese. As Le Duc Tho said on January 25, 1973, "In the end, we reached an agreement not to use the term 'structure of power' or 'administrative structure' but to call it directly the National Council of Reconciliation and National Concord, for the importance of the body lies in its way of proceeding in its work."

With such insignificant difference between the 1969 proposal and the 1973 deal, we can only conclude that many tens of thousands died for very little, or simply while waiting for Thieu to give in because Nixon had allowed him to remain in office because Nixon believed that there was no acceptable American alternative to Thieu. Nixon feared that anyone else would not accept the American guarantee of continuous war under the guise of a paper peace. Thieu was their man to punch the ticket for the return of the B-52s. In the end, Thieu was betrayed not just by Watergate but by the men who kept him in power and made him sign the so-called peace agreement.

Vice President Ky later reflected on the Paris agreement, "In fact, the Paris agreement gave the world an entirely wrong impression. Though it was the end of the war for America, it was never regarded as the end of the war by Hanoi. . . . The North Vietnamese seized on one fact: that the U.S. was not really concerned with peace at all; it was only concerned with getting out of Vietnam."

It is true that both sides made concessions in order to produce the final accord. That Thieu remained in power was the major concession of the communists. "We thought that an agreement that left him in office, and in which he was legitimized by the North Vietnamese, was such a spectacular success that he would not pay attention to all the other surrounding circumstance," is how Kissinger explained it two decades later.

But the concessions made by the United States were much greater and far more detrimental. The United States abandoned the principle of mutual withdrawal, which allowed the North Vietnamese to pursue their long-range goals of unification. It also botched the implementation completely. Because of Kissinger's and Nixon's suspicion of the bureaucracy and dedication to secrecy, there was no agreed on position within the government for implementing and enforcing a cease-fire in place. The accord became a protocol for the disengagement of U.S. troops and the return of the POWs, but not for a sustained peace.

For the 60 days immediately following the agreement, the JMC, composed of representatives from four parties, the U.S., PRG, DRV, and GVN, was responsible for overseeing the implementation of the agreement and related issues of securing the peace. After 60 days, provided that all U.S. and allied troops were withdrawn and all military and foreign civilian prisoners were released, the DRV and U.S. teams would terminate their roles. The Two-Party JMC of Saigon and PRG representatives would supersede the four-party group.

The American team in Saigon, which had been working in absolute secrecy imposed by Kissinger, had five major goals to accomplish in the 60 days. The most central was the return of POWs, followed by the orderly and safe withdrawal of all remaining troops, including the sizable number of outside forces. The third goal was to reduce the level of fighting in Vietnam, the fourth to stabilize the conflict as much as possible by creating a forum for talks, and the fifth to provide the South Vietnamese with a reasonable chance to survive on their own. The official historian of the U.S. delegation, Lieutenant Colonel Walter Scott Dillard, concluded that in "pursuing this last goal, the United States violated the spirit of the provisions of the Paris agreement and protocols. Article 6 of the basic agreement required the dismantlement of the American military bases in South Vietnam within 60 days of the signing of the agreement. By no stretch of the imagination can the argument be sustained that these bases were dismantled. . . . A subterfuge was invented in which the US transferred and the South Vietnamese accepted ownership of the bases. . . . Appropriate documents were subsequently signed formalizing the transfer but, until their actual physical withdrawal, American forces retained the same rights and privileges they had enjoyed before, as if ownership had been retained—occupancy, complete control, reentry, use of all facilities." Nonetheless, the U.S. did very little to slow the Northern encroachment.

On February 22, 1973, Major General Woodward received from George Aldrich a secret memorandum, "'Interpretations' of Viet-Nam Peace Agreement." In his covering note, Aldrich explained that the "secret attachment" provided an interpretation of "some of the less obvious points in the Agreement on Ending the War and Restoring Peace in Vietnam of January 27, 1973." What it really shows is how unprepared the U.S. was for implementing the treaty—and how the treaty masked enormous disagreements, as the following excerpts demonstrate:

> *Aerial Reconnaissance:* North Vietnam: Secret—with respect to reconnaissance activities over North Viet-Nam, we have assured the DRV that such activity "will cease completely and definitely." With respect to GVN reconnaissance over South Viet-Nam, the DRV has told us that the PRG will not tolerate reconnaissance over areas controlled by the PRG and will fire at any GVN aircraft overlying such areas. We have responded that we would consider such firing a violation of the cease-fire.
>
> *Other Aircraft Operations:* South Viet-Nam. In South Viet-Nam, I interpret Article 3 of the Cease-Fire Protocol as limiting U.S. and GVN over flights of South Viet-Nam only by preventing flights of armed combat aircraft. To the extent the Joint Military Commissions may agree on corridors or other regulations pursuant to Article 3 (b), there might of course be further limitations.
>
> *Confidential*—From our negotiations with the DRV it seems clear that they do not accept this interpretation of the assurance of freedom of movement in Article 3 (a) (1) and will assert that any over flight of PRG controlled areas is illegal. The DRV/PRG will press for agreement on cor-

ridors and restrictions. So long as the PRG is not provided with a substantial air capability, I would doubt that the GVN would agree to any such corridors or restrictions.

Cease-Fire in Place: Article 3 paragraphs (a) and (b) of the Agreement call for a cease-fire in place in South Vietnam and paragraph (c) prohibits certain specified offensive activities. Articles 2–6 of the Cease-Fire Protocol give meaning to these obligations. Article 2 (a) is perhaps most important in defining the cease-fire in place as meaning "no major redeployments or movements that would extend each party's areas of control or would result in contact between opposing armed forces and clashes which might take place." Therefore, other military movements not of this type are permitted unless they are the type of hostile action specifically prohibited.

Areas of Control: The concept of separate areas of control by the two South Vietnamese parties is critical to the definition of the cease-fire and is one of the basic assumptions of the Agreement. Article 3 (b) of the Agreement provides that the Two-Party Joint Military Commission "shall determine the areas controlled by each party." We tried unsuccessfully to include in the Cease-Fire Protocol an article making it clear that the Two-Party Joint Military Commission should base its determination on a census of military forces, including their location, strength, and deployment. The DRV refused to accept this concept and clearly preferred a political exercise of drawing lines on a map. In view of this unresolved disagreement, the Two-Party Joint Military Commission is left with no guidance on how to determine the areas of control in South Viet-Nam.

Withdrawal of U.S. and Allied Forces—Equipment Left Behind: Article 5 of the Agreement requires the withdrawal within 60 days of foreign military personnel and "armaments, munitions, and war material of the United States and those of the other foreign countries mentioned in Article 3 (a)." The question arises whether these forces may leave behind in Viet-Nam for the benefit of the Government of the Republic of Viet-Nam any military equipment. It was the understanding of the U.S. in negotiating the text of this article that the phrase "of the United States" implied ownership by the United States and, therefore, that equipment not owned by the U.S. at the time of the entry into force of the Agreement or subsequent thereto could be left in South Viet-Nam under Article 5. This point was also dealt with in Article 8 (a) of the protocol on the cease-fire and joint military commissions. That article referred to the obligations of Article 5 to withdraw armaments, munitions and war material and stated "transfers of such items which would leave them in South Viet-Nam shall not be made subsequent to the entry into force of the Agreement . . ." This article makes it clear that equipment transferred prior to the cease-fire raises no problem; it does not, however, clarify the question whether transfer of title or transfer of possession is the critical act.

Confidential—We tried during the negotiations to lay a foundation for our theory that transfer of title was adequate to take equipment out of the requirements of these articles, but we decided that we could not make this explicit without running an unacceptable risk that the North Vietnamese would object and make the issue a major one in the negotiations. Therefore, we did not explain to the DRV negotiators our interpretation of the phrase "of the United States." On the other hand, the North Vietnamese said nothing to us inconsistent with our interpretation. On the basis of the language and the absence of any relevant negotiating history, we can make a reasonable case, but we must recognize that it is far from compelling and that the International Commission may or may not agree with our view. We should anticipate that the North Vietnamese and the PRG will press the issue.

Destruction of Bases: Article 6 of the Agreement requires the dismantlement of all military bases in South Viet-Nam "of the United States and of the other foreign countries mentioned in Article 3 (a)," and this obligation is reiterated in Article 9 of the Cease-Fire Protocol, which requires the U.S. to supply necessary information to the Four-Party Joint Military Commission and the ICCS. We have interpreted this provision as meaning that bases which are owned by the U.S. must be dismantled, but that bases title to which was transferred to the GVN or to the U.S. Embassy for civilian use prior to the conclusion of the Agreement need not be dismantled. Since we transferred title to all U.S. bases prior to the conclusion of the Agreement, we intend to dismantle no bases.

Confidential: We avoided making this intention clear to the DRV during the negotiations, but we consider the phrase "bases of the U.S." synonymous with bases owned by the U.S. Moreover, it was clear from discussions with the DRV concerning such issues as points of entry that they did not expect the dismantlement of installations such as Cam Ranh Bay and Than Son Nhut. Nevertheless we can expect a dispute on this issue. End Confidential.

Recall Kissinger's many private assurances to Le Duc Tho that the Nixon administration had no interest in maintaining bases or even Nixon's promise to Mao and Chou that the U.S. would leave no "tail" behind after its withdrawal. These were, as the Aldrich memo documents, all lies. In fact, the ambiguities in the details of the agreement virtually guaranteed that the Vietnamese parties themselves would reach no agreement, and that once it was violated, the terms of Nixon's secret assurances would be activated.

The U.S. delegation succeeded admirably in the area of prisoner returns and troop withdrawals, but they lacked power to enjoin all three Vietnamese parties to implement, much less enforce, a complete and effective cease-fire. "This failure cannot be emphasized too strongly. It meant that the war would continue unabated and unchecked until one Vietnam conquered the other," observed Dillard in the official military history of the period.

The North Vietnamese wanted the United States out of Vietnam, so on the one issue most important to the Americans, return of the POWs, Hanoi cooperated with the United States because jeopardizing the safety or release of the POWs would result in a brutal response.

* * *

When the Americans departed Vietnam 60 days after the Paris agreement had been signed, the level of violence had not significantly declined. One report from the field dated April 4, 1973, focused on a military flare-up at Tong Le Chan, a Ranger camp in Tay Ninh Province on the Saigon River near the Cambodian border. Elements of the North Vietnamese 9th Division had launched ground attacks supported by artillery trying to overrun the 260 Rangers. A fierce South Vietnamese counterattack included 97 tactical air sorties by the Republic of Vietnam Armed Forces (RVNAF). It was impossible for outsiders to agree on who started these hostilities because the NVA attacks began only after the NVA forces and supply units suffered heavy losses from ARVN artillery and air strikes.

"We in the Consulate General never really expected the ICCS to stop the war completely, but thought that it would at least bring about a noticeable decease in the level of violence. Unfortunately, neither the FPJMC [Four-Party JMC] nor the ICCS has had a restraining effect on combat. Based on the Tong Le Chan and Rach Bap experience, we do not believe that the TPJMC [Two-Party JMC] or ICCS will either. A genuine cease-fire, and then possibly peace, will come to Viet-Nam only when the Vietnamese belligerents are ready. We do not believe that they are ready now, nor will they be ready at any time in 1973. . . . The leaders of the DRV believe that they were cheated out of final victory by legalities in 1947 and 1954. Those men (using the 11 presently serving on the Politburo) have spent a total of approximately 75 years in prisons and 135 years living in the jungles of Indo-China. One objective has kept them going these many years, and they may not settle in the end for anything less than that objective: a reunified Viet-Nam under their control. . . . On the other side, the GRVN does not appear at the moment to want to even try to reach some murky Vietnamese accommodation with its enemies, and wants to settle in the end for nothing less than driving the NVA out of the RVN and crushing the PRG and its forces."

This was just as President Thieu had warned Kissinger throughout their negotiations.

On June 10, Charles Whitehouse cabled Kissinger with an appraisal of the situation in Vietnam. The principal actors in the GVN "are deeply disappointed by the communists' non-compliance with the Paris Agreement and extremely upset by the emergence of a 'three Vietnams' situation. . . . Illogically, they do not see it as the inevitable result of their military failure to eject the NVA from the South but blame it instead on the Paris Agreement itself. I think GVN disappointment in the Paris Agreement is understandable for many reasons. The GVN believed when they signed that the Agreement would lead to a freezing of the military situation—and eventually to the attrition of NVA forces remaining in South Vietnam—and that this would set the stage for a political solution in South Vietnam. . . . They were also told that, if there was massive violation of the Paris Agreement, we would mete out dire punishment to the North Vietnamese. None of these has happened in the more than four months since January 27. . . . The U.S. response has seemed very mild and quite ineffective in persuading Hanoi to live up to its commitments under the Paris Agreement. Thieu and his advisors of course understand the problems that President Nixon faces domestically in responding strongly to Hanoi's subversion of the Paris Agreement, but they cannot escape feeling that the peace we sold them with so much vigor last autumn has left them with less than they had before and the North Vietnamese with more. . . . The leadership here is also suspicious of your negotiations with Le Duc Tho. They resent drafts which are in concrete, short deadlines, the muscle applied through Presidential letters and the apparent warmth of your relations with the other side. They believe you put more negotiating heat on Saigon than you do on Hanoi and are prone to accept Le Duc Tho's intransigence while castigating theirs."

* * *

Article 8 (c) of the Paris agreement stipulated that the two South Vietnamese parties would do their best to resolve the question of the return of the Vietnamese civilian personnel captured and detained in South Vietnam within 90 days after the cease-fire. In an accompanying protocol, it was further stipulated that each party would return all captured persons without denying or delaying their return for any reason; in fact, the protocol specifically called for facilitating the return of those captured and detained. All personnel were to be treated humanely at all times and in accord with international practice.

Yet President Thieu had very little incentive to release the prisoners since he had been told by Haig and Kissinger to hold them hostage for the removal of North Vietnamese troops from South Vietnam. Indeed, in these 60 days between cease-fire and the American withdrawal, Thieu's government reclassified many military prisoners as political detainees so as not to have to release them.

When Kissinger cabled Bunker on January 31 that "it would help me very much in other matters if, prior to my visit to Hanoi, the GVN could release some civilian prisoners," Bunker immediately responded, "I think we may find some reluctance on Thieu's part to granting amnesty to civilian prisoners before he has had an opportunity to bargain on the presence of NVA troops in South Vietnam. You will recall that we suggested to him that this was one of the ploys he might use."

Kissinger cabled Bunker on February 24 that "the North Vietnamese have again complained to us on the question of civilian prisoners. They recall my promise during my visit to Hanoi that 5000 civilians would be released shortly, and notes that not a single civilian has yet been returned by the GVN." Why he should have expected otherwise is unclear.

By February 28, Bunker met with Thieu and told him that Nixon was "very much concerned about the hold-up of the release of American prisoners. He is also concerned about the unsatisfactory implementation of the cease-fire. He cannot have the agreement, most particularly the release of American prisoners, threatened by actions which are under the control of our side."

By March Kissinger cabled Bunker that Le Duc Tho had again questioned him on civilian prisoners: "I know that you have taken this up with Thieu on several occasions, but absolutely nothing seems to have happened. Although Le Duc Tho conveniently overstates the precision of our obligations, there is no question that we are committed to making a maximum effort with the GVN on this issue. So far, there have been no results whatsoever and no progress seems to be in sight." On March 4 Bunker cabled Charles Whitehouse that "I think it is clear that GVN has not been frank with us on their handling of this issue (sentencing political prisoners as common criminals is certainly contrary to Agreement) . . . and it is time that they gave us a clear statement of what they have done and propose to do in the matter. At same time I have no doubt other side is equally tricky."

By June, key members of the United States Senate had taken up the issue. Frank Moss wrote Secretary Rogers on June 18 "I am becoming increasingly concerned about information becoming available about the condition of political prisoners in South Vietnam. It appears that thousands of political prisoners are still being detained in South Vietnam and that new prisoners are very probably being added to the list." By December 20, 1973, Senator Fulbright, chair of the Foreign Relations Committee, would write Secretary Kissinger that "regardless of difference in views regarding past U.S. involvement in Vietnam, the continuing reminders of the practice of political detention and of the maltreatment of prisoners by South Vietnamese authorities should weigh heavily on the conscience of all Americans. . . . I simply do not see how we can now, in good conscience, deny any responsibility for the heinous acts of a government which owes its total existence to our support."

In the end, Le Duc Tho's warning to Kissinger on January 23, 1973, would be prophetic.: "Article 8.c will be following you for a long time after the ceasefire."

* * *

By late February 1973 photographic evidence revealed that the North Vietnamese had introduced surface-to-air missiles (SA-2) into the Khe Sanh area. Just as Nixon, Haig, and Kissinger had anticipated, the communists were intent on violating the agreement—not just with a modest territory grab but with a major offensive that could restart the war. General Woodward warned the PRG delegation that these types of violations could not be tolerated, but the communists denied the existence of the missiles in the teeth of the photographs. Woodward told them that "the United States considered this to be worse than a cease-fire violation; it was a provocation."

Despite pleas by the South Vietnamese for an on-site investigation at Khe Sanh, none occurred because the last American POWs were soon to be withdrawn and the American delegation would soon be going home.

For years, Nixon and Kissinger maintained this line: that they intended to punish transgressions but were tied by Watergate. Although it is difficult to believe that public opinion would have supported renewed bombing for long, even without Watergate, Nixon most likely did intend to give it a try. On March 21, 1973, Kissinger wrote Scowcroft that "there is one principal argument for conducting the strikes at this time and that is to make it clear to the North Vietnamese that we may do something totally unexpected if pressed in defense of the agreement. If the North Vietnamese believe we will not act after the POWs are out, an offensive by the end of the year is almost a certainty. If an offensive succeeds, all those who have fought every move the President has made will be vindicated and the whole basis of the President's policy undermined."

Options for U.S. air strikes against infiltration routes in southern Laos were under consideration, but the question was whether to risk a strike before the POWs were returned. On March 14, Kissinger wrote Nixon on the subject of "North Vietnamese Infiltration and Logistic Activity in South," which, in his mind, constituted a "clear violation of both the letter and the spirit of the January 27 Agreement." Kissinger raised three possible motivations, but "whatever their motivations, their actions are a clear challenge. . . . We have given the North Vietnamese a clear signal that they cannot continue this course with impunity, but they have not responded and we have seen no evidence of a cessation." On the diplomatic side, it would be useless to go to the four-Party JMC or the ICCS since "neither of these bodies has been able up to now to successfully undertake on a timely basis investigations of major violations."

Kissinger reported that the North Vietnamese infiltration violations were so great that they were operating in daylight and the traffic was so heavy as to be congested: "They clearly are taking advantage of the fact that all air action against them has ceased. A series of heavy air strikes over a 2 or 3 day period in either of these areas would be very costly to them in both personnel and material." Kissinger recommended a "prompt and violent response" and reviewed military options for strikes. The declassified record shows that Nixon favored actions similar to May 8 and Christmas 1972: "A strike would, by its very surprise, have a devastating effect. It would dramatically inhibit the infiltration of both personnel and equipment. It would signal clearly that we will not tolerate continued violations and will react decisively to them. It is precisely this sort of U.S. reaction on May 8 and again in December, which caused the North Vietnamese to reexamine the course on which they were then bent. If they now believe that we may not react and we fail to do so, we will encourage increasing and even more blatant violations. If we react we will demonstrate the costs, which they must expect to bear if they abrogate the Agreement. It will help make clear once again that they have a stake in keeping the Agreement." If no action was taken, then "the Agreement may well break down precisely because we did not," warned Kissinger.

Kissinger recommended and Nixon approved a two- to three-day series of intensive U.S. air strikes against the trail area of southern Laos immediately after the release of the third increment of POWs, expected to occur on March 16. But that release was delayed by the Vietnamese, and the bombing was deferred. One of the small ironies that had to be weighed during this period was that President Thieu, who had been promised a presidential visit to San Clemente and Washington if he agreed to the Paris Accords, was soon due in Washington, and Kissinger mused that if the strikes occurred while Thieu was in Washington, "we thus would be seen as reacting to Thieu's pressure and be pictured as captive of his policies. The benefit of independent reaction would be substantially diluted."

In retrospect, Thieu's visit to San Clemente and Washington offered several telltale signs of the forthcoming betrayal. Thieu had been promised the visit in return for his agreement to the Paris Accords. He chartered a Pan American Boeing 707 and, in an effort to present the image of Vietnam independence and sovereignty, had the Vietnamese flag painted on the plane. Thieu was unhappy that he would meet Nixon in San Clemente and not Washington, but he managed to negotiate a number of concessions from Nixon relating to his Washington activities, such as a National Press Club appearance and meetings on Capitol Hill.

When Thieu arrived at San Clemente, he was told that there would be no joint communiqué, which had been promised as a standard matter of protocol. But Nixon was already feeling the political pressures of Watergate and must have understood that the strong language required in the communiqué might no longer have any authority. So furious was Thieu that he ordered Nha to get their plane refueled because they would be departing immediately. When Nixon learned of the threat, he ordered that the communiqué be issued. The communiqué promised economic aid and assistance for South Vietnam, but Thieu was concerned that the pledge of "vigorous reaction" to communist violations was not made as clearly as in any of Nixon's private letters to Thieu.

That evening, Nixon hosted a cocktail party for Thieu at Casa Pacifica, the Western White House. Nha recalled two conversations. The first was with Kissinger, who greeted him warmly and said, "The past is behind us. I realize now that I moved too fast and that October was a mistake."

"I could make a lot of money if I released your admission of a mistake in October to the press right now," said Nha.

"I know you wouldn't do that sort of thing," said Kissinger.

The other conversation was with John Negroponte and was much more telling than the chitchat between Kissinger and Nha. "I have to apologize," said Negroponte. "We really screwed you guys."

Before leaving for Washington, Ronald Reagan, governor of California, hosted a reception for Thieu in Los Angeles. Although Thieu was the guest of honor, Nha recalls that the highlight of the evening was meeting one of his great movie heroes, John Wayne, who told Thieu and Nha, "I agree with you, we will break the communists!" Wayne then made believe he was picking up the communists and breaking them in his two hands. Nha remembers the moment as if it were yesterday.

On March 15 Kissinger cabled Bunker that "it is imperative that you understand our strategy. . . . We are considering resuming air strikes in Laos next week for a few days along the Ho Chi Minh trail. We will not be in a position to do this, however, unless we are able to demonstrate meticulous observance of the agreement on our side." On March 16, Bunker met with Thieu to explain the strategy.

In Washington on March 16 at a meeting at the Pentagon concerning military aid to Vietnam, Kissinger insisted, "We can't permit a total flouting of the agreement within weeks. We will have lost all we won in the last 4 years. The idea is to get a pause and get the thought into their head that the President is hair-trigger. The President wants a strike next week, while they still have the POW's. A strike Thursday and Friday along the Trail right up to the passes." But Secretary of Defense Elliot Richardson doubted that bombing was necessary and argued that "South Vietnam ought to be able to handle anything North Vietnam can throw this year. Bombing the Trail will do little good."

Kissinger responded, "That is not the point. It is a psychological reprisal point we must make."

The press was now reporting that Nixon was considering a resumption of the bombing. R. W. Apple reported in the *New York Times* that at an unscheduled news conference in the West Wing, the president said that "based on my actions over the past four years, the North Vietnamese should not lightly disregard such expressions of concern, when they are made with regard to a violation. . . . The leaders of North Vietnam should have no doubt as to the consequences if they fail to comply with the Agreement."

James Reston wrote on March 18 that "once the withdrawal of American prisoners and troops is complete—and it will be within a few weeks—there will be an interesting legal question: what legal authority would the President then have to order American men and bombers back into battle?" The administration was quick to respond. Secretary of Defense Richardson stated that the president retained "residual authority" to bomb in order to maintain the peace and that such bombing was merely a "mopping up exercise." He provided an elaboration on this crucial point: "If he had the authority up to the moment the documents were signed, he has the authority in the following weeks to see that those agreements are lived up to."

But there would be no strikes in March after all. Nixon decided he did not want to jeopardize the return of the final group of American POWs, which finally occurred on March 29, 1973.

By April 1973 Nixon and Kissinger were again considering bombing Khe Sanh. On April 16, Bunker tried to talk Kissinger and Nixon out of it because it would "effectively destroy the cease-fire. I question whether the ICCS would survive bombing attacks in SVN or Laos. . . . Our resuming the bombing of SVN or Laos would also destroy the cease-fire in the minds of the South Vietnamese." Besides, in Bunker's view, the rainy season was about to start and there was no need to restart the bombing in South Vietnam. "In fact, the communists may regard this infiltration effort as compensating for our Enhance and Enhance Plus."

On April 17, Bunker backed off a bit: "I have no problem with 'massive strikes' in Laos and Cambodia. . . . I question the effectiveness of bombing the Trail in Laos and the advisability of bombing either the Trail or Khe Sanh before your meeting with Le Duc Tho." (Kissinger was scheduled to meet again with Le Duc Tho in order to hammer out problems in the agreement.) Kissinger cabled right back with his long-held belief that "it is our judgment that the North Vietnamese will break the cease-fire whenever and however it suits their purpose. They need no provocation. We are therefore considering massive strikes in Laos [to] leave no doubt as to their chances of getting away with flagrant disregard of the agreements."

* * *

Five days before he had been sworn in for his second term as the nation's thirty-seventh president, Nixon had written in his diary, "It is ironic that the day the news came out stopping the bombing of North Vietnam, the Watergate Four plead guilty." Unbeknown to anyone, as Henry Kissinger was negotiating with Le Duc Tho in Paris, "Watergate was changing from amber to red," recalled Admiral Zumwalt. "The private commitments made by Nixon to Thieu were unraveling alongside Nixon's presidency."

More than a private commitment was at stake; a secret plan was being overtaken by events. By April 30, Nixon had told the country that he accepted responsibility for the Watergate incident, but he also denied any personal involvement in either the break-in or cover-up. He said that he had been misled by subordinates who had made an "effort to conceal the facts." Nixon announced the nomination of Elliot Richardson as attorney general and that Richardson would have authority to appoint a special prosecutor. The White House also announced that the president had accepted the resignations of Ehrlichman, Haldeman, Attorney General Richard Kleindienst, and the president's counsel, John Dean. As Kissinger later told Stanley Karnow, "After June 1973 I did not believe that the cease-fire would hold. I certainly did not after July 1973. Watergate was in full strength. We had intelligence documents from North Vietnam decoded that Nixon could not honor his pledge and do what he had done in 1972 because of domestic situations."

Watergate would have another effect. Kissinger later stated that this was a "different Nixon. He approached the problems of the violations in a curiously desultory fashion. He drifted. He did not home in on the decision in the single-minded, almost possessed manner that was his hallmark. The rhetoric might be there, but accompanied this time with excuses for inaction. In retrospect, we know that by March, Watergate was boiling."

There is no question now, nor was there then, that Watergate sapped any resolve that Nixon may have had to bomb again. For decades, Henry Kissinger has used that fact to justify his argument that the administration—including himself—never intended to abandon South Vietnam. Yet something is hard to swallow in that argument. Nixon, the die-hard anticommunist, may have convinced himself that the American people would support South Vietnam in the face of the new—and newly illegal—Northern aggression no matter what. But most Americans were weary of the war, and the public no longer held the same zeal for anticommunism that it had had in the late 1940s and 1950s.

Could Kissinger, the realist, the pragmatist, have failed to see this? Indeed, two newly released records of conversations at meetings suggest a more devious plan. The first, a meeting with Lee Quan Yew, prime minister of Singapore, on August 4, 1973, reveals, in Kissinger's own words, the belief that bombing was the only way to make certain that the South would not fall.

The secret meeting occurred in the Captain's Conference Room of the New York Port Authority Policy Building at Kennedy Airport. The euphoria of January's peace with honor was now a distant memory. Lee had just returned from meeting Nha.

Kissinger told Lee that "[Nha] dislikes me intensely!"

"That is not important—personal likes and dislikes. The important thing is the job to be done. I told him it would be useful if Thieu met me. He said, 'why not just meet me?'"

"What is your impression of Nha?" asked Kissinger.

"He is bright, ambitious. With full confidence that what he says will carry weight with the President," said Lee.

"That is true. He is also immature. Emotional," concluded Kissinger

But Kissinger had come to talk about Watergate and Vietnam, not Mr. Nha. "Our objectives are still the same. We have suffered a tragedy because of Watergate. . . . We were going to bomb North Vietnam for a week, then go to Russia, then meet with Le Duc Tho. Congress has made it impossible." Then Kissinger made the tell-tale confession of his dashed hopes: "In May and June I drew the conclusion that the North Vietnamese were resigning themselves to a long pull of 5-to-6 years. . . . And it would have been a certainty if we had given them one blow." In other words, a little bombing now might have slowed them down, which would be a decent interval before losing the South. Nixon and Kissinger would not be directly tied to it.

One more blow was a far more realistic expectation on Kissinger's part. Kissinger told Lee that "the last three months were the most difficult period for us. We couldn't say anything because we could never be sure what some junior aide would say next. But as soon as the hearings are over, we will go on the counter-offensive. We are already in the process. While we are in these difficulties, we have to stay cool. But we won't give up our foreign policy. We will regain the initiative. In Southeast Asia, we haven't gone through all this for four years to abandon it. Sixty-one percent voted in November 1972 not to abandon Southeast Asia. It was a clear issue."

The meeting ended with Lee Kuan Yew's saying how important it was that South Vietnam survive through 1976. "My concern is to have it last through 1976 so that you will have a strong President. If it falls, you will have a new President who says, 'that's what tore American society apart.'"

Kissinger must have been reassured, because he told Lee, "You are an asset to us in that part of the world and we have no interest in destroying you. We won't leave any documents around. They stay in my office."

A little more than a month later, on September 26, Kissinger met with Nguyen Phu Duc in the Waldorf Towers in New York. Kissinger was now secretary of state, and Duc asked Kissinger what the United States planned to do with respect to the North's violations of the Paris Accord. "If it were not for domestic difficulties, we would have bombed them. This is now impossible. Your brothers in the North only understand brutality," said Kissinger. The secretary then spoke about how the Congress had acted "irresponsibly" by cutting off support for bombing, but North Vietnamese "suspiciousness is playing into our hands. They don't completely understand the restrictions placed on us by Congress. President Nixon has fooled them so often that they are probably more concerned that you believe. It is important that you show confidence and behave strongly." He ended with a joke: "Treat them like you treat me."

The conversation then got much more revealing. Kissinger made a startling admission: "I came away from the January negotiations with the feeling that we would have to bomb the North Vietnamese again in early April or May." He did not say, "If the North violated the accord, we would bomb." He confirmed what Haig had told Phouma, what Nixon had said to Thieu and what Zumwalt had concluded in November 1972 at the JCS meeting: it was a sham peace held together with a plan to deceive the American public with the rhetoric of American honor. He knew the North would cheat and was planning on resuming the bombing.

As Kissinger toasted Le Duc Tho with words of peace in January 1973 and as Richard Nixon addressed the nation with news of an honorable peace in Vietnam, both men knew that as soon as the last American POW was home, the bombing would be renewed. For Nixon, the bombing would continue right through 1976, and for Kissinger, just long enough to pick up his Nobel Peace Prize.

Writing in the *Wall Street Journal* on April 27, 1975, William Buckley noted that Watergate had derailed the president's plan to pulverize Hanoi and that Nixon at the time was too emotionally unstable to renew the bombing: "What would Nixon, under Kissinger's prodding, have done, if his reactions had been healthy, when only a few weeks after the Paris Accord was executed, North Vietnam began its blatant disregard of it. My own information is that it was planned, sometime in April, to pulverize Hanoi and Haiphong," wrote Buckley. Indeed, the plans were made even earlier.

One final question remains: Would even short-term bombing support for the South have been accepted by the public? In interviewing done on the day of the Vietnam agreement, a Gallup Poll asked the following questions:

• "When United States troops are withdrawn from Vietnam, do you think a strong enough government can be maintained in South Vietnam to withstand Communist political pressure, or not?" Fifty-four percent believed that government in the South would not survive; 27 percent believed South Vietnam would last; 19 percent had no opinion.

• "After United States troops are withdrawn from Vietnam, do you think North Vietnam in the next few years is likely to try to take over South Vietnam again, or not?" Seventy percent thought that the North would try to take over the South, 16 percent thought no, and 14 percent had no opinion.

• "Suppose when the United States troops are withdrawn, North Vietnam does try to take over South Vietnam again, do you think the United States should send war materials to South Vietnam, or not?" Fifty percent believed the U.S. should not send war materials, while 38 percent said yes, and 12 percent had no opinion.

• "If North Vietnam does try to take over South Vietnam again, do you think the United States should bomb North Vietnam, or not?" Seventy-one percent said no to bombing, while 17 percent said yes, and 12 percent had no opinion.

• "If North Vietnam does try to take over South Vietnam again, do you think the United States should send troops to help South Vietnam, or not?" Seventy-nine percent were opposed to sending troops, while 13 percent favored such an action, and 8 percent had no opinion.

Kissinger later acknowledged that he had misjudged the willingness of the American people to defend the agreement. "But I admit this: we judged wrong. And what we judged wrong above all was our belief that if we could get peace with honor, that we would unite the American people who would then defend an agreement that had been achieved with so much pain. That was our fundamental miscalculation. It never occurred to me, and I'm sure it never occurred to President Nixon, that there could be any doubt about it, because an agreement that you don't enforce is a surrender; it's just writing down surrender terms."

TWENTY-FIVE YEARS LATER

On the occasion of the twenty-fifth anniversary of the Paris agreement, the Nixon Center in Washington, D.C., convened a conference, "The Paris Agreement on Vietnam: 25 Years Later." Noticeable by their absence were those who in the intervening years had questioned "peace with honor." Kissinger attended and spoke about the many letters and private assurances given by Nixon to Thieu in which he promised to enforce the agreement: "I would simply ask some honest researcher sometime to compare the letters that President Nixon wrote to Thieu with the letters that still have not been published that President Kennedy or Johnson wrote to other leaders to see who made the bigger commitments. Or even other Presidents, in other circumstances. These were never treated as national commitments. These were expressions of the intentions of the President. Every senior member of the administration—including myself, the Secretary of Defense, the Secretary of State—is represented in compendiums of statements that said publicly every week that we intended to enforce the agreement. There was nothing new about that. . . . If I had any idea that all this was possible, I would not have participated in, and President Nixon would never have authorized, any sort of agreement. I believe it could otherwise have been maintained for a long enough period of time to give the South Vietnamese an opportunity, as the South Koreans were given, to develop their own future."

With respect to consultations with President Thieu, Kissinger's position remained unchanged: "There were all kinds of proposals that we made during that period—the last one made publicly in January 1972 by President Nixon when he disclosed the secret talks which had been going on, and which had been preceded by a secret proposal in May 1971 (all of which, incidentally, President Thieu, approved, probably thinking they would never be accepted). It was not as if we just slipped a proposal to the North Vietnamese that the South Vietnamese had never seen. In fact, I believe that Al Haig took every proposal to Saigon before we made it, and that was approved—although I will admit that the speed with which we moved at the end undoubtedly surprised the South Vietnamese."

The records that Kissinger and Nixon chose to omit from their respective memoirs offer a far more devious explanation. Hoang Duc Nha once employed a Vietnamese proverb to describe his dealings with Kissinger, translated as, "We are like frogs looking up from the darkness at the bottom of the well," meaning that the Vietnamese were in the dark about Kissinger's motives and intentions. Even today, almost three decades since the Paris Accords were signed, Kissinger would prefer that we all remain, like the South Vietnamese, in the dark.

Epilogue

**The signing of the Agreement created the false
impression that the cease-fire had ended the war.**

Sir Robert Thompson

Twenty-seven months after the signing of the Paris Accords, the new American president, Gerald Ford, wrote Khurkrit Pramot, prime minister of Thailand, "I am extremely concerned about North Vietnam's current military campaign against the Republic of Vietnam. North Vietnam now has shed all pretense of adherence to the Paris Agreements. It is openly invading South Vietnam with its regular Army divisions. I assure you, Mr. Prime Minister, that the United States remains determined to give South Vietnam the tools it must have to resist. We intend to help our friends."

Ford had now decided to send Army Chief of Staff General Fred Weyand to South Vietnam in order to assess the situation and make recommendations for future action. Weyand visited Vietnam from March 28 to April 4. His conclusion was that "the current military situation is critical, and the probability of the survival of South Vietnam as a truncated nation in the southern provinces is marginal at best." Weyand believed that the United States owed it to the South Vietnamese to do everything possible with respect to providing materials and equipment that would allow them to replenish their resources in the face of the offensive. "We went to Vietnam in the first place to assist the South Vietnamese people—not to defeat the

North Vietnamese. We reached out our hand to the South Vietnamese people, and they took it. Now they need that helping hand more than ever."

What was now needed, according to Weyand, was an additional $722 million that would bring the South Vietnamese to a minimal defense posture to meet the invasion. "Additional U.S. aid is within both the spirit and intent of the Paris Agreement, which remains the practical framework for a peaceful settlement in Vietnam." Weyand concluded his recommendations by noting that "United States credibility as an ally is at stake in Vietnam. To sustain that credibility we must make a maximum effort to support the South Vietnamese now."

Ten days later, the situation was worse. The communists were entering the last stage of their all-out assault. "Why in the hell don't we drop the bomb on North Vietnam?" asked Senator James Eastland of Mississippi. Yet a majority of legislators had no interest in sending any aid, let alone drop an atomic bomb on North Vietnam.

Eleven days later, in a last-ditch effort to secure aid, Kissinger appeared before the Senate Foreign Relations Committee. Senator Sparkman asked if "we have any obligations under the Paris Accords." Kissinger responded that, "the Accords had not obligations but authorities, that is, Article 7. President Nixon and others judged that permitting the United States to extricate itself would permit the United States to provide aid and enforce the Agreements. Under the Paris Accords we have no obligation. To the GVN we said that if they let us get our forces out it would enhance our chances of getting aid for them and enforcing the agreement. It was in this context, not that of a legal obligation. We never claimed an obligation; we never pleaded an obligation. But some of us think there is a moral obligation."

The next day, Kissinger met in the Oval Office with President Ford and his NSC deputy, Brent Scowcroft. Congress had made it clear it would not approve the funds necessary to keep South Vietnam afloat. "We have no chips left," says Kissinger. "If we could tell Le Duc Tho we would re-enter if they didn't calm down, he might stare us down, but I don't think he would cave in." Kissinger feared that once Congress turned down the aid package, "people may start killing Americans to ingratiate themselves with the communists. Whole divisions may switch."

Meeting with the cabinet in the White House the next day, Kissinger reported that "the entire North Vietnamese Army is in the South at the present time. . . . One Marine brigade could take all of North Vietnam. There has been a terrible violation of the Paris Peace Accords."

The first weeks of April also provided the opportunity for behind-the-scenes attempts to oust President Thieu. The events show that in the end, the South Vietnamese dealt with two enemies: the Communists and the U.S. government.

On April 2, 1975, the CIA station chief in Saigon Thomas Polgar sent a cable to CIA headquarters recommending that President Thieu be ousted in order to pave the way for Big Minh (General Duong Van Minh) to take over—thus facilitating the formation of the coalition government and supposedly stopping the North Vietnamese invasion. Polgar insisted that he had heard from the chief of the Hungarian delegation to the four-party peace accords supervision team that if President Thieu immediately stepped aside, then the North Vietnamese would be willing to negotiate.

About the same time, General Ky, whom President Thieu suspected was working with the CIA, approached South Vietnam's chief of general staff, General Cao Van Vien, to stage a coup against President Thieu. General Vien did not want to do anything without consulting General Tran Thien Khiem (who had stepped down 6 months ago as prime minister). Khiem immediately sought the advice of a longtime CIA operative, General Timmes, who was a very well-known figure in South Vietnam's politics and rumored as the instigator of quite a few coup attempts. President Thieu had always regarded Timmes as the godfather of General Khiem and believed that Khiem would do things only if the CIA agreed. Polgar was nervous at the turn of events and did not want Ky, Vien, and Khiem to mess up his own plans and told Timmes to turn them down. Khiem saw that the CIA did not want to move against President Thieu and in an effort to ingratiate himself with the President, told him about Ky's plans for the coup. "Talk about 'honor among thieves'" Nha commented when he recalled the episode.

The period from April 5 to 19 saw a flurry of activities between the U.S. Embassy in Saigon and Washington D.C. Polgar managed to convince Graham Martin that President Thieu should be ousted in order to save the country. Martin cabled Kissinger with his recommendation. At that time, Nha got a tip from a friendly Australian journalist that some type of coup was planned by the CIA and the South Vietnamese generals. The French ambassador in Saigon, Jean Marie Merillon, invited Nha to lunch and asked him to consider joining the so called "Third Force" and participating in the coalition government being planned. The ambassador told Nha that the French Ministry of Foreign Affairs got word from the North Vietnamese that should President Thieu be removed they would bless the coalition government. Ambassador Merillon also told Nha that he had passed those words to Ambassador Martin. Nha was incredulous and told the ambassador: "my friend, it is a bit late in the game for France to play power politics. You would be quite naïve to believe that the communists would give the so called NLF any say in the settlement. They do not care a bit for a negotiated settlement and intend to finish South Vietnam off militarily." Nha further told Ambassador Merillon that he would never work with the Third Force.

Meanwhile, upon receiving Martin's recommendation on the ouster of President Thieu, Kissinger told Martin not to precipitate anything because he (Kissinger) wanted to consult with Russian ambassador Dobrynin. On April 19 Martin went to see President Thieu to tell him that he should resign and that the U.S. would guarantee his safeguard. Ambassador Martin went on to tell President Thieu that if he were to go, then, in accordance with South Vietnam's constitution, Vice President Huong would succeed him, but that he would step down right away so that the President of the Senate, Tran Van Lam (former Minister of Foreign Affairs) could become the interim president and pave the way for a coalition government.

Apparently, Ambassador Martin also told Vice President Huong of this scenario, but Vice President Huong refused to go along, thus exposing the CIA and embassy's plan for a coup to grave danger. At that time, April 19, Nha had already gone to Singapore to meet with his contact who confirmed that a coup was being planned against the president and was blessed by the U.S. Nha then called Thieu from Singapore to relay the news, and they discussed options. "Both of us knew that it was another naïve option laid out by the U.S., in the desperate hope to save the so-called Peace Accords, given the blatant violation by the Communists," recalled Nha.

The CIA was now encouraging Gen. Vien and Gen. Khiem to stage the coup to remove President Thieu, and that such a coup would be launched on April 23. On April 21 President Thieu put an end to all the plans of his generals and of the U.S.: He resigned. The irony was that the U.S. Embassy did not know about this decision until a few hours before President Thieu made his announcement to the nation.

By April 17, Ambassador Martin was searching for ways of preventing the inevitable in Saigon. He pleaded with Kissinger to secure a loan from the Saudis as a way of privatizing foreign policy. Martin informed Kissinger that the National Bank of Vietnam had now promised to send billions in gold reserves to the Federal Reserve Bank in New York. But Martin warned that everything could fall apart at the slightest appearance of panic in Washington. "The one thing that would set off violence would be a sudden order for American evacuation. . . . It will be universally interpreted as a most callous betrayal, leaving the Vietnamese to their fate while we send in the marines to make sure that we get all ours out." Martin ended his message by reporting, "This is being personally typed. There will be no record except in Washington."

The next day, Martin received a cable from Henry Kissinger instructing him to reduce the number of Americans in the mission to 1,100. "I know that this decision will come as a blow to you. It is so for me. I can assure you that once we reach this level, I shall not press you again for further reductions except on the day, God forbid, if and when you are instructed completely to close down the mission."

Martin responded with a warning. "My ass isn't covered," he told Henry Kissinger. "I can assure you that I will be hanging several yards higher than you when this is all over." It was less than two weeks before the final evacuation of the U.S. embassy, and the American ambassador was at the end of his mental and physical rope. He needed to find a way of getting all Americans and as many loyal Vietnamese locals as possible out of Saigon. "Not to take them would be one last act of betrayal that would strip us of the last vestige of honor," Martin warned Kissinger.

On April 21, President Thieu announced his resignation to the legislature and the Supreme Court. He told his closest advisers that the military situation was hopeless and that his continued presence in office could conceivably be a block to a resolution of the conflict. Vice President Huong assumed the presidency.

Kissinger told President Ford that Thieu "warned me in '72 that leaving North Vietnamese troops in the South was dangerous. He said we said we would cut off aid if they didn't sign. Both of these are true, but to ask them to withdraw when the North had agreed not to reinforce or add equipment would have been impossible. I don't think Congress would have stood for continued fighting under these conditions."

"I will get a question on did we force him out," said Ford.

"Say no," answered Kissinger. "All our commitments are on the public record. It was always understood. President Nixon's correspondence is perfectly normal and reflects his intentions as President. Where they involve national commitments, they must go to the Congress."

At a Special Action Group meeting that day, the consensus was that the best that could now be hoped for was a negotiated surrender under the guise of a political solution. But that type of orderly transfer in power was unlikely to occur if the communists did not halt their military advance.

On April 23, Henry Kissinger received a memo on the subject, "North Vietnamese Troops in South Vietnam/Cambodia." The news was not good: "Since the ceasefire on January 28, 1973, over 120,000 NVA infiltrated South Vietnam. The current NVA strength in South Vietnam is approximately 207,000. The total enemy strength in South Vietnam (including VC) is approximately 280,000."

On April 25, Ambassador Martin cabled Kissinger that he had found a way to get Thieu and Kheim out of the country secretly. At 9:20 P.M. that day, they boarded a C-118, Tail Number 231, from Tan Son Nhut, headed for Taipei. Rumors swirled that Thieu had also transported over 16 tons of South Vietnam's gold reserves out of the country. But two days later, Martin cabled Kissinger that the Vietnamese gold was not going to New York. Those who had it did not want the Americans to get it: "The products of Harvard Business School and Hautes Etudes Commercials appear now to be obeying an earlier instinct that teaches the false security of physical possession."

The next day, reports arrived that Ton Son Nhut had been attacked and that the bombing was probably carried out by South Vietnamese defectors or VNAF pilots who were upset at the transition to the new Minh government. Although planes had flown over the palace, they dropped no ordnance, and therefore no targets were hit. Kissinger wryly said, "Why should they now. They never hit anything before."

On April 28, General Duong Van Minh sent a letter to Ambassador Martin. "I respectfully request that you give the order for the personnel of the Defense Attaché's Office (DAO) to leave Vietnam within 24 hours beginning April 29, 1975 in order that the question of peace for Vietnam can be settled early." Ambassador Martin replied to President Minh: "This is to inform your Excellency that I have issued orders as you have requested. I trust your Excellency will instruct the armed forces to the government to cooperate in every way possible in facilitating the safe removal of the personnel of the Defense Attaché Office. I also express the hope that your Excellency may intervene with the other side to permit the safe and orderly departure of the Defense Attaché and his staff."

Still, Martin did not want to leave. He beseeched Kissinger to "permit me and about twenty of my staff to remain behind, at least for a day or two to at least give some dignity to our departure and to facilitate an orderly disposition of our extensive properties here." Yet at a meeting of the NSC, CIA director William Colby reported that Minh's cease-fire offer had been rejected. "It is a very dangerous situation." Kissinger told the NSC that "the North Vietnamese have the intention of humiliating us and it seems unwise to leave people there."

On April 29, Ambassador Martin was ordered to leave and to make sure that everyone else was out. He refused to comply. Kissinger was livid. "There is no reason for Americans to still be there. He has been ordered by the President of the United States to get them the hell out of there. . . . What the hell is going on?"

At 6:30 A.M. on April 29 Secretary of Defense James Schlesinger announced publicly that "the President ordered the final withdrawal of the Americans from Vietnam at approximately 11:00 last night on the advice of the Ambassador and subsequent to the closing of Tan Son Nhut making it necessary to go to a helicopter lift."

The previous day, George S. Brown, JCS chairman, had warned those responsible for the evacuation, "I do not want to see Americans standing there waiting for the last plane."

A furious Kissinger cabled Martin, "You are immediately to resort to helicopter evacuation of all, repeat all, Americans."

On April 30, a sign was posted on the courtyard of the embassy in Saigon: "Turn off the light at the end of the tunnel when you leave."

The top-secret transmissions came in quick bursts from the CH-46 Sea Night helicopters and the larger CH-53 Sea Stallions that were ferrying evacuees from the American embassy rooftop to the U.S. fleet offshore. All communications between the pilots and their Airborne Battlefield Command and Control Center were simultaneously transmitted to U.S. command and control authorities in Hawaii and Washington. The final transmissions confirmed the bitter end of the evacuation.

"All of the remaining American personnel are on the roof at this time and Vietnamese are in the building," reported the pilot of a CH-53.

"The South Vietnamese have broken into the Embassy; they are rummaging around . . . no hostile acts noticed," reported another transmission. From the embassy rooftop, Marine Major James Kean described the chaos below as similar to a scene from the movie *On the Beach*.

Finally, at 0751 Saigon time, the embassy's Marine ground security force spotted the CH-46 and its call sign, "Swift 22." The last flight from Saigon would take the Marines home.

The final transmission from the CH-46 arrived with just seven words: "All the Americans are out, Repeat Out."

But not everyone was out. On the embassy rooftop, over 420 Vietnamese stared into the empty skies looking for any sign of returning American helicopters. Just hours earlier, they had been assured by well-intentioned Marines, "Khong ai se bi bo lai" ("No one will be left behind!"). Sensing the worst, however, many parents had pinned notes to their young child's clothing with final parental instructions that the child should study engineering or become a doctor in America. But a breakdown in communication had occurred among those running the evacuation from the ground, those offshore with the fleet controlling the helicopters, and those making the decisions in Hawaii and Washington. "It was the Vietnam war all over again," observed Colonel Harry G. Summers, Jr. "It was not a proud day to be an American."

The helicopters would not return. All the Americans were out. Repeat out.

From the White House, President Gerald Ford issued an official statement: "The evacuation has been completed. . . . This action closes a chapter in the American experience."

The six-story U.S. embassy on Thong Not Boulevard was left teeming with throngs of South Vietnamese pillaging whatever remained of the American presence. Rolls of green Bank of America embassy payroll checks were strewn across the parking lot. The embassy safe, days earlier emptied of its contents, was turned on its face. Smashed typewriters, file cabinets, broken desk fixtures lay everywhere, empty folders marked "top secret" scattered across the floor. Looters had carried away the embassy's kitchen sinks as well as the document shredder, which had been used almost nonstop by embassy employees to destroy not only diplomatic secrets but also the names of Vietnamese friends and collaborators. Amid the pile of rubble on the floor was a bronze plaque engraved with the names of five American servicemen who had died defending the embassy from Vietcong assault in 1968.

At 12:10 P.M. the first tanks of the People's Liberation Armed Forces (PLAF) broke through the palace gates. For years, the president had been protected by the ornamental wrought iron fences bolstered by tangles of rusting barbed wire and guarded by combat police and special palace guards. This time, it took only minutes for the PRG flag to be raised. At 12:30, PRG soldiers walked into the plush carpeted office where the newly installed president of South Vietnam, Big Minh, had been waiting to transfer power officially. Big Minh could not transfer what he did not possess; his only choice was unconditional surrender. "The old administration has totally collapsed, "said Colonel Bui Tin. "You cannot hand over what you do not have. You must surrender immediately." To ease the tension, Bui Tin asked Big Minh if he still played tennis and about Minh's orchid collection, reputed to have over 600 species. Also present in the room was Vu Van Mau, South Vietnam's prime minister designate. Bui Tin asked Vu Van Mau why his hair was so long, since he had promised to wear it short for as long as Thieu remained president. Bui Tin later recalled that Big Minh laughed at this and said, "No wonder we [the North Vietnamese] had won the war because we knew everything."

Big Minh was driven to a radio station near the palace and forced to broadcast a message requesting that all armed forces of the Republic of Vietnam lay down their arms and surrender unconditionally. "I declare that the Saigon government, from central to local level, has been completely dissolved."

South Vietnam had ceased to exist.

Back at the White House, a cabinet meeting was convened. The mood was somber, but Henry Kissinger could see something positive: "We have maintained our honor by taking out 42,000–45,000 Vietnamese."

Brigadier General Vernon Walters, the military attaché who took Kissinger in and out of Paris on the secret "walks in the night," did not see it that way. To this day he keeps a little South Vietnamese flag in his office. When asked about it, he explains that it stands for "unfinished business. We let 39 million people fall into slavery." Such was one legacy of "peace with honor."

APPENDIX A

White House Fact Sheet

Basic Elements of the Vietnam Agreement,
January 24, 1973

STRICTLY EMBARGOED FOR WIRE MOVEMENT   JANUARY 24, 1973
AND RELEASE UNTIL 10:00 AM EST

Office of the White House Press Secretary

THE WHITE HOUSE

FACT SHEET

BASIC ELEMENTS OF VIETNAM AGREEMENT

Military Provisions

Cease-fire
—International-supervised cease-fire throughout South and North Vietnam, effective at 7:00 PM EST, Saturday, January 27, 1973.

American Forces
—Release within 60 days of all American servicemen and civilians captured and
held throughout Indochina, and fullest possible accounting for missing in action.
—Return of all United States forces and military personnel from South Vietnam
within 60 days.

Security of South Vietnam
—Ban on infiltration of troops and war supplies into South Vietnam.
—The right to unlimited military replacement aid for the Republic of Vietnam.
—Reunification only by peaceful means, through negation between North and
South Vietnam without coercion or annexation.
—Reduction and demobilization of Communist and Government forces in the
South.
—Ban on use of Laotian or Cambodian base areas to encroach on sovereignty
and security of South Vietnam.
—Withdrawal of all foreign troops from Laos and Cambodia.

Political Provisions
—Joint United States–Democratic Republic of Vietnam statement that the South
Vietnamese people have the right to self-determination.
—The Government of the Republic of Vietnam continues in existence, recog-
nized by the United States, its constitutional structure and leadership intact
and unchanged.

—The right to unlimited economic aid for the Republic of Vietnam.

—Formation of a non-governmental National Council of National Reconciliation and Concord, operating by unanimity, to organize elections as agreed by the parties and to promote conciliation and implementation of the Agreement.

Indochina

—Reaffirmation of the 1954 and 1962 Geneva Agreements on Cambodia and Laos.

—Respect for the independence, sovereignty, unity, territorial integrity and neutrality of Cambodia and Laos.

—Ban on infiltration of troops and war supplies into Cambodia and Laos.

—Ban on use of Laotian and Cambodian base areas to encroach on sovereignty and security of one another and of other countries.

—Withdrawal of all foreign troops from Laos and Cambodia.

—In accordance with traditional United States policy, U.S. participation in post-war reconstruction efforts throughout Indochina.

—With the ending of the war, a new basis for U.S. relations with North Vietnam.

Control and Supervision

—An International Commission of Control and Supervision, with 1160 international supervisory personnel, to control and supervise the elections and various military provisions of the Agreement.

—An International Conference within 30 days to guarantee the Agreement and the ending of the war.

—Joint Military Commissions of the parties to implement appropriate provisions of the Agreement.

APPENDIX B

The Lessons of Vietnam

Henry Kissinger to President Ford

MEMORANDUM   3173-X

THE WHITE HOUSE

WASHINGTON

~~SECRET~~/SENSITIVE/EYES ONLY

MEMORANDUM FOR: THE PRESIDENT

FROM: HENRY A. KISSINGER

SUBJECT: Lessons of Vietnam

At your request, I have prepared some thoughts on the "lessons of
Vietnam" for your consideration and for your background information in dealing with further press questions on the subject.

It is remarkable, considering how long the war lasted and how
intensely it was reported and commented, that there are really
not very many lessons. from our experience in Vietnam that
can be usefully applied elsewhere despite the obvious temptation
to try. Vietnam represented a unique situation, geographically,
ethnically, politically, militarily and diplomatically. We should
probably be grateful for that and should recognize it for what it is,
instead of trying to apply the "lessons of Vietnam" as universally
as we once tried to apply the "lessons of Munich".

The real frustration of Vietnam, in terms of commentary and evaluation, may be that the war had almost universal effects but did not
provide a universal catechism.

A frequent temptation of many commentators has been to draw
conclusions regarding the tenacity of the American people and the
ultimate failure of our will. But I question whether we can accept
that conclusion. It was the longest war in American history, the
most distant, the least obviously relevant to our nation's immediate
concerns, and yet the American people supported our involvement
and its general objectives until the very end. The people made
enormous sacrifices. I am convinced that, even at the end, they
would have been prepared to support a policy that would have saved
South Vietnam if such an option had been available to use.

~~SECRE~~T/SENSITIVE/EYES ONLY - XGDS

It must not be forgotten that the decisions of American administrations that involved this nation in the war were generally supported at the time they were taken, and that they were supported not only among the people at large but among the political elements and among the journalists who later came to oppose the war. The American people generally supported and applauded President Eisenhower for a decision to partition Vietnam and to support an anti-Communist government in the South. The American people, and particularly the American media, supported President Kennedy's decision to go beyond the restrictions on American involvement that President Eisenhower had set and they also supported his decision to permit American involvement in the removal of President Diem -- although the extent of that involvement was not clear at the time. Many who were later to be labeled as "doves" on Vietnam then insisted that South Vietnam had to be saved and that President Diem's removal was essential to save it. You yourself will remember the strong support that the Tonkin Gulf resolution won on the Hill and the general support for President Johnson's decision to send troops. President Nixon won an outpouring of support for the decision to withdraw American forces at a gradual pace, as well as for the Paris Peace Agreement.

If one could offer any guidelines for the future about the lessons to be drawn regarding domestic support for foreign policy, it would be that American political groups will not long remain comfortable in positions that go against their traditional attitudes. The liberal Democrats could not long support a war against a revolutionary movement, no matter how reactionary the domestic tactics of that movement. They had accepted the heavy commitment to Vietnam because of President Kennedy, whom they regarded as their leader, but they withdrew from it under President Johnson.

One clear lesson that can be drawn, however, is the importance of absolute honesty and objectivity in all reporting, within and from the Government as well as from the press. U.S. official reports tended for a long time to be excessively optimistic, with the result that official statements did not make clear to the American people how long and how tough the conflict might turn out to be. After a while the pessimistic reports from journalists began to gain greater credence because such positive trends as did emerge came too slowly to justify optimistic Washington assessments. In Vietnam, the situation was generally worse than some reported and better than others reported. But the pessimistic reports, even if they were

inaccurate, began to look closer to the mark until almost any
government statement could be rejected as biased, not only by
the opposition but by an increasingly skeptical public.

Another lesson would be the absolute importance of focusing our
own remarks and the public debate on essentials -- even if those
essentials are not clearly visible every night on the television
screen. The Vietnam debate often turned into a fascination with
issues that were, at best, peripheral. The "tiger cages" were
seen as a symbol of South Vietnamese Government oppression,
although that Government was facing an enemy who had assassinated, tortured and jailed an infinitely greater number; the
"Phoenix" program became a subject of attack although North
Vietnamese and Viet Cong tactics were infinitely more brutal.
The Mylai incident tarnished the image of an American Army that
had generally -- through not always -- been compassionate in
dealing with the civilian population. Even at the end, much of
the public discussion focused on President Thieus's alleged failure
to gain political support, but it was the Communists who rejected
free elections and who brought in their reserve divisions because
they did not have popular support. And at home, it was argued that
your aid request meant American reinvolvement when nothing was
further from your mind.

Of equal importance may be a dedication to consistency. When the
United States entered the war during the 1960's, it did so with
excesses that not only ended the career and the life of an allied leader
but that may have done serious damage to the American economy and
that poured over half a million soldiers into a country where we never
had more than 100,000 who were actually fighting. At the end, the
excesses in the other direction made it impossible to get from the
Congress only about 2 or 3 percent as much money as it had earlier
appropriated every year. When we entered, many did so in the name
of morality. Before the war was over, many opposed it in the name of
morality. But nobody spoke of the morality of consistency, or of the
virtue of seeing something through once its cost had been reduced to
manageable proportions.

In terms of military tactics, we cannot help draw the conclusion that
our armed forces are not suited to this kind of war. Even the Special
Forces who had been designed for it could not prevail. This was partly
because of the nature of the conflict. It was both a revolutionary war

4

fought at knife-point during the night within the villages. It was
also a main force war in which technology could make a genuine
difference. Both sides had trouble devising tactics that would be
suitable for each type of warfare. But we and the South Vietnamese
had more difficulty with this than the other side. We also had
trouble with excesses here: when we made it "our war" we would
not let the South Vietnamese fight it; when it again became "their
war", we would not help them fight it. Ironically, we prepared
the South Vietnamese for main force warfare after 1954 (anticipating
another Korean-type attack), and they faced a political war; they
had prepared themselves for political warfare after 1973 only to be
faced with a main force invasion 20 years after it had been expected.

Our diplomacy also suffered in the process, and it may take us
some time to bring things back to balance. We often found that
the United States could not sustain a diplomatic position for more
than a few weeks or months before it came under attack from the
same political elements that had often advocated that very position.
We ended up negotiating with ourselves, constantly offering concession after concession while the North Vietnamese changed nothing
in their diplomatic objectives and very little in their diplomatic
positions. It was only in secret diplomacy that we could hold anything approaching a genuine dialogue, and even then the North
Vietnamese could keep us under constant public pressure. Our
diplomacy often degenerated into frantic efforts to find formulas
that would evoke momentary support and would gloss over obvious
differences between ourselves and the North Vietnamese. The
legacy of this remains to haunt us, making it difficult for us to
sustain a diplomatic position for any length of time, no matter how
obdurate the enemy, without becoming subject to domestic attack.

In the end, we must ask ourselves whether it was all worth it, or
at least what benefits we did gain. I believe the benefits were
many, though they have long been ignored, and I fear that we will
only now begin to realize how much we need to shore up our positions elsewhere once our position in Vietnam is lost. We may be
compelled to support other situations much more strongly in order
to repair the damage and to take tougher stands in order to make
others believe in us again.

I have always believed, as have many observers, that our decision
to save South Vietnam in 1965 prevented Indonesia from falling to
Communism and probably preserved the American presence in Asia.

SECRET/SENSITIVE/EYES ONLY   5

This not only means that we kept our troops. It also means that
we kept our economic presence as well as our political influence,
and that our friends -- including Japan -- did not feel that they
had to provide for their own defense. When we consider the
impact of what is now happening, it is worth remembering how
much greater the impact would have been ten years ago when the
Communist movement was still widely regarded as a monolyth
destined to engulf us all. Therefore, in our public statements,
I believe we can honorably avoid self-flagellation and that we
should not characterize our role in the conflict as a disgraceful
disaster. I believe our efforts, militarily, diplomatically and
politically, were not in vain. We paid a high price but we gained
ten years of time and we changed what then appeared to be an
overwhelming momentum. I do not believe our soldiers or our
people need to be ashamed.

Text of Address by President Nixon on the Vietnam Agreement

FOR IMMEDIATE RELEASE   JANUARY 23, 1973

Office of the White House Press Secretary

THE WHITE HOUSE

TEXT OF A RADIO AND TELEVISION ADDRESS
BY THE PRESIDENT
ON
AN AGREEMENT ON ENDING THE WAR
AND RESTORING PEACE IN VIETNAM

I have asked for this radio and television time for the purpose of announcing that we have today concluded an agreement to end the war and bring peace with honor in Vietnam and Southeast Asia.

The following statement is being issued at this moment in Washington and in Hanoi:

"At 12:30 p.m. Paris time today, January 23, 1973, The Agreement on Ending the War and Restoring Peace in Vietnam was initialed by Dr. Henry Kissinger on behalf of the United States and Special Advisor Le Duc Tho on behalf of the Democratic Republic of Vietnam.

"The Agreement will be formally signed by the Parties participating in the Paris Conference on Vietnam on January 27, 1973, at the International Conference Center in Paris. The cease-fire will take effect at 2400 Greenwich Mean Time January 27, 1973.

"The United States and the Democratic Republic of Vietnam express the hope that this Agreement will ensure stable peace in Vietnam and contribute to the preservation of lasting peace in Indochina and Southeast Asia."

Throughout the years of negotiations, we have insisted on peace with honor. In my addresses of January 25 and May 8, I set forth the goals that we considered essential to peace with honor. In the settlement that has now been agreed to, the conditions that I laid down then have all been met:

—A cease-fire, internationally supervised, will begin at 7:00 p.m. this Saturday, January 27, Washington time.

—Within 60 days from this Saturday, all Americans held prisoner throughout Indochina will be released. There will be the fullest possible accounting for all those who are missing in action.

—During the same 60-day period, all American forces will be withdrawn from South Vietnam.

—The people of South Vietnam have been guaranteed the right to determine their own future without outside interference.

By joint agreement, the full text of the Agreement and of the protocols to carry it out will be released tomorrow.

Throughout the negotiations, we have been in the closest consultation with President Thieu and other representatives of the Republic of Vietnam. This settlement meets the goals and has the full support of President Thieu and the Government of the Republic of Vietnam, as well as that of our other allies who are affected.

The United States will continue to recognize the Government of the Republic of Vietnam as the sole legitimate government of South Vietnam.

We shall continue to aid South Vietnam within the terms of the Agreement, and we shall support efforts by the people of South Vietnam to settle their problems peacefully among themselves.

We must recognize that ending the war is only the first step toward building the peace.

All parties must now see to it that this is a peace that lasts, a peace that heals—and a peace that not only ends the war in Southeast Asia, but contributes to the prospects of peace in the world.

This will mean that the terms of the Agreement must be scrupulously adhered to. We shall do everything the Agreement requires of us, and we shall expect the other parties to do everything it requires of them. We shall also expect other interested nations to help ensure that the Agreement is carried out and the peace maintained.

As this long and difficult war ends, I would like to address a few special words to each of those who have been parties to the conflict.

To the people and the Government of South Vietnam:

By your courage, by your sacrifice, you have won the precious right to determine your own future. You have developed the strength to defend that right. We look forward to working with you in the future, friends in peace as we have been allies in war.

To the leaders of North Vietnam:

As we have ended the war through negotiations, let us build a peace of reconciliation. For our part, we are prepared to make a major effort to help achieve that goal. But just as reciprocity was needed to end the war, so too will it be needed to build and strengthen the peace.

To the other major powers that have been involved, even indirectly:

Now is the time for mutual restraint, so that the peace we have achieved can be kept.

And finally, to the American people:

Your steadfastness in supporting our insistence on peace with honor has made peace with honor possible. I know that you would not have wanted that peace jeopardized.

With our secret negotiations at the sensitive stage they were in during this recent period, for me to have discussed publicly our efforts to secure peace would not only have violated our understanding with North Vietnam; it would have seriously harmed and possibly destroyed the chances for peace. Therefore, I know that you now can understand why, during these past several weeks, I have not made any public statements about those efforts. The important thing was not to talk about peace, but to get peace—and to get the right kind of peace. This we have done.

Now that we have achieved an honorable agreement, let us be proud that America did not settle for a peace that would have betrayed our allies, that would have abandoned our prisoners of war, or that would have ended the war for us but would have continued the war for the 50 million people of Indochina.

Let us be proud of the two and a half million young Americans who served in Vietnam—who served with honor and distinction in one of the most selfless enterprises in the history of nations.

Let us be proud of those who sacrificed—who gave their lives—so that the people of South Vietnam might live in freedom and so that the world might live in peace.

In particular, I would like to say a word to some of the bravest people I have ever met: the wives, the children, the families, of our prisoners of war and of the missing in action.

When others called on us to settle on any terms, you had the courage to stand for the right kind of peace, so that those who died and those who suffered would not have died and suffered in vain, and so that where this generation knew war the next generation could know peace.

Nothing means more to me now than the fact that your long vigil is coming to an end.

Just yesterday, a great American died.

In his life, President Johnson endured the vilification of those who sought to portray him as a man of war. But there was nothing he cared about more deeply than achieving a lasting peace in the world.

I remember the last time I talked with him, just the day after New Year's. He spoke then of his concern with bringing peace, and with making it the right kind of peace, and I was grateful that he once again expressed his support for my efforts to gain such a peace.

No one would have welcomed this peace more than he. And I know he would join me in asking—for those who died, and for those who live—let us consecrate this moment by resolving together to make the peace we have achieved a peace that will last.

*   *   *

NOTES

"Historians will eventually dig it all out. . . . There is a hell of a story there that is yet to be told." That is how Graham Martin, the last American ambassador to Vietnam, described the paper trail of documents labeled "Top Secret/Sensitive," which he hoped one day would illuminate the public events and private decisions concerning America's exit from Vietnam. That story is now emerging, and as Martin knew, it is a far different one than either Richard Nixon or Henry Kissinger offered in their respective memoirs. In the material that follows, I offer documentary evidence of a massive historical shell game called "peace with honor."

I conducted research in the following archival depositories. Every document and interview transcript utilized in this book will be deposited by Deed of Gift to the Vietnam Archive at Texas Tech University so that others might use these resources.

At the Hoover Archives, located on the campus of Stanford University, I used the files of Allan Goodman, author of a 1978 book, *The Lost Peace*. These contain notes, interview transcripts and research materials bearing on the political and military elements of the Paris negotiations. They are cited as Goodman Files.

At the Gerald Ford Library, located on the campus of the University of Michigan, I focused on the Henry Kissinger–Brent Scowcroft Memcons—transcript-like memoranda of high level conversations, National Security Agency declassifications of radio messages from helicopter pilots shuttling to and from the Saigon embassy in April 1975, Ron Nessen's notes of meetings with Kissinger and Ford, Gerald Ford's Congressional Papers (Ford was Minority Leader at the time of the Paris Accords), and the papers of Ambassador Graham Martin. I spent much time in the NSC Convenience Files. These are materials from the U.S. Embassy, Saigon: 1963–75 (1976), copies of State Department telegrams and White House backchannel messages between U.S. ambassadors in Saigon and White House national security advisers, talking points for meetings with South Vietnamese officials, intelligence reports, drafts of peace agreements, and military status reports. The Graham Martin papers and the fall of South Vietnam files are key parts of this record. The Kissinger-Scowcroft files and an extraordinary set of MEMCONS are available in the Ford Library. See also Henry Kissinger and Brent Scowcroft Parallel File of documents opened from unprocessed collections; National Security Council, Kissinger-Scowcroft West Wing Office File; National Security File—NSC meetings; and National Security File—Saigon Embassy file. Recent declassifications include files from the National Security Adviser, Presidential Name file; National Security Council Meetings file; presidential country files for East Asia and the

Pacific; State Department telegrams; backchannel messages—Martin channel; Kissinger-Scowcroft West Wing Office Files and Camp David Files.

At the LBJ Library, located on the campus of the University of Texas, I was able to review the papers of Paul Warnke, Clark Clifford and George Elsey's notes of Secretary Clifford's morning staff conferences. I also obtained copies of recently declassified materials from the Anna Chennault files that are cited as Chennault folder.

In the Legislative Records Division of the National Archives, I accessed the depositions and affidavits of the principals from the Congressional inquiry into the status of American MIAs—depositions are available for Henry Kissinger, Alexander Haig, Brent Scowcroft, Vernon Walters, William Rogers, Heyward Isham, Winston Lord, John Negroponte, Roger Shields, George Aldrich, Paul Miles, Thomas Moorer, William Sullivan, Peter Rodman, and others. I also reviewed declassified conversations between Henry Kissinger and Le Duc Tho, but only those segments bearing on prisoners of war (POW) or those missing in action (MIA). These are cited in *Records Relating to American Prisoners of War and Missing in Action from the Vietnam War*, compiled by Charles E. Schamel, National Archives and Records Administration, Washington D.C., 1996. See Neal Kravitz Investigative Counsel Witness Files, Boxes 1–14; Senate Select Committee on POW/MIA Affairs, Investigative Case Files, Papers of John Erikson, boxes 1–5. I also made extensive use of Records subgroup 13— Records of the Peace Accords team, Department of State. These are records of selected transcripts of the Paris Accords meetings and related documents from May 1968–January 1973. These include telegrams to the State Department, texts of speeches, analyses, and memorandums. Documents passed to the other side are also available. In subgroup 14—Paris Embassy cable (TWX) traffic relating to the Paris Peace accords, there are selected TWX files on POW/MIA affairs as they related to the Paris Accords, originating from Washington. In subgroup 15—Paris Embassy Cable TWX, I found records originating from the U.S. Embassy in Paris, France. In subgroup 16—Selected records of Frank Sieverts, I made use of his extensive clippings, messages, and telegrams. In subgroup 20—Copies of selected papers of Henry Kissinger, I found copies from the personal papers of Henry Kissinger housed in the Library of Congress. They included declassified memorandums for the president, memorandums of conversations, memorandums to file, texts of cable traffic and reports relating to the negotiations in Paris, negotiating strategies, and prisoner issues, cited as Kissinger papers.

At the National Security Archive at George Washington University, I read the Joint Chiefs of Staff Command History for the Vietnam War, cited as JCS *History*.

In the Mudd Library at Princeton University, I received unrestricted access to the personal papers of George McGovern and these are cited as McGovern papers.

At the National Archives II, I focused initially on the papers of Tony Lake, as well as the State Department files on the Paris negotiations. The Nixon Presidential Materials Staff has released "Documents Relating to POW/MIA Matters Among the Nixon White House Files in the National Security Council." I drew extensively from the Vietnam Country Files, Paris Talks/Meetings, Backchannel Messages; For the President Files—Winston Lord, Vietnam Negotiations, Alexander Haig–Special File, Files for the President—Vietnam Negotiations; Henry Kissinger Office Files—HAK Administration and staff files—memorandums dispatched from west basement and HAK trip files. The Paris Talks/Meetings, boxes 165–192 cover the period May 1968—March 1973, and these files consist of Department of State cables, memorandums, and other materials relating to the Vietnam Peace talks. The bulk are cables between the American Embassy in Paris and the Department of State. The Lake Chron Files series contains the staff files of Tony Lake, an NSC staff member from 1970 to 71. The HAK Trip Files include memorandums of conversations, cables, telegrams, and correspondence pertaining to Kissinger's trips to Vietnam, Paris, and Cambodia. I made extensive use of the Haldeman Diaries, a daily record of events and conversations and thoughts by the assistant to the president and chief of staff. I also utilized the cd-rom *Haldeman Diaries*. In April 2000, the NARA opened 130,000 pages of previously classified materials primarily from the NSC files.

The Nixon Presidential Library is the only presidential library that does not accept government funds. The Library raises all of its revenue from private sources, museum admissions, and Museum Store sales to fund the Library and Birthplace in Yorba Linda and the Nixon Center in Washington, D.C. My readers need to understand that this not only makes the Nixon Library an official "rehab center" for their President's place in history, but also the central PR control room for countering virtually anything that challenges Nixon's legacy. The Nixon Library's mission is "preserving and protecting the legacy of the 37th President." Any visitor to the Nixon Library web-site can see firsthand just how far the Library goes in discrediting those writers who have challenged the official historical legacy of Richard Nixon.

At Archives II, I also discovered a trove of material used by Walter Scott Dilliard in writing the official MACV history, *Sixty Days to Peace: Implementing the Paris Accords.* See "Final Report, US Delegation, Four-Party Joint Military Commission." This document was prepared in Saigon and Washington from February to June 1973. It was originally located in Record Group 319, Boxes 10–41 in the Washington National Records Center and now transferred to Archives II. I made extensive use of Dilliard's interviews, the lengthy first draft which contained substantive material that was later deleted from the final publication, and all of his research questions and related observations.

I benefited greatly from declassifications in RG 59—General Records of the Department of State. I cite from POL VIET S and boxes 2693–2715; US Kissinger-Nixon and US-Nixon. Also 2773–2832 on Vietnam. In RG 59 boxes 2774–2809 and 2820–2832 Political and Defense and the TS Top Secret file, boxes 20–22-POL Viet. Record Group 84 contains much Bunker-Embassy traffic, boxes 1–7. Most of the Ellsworth Bunker cables to Kissinger are found in this series, and are cited as such.

At the Vietnam Archive located at Texas Tech University, I used the Doug Pike collection bearing on the Paris Accords as well as North Vietnamese assessments of the Accords. The Pike collection was especially valuable for North Vietnamese perspectives.

I made frequent use of the complete interview transcripts done by Stanley Karnow in preparation for *Vietnam: A Television History,* the major documentary produced by WGBH Television in Boston and aired on PBS in the United States. The transcripts as well as other materials from the PBS series are located in the William Joiner Center for the Study of War and Social Consequences at the University of Massachusetts–Boston. Karnow provided me with his set of interviews done for the show and his book.

PROLOGUE

Full book references are furnished with the first citation. After that, the reference is shortened, but the complete citation can be found in the Bibliography. Documents cited with a date in the text, such as a Haldeman diary entry, are referenced only the first time. References are in order of appearance in the book. In many instances I have shortened archival citations, but provided the Library that I consulted.

The Nixon diary entry is found in Richard Nixon. *The Memoirs of Richard Nixon*, p. 742 (cited hereafter as *RN*). The conversation between Cho and Tho is in *77 Conversations Between Chinese and Foreign Leaders on the Wars in Indochina, 1964–1977*, edited by Odd Arne Westad, Chen Jian, Stein Tonnesson, Nguyen Vu Tung, and James G. Hershberg. Working Paper No. 22, Cold War International History Project (Washington, D.C.: Woodrow Wilson International Center for Scholars, May 1998) (cited hereafter as *77 Conversations*. These are top-level conversations among Chinese, Vietnamese, Cambodian, and Laotian leaders during the 1960s and 1970s from archival documents and internal Communist party documents. Also see Qiang Zhai, *Beijing and the Vietnam Peace Talks, 1965–68, New Evidence from Chinese Sources,* working paper 18, and *China and the Vietnam Wars, 1950–1975* (Chapel Hill: University of North Carolina Press, 2000).

The Thurmond letter is part of the massive Record Group (RG) declassification relating to "American Prisoners of War and Missing in Action from the Vietnam War." Many documents relating to POW/MIA matters are in the Nixon White House files of the National Security Council in the Nixon Presidential Materials. The National Security Files were the working file of the president's special assistant for national security affairs, Henry Kissinger. The materials include letters, memorandums, telegrams, memorandums of conversations, and related documentation created and received by Kissinger and his staff. Many of these documents concerned the ongoing Paris negotiations. These included the following NSC files: President's Daily Briefing, Vietnam Subject Files, Vietnam Country Files, Paris Talks/Meetings, Back-Channel for the President's Files–Winston Lord, Vietnam Negotiations, Alexander M. Haig Special File, Files of the President–Vietnam Negotiations, Jon Howe Vietnam Subject Files, and Henry Kissinger Office Files. A fraction of the material is open.

The Kissinger remark to Tho about North Vietnamese troops can be found in the transcript of conversation from the private meeting, January 23, 1973, Small Meeting Room, International Conference Center, Hotel Majestic, NSC Files, Nixon Project "Paris Talks/Meetings 189–192" and in RG 59, State Department Files, RG 59 "Records Relating to South Vietnam and the Central File of the Department of State (RG 59) 1910–73. See especially No. 59, Stack Area 150, Row 67 Central Policy File

Top Secret Box, 20–22, Def Viet; Boxes 2703–2704 US-Nixon 6/2/72–5/23/73 US-Nixon 9/1/72–10/23/73; boxes 2711–2714, 2775–2832 are all Vietnam POL 2782–3; 2792–99, 2807–8, 2820–32; RG 59 TOP SECRET (TS) Files, box 9, 20–22.

The Thieu letter to Nixon is in Nguyen Tien Hung and Jerrold L. Schecter. *The Palace File* (New York: Harper & Row, 1978). The letters can be found in files at the Ford Library. Readers should understand that President Thieu viewed the letters from Nixon as "a pledge of honor." Kissinger told the Senate Foreign Relations Committee in 1975 that the letters were "not a legal commitment. We never said there was." The Ford speech draft and related files are at "Address by President Gerald R. Ford to the Joint Session of Congress, April 10, 1975 On Foreign Policy," April 8, 1975. See papers of Ron Nessen and Robert Hartman in the Ford Library. The Mitak letter and the documents bearing on the evacuation and Martin cables are located in the Ford Library. See Martin's testimony on January 27, 1976, House of Representatives, Special Subcommittee on Investigations of the Committee on International Relations. P. 540. For a fascinating "fictional" account of the final months, see Bernard Kalb and Marvin Kalb, *The Last Ambassador* (Boston: Little, Brown, 1981). The intercepts are messages pertaining to the evacuation of Saigon and were in possession of NSA and later transferred to the Center for Cryptologic History. The special file is available at the Ford Library. For the final days, see Harry G. Summers, Jr., "The Bitter End," in a special issue of *Vietnam,* "The Fall of Saigon," April 1995. In that same issue, see Major General Homer D. Smith, "The Final 45 Days in Vietnam," p. 26. See David Butler, *The Fall of Saigon* (New York: Simon & Schuster, 1985); Alan Dawson. *55 Days: The Fall of South Vietnam* (Englewood Cliffs, NJ: Prentice Hall, 1977); James Kean, "Last Flight Out of Saigon," *California Monthly* (April 1995); James H. Willbanks, "The Last 55 Days" (paper presented at 3d Triennial Vietnam Symposium, Texas Tech University, April 15–17, 1999); Stuart A. Herrington, *Peace with Honor?* (Novato, Calif.: Presidio Press, 1983); General Cao Van Vien, *The Final Collapse* (Center for Military History, 1983). The Speakers' Kit and Media Kit are in the Douglas Pike Collection in Texas Tech's Vietnam Archive. Unit IV Political Settlement; Box 26 has Hanoi's statements on the treaty. Peter Arnett, "The Last American Handout—US Embassy Stripped Bare," *Washington Star,* April 30, 1975 for the embassy being looted.

The Dong interview with Cronkite is from a February 25, 1985 CBS interview in Hanoi later published in *"Vietnam Courier,"* no. 4 (April 1985): 5–6. The postcard is from the Pike Collection. Nixon's comment to Crowley is at Monica Crowley, *Nixon in Winter* (New York: Random House, 1998), pp. 237–238. See *The Paris Agreement on Vietnam: Twenty-Five Years Later* (Nixon Center, Washington, DC, April 1988). For the decent interval see Frank Snepp, *Decent Interval* (New York: Random House, 1977) and Col. William E. Le Gro, *Vietnam from Cease-Fire to Capitulation* (Washington, D.C.: U.S. Army Center Military History, 1981). The Kissinger response to Negroponte is from Stanley Karnow in Peter Braestrup, ed., *Vietnam as History: Ten Years After the Paris Peace Accords* (Washington, D.C.: Woodrow Wilson International Center for Scholars, 1984), p. 83. The fullest account of Tonkin Gulf is Edwin E. Moise, *Tonkin Gulf and the Escalation of the Vietnam War* (Chapel Hill: University of

North Carolina Press, 1996). Kissinger has rebutted these charges in a letter to the editor, *Foreign Affairs* 78, no. 4 Sept./Oct. 1999, pp. 152–3. See Philip Zelekow, "The Statesman in Winter," *Foreign Affairs* 78, no. 3, 1999, and William Burr, "The Kissinger Papers," *New York Review of Books,* May 20, 1999. According to Kissinger, "When somebody studies it, they will find that our position in the negotiations was consistent from the first day onwards." See his deposition to Kerry Committee. Peter Rodman, Kissinger's former assistant, told me that "revisionist history of the negotiations in Paris will reveal that what we said happened, actually happened. Kissinger's memoirs give the actual story of our dealings with Tho and Thieu."

The Zumwalt assessment is from an interview with me and is consistent with Zumwalt's theory of "Kissingerology" from his memoir *On Watch* (New York: Quadrangle, 1976), chap. 18. See Records Relating to American Prisoners of War and Missing in Action from the Vietnam War era, 1960–1994, compiled by Charles E. Schamel, Senate Select Committee on POW/MIA Affairs at the Center for Legislative Archives in National Archives Building, 102d Congress; see especially vol. 1(f). Deposition Files and (g) Records of the Chief Clerk: depositions and Witness case files. Files of Investigator William Legro. Records of the Senate Select Committee on POW/MIA Affairs, Selected Records of Frank Seiverts, boxes 3–23. Records of the Senate Select Committee on POW/MIA Affairs, Paris Embassy TWX Traffic (1968–72), boxes 7–13; boxes 1–6, Plenary Sessions of meetings with transcripts; 7–113 embassy traffic; Embassy TWX Traffic boxes 1–27; Paris Emb TWX Traffic 22–27; Records of the Paris Peace Accords Team, boxes 1–7; Washington Saigon TWX traffic, 1973–92 boxes 1–4.

Luu Van Loi and Nguyen Anh Vu, *Le Duc Tho–Kissinger Negotiations in Paris* (Hanoi: Gioi Publishers, 1996). "The public knows only half the truth from Western writing," is how the authors begin their important contribution (hereafter referred to as Loi and Vu, *Negotiations*). A note on my use of Loi and Vu's translations of Hanoi's records from the Tho-Kissinger meetings: I made every attempt to obtain multiple sources for verification purposes, but the sad fact is that many of the U.S. documents remain classified and Kissinger's personal papers are still locked away in the Library of Congress. I recognize that the complete record is still not available and eagerly await the day that Kissinger decides to open his materials for research. Until that day, however, I have done the best with the hand dealt me.

CHAPTER ONE

"Search For Peace"

The Johnson attribution is from Nixon in Crowley, *Nixon in Winter,* p. 237. The story of Tet is best told in Don Oberdorfer's *TET,* (Baltimore: Johns Hopkins University Press, 2001). See also Marc Jason Gilbert and William Head, eds., *The Tet Offensive* (New York: Praeger, 1996). Larry Berman, *Lyndon Johnson's War: The Road to*

Stalemate in Vietnam (New York: Norton, 1969). Herbert Y. Shandler, *The Unmaking of a President: Lyndon Johnson and Vietnam* (Princeton, N.J.: Princeton University Press, 1977). William C. Westmoreland, *A Soldier Reports* (Garden City, N.Y.: Doubleday 1976). For Clifford's role, see Clark Clifford, *Counsel to the President* (New York: Random House, 1991). I relied on the excellent works of Robert Dallek, *Flawed Giant: Lyndon Johnson and His Times, 1961–1973* (New York: Oxford University Press, 1998); Lloyd C. Gardner, *Pay Any Price: Lyndon Johnson and the Wars for Vietnam* (Chicago: Ivan R. Dee, 1995, George Herring, *LBJ and Vietnam: A Different Kind of War* (Austin: University of Texas Press, 1994); Robert D. Schulzinger, *A Time for War: The United States and Vietnam, 1941–1975* (New York: Oxford University Press, 1977).

On the search for peace see Robert K. Brigham, *Guerrilla Diplomacy: The NLF's Foreign Relations and the Viet Nam War* (Ithaca, N.Y.: Cornell University Press, 1999). Also see Allan Goodman, *The Search for a Negotiated Settlement of the Vietnam War* (Berkeley, Calif.: Institute of East Asian Studies, 1986). See also Goodman's *The Lost Peace: America's Search for a Negotiated Settlement of the Vietnam War* (Palo Alto, Calif.: Hoover Institution, 1978). Gareth Porter, *A Peace Denied: The United States, Vietnam, and the Paris Agreement* (Bloomington: Indiana University Press, 1975). The Chinese assessments are in *77 Conversations*. For accounts of Ho and 1945, see Truong Nhu Tang, with David Chanoff, and Doan Van Toai *A Viet Cong Memoir* (New York: Vintage Books, 1985). Bui Tin, *Following Ho Chi Minh* (Honolulu: University of Hawaii Press, 1995). Bill Duiker, *Ho Chi Minh* (New York: Hyperion, 2000). The observations of Nguyen Khac Huyen and Luu Doan Huynh are from Robert McNamara, *Argument Without End* (New York: Public Affairs Press, 1999); the Dong observation is from *77 Conversations*. For Geneva, see Philippe Devillers and Jean Lacouture, *End of a War, Indochina 1954* (New York: Praeger, 1969).

For President Johnson's televised speech of March 31, 1968, See *Public Papers of the Presidents of the United States: Lyndon B. Johnson, 1968–1969,* book I (Washington, D.C.: Government Printing Office, 1970), p. 476. On getting the talks started, see the JCS *Command History* and also see Ilya V. Gaiduk. *The Soviet Union and the Vietnam War* (Chicago: Ivan R. Dee, 1996). The NLF perspective is best presented in Brigham, *Guerrilla Diplomacy,* chap. 3. "He might cry again" is from cable traffic in the Chennault file at the LBJ Library. I used several key files on the October 31, 1968 bombing halt in the LBJ Library: Meeting Notes File, box 3; National Security File, Files of Walt Rostow; "Richard Nixon—Vietnam," box 5; "Vietnam: July–December 1968," box 6. See also the Reference File: "Anna Chennault" and the Diary Backup for October 31, 1968, box 114; November 11, 1968, box 115. Several oral histories contain valuable information: William Bundy, Clark Clifford, Averell Harriman, Harry McPherson, Walt Rostow, Dean Rusk, and Cyrus Vance. Several documents have been declassified through the mandatory review program at the LBJ Library. See National Security File, Country File, Vietnam, boxes 21–44; Vietnam, NODIS_LOR, boxes 45–47; Vietnam, 6E, Bombing Pause Discussion by US, box 95; Vietnam, 6g(4) a, talks with Hanoi, box 96; Vietnam, Memos to the President, Bombing Halt Decision, vols.

2–7, boxes 137–138; Vietnam, HARVAN-Double Plus, Chronological Papers and Other Miscellaneous material, box 260; Tom Johnson's Notes of Meetings, especially box 4; Papers of Clark Clifford, boxes 2–6, especially Memos of Vietnam: April–May 1968, box 4, and Presentation on Paris Peace Talks, November 18, 1968, box 6; Minutes of Secretary of Defense Staff Meetings, March–September 1968, box 18; and Vietnam, box 26. In the Clifford Papers, see State Department cable traffic regarding the Paris negotiations during October 1968. Not yet processed are the Papers of Morton Halperin, Box 14, Vietnam Negotiations, FRC #4, 3 folders, documents 1–87. See Peter Rodman, "Nixon and the 1968 Bombing Halt," United Press International, September 19, 2000. Rodman is Director of National Security Programs at the Nixon Center, and his article was in response to what he described as "a new and unsympathetic book about Richard Nixon" (by Anthony Summers).

On the negotiations before the October bombing halt, see "Instructions for Governor Harriman (draft as reviewed at the White House April 6, 1968)," Warnke Notebook on Vietnam, 1968, folder 5, Papers of Paul C. Warnke, Box 9, LBJ Library. See "Memorandum: Immediate Issues Requiring Policy Guidance," Warnke Notebook on Vietnam, 1960, folder 5, Papers of Paul C. Warnke, Box 9, LBJ Library. Rusk's and Johnson's statements in "Meeting of the President with Foreign Policy Advisors," May 6, 1968, Papers of Lyndon B. Johnson, Meeting Notes File, box 3, LBJ Library, and in "Notes of Tuesday Luncheon, May 7, 1968," Tom Johnson's Notes of Meetings, box 3, LBJ Library. For the text of Harriman's opening statement, see "Texts of Statements by Envoys of North Vietnam and U.S. at Their Paris Meeting," New York Times, May 14, 1968, p. 18. "Notes on President's Meeting of Foreign Policy Advisors, Saturday, June 21, 1968, "Tom Johnson's Notes of Meetings," box 3, LBJ Library. A summary of Vance's report on the June 28 meeting is provided in "US/Soviet Exchanges on Two-Phase Proposal," Harvan 10/11-16/68, vol. I, National Security File, Vietnam Country File, box 124, LBJ Library. See Memo, W.W. Rostow to the President, "[Vietnam: July–December 1968]," National Security File, Files of Walt W. Rostow, box 6, LBJ Library. Vance's report on the July 15 meeting, Embtel 18012 (Paris) Vance to Rusk, 7/16/68, "South Vietnam Trip, July 13–17, 1968: Cables," Papers of Clark Clifford, box 5, LBJ Library. Cable CAP82363 from W.W. Rostow to the President, 9/3/68, "[Vietnam: July–December 1968]," National Security File, Files of Walt W. Rostow, box 10, LBJ Library. See Memo, W.W. Rostow to the President, "Literally Eyes Only for the President and Secretary Rusk, "9/16/68, 9:00 A.M., "Kosygin" [folder 3], National Security File, Files of W.W. Rostow, box 10, LBJ Library. Draft statement, 9/16/68, "Kosygin" [folder 3], National Security File, Files of Walt W. Rostow, box 10, LBJ Library. See "Sept. 25, 1968–12:17 P.M." National Security Council Meeting, "Tom Johnson's Notes of Meetings," box 4, LBJ Library, and "Summary Notes of 591st NSC Meeting, September 25, 1968: 12:05 to 1:40 P.M.," taken by Bromley Smith, Secretary to the NSC, National Security File, NSC Meetings File, Vol. 5, Tab 73, box 2, LBJ Library. See Memo, W.W. Rostow to the President, 10/2/68, "Memorandum for the Record: Meeting with Ambassador Vance, October 3, 1968, 9:00–10:30 A.M.," in [Vietnam: July–Dec. 1968]," National Security File, Files of Walt

W. Rostow, box 6, LBJ Library. For Rusk's view, see "Notes of the President's Meeting with Foreign Policy Advisers," September 4, 1968, Papers of Lyndon B. Johnson, Meeting Notes File, box 3, LBJ Library. For Rostow, see Memo, W.W. Rostow to the President, 10/11/68, 12:30 P.M., "Memo to President/Bombing Halt Decision 10/23-28," Volume I, National Security File, Vietnam Country File, box 137, LBJ Library. "The President's Address to the Nation Upon Announcing His Decision to Halt the Bombing of North Vietnam, October 31, 1968," in *Public Papers,* book II.

The Xuan Thuy–Harriman exchange is in Loi and Vu, *Negotiations,* and JCS *History* documents. Nixon's meeting with LBJ are taken from Tom Johnson's meeting notes, box 3. See also A. J. Languth, *Our Vietnam* (New York: Simon & Schuster, 2000); Anthony Summers, *The Arrogance of Power* (New York: Viking, 2000); Jeffrey Kimball, *Nixon's Vietnam War* (Lawrence: University of Kansas Press, 1998). See Anatoly Dobrynin, *In Confidence: Moscow's Ambassador to America's Six Cold War Presidents* (New York: Random House, 1995), pp. 174–77. On Le Duc Tho's strict instructions from Hanoi, see Loi and Vu, *Negotiations.* pp. 46–47. See Bui Diem, *In the Jaws of History* (Boston: Houghton Mifflin, 1987). The Chen Yi and Tho conversation is in *77 Conversations.* The Thieu quote about history is from the special Chennault file. The Abrams insight is from Lewis Sorley, *Thunderbolt* (New York: Simon & Schuster, 1992), and Lewis Sorley, *A Better War* (New York: Harcourt Brace, 1999). "No honor talking to thieves" is Thieu's comment in Chennault file cable traffic. The Clifford comments are in the staff meeting notes taken by George Elsy. For the Chennault affair, see Sommers, *The Arrogance of Power,* and William Bundy, *A Tangled Web: The Making of Foreign Policy in the Nixon Presidency* (New York: Hill and Wang, 1998). Also see Anna Chennault, *The Education of Anna* (New York: Times Books, 1980), pp. 170–185; Bui Diem, *In the Jaws of History,* pp. 236–240. The tape transcripts are from Stanley Kutler, ed., *Abuse of Power: The New Nixon Tapes* (New York: Free Press, 1997). The Ky quote is from his book, *How We Lost the Vietnam War,* published in hardcover under the title, *Twenty Years and Twenty Days* (New York: Stein and Day, 1976). See also Christopher Hitchens, "The Case Against Henry Kissinger," *Harpers* magazine, February 2001, pp. 33–58.

CHAPTER TWO
Nixon Takes Control

The Sainteny materials and all documents in this discussion, unless otherwise noted, are from newly released documents in the Ford Library. See National Security Advisor, Kissinger-Scowcroft West Wing Office Files, box 34 Vietnamese War–Secret Paris Peace Talks, *Mr. S. File.* In *The White House Years,* pp. 277–278, Kissinger discusses Sainteny. All of the Kissinger to Nixon and Sainteny to Nixon cables and letters are in the Mr. S. file. Stanley Karnow noted that Ho had warned Sainteny on the eve of the

French war: "I will lose ten men to every one of yours, but I will win and you will lose." See Braestrup, ed., *Ten Years After,* p. 79. The Kissinger back channel to Ehrlichman from Haig is from the Mr. S. file, as are the Ho letter and draft. For the August 4, 1969, first meeting with Mai Van Bo, see Tony Lake Chronological File, 1969–70, NSC Files, Nixon Presidential Materials, Camp David File, and Kissinger Office Files Archives II, College Park, MD. See Loi and Vu, *Negotiations,* as well as Vernon A. Walters, *Silent Missions* (Garden City, NY: Doubleday, 1978). Walters recalled, "I reported to Kissinger through an unbreakable form of code. It was a very tedious thing to encode and decode; it took hours and hours. Kissinger obviously didn't want this to go through the usual government channels." See Gerald Strober and Deborah Strober, *Nixon* (New York: Harper Collins, 1994), p. 174.

The Isham observation is from his deposition for the Kerry Committee. For Nixon's offhand remark to Southern delegates, see "What Dick Nixon Told Southern Delegates," *Miami Herald,* August 7, 1968, 22A. See Jonathan Aiken, *Nixon: A Life* (Washington, D.C.: Regnery, 1993), p. 352; Stephen E. Ambrose, *Nixon: The Triumph of a Politician 1962–1972* (New York: Simon & Schuster, 1989). Herbert S. Parmet, *Richard Nixon and His America* (New York: Smithmark, 1990). See Kissinger, *The White House Years* (Boston: Little, Brown, 1979), chap. 1, for "fighting seemed stalemated," and *RN* for first morning in White House, p. 369. Much has been written on Kissinger: Seymour M. Hersh, *The Price of Power: Kissinger in the Nixon White House* (New York: Summit Books, 1983); Joan Hoff, *Nixon Reconsidered* (New York: Basic Books, 1994); Danielle Hunebelle, *Dear Henry* (New York: Berkeley Medallion Books, 1972); Walter Isaacson, *Kissinger* (New York: Simon & Schuster, 1992); Kalb and Kalb, *Kissinger;* Kimball, *Nixon's Vietnam War;* William Shawcross, *Sideshow: Kissinger, Nixon and the Destruction of Cambodia* (New York: Simon & Schuster, 1979). The Nessen quote is from Ron Nessen, *It Sure Looks Different from the Inside* (Chicago: Playboy Press, 1978). The Zumwalt quote is in Elmo R. Zumwalt, Jr., *On Watch.*

See Kissinger to Nixon, "Possible Private Talks at the Paris Negotiations," March 1, 1969, in folder Paris Talks—misc. What I began to see from my interviews and the declassified record was a pattern that seemed to conform with the South Vietnamese accounts of Kissinger's core character. According to Nguyen Tien Hung's account, the Vietnamese gradually came to view Kissinger as a man who could not be trusted. In Confucian tradition, a person's honor is related directly to his trust—*chu tin* is the highest of all qualities. Every Vietnamese school child learns the Confucian maxim concerning the words of an honorable person, *hu danh dong cot* (words, once spoken, are "like a spike driven into a post"). In another Confucian maxim, "Not even four speedy horses can catch the words of an honorable person once they have left the mouth." This account is from Nguyen Tien Hung and Jerrold L. Schector, *The Palace File* (New York: Harper and Row, 1978).

Tan Van Lam, Vietnam's minister of foreign affairs, had just returned from Paris and told Anna Chennault, "He's going to sell us down the river. Also, his ambition is so large, it'll claim more than one victim. Not just the United States, but Vietnam as well." Lam described Kissinger as a "clever liar." See Chennault, *The Education of Anna.*

On the transition, I drew heavily from interviews with Dan Ellsberg and Mort Halperin's written materials, as well as Halperin's interview with Karnow. Halperin later told the Strobers that "it became clear to me, in retrospect, that Nixon's [secret] plan was to threaten the Russians with the destruction of North Vietnam unless they cooperated. But, at the time, it wasn't clear to me that he had any plan at all" (p. 172). The December 27, 1968 Options Paper is available in an NSC file Vietnam–RAND, box 3, NSC: Kissinger's Office Files. See Walter Isaacson, *Kissinger: A Biography* (New York: Simon & Schuster, 1997).

The Mai Van Bo comment to Sainteny was made at Ho's funeral and sent to Kissinger by Sainteny and is in the Mr. S. File, Ford Library. Roger Morris, *Uncertain Greatness: Henry Kissinger and American Foreign Policy* (New York: Harper and Row, 1977). For Nixon's perspective see *RN*, pp. 348–349. The memo of the conversation with Dobrynin is from recently declassified NSC files of Ken Hughes, supplied to me by Dan Ellsberg. For the discussion on Vietnamization, see Jeffrey J. Clarke, *United States Army in Vietnam: Advice and Support: The Final Years, The U.S. Army in Vietnam* (Washington, D.C.: Center of Military History, 1988. I drew extensively from the JCS *History* at the National Security Archive. For MENU and Cambodia see The JCS History; Shawcross, *Sideshow,* Arnold R. Isaacs, *Without Honor: Defeat in Vietnam and Cambodia* (Baltimore: Johns Hopkins University Press, 1983), and Hersh, *Price of Power.* For Midway meetings, see Hung and Schecter, *The Palace File,* who reported that Thieu arrived at the meeting room about fifteen minutes before Nixon and saw that three of the chairs were the same height but that the one reserved for Nixon had a higher back. Thieu was amused. He went into the dining room and grabbed a chair that was the same size as Nixon's and placed it opposite from where Nixon would sit. Now, the two presidents would be at eye level. This story was later confirmed to me by Nha, who was present.

On NLF and PRG, see Brigham, *Guerrilla Diplomacy,* chap. 3–4. On Nixon visit to Saigon the MEMCON is from Ford Library in MEMCON files. My interview with Nha confirmed that Nixon's reference was to the bombing program. Lodge's comments to Kissinger are in the MEMCON. See Richard Morris, *Uncertain Greatness,* 1977 and Tad Szulc, *The Illusion of Peace: Foreign Policy in the Nixon Years* (New York: Viking, 1978). For Duck Hook background and precedents, see the excellent discussion in John Prados, *The Blood Road* (New York: Wiley, 1999). The Duck Hook file and other speech files are in the Ford Library and the November 3 file. See Tom Wells, *The War Within* (Berkeley: University of California Press, 1994). See Tony Lake Chronological File, June 1969–May 1970 (6 of 6). Nha confirmed that Nixon did indeed tell them about Duck Hook. The tape is from a posting by Jeffrey Kimball on the H-DIPLO web site. Kimball transcribed the tape. "Don't get rattled" is from Aiken, *Nixon, A Life,* 1983, and Nixon Project Files, President's November 3 Speech. Nixon told Monica Crowley, *Nixon in Winter,* that "the silent majority speech was probably my greatest speaking triumph. . . . The support was overwhelming and made my job of ending the war in an honorable way easier" (p. 252).

CHAPTER THREE

"You Cannot Hide an Elephant with a Basket"

The chapter title is from Loi and Vu, *Negotiations,* p. 136. Kissinger's instructions to Walters are in Mr. S. files at the Ford Library. Readers may ask why so many of Kissinger's files from the Nixon years are located in the Ford Library. Archivists at the Ford Library have made Vietnam file declassifications one of their highest priorities; many of Kissinger's papers followed him to the Ford administration, where he served as secretary of state. See Walters, *Silent Missions,* for the conversation with Mai Van Bo. Nixon's description of cloak and dagger are from *RN,* and the Midnight Diplomat is from Hung and Schecter, *The Palace File.* The itinerary details are in the Lake papers. Here is a sampling of the detailed schedule and points of contact:

9:15 A.M. (Friday)

Mr. Kissinger and Tony Lake to depart the Ellipse by helicopter for Andrews, with cover story they are departing for Camp David (Dianne will go by sedan directly to Andrews, with necessary supplies and equipment) and will be on board for take-off as soon as the helicopter arrives at Andrews.

10:00 P.M. (local)

Arrive Avord French Strategic Air Command Air Base in Central France. Will be met by Colonel Guignard, French Air Force, who will escort Dr. Kissinger and Mr. Lake to a civilian Mystere 20 (Air Force One will proceed to Wiesbaden Air Base in Germany and remain there until return flight from Avord.)

Mr. Lake should obtain from the pilot, Colonel Albertazzi, precise information on how to contact him in Wiesbaden, should there be any changes in schedule. It is possible that we will not have confirmation of meeting with Pompidou on Saturday afternoon prior to party's arrival at Avord. If so, it may be necessary to contact Colonel Albertazzi to modify takeoff time Saturday afternoon or evening.

10:30 P.M. (local)

Arrive Villa Coublay Air Field. Will be met by General Walters in rented civilian automobile and will be driven directly to General Walters's apartment at 49 Boulevard Commandant Charcot in Nevilly District.

General Walters will turn over one bedroom to Mr. Kissinger and Mr. Lake will share a second bedroom with General Walters.

10:00 A.M., Saturday morning (local)

Mr. Kissinger, General Walters, Mr. Lake will meet the other side at 11 Rue Darthe in Choisy District.

3:00 P.M. or later, Saturday (local)

To be confirmed by President Pompidou's Diplomatic Advisor, M'sieur. Gaucher to General Walters. The party may have an appointment with President Pompidou for the purpose of discussing last minute arrangements for Pompidou's visit to the U.S. For this reason, in addition to what other Vietnam papers

wishes to take off of Air Force One, it will be necessary to carry the Pompidou visit book, as well as the NSC issues paper which will be aboard Air Force One.
Saturday Afternoon or Evening (local)
Depart Villa Coublay by Mystere 20 aircraft for Avord Air Base. Air Force One will be at Avord. Because of the uncertainty of the meeting with President Pompidou, it is necessary that General Walters knows how to contact Colonel Guignard throughout Saturday to insure that the civilian airplane will be ready as needed at Villa Coublay. It will also be necessary for General Walters to provide for the movement of his baggage to Air Force One since he will return with the party to Washington.

Finally, General Walters should arrange to have his rented automobile disposed of following takeoff from Villa Coublay. Attached is a memorandum prepared by Colonel Albertazzi, which outlines the scope of the training flight, which has been established as cover for Air Force One. There will be, according to General Hughes, adequate food for all meals on Air Force One, as well as a tape recorder and tapes available. Classified documents can be stored in the safe on Air Force One, which will be physically guarded throughout the period. Colonel Albertazzi will also make arrangements for accommodations for Dianne Matthews at the Von Steuben Hotel in Wiesbaden on Friday night. She should be instructed to stay in continuous contact with Colonel Albertazzi on Saturday in case there should be a change in departure time.

For the first meeting and all others, I have triangulated the notes from the Paris Peace Files, the Loi and Vu translations, the Lake files, the Ellsworth Bunker files and compared these with the accounts in both Kissinger's and Nixon's memoirs. I have retained a detailed "road map" of this exercise that now stretches over 15 feet of paper; it is archived with my materials at Texas Tech's Vietnam Archive. On "Henry A. Kirshman," Walters recalled, "I had a housekeeper who was very interested in everything and one day she came home and said, 'I've just seen this man on television that you gave your bedroom to.' I replied, 'You think this man is Dr. Kissinger. Dr. Kissinger is the principal advisor to the president of the United States. If he came to Paris, he would be in the big embassy downtown, not in my apartment." (Strober and Strober, *Nixon,* p. 174).

The Kissinger observation is from Kissinger-Scowcroft files, Ford Library. The Negroponte quote is from the interview with Karnow. Kissinger to Nixon and the Bunker briefing of Thieu are in the back channel files, see Tony Lake Chronological File (June, 1969–May 1970), 6 boxes; Archives II. The Lake warning is in the Lake papers, March 13, 1970, Memo to Kissinger. The second meeting, "how to proceed," is from Kissinger Office Files. For the March 16 meeting, see Loi and Vu. The post–March 16 assessments are from Kissinger to Nixon and Bunker's briefings of Thieu—a note on my source compilations. Kissinger would meet secretly with Tho and would then communicate to Bunker what had been discussed. We already know from what has been declassified that Bunker was not fully briefed. Nevertheless, Bunker would then brief Thieu on the secret negotiation with Tho. Bunker would then cable Kissinger with a detailed account and narrative of his meetings with Thieu. For the April 4 meeting see Loi and Vu, *Negotiations,* and Lake Chron. The description of Bruce is from Kissinger's memoirs, as are Kissinger's assessments of Lake and Morris; the narrative is from Lake papers. The Morris recollections on Nixon's drinking are from Wells, *The War Within,* pp. 417–418. The Bunker visit to Thieu on a cease-fire in place and all documents are in RG-59. The Binh observation is made by Brigham, *Guerrilla Diplomacy,* p. 86. On Kissinger's assessment of Binh see Kissinger's *White House Years,* Bunker to Rogers is in RG-59, and the September 19 Dong-Chou meeting is in *77 Conversations.* September 20 Bunker to Kissinger in Paris Talks file. I made extensive use of the Lake files as well as the Paris Talks file and both of the Kerry materials. The Bunker-Thieu materials are from the State Department records Group 59.

CHAPTER FOUR
McGovern's October Surprise

Nixon had Charles Colson investigate the accuracy of McGovern's war record. According to Colson's investigation, "There is nothing in the folder that would be of interest to us or anyone. The information is routine and clean. McGovern flew 35 combat missions as an Army Air Corps Pilot in World War II. He earned several air medals and the Distinguished Flying Cross." The memo is in Bruce Oudes, *From the President: Richard Nixon's Secret Files* (New York: Harper and Row, 1989).

The bulk of materials in this chapter, unless otherwise noted, are from the Mudd Library, Princeton University. I consulted the following McGovern files: George McGovern Papers, 1948–1978 MC #181. These contain over 1,000 cubic feet of records, much of which are uncataloged and unprocessed. Box 24, Vietnam, and I-10-McGovern 1971 Issues; for McGovern trip itinerary see I-9 Vietnam with all schedules and notes and interviews. The press conference at airport and others are in box 58, September 1971. See also box 32, Nixon (5 of 5); box 25 McGovern Vietnam and 26 Misc. Memo on dinner discussion.

Gloria Emerson, *Winners and Losers* (New York: A Harvest/HBJ Book, 1976). McGovern also spent time with Emerson in Saigon. Background details from my interview with Pierre Salinger. See Loi and Vu, *Negotiations,* for Kissinger's meeting without Tho. I shared all of these materials on Thieu's resignation with Nha, who confirmed my version of events and provided additional details. See Brigham, *Guerrilla Diplomacy,* on NLF strategy. My interview with Nha confirmed what was discussed between Thieu and McGovern. Ky said the "election was rigged." See Ky, *How We Lost the War,* p. 193. On the meeting on the thirteenth, see Loi's detailed account. The Bunker cable to Kissinger re strategy and Kissinger to President on September 18 is in the Paris File, Archive II. Tape from October 2000 release, transcript from Nixon Library Web site. For Haig's September 23 visit, see *Inner Circles* (New York: Warner

Books, 1992), pp. 278–283 and the new declassifications of MEMCONS of Haig with Thieu; cables of Kissinger to Bunker and back on the coup are in the Bunker files and filed as MEMCONS in Berman collection at Texas Tech. The McGovern letter to Thuy and Thi to McGovern are in the Mudd collection.

CHAPTER FIVE
A Chess Match

See William Burr, ed., *The Kissinger Transcripts: The Top Secret Talks with Beijing and Moscow* (New York: New Press, 1998); James Mann, *About Face: A History of America's Curious Relationship with China: From Nixon to Clinton* (New York: Knopf, 1999). I learned much from the account in Zhai, *China and the Vietnam Wars, 1950–1975.* Kissinger's observation to Karnow is in PBS interview transcript. Kissinger's account of President Yahya directing the script is in his memoirs, *The White House Years,* pp. 738–740. Haldeman diary for July 8 about lying to Billy Graham. For the July 9–11 meetings in China, see Mann, *About Face,* and Burr, *Transcripts.* Burr provides the declassified transcripts of these meetings. Smyser's observation is in Languth, *Our Vietnam.* See Qiang Zhai for Chou Enlai, as well as *77 Conversations.* The transcript of the July 12, 1971, meeting with Le Duc Tho is translated in Loi and Vu, *Negotiations,* and cross-referenced with the U.S. record in the Paris correspondence file and in the Kerry Committee Files. See Kissinger memoirs, *The White House Years,* for "Le Duc Tho did not yet know this." The July 17, 1971, Trinh message to Le Duc Tho is in Loi and Vu, *Negotiations,* p. 195. The new tape is from the Nixon Library web page. For Lam Son, see Haig, *Inner Circles,* pp. 273–274. For the July 26 meeting, see Loi and Vu, *Negotiations,* p. 195. The Bunker to Kissinger cables on keeping Thieu out of loop as well as the Kissinger and Nixon responses are at Paris Files, Archives II. See Winston Lord deposition for Kerry Committee as well as Lord's interview with Strober and Strober, *Nixon,* p. 178.

CHAPTER SIX
Nixon Goes Public

For Kissinger's assessment of the president's January speech, see his memoirs, *The White House Years,* p. 1044. The editorial reactions and materials dealing with the January announcement were obtained from the Pike collection, especially Unit II. The newly declassified files used in this chapter are all from Paris Talks/Meetings Files and NSC Files. See Mann, *About Face,* p. 40, for Nixon handwritten notes. Partial and misleading accounts of the private negotiations with Thieu are offered in both *RN* and

Kissinger's memoirs, *The White House Years.* Haig's account is in *Inner Circles,* pp. 278–280. Kissinger's description of Thieu's opposition as "pretext" is from *White House Years,* p. 1043. The Bunker cables to Kissinger and the entire sequence of meetings with Thieu that were reported to Kissinger and then to Nixon are located in the Bunker files. For future researchers, I have created a separate file on the case in the Texas Tech archive. The meetings in the Great Hall are in Burr, *Transcripts.* The Walters message is in Walters, *Secret Missions,* the Thieu observation about a "better mistress" is from *The Palace File.*

CHAPTER SEVEN
The Easter Offensive

The best account of the Easter Offensive is Dale Andrade, *Trial by Fire* (New York: Hippocrene Books, 1995). See also Colonel G. H. Turley, *The Easter Offensive* (Novato, Calif.: Presidio Press, 1985). Lieutenant General Ngo Quang Truong, *The Easter Offensive of 1972.* Center for Military History, Indo China Monographs, 1972. Also see Stanley Karnow, *Vietnam* (New York: Penguin Books, 1991), pp. 654–656. See *77 Conversations* for Chou confiding in Nguyen Tien. For Freedom Train see Mark Clodfelter, *The Limits of Air Power* (New York: Free Press, 1989). On April 20 Kissinger secretly departed for Moscow; see Tad Szulc, *Illusion of Peace* (New York: Viking, 1978). Bunker's briefing of Thieu and reports to Kissinger regarding what was said in Moscow and Bunker's reports and cables to Kissinger have been placed in a separate file at Texas Tech archive. The Konstantin Katushev information is translated in Loi and Vu, *Negotiations,* p. 224. Accounts of the May 2 meeting can be found in Loi and Vu, *Negotiations,* and in Kissinger's memoirs, *The White House Years.* Kissinger's description of Le Duc Tho as "insolent and unbearable" needs examination. In the view of Arnold Isaacs, the word "insolent is a word customarily used about persons in unequal relationships. . . . The word suggests defiance to a rightful authority." (Unpublished papers, provided by Isaacs to author.)

"If it works, I'm for it; if it fails, I'm against it," is documented in Haig, *Inner Circle,* and *RN,* although Haig gets right to the meaning. The meeting with congressional leadership is described in detail in Haig, *Inner Circle,* and *RN.* The Chinese mine investigation team information is from Zhai, *China and the Vietnam Wars;* see Hersh, *Price of Power,* p. 505; Kissinger, *White House Years,* p. 1100; Clodfelter, *Limits of Air Power,* pp. 150–160; *RN,* pp. 192–193. Speaking to the nation, see Richard Nixon "The Situation in Southeast Asia," President's Address to the Nation, May 8, 1972, *Weekly Compilation of Presidential Documents,* May 8, 1972, p. 839. Also see Henry Kissinger, news conference of May 9, 1972, in *Weekly Compilation of Presidential Documents,* May 15, 1972, p. 846. See Kissinger, *White House Years,* p. 1181. The State Department document is cited in Andrade, *Trial by Fire.* Tho's meeting in

Beijing on July 12, 1972, with Chou Enlai is in 77 *Conversations*. Regarding Jimmy Hoffa, Loi and Vu, *Negotiations,* note that "Kissinger raised in vain the question of Vietnamese delivering American prisoners to the opposition party hoping to prevent us from doing this" (p. 245). On Hoffa, see Jack Anderson, "Haldeman Arranged Hoffa's Release," *Washington Post,* May 3, 1973, p. C. 11; Murray Mander, "Hoffa Trip to Hanoi Set, Then Barred," *Washington Post,* September 8, 1972, p. A. 1; and "Hoffa Says Hanoi Trip Would Have Been Successful," *Washington Post,* February 15, 1973, p. A. 2.

The meeting accounts are from Loi and Vu, *Negotiations,* and from the Paris Peace Talks file in the declassified transcripts made available from the POW/MIA investigation. Readers may note that as a consequence of the POWs becoming more and more part of the discussions between Tho and Kissinger, there was more declassified for the Kerry Committee investigation.

CHAPTER EIGHT

"They Have Concluded They Cannot Defeat You"

The meetings in this chapter are all from the declassified files and have been checked for accuracy with Nha and with the detailed accounts provided by Tran Van Don in *Our Endless War: Inside Vietnam* (Novato, Calif.: Presidio Press, 1978) and with Hung and Schecter, *Palace File.* Nha read this chapter, consulted his own records, and offered valuable insights and corrections on my sequencing of events. I then cross-checked the accounts with Bunker's detailed cables to Kissinger on his briefings of Thieu about the meetings. I also received recently declassified MEMCONS of the meetings. Kissinger's account of returning from Switzerland is from his memoir *The White House Years.* "I sympathized with Thieu" is from *RN.* Kissinger's frustration with Le Duc Tho is from *The White House Years* and reinforced even more powerfully in his interview with Karnow. The August 19 Kissinger cable to Bunker and the meeting in Oahu with the related speech drafting (with Rodman) are in the Kissinger-Scowcroft files and in the Kissinger Office files. On September 16, 1972, Bunker reported on the NCRC and Thieu's concerns; Kissinger cabled Bunker on September 23 that "it is essential that Thieu stay close to us." See Record Group 59. For the September 26 and 27 meetings, see Loi and Vu, *Negotiations.* "Appreciation for services rendered" is what Kissinger wrote in his memoirs. "Kissinger couldn't handle Thieu" is how Haig described it to Strober and reinforced in his deposition. Haldeman diary, October 4, 1972. The Bunker-Thieu exchanges are in the Bunker files. Nixon's warnings to Thieu and Kissinger's messages are in the Nixon project files. The October meeting is from Loi and the Paris Peace Talks files. Negroponte's description is from the Karnow interview. The files from both the October 2 and 4 meetings are in a special file created for researchers at Texas Tech in Berman collection.

Differences between the Vietnamese-language (DRV) text and the original English version are as follows:

1. Chapter II, Article 2, third paragraph: "unconditional durable, and without limit of time" (lau dai va vung chac = lasting and durable).
2. Chapter II, Article 4: "or *intervene* in" (va can thiep vao = or *intervention* in)
3. Chapter V, Article 10, third paragraph: "*various* fields" (moi mat = *all* fields)
4. Chapter VI, Article 11a, first paragraph: "task of *ensuring*" (nhiem vu *phoi hop* = task of *coordinating*)
5. Chapter VI, Article 12, first paragraph: "task of *ensuring*" (nhiem vu *phoi hop* = task of *coordinating*)
6. Chapter VI, Article 11a, paragraph 7: "military personnel and innocent civilians" (nguoi = persons)
7. Chapter VI, Article 13 b, paragraph 7: same as item 6
8. Chapter VI, Article 14, first sentence: "*within* 30 days" (trong *vong* 30 days = *within about* 30 days)
9. Chapter VII, Article 15a, first sentence: "agreements on *Cambodia*" (ve dong duong = on *Indochina*)
10. Chapter VIII, Article 16, first sentence: "United States *expects* that" (nuoc my mong rang = the United States *hopes* that)

CHAPTER NINE
Thieu Kills the Deal

As context, on October 8, 1970, Kissinger was asked at a press conference, "Are we abandoning the previous requirement for mutual withdrawal?" His answer was, "No, of course, a lot depends on how you define 'mutuality.' But we are not abandoning the general principle." I could not help but recall President Clinton's "It depends on what the meaning of the word *is*, is." Now, on October 23, 1972, Kissinger would cable Nixon that "the ceasefire leaves the North Vietnamese forces in the South. This is Thieu's single greatest problem. We long ago gave up the principle of mutual withdrawal and no American proposal since May 1969 has specified the withdrawal of North Vietnam forces. Hanoi, of course, has never formally acknowledged the presence of its troops in South Vietnam. . . . While this is absurd, and holds certain disadvantages, this position does have the advantage that they cannot claim a legal right to have their troops there." By December 19, 1972, Haig could claim "there is no language in the draft agreement which authorizes the continued presence of North Vietnamese troops in the South."

Nha told me that Kissinger tried the tactic of sending Thieu an earlier draft with harsher terms so that Thieu would jump to sign the new one. "General Instructions for

a Cease-Fire" is from Hung and Schector's account in *The Palace File* and later confirmed by interviews and the subsequent Bunker cable to Kissinger. I have relied on Loi
and Vu's account in *Negotiations* but have also cross-checked his translation with the
available parts of declassified records in the archives. John Negroponte's recollection
is from interview with Karnow. Kissinger's cable to Haig on October 22, "It is hard to
exaggerate," is from Bunker files. The notes of the private luncheon with Kissinger on
February 21, 1975, in the Secretary of State's dining room were made by McGovern
and are located in the Mudd Library. See Brigham, *Guerrilla Diplomacy,* for this analysis. See Walter Scott Dillard, *Sixty Days to Peace* (Washington, D.C.: National Defense
University Press, 1982). Records of the U.S. Delegation to the Four Party Joint Military Commission (FPJMC), January 27, 1973–March 31, 1973. The FPJMC was established under Article 6 of the Paris Peace Accords. See Historians Background Files,
Boxes 1–16. I made extensive use of RG 472, especially the Historians Background
Files and related materials.

CHAPTER TEN
Peace Is at the End of a Pen

"If anyone had told me," is from my interview with George McGovern. The Haig observation was made to Strober and Strober, *Nixon,* p. 184, and repeated in Haig's
memoir, *Inner Circles.* The Bunker appraisals to Thieu of General Weyand's work are
in the papers of the FPJMC. Details provided to me by Nha and confirmed by primary
source documents. The letter to Nixon was drafted by Nha and can be found in *Palace
File* and in Kissinger's memoirs, *The White House Years.* Haig met with Lon Nol in the
private residence. See MEMCON file from Ford Library. The Bunker cables are available in Berman files. *The Palace File* is the source for the Vietnamese community's
views of Kissinger. Interview with Oriana Fallaci was published on December 16,
1972, in *New Republic,* p. 17. That the Executive Office of the President, the Oval Office, and the Lincoln Room were bugged is from a Nixon tape in Kutler, *Abuse of
Power.* The MEMCONS on the meeting in the library at the private residence of ambassador are declassified at PARIS TALKS File. On Nguyen Phu Duc's meetings in
Washington, extensive new documentation is now available. The November 30 Joint
Chiefs of Staff meeting transcript is recently declassified in NSC Files, Archive II. See
Zumwalt, *On Watch,* pp. 412–413. Westmoreland had already warned Nixon about
the shortcomings of the text. During their October 20 meeting, he "urged the President to delay action on the new agreement and to hold out for better terms. . . . I emphasized that it was vital that North Vietnamese troops be compelled to withdraw
from South Vietnam. It was obvious that if they were allowed to retain the positions
they had gained in their 1972 offensive, they would continue to pose an immediate
threat to Hue and their troop dispositions in the Central Highlands would outflank
the entire two-thirds of South Vietnam. . . . If South Vietnam was to survive, the mat-

ter had to be squarely faced." See Westmoreland, *A Soldier Reports* (New York: Doubleday, 1976), p. 479.

CHAPTER ELEVEN
Linebacker II

Richard Nixon's diary entry for December 4, 1972, is in *RN*. See Kutler, *Abuse of Power*. Bunker to Kissinger, December 4, is in the Kissinger-Scowcroft files and in Kissinger's Office File. Kissinger cabled Nixon that the North Vietnamese were more intransigent than ever before. See Brigham, *Guerrilla Diplomacy,* chap. 6, for NLF strategy during this period. On Kissinger's meeting with the Vietnamese delegation, see MEMCON file. I have relied on Loi and Vu's translations, *Negotiations,* for the meeting accounts. On December 13, Kissinger cabled Nixon, "just more ludicrous and insolent in form," Kissinger Office Files. December 14, "do not let the palace to deflect you," is from Paris Peace Talks cable file. Much has been written on the Christmas bombing, but by far the best account is Clodfelter, *Limits of Air Power.* Nixon's remarks to Moorer need to be understood as a reference to LBJ's restraints on the air war.

When Clifford, Harriman, and Vance spoke out against the attacks, Vice President Spiro Agnew attacked them as "men whom history has branded as failures . . . the men who were bluffed, raised, called, whipped, and cleaned out at the tables in Paris, who are the ones who are now standing behind President Nixon yelling, 'fold, fold.' Well, the President isn't going to fold." (*The New York Times,* June 21, 1970; see also Clifford, *Counsel to the President,* p. 611). Commander James B. Stockdale's recollection was made by Nixon in a meeting with POW families in the White House. See Neil Sheehan, *After the War Was Over* (New York: Vintage Books, 1992).

CHAPTER TWELVE
Nixon's Peace with Honor

See Louis A. Fanning, *Betrayal in Vietnam* (New Rochelle, N.Y.: Arlington House Publishing, 1976). The secret meeting with Le Duc Tho is from *77 Conversations.* Sullivan's observation about "hang dog" is in his Kerry deposition. President Thieu's letter is in Hung and Schecter, *Palace File.* Nixon's instructions to Kissinger are detailed in *RN* and Kissinger's *The White House Years.* Haldeman's diary records Nixon's concern with Kissinger's own records. Loi and Vu's translation, *Negotiations,* is the source for January 6 Le Duc Tho comments, as well as, "Stupid, Stupid, Stupid." See Kissinger deposition for this assessment of Tho after the bombing. The Thieu shenanigans are from Bunker cables to Kissinger, January 9–11. "I have one consolation" is from U.S.

declassifications in Paris Meeting Files. Memorandum of Conversation between Haig and Prime Minister Souvanna Phuoma at the Prime Minister's residence in Vientiane and the message to Field Marshal Thanom Kittikachorn are in the PARIS TALKS Files. Bunker cabled Kissinger, "I did not give Nha or Duc any encouragement" is in Bunker papers. See Paris Transcripts and Loi and Vu, *Negotiations.* Ky's assessment is from *How We Lost the Vietnam War.* Nixon told Monica Crowley, *Nixon in Winter,* p. 256. See *RN* for Nixon's account of LBJ's death. Former Japanese prime minister Eisaku Sato's comments are in meeting notes from the Nixon Project at xxxx John Colville, *Footprints in Time* (London: Collins, 1976), pp. 62–63.

CHAPTER THIRTEEN
The Jabberwocky Agreement

See Porter, *A Peace Denied;* Allan Goodman, *The Lost Peace;* Dilliard, *Sixty Days to Peace.* The "guidebooks" are from the Pike Collection, Unit II. Donald Kirk. *Tell It to the Dead* (New York: M. E. Sharpe, 1996). The Rusk meeting with Pompidou was recently declassified in the Nixon Project. Cao Van Vien and Lt. General Dong Van Khuyen, *"Reflections on the Vietnam War."*

Also see February 22, 1973 George Aldrich "Interpretations" of Viet-Nam Peace Agreement," Kerry Committee files/POW. April 4, 1973, Flare-up at Tong Le Chan. The following documents—June 10, 1973 Charles Whitehouse to Kissinger, Kissinger to Bunker on January 30. February 28, 1973 Bunker met with Thieu—are in Paris Talks file. Frank Moss wrote Secretary Rogers on June 18, and related issues on political prisoners are in the Paris Talks file and records Group 59. Kissinger a "different Nixon" is in *"With Back to the Abyss,"* *Newsweek,* October 19, 1998, p. 42.

At the Richard Nixon Library in Whittier, California, John Taylor, executive director of the Nixon Foundation, told a 1998 Memorial Day gathering of POW families that "the United States made three promises in connection with the Paris Peace Accords." In Taylor's history, "We promised to continue to support South Vietnam with weapons and other aid to the same extent the Soviets supported the North. And we promised to send the B-52s again if the North violated the treaty, either by sending more troops into the South or failing to account fully for POWs and MIA. We all know what happened instead. Watergate—the scandal whose very roots were in America's argument with itself over Vietnam, and the elite's outrage at President Nixon's war policies. The president's ability to keep the promises he had made evaporated. Congress took away his right to use air power and slashed aid to Saigon. The North Vietnamese, delighted by this turn in events, launched new offensives. . . . In April 1975 Saigon fell, after its under-supplied troops had fought bravely for over a year against an enemy still fat with Soviet largess. For the first time in its history, the United States had let an ally it had sworn to defend run out of bullets."

Kissinger also admitted that he misjudged the willingness of the American people to defend the agreement: "But I admit this: we judged wrong. And what we judged wrong above all was our belief that if we could get peace with honor, that we would unite the American people who would then defend an agreement that had been achieved with so much pain. That was our fundamental miscalculation. It never occurred to me, and I'm sure it never occurred to President Nixon, that there could be any doubt about it, because an agreement that you don't enforce is a surrender; it's just writing down surrender terms. And that we never intended. Nixon wrote letters to Thieu that were not public in which he promised we would enforce the agreement. This was later criticized. I would simply ask some honest researcher sometime to compare the letters that President Nixon wrote to Thieu with the letters that have still not been published that President Kennedy or Johnson wrote to other leaders to see who made the bigger commitments. Or even other Presidents, in other circumstances. These were never treated as national commitments. These were expressions of the intentions of the President. Every senior member of the Administration—including myself, the Secretary of Defense, the Secretary of State—is represented in compendiums of statements that said publicly every week that we intended to enforce the agreement. There was nothing new about that." "The Paris Agreement on Vietnam: Twenty-five Years Later." Washington, D.C.: Nixon Center, April 1998.

Late in 1974, Prime Minister Pham Van Dong was meeting in the Politburo to discuss the military campaign that would end the war in two years: "For over a week I have been thinking about the ability of the American administration to react and I have come to the conclusion that even if we offered the Americans a bribe to intervene again, they would not accept it. So let's go ahead with the campaign in the South. Yes, even a bribe cannot induce the Americans to return again." Then he laughed. (Stanley Karnow, interview.)

EPILOGUE

"So this is it, this is what it comes to. Fifty thousand Americans dead, three hundred Americans wounded, a hundred and fifty billion dollars in military aid, the U.S. ripped by years of violence on the campuses, a President driven out of office. Now this—from Washington: Sorry, Viet Nam, but I have another engagement. Let's have lunch some day. Don't call me. I'll call you.

"Why did we ever bother sending in all those troops here ten years ago?" Walker asked angrily. "Why didn't we just send in gravediggers at the very outset and they could have buried South Viet Nam in 'sixty-five, nice and simple. Been much cheaper, too. In all ways." Kalb and Kalb, *The Last Ambassador.*

See Anthony T. Bouscaren, ed., *All Quiet on the Eastern Front: The Death of South Vietnam* (Old Greenwich, Conn.: Devin-Adair Company, 1977). David Butler, *The Fall of Saigon* (New York: Simon & Schuster, 1985). General Van Tien Dung, *Our Great Spring Victory: An Account of the Liberation of South Vietnam* (New York: Monthly Review Press, 1977). Larry Engelmann, *Tears Before the Rain: An Oral His-*

tory of the Fall of South Vietnam (New York: Oxford University Press, 1990). Fanning, *Betrayal in Vietnam*. Stephen T. Hosmer, Konrad Kellen, and Brian M. Jenkins, *The Fall of South Vietnam: Statements by Vietnamese Military and Civilian Leaders* (New York: Crane, Russak & Company, 1980). Kalb and Kalb, *The Last Ambassador*. Nessen, *It Sure Looks Different from the Inside*. Snepp. *Decent Interval*. Oliver Todd. *Cruel April: The Fall of Saigon*. (New York: Norton, 1987).

The documents used in this epilogue are from the Graham Martin Files in the Ford Library. See especially the May 2000 declassifications under the subjects:

Deterioration of the Situation in South Vietnam, Cambodia, Laos:
Analysis of intelligence reports regarding North Vietnamese aggression
Reports re surrounding of Phnom Penh
Perception of corruption in South Vietnam, demands for change of government
Question of Ambassador Graham Martin's recognition of gravity of situation
Evacuation of Danang and other northern areas
Weyand mission
Position of religious groups and voluntary agencies in South Vietnam
Influence of U.S. Labor movement in South Vietnam
Possibility of negotiated settlement, possible intermediaries
Laos—problem of refugees and special arrangements with certain tribes
Cambodia—Sihanouk's influence, What would happen if Communists took
    over, Plans for and U.S. evacuation of Phnom Penh

Fall of South Vietnam
Contingency planning and execution of evacuation plans
Civil aviation issues (insurance)
Treatment of high government officials who left Vietnam or Cambodia
Attempt to get South Vietnamese gold out of the country
Musing re America's image if we deserted Indochina

Refugees
Treatment of boat people
Temporary quarters and permanent resettlement
Relations with other governments over settlement of refugees
Special refugee cases
Refugees who wanted to repatriate
Indochina Interagency Task Force on Indochina Refugees-Julia Vadala Taft

MIA/POW issues
Contacts with National League of Families
Attempts to get accounting and return of remains

At a White House meeting with congressional leaders on April 14, Kissinger insisted, "Under the Paris Accords we have no obligations. To the GVN (Government of

Vietnam) we said that if you let us get our forces out it would enhance our chances of getting aid for them and enforcing the Agreement. It was in this context, not that of a legal obligation. We never claimed an obligation; we never pledged an obligation. But some of us think there is a moral obligation."

As he sat in the White House watching the evacuation of Hue, Kissinger wryly observed, "To have the United States as an ally is really a joy these days."

BIBLIOGRAPHY

Aitken, Jonathan. *Nixon: A Life*. Washington, D.C.: Regnery Publishing, 1993.

Ambrose, Stephen E. *Nixon: The Triumph of a Politician, 1962–1972*. New York: Simon & Schuster, 1989.

———. *Nixon: Ruin and Recovery, 1973–1990*. New York: Simon & Schuster, 1991.

Andrade, Dale. *Trial by Fire*. New York: Hippocrene Books, 1995.

Bouscaren, Anthony T., ed. *All Quiet on the Eastern Front: The Death of South Vietnam*. Old Greenwich, Conn.: Devin-Adair Company, 1977.

Brigham, Robert K. *Guerrilla Diplomacy: The NLF's Foreign Relations and the Viet Nam War*. Ithaca, N.Y.: Cornell University Press, 1999.

Bundy, William. *A Tangled Web: The Making of Foreign Policy in the Nixon Presidency*. New York, N.Y.: Hill and Wang, 1998.

Butler, David. *The Fall of Saigon*. New York: Simon & Schuster, 1985.

Chanoff, David, and Van Toai, Doan. *"Vietnam": A Portrait of Its People at War*. New York: I. B. Tauris Publishers, 1986.

Chayes, Abram; Fritchey, Clayton; Kaplan, Morton A.; Nutter, G. Warren; Roche, John P.; and Warnke, Paul C. *Vietnam Settlement: Why 1973, Not 1969?* Washington, D.C.: American Enterprise Institute for Public Policy Research, 1973.

Clodfelter, Mark. *The Limits of Air Power*. New York: Free Press, 1989.

Crowley, Monica. *Nixon in Winter*. New York: Random House, 1998.

Dallek, Robert. *Flawed Giant: Lyndon Johnson and His Times, 1961–1973*. New York: Oxford University Press, 1998.

Dawson, Alan. *55 Days: The Fall of South Vietnam*. Englewood Cliffs, N.J.: Prentice Hall, 1977.

Devillers, Philippe, and Lacouture, Jean. *End of a War: Indochina, 1954*. New York: Praeger, 1969.

Diem, Bui, with Chanoff, David. *In the Jaws of History*. Boston: Houghton Mifflin, 1987.

Dillard, Walter Scott. *Sixty Days to Peace*. Washington, D.C.: National Defense University Press, 1982.

Divine, Robert A., ed. *The Johnson Years, vol. 3: LBJ at Home and Abroad*. Lawrence: University Press of Kansas, 1994.

Dobrynin, Anatoly. *In Confidence: Moscow's Ambassador to America's Six Cold War Presidents*. New York: Random House, 1995.

Don, Tran Van. *Our Endless War: Inside Vietnam*. San Rafael, Calif.: Presidio Press, 1978.

Dung, General Van Tien. *Our Great Spring Victory: An Account of the Liberation of South Vietnam*. New York: Monthly Review Press, 1977.

Emerson, Gloria. *Winners and Losers*. New York: a Harvest/HBJ Book, 1976.

Engelmann, Larry. *Tears Before the Rain: An Oral History of the Fall of South Vietnam*. New York: Oxford University Press, 1990.

Fanning, Louis A. *Betrayal in Vietnam*. New Rochelle, N.Y.: Arlington House Publishing, 1976.

Gaiduk, Ilya V. *The Soviet Union and the Vietnam War*. Chicago: Ivan R. Dee, 1996.

Gardner, Lloyd C. *Pay Any Price: Lyndon Johnson and the Wars for Vietnam*. Chicago: Ivan R. Dee, 1995.

Haig, Alexander M., with McCarry, Charles. *Inner Circles*. New York: Warner Books, 1992.

Haldeman, H. R. *The Haldeman Diaries: Inside the Nixon White House*. New York: Putnam, 1994.

Herring, George C. *LBJ and Vietnam: A Different Kind of War*. Austin: University of Texas Press, 1994.

Herrington, LTC Stuart A. *Peace with Honor? An American Reports on Vietnam 1973–1975*. Novato, CA.: Presidio Press, 1983.

Hersh, Seymour M. *The Price of Power: Kissinger in the Nixon White House*. New York: Summit Books, 1983.

Hoff, Joan. *Nixon Reconsidered*. New York: Basic Books, 1994.

Hosmer, Stephen T., Kellen, Konrad; and Jenkins, Brian M. *The Fall of South Vietnam: Statements by Vietnamese Military and Civilian Leaders*. New York: Crane, Russak & Company, Inc., 1980.

Hunebelle, Danielle. *Dear Henry*. New York: Berkeley Medallion Books, 1972.

Hung, Nguyen Tien, and Schecter, Jerrold L. *The Palace File*. New York: Harper & Row, 1978.

Isaacs, Arnold R. *Without Honor: Defeat in Vietnam and Cambodia*. Baltimore, Md.: Johns Hopkins University Press, 1983.

Isaacson, Walter. *Kissinger*. New York: Simon & Schuster, 1992.

Kalb, Bernard, and Kalb, Marvin. *The Last Ambassador*. Boston: Little, Brown, 1981.

Karnow, Stanley. *Vietnam: A History*. New York: Penguin Books, 1991.

Kimball, Jeffrey. *Nixon's Vietnam War*. Lawrence: University of Kansas Press, 1998.

Kirk, Donald. *Tell It to the Dead*. Armonk, N.Y.: M. E. Sharpe, 1996.

Kissinger, Henry. *Diplomacy*. New York: Simon & Schuster, 1994.

———. *Years of Renewal*. New York: Simon & Schuster, 1999.

———. *Years of Upheaval*. Boston: Little, Brown, 1982.

———. *White House Years*. Boston: Little, Brown, 1979.

Kutler, Stanley, ed. *Abuse of Power: The New Nixon Tapes*. New York: Free Press, 1997.

Ky, Nguyen Cao. *How We Lost the Vietnam War*. New York: Scarborough Books, 1978.

Logevall, Fredrik. *Choosing War*. Berkeley: University of California Press, 1999.

Loi, Luu Van, and Vu, Nguyen Anh. *Le Duc Tho-Kissinger Negotiations in Paris.* Hanoi: Gioi Publishers, 1996.

Maclear, Michael. *The Ten Thousand Day War.* New York: St. Martin's Press, 1981.

Mankiewicz, Frank. *Perfectly Clear: Nixon from Whittier to Watergate.* New York: Quadrangle/New York Times Book Co., 1973.

McNamara, Robert. *Argument Without End.* New York: Public Affairs, 1999.

Nessen, Ron. *It Sure Looks Different from the Inside.* Chicago: Playboy Press, 1978.

Nixon, Richard. *The Memoirs of Richard Nixon.* New York: Grosset & Dunlap, 1978.

Parmet, Herbert S. *Richard Nixon and His America.* New York: Smithmark, 1990.

Porter, Gareth. *A Peace Denied: The United States, Vietnam, and the Paris Agreement.* Bloomington: Indiana University Press, 1975.

Prados, John. *The Blood Road.* New York: Wiley, 1999.

Record, Jeffrey. *The Wrong War.* Annapolis, Md.: Naval Institute Press, 1998.

Reporting Vietnam: American Journalism 1959–1969, Part One. New York: Library of America, 1998.

Reporting Vietnam: American Journalism 1969–1975, Part Two. New York: Library of America, 1998.

Schell, Jonathan. *Observing the Nixon Years.* New York: Pantheon Books, 1989.

Shafer, Morley. *Flashbacks: On Returning to Vietnam.* New York: Random House, 1990.

Shapler, Robert. *Bitter Victory.* New York: Harper & Row, 1986.

Shawcross, William. *Sideshow: Kissinger, Nixon and the Destruction of Cambodia.* New York: Simon & Schuster, 1979.

Sheehan, Neil. *After the War Was Over.* New York: Vintage Books, 1992.

Snepp, Frank. *Decent Interval.* New York: Random House, 1977.

Sorley, Lewis. *Thunderbolt.* New York: Simon & Schuster, 1992.

———. *A Better War.* New York: Harcourt Brace & Company, 1999.

Strober, Gerald S., and Strober, Deborah Hart. *Nixon: An Oral History of His Presidency.* New York: HarperCollins, 1994.

Tang, Truong Nhu, with Chanoff, David, and Toai, Doan Van. *A Viet Cong Memoir.* New York: Vintage Books, 1985.

Thompson, Sir Robert. *Peace is Not at Hand.* New York, N.Y.: David McKay, 1974.

Tin, Bui. *Following Ho Chi Minh.* Honolulu: University of Hawaii Press, 1995.

Todd, Oliver. *Cruel April: The Fall of Saigon.* New York: Norton, 1987.

Turley, Colonel G. H. *The Easter Offensive.* Novato, Calif.: Presidio Press, 1985.

Vien, General Cao Van. *The Final Collapse.* Washington, D.C.: Center for Military History, United States Army, 1983.

Walters, Vernon A. *Silent Missions.* Garden City, N.Y.: Doubleday, 1978.

Wested, Odd Arne; Jian, Chen; Tonnesson, Stein; Tung, Nguyen Vu; and Hershberg, James G. *77 Conversations Between Chinese and Foreign Leaders on the Wars in Indochina,* Working Paper No. 22, Cold War International History Project (Washington, D.C.: Woodrow Wilson International Center for Scholars, May 1998).

Westmoreland, William C. *A Soldier Reports.* Garden City, N.Y.: Doubleday, 1976.

Willenson, Kim. *The Bad War: An Oral History of the Vietnam War.* New York: New American Library, 1987.

Zhai, Qiang. *China and the Vietnam Wars, 1950–1975.* Chapel Hill: University of North Carolina Press, 2000.

Zumwalt, Jr., Elmo R. *On Watch.* New York: Quadrangle/New York Times Book Co., 1976.

Zumwalt, Jr., Elmo R. and Zumwalt, III, Elmo R. with Pekkanen, John. *My Father, My Son.* New York: Macmillan, 1986.

ACKNOWLEDGMENTS

There is a scene in Lewis Carroll's Alice's Adventures in Wonderland when Alice remarks, "I don't want to go among mad people."

To which the Cat replies, "Oh, you can't help that, we're all mad here. I'm mad. You're mad."

"How do you know I'm mad?" asks Alice.

"You must be or you wouldn't have come here," says the Cat.

* * *

I came here and it is now my pleasure to acknowledge the individuals and institutions who provided guidance along the way.

At the Hoover Archives, located on the campus of Stanford University, Carol Leadenham provided guidance on the files of Allan Goodman, author of a 1978 book, *The Lost Peace*, which remains a seminal contribution on the Paris negotiations. Allan's notes, interview transcripts, and research materials helped me to understand the complex political and military elements of the Paris negotiations. His precedent led me to deed all of my research materials, which include thousands of declassified documents and transcripts, to the Vietnam Archive at Texas Tech University.

At the Gerald Ford Library, located on the campus of the University of Michigan, I benefited from the guidance of Karen Holzhausen, who led me to such important materials as the Henry Kissinger–Brent Scowcroft Memcons—transcript-like memoranda of high-level conversations, important "top-secret" back-channel messages, the National Security Agency declassifications of radio messages from helicopter pilots shuttling to and from the Saigon embassy in April 1975, Ron Nessen's notes of meetings with Kissinger and Ford, Gerald Ford's congressional papers (Ford was minority leader at the time of the Paris Accords), and the papers of Ambassador Graham Martin. I returned to Ann Arbor in June 2000 in order to review thousands of pages of newly declassified materials.

Thanks to Richard Holzhausen for my jacket photo.

Graham Martin's story bears repeating. In January 1978 the North

Carolina State Police found a cache of 6,000 classified "TOP-SECRET" documents in the trunk of a car that had been stolen from Martin, the last American ambassador to South Vietnam. Martin was the original culprit, having illegally removed the documents from Saigon in order to protect himself from being made the scapegoat for the way things ended during the evacuation from the American embassy in April 1975. He expected that Kissinger or Nixon would assign him the blame. "My ass isn't covered," Martin cabled Kissinger on April 19, 1975. "I can assure you that I will be hanging several yards higher than you when this is all over."

At the LBJ Library, located on the campus of the University of Texas, I was able to review documents bearing on the first efforts at securing a settlement, especially in the papers of Paul Warnke, Clark Clifford, and George Elsey's notes of Secretary Clifford's morning staff conferences. Ted Gittinger and Regina Greenwell provided more help than I can ever thank them for, especially as I approached deadline and new Chennault documents were sent overnight for inclusion.

In Washington, D.C., at the Center of Military History, I benefited from the direction and knowledge of John Carland who introduced me to Dale Andrade and Graham Cosmas. John provided a copy of Tran Van Tra's *Vietnam: History of the Bulwark B2 Theatre, Concluding the 30-Year War,* and Colonel William E. LeGro's *Vietnam from Cease-Fire to Capitulation.*

At the National Archives, I was helped immensely by Ed Schamel in the Legislative Records Division. Ed guided me to the depositions and affidavits of the principals from the congressional inquiry into the status of American MIAs. For the first, but certainly not the last, time, I read declassified conversations between Henry Kissinger and Le Duc Tho, but only those segments bearing on POWs or MIAs. A paper trail now existed from which I could begin. Five years later, pieced together from several sources, I am in possession of most of what was said at the private meetings. At the Legislative Records Division, I was also advised by Ken Kato, Michael Gillette, and Richard McCulley.

At the National Security Archive at George Washington University, I read the Joint Chiefs of Staff Command History for the Vietnam War. William Burr shared with me his detailed knowledge of the declassified records. A generation of scholars owes much to the declassification efforts of the National Security Archive.

At the State Department, David Humphrey, who in previous years guided me through the LBJ files in Austin, put me in touch with Ed Keefer and Kent

Seig in the Office of Historian. From these conversations, I learned about the procedures for reviewing the Kissinger papers in the Library of Congress and how long it was going to be before the complete records were available.

In the Mudd Library at Princeton University, I received unrestricted access to the personal papers of George McGovern, where transcripts of his secret meetings with Xuan Thuy in Paris in September 1971 shed new light on the political maneuvering of 1972. I also found a revealing memo for the record bearing on Kissinger's October 1972 observation, "Peace is at hand." Ben Primer, university archivist at Seeley G. Mudd Library, was very helpful.

At the National Archives in College Park, Maryland, I benefited from access to the recently declassified papers of Tony Lake, as well as the State Department files on the Paris negotiations. I also discovered a trove of material used by Walter Scott Dilliard in writing the official MACV history, *Sixty Days to Peace: Implementing the Paris Accords*. I spent countless hours reviewing the diplomatic and military files relating to the Paris negotiations as well as Dilliard's original notes from interviews with members of the Four-Party Joint Military Commission, including a set of remarkably candid interviews with Generals Woodward, Weyand, and Wickham. I am very grateful to Richard Boylan, senior military archivist at NARA, and to Milton Gustafson for explaining Record Group 59.

The Nixon Project at Archives II offered access to the H. R. Haldeman diaries, which, when supplemented with the rest of the available record, provided important insight into the complexities of the Kissinger-Nixon relationship, as well as interactions within the White House. Recently released tapes offer glimpses into Nixon's views on Vietnam, but it will be years before that record is completely available. The Nixon Presidential Materials Staff, especially Pat Anderson and Ron Sodano, were very helpful in answering my questions and directing me to the appropriate files.

At the Vietnam Archive located at Texas Tech University, I spent many days going through the papers and materials of Professor Douglas Pike bearing on the Paris Accords, as well as North Vietnamese assessments of the accords. Doug spent several sessions answering my questions and offered counterpoints from which I always benefited.

Under the directorship of James Reckner, the Vietnam Archive at Texas Tech has become a special home for scholars and veterans to discuss all aspects of the Vietnam War. By a deed of gift, I have given all primary source materials used in the preparation of this book, as well as my previous books on Vietnam, to the Vietnam Archive at Texas Tech. I hope that students and scholars of the Vietnam period will find these materials useful.

I conducted many interviews for this book—all on the record and for attribution. Despite my repeated efforts, Henry Kissinger refused to be interviewed.

I traveled to Paris to interview Bui Tin, whose views on Le Duc Tho and the Paris negotiations brought focus to my thinking about the period.

I spent several hours with Hoang Duc Nha, and he answered my questions with grace and humor. Nha read every page of my final draft manuscript and made many helpful suggestions for improving the record and passed several of my questions on to President Thieu.

I thank John Negroponte, Peter Rodman, Douglas Pike, Harry Summers, Don Oberdorfer, Herb Schandler, Mark Clodfelter, Bui Diem, Chris Gocca, Arnold Isaacs, Philip T. K. Hughes, Morton Halperin, George McGovern, Pierre Salinger, Nguyen Manh Hung, Nguyen Ngoc Bich, General Nguyen Khanh, James Willbanks, Thach H. Nguyen, and David Marr for taking time to talk with me.

My friend and a distinguished author John Prados helped in many ways, especially in providing insight into the plans for Duck Hook and the Kissinger-Nixon relationship. John also read the draft manuscript and offered many valuable suggestions. He also shared key declassified documents from the Nixon papers and the Chennault file.

I owe a special debt of gratitude to the late Admiral Elmo Zumwalt, who agreed to sit with me for a C-Span interview and, when I was a fellow at the Wilson Center, would call me with advice and encouragement, saying that Henry Kissinger should not write the final draft of "peace with honor."

I have three special debts:

Stanley Karnow provided me with his complete set of transcribed interviews conducted in preparation of his seminal book and television series on Vietnam. These are interviews with the Vietnamese and American principals from the period. I deeply appreciated the time Stanley spent discussing with me his own recollections and impressions. Stanley also secured for both of us the English translation of Luu Van Loi and Nguyen Anh Vu's *Le Duc Tho–Kissinger Negotiations in Paris*.

Colonel Paul L. Miles walked me through the work of the Four-Party Joint Military Commission—the soldier-negotiators—charged with implementing the Paris agreement. In 1972 he played a central role in the planning group formed by the MACV chief of staff, Major General Gilbert H.

Woodward. Paul became a trusted confidant on matters dealing with Vietnam and the personalities of the period. He helped me understand the linkages between issues not settled in Paris and the eventual failure of the accords, although the conclusions are mine alone.

Dan Ellsberg engaged me in hours of conversation about what Kissinger and Nixon might really have been up to during this period. Even while working on deadline for his memoirs, Dan never hesitated to answer my questions or to initiate new and creative lines of inquiry. Dan critiqued several early drafts and arranged for me to interview Mort Halperin in the State Department. Halperin was, I believe, the first to write that Nixon and Kissinger never really intended to leave Vietnam. I also learned much from the early path-breaking work of Seymour Hersh, *The Price of Power: Kissinger in the Nixon White House.*

My intellectual debts include a group of scholars who have previously blazed the path in archives in Hanoi, Russia, China, and other international depositories. Ilya V. Gaiduk, Jeffrey Kimball, Robert Brigham, Qiang Zhai, and Fredrik Logevall are authors of seminal works on Vietnam, and their influence on my thinking has been profound. Fred Logevall's Cold War History Group at the University of California, Santa Barbara, provided me with a venue for sharing my ideas on the Jabberwocky agreement. Nguyen Tien Hung and Jerrold Schecter's *The Palace File* proved an invaluable resource not only for the exchange of letters between Nixon and Thieu, but for insight into how the South Vietnamese viewed Kissinger and Nixon.

I was the beneficiary of two extraordinary opportunities for research, writing, and reflection. I spent the 1998–1999 year in residence as a fellow at the Woodrow Wilson International Center for Scholars in Washington, D.C. I owe a special debt to Sam Wells, Rob Litwak, and Christian Ostermann. This book owes so much to the Wilson Center's Cold War History Project, especially the declassifications of conversations on Vietnam from Chinese and Soviet archives. Robert Hathaway's questions helped me to refocus some of my points.

My fellowship at the Wilson Center was preceded by residency at the Rockefeller Foundation Research and Study Center in Bellagio, Italy. Special thanks to Gianna Celli of the Villa Sorbelloni for her hospitality and for introducing me to bocce and to Susan Garfield for special arrangements.

My research interns at the Wilson Center—Nick Conway, Elizabeth Bellardo, and Erik Schelzig—provided indispensable assistance. At the University of California, Davis, I benefited from the work of research assistants

Josh London, J. G. Lallande, Cyndi Boaz, and Loren Wallin. Tan Dinh was the first of my U.C. Davis students to share with me the personal story of courage and strength that began on April 30, 1975. Jason Newman, a doctoral student in history at the University of California Washington Center, was with me for the crucial final push. Jason ranks in the very top cohort of research assistants, and by the end of this book we were colleagues.

At the University of California Washington Center, I thank my friends Lee Klug, Rodger Rak, Alverta Scott, Diane Rouda and Dianne Lessman for their support and good nature. I work with a wonderful group of people. I thank my administrative assistant at UCDC, Channa Threat, for her efforts in preparing the final manuscript, processing my paper flow, and always accepting graciously the reality that there was no such thing as a "final" draft. Channa saved the day more than once, and I am eternally grateful for her commitment.

Sylviane Ostermeyer in Paris provided emergency dental care when I thought it would not be possible to conduct my research. I promised the good *docteur* that if she relieved my pain, I would be able to write the book in Bellagio.

At the Free Press I thank Bruce Nichols for his guidance, patience, and involvement in this book. Bruce helped me see the importance of linking disparate events into a storyline that readers could follow without a map. His editorial guidance and collegiality were invaluable. I cannot imagine working with a better editor than Bruce. I also want to thank Dan Freedberg and Beverly H. Miller.

Thanks to Edmund S. Costantini for reading and editing several chapters and Ed and Aggie Costantini for use of their Echo Lake cabin when I needed time to think and revise parts of the manuscript, but not before catching my limit at "Berman Point," where I often shared wonderful moments with my children, Lindsay and Scott.

My wife, Nicole Costantini Berman, encouraged me to take the time to develop this book fully. Nicole also translated from French to English the Karnow interviews with Tran Van Don and General Giap and assisted me in Paris with my interview with Bui Tin.

This book is dedicated to Bertha Costantini and Selma Berman, our mothers, who passed away before I was able to finish this book. I drew friendship, laughs, and support from Bert; from Selma I drew a lifetime of encouragement and love.

INDEX